Pitching, Defense, and Three-Run Homers

Memorable Teams in Baseball History

Pitching, Defense, and Three-Run Homers
The 1970 Baltimore Orioles

Edited by **Mark Armour and Malcolm Allen**

Published by the **University of Nebraska Press** Lincoln & London, and the **Society for American Baseball Research**

© 2012 by the Society for American Baseball Research

Portions of chapter 1 are adapted from Warren Corbett's *The Wizard of Waxahachie: Paul Richards and the End of Baseball as We Knew It* (Southern Methodist University Press, 2009).

Chapter 17 is adapted from a biography by Rory Costello that originally appeared on the website *Baseball in the Virgin Islands* (http://home.roadrunner.com/~vibaseball/).

Chapter 44 is based on a short biography by Todd Newville titled "Beeney!" that originally appeared on *Baseball Todd's Dugout* (http://www.baseballtoddsdugout.com/fredbeene2.html).

All photographs are courtesy of the National Baseball Hall of Fame Library, Cooperstown, New York.

Player statistics are courtesy of Baseball-Reference.com.

Library of Congress Cataloging-in-Publication Data

Pitching, defense, and three-run homers: the 1970 Baltimore Orioles / edited by Mark Armour and Malcolm Allen.
p. cm. — (Memorable teams in baseball history)
Includes bibliographical references.
ISBN 978-0-8032-3993-7 (pbk.: alk. paper)
1. Baltimore Orioles (Baseball team)—History.
I. Armour, Mark L. II. Allen, Malcolm, 1970–
GV875.B2P58 2012
796.357'64097526—dc23
2011042433

Set in Sabon.

Table of Contents

Introduction

Mark Armour

This book was conceived a few years ago by life-long Orioles fan Malcolm Allen, who organized the project and edited early drafts of many of the chapters herein. In 2010 Malcolm had to bow out, and he passed the baton to me. I hope that the finished product is worthy of his original vision. Bill Nowlin helped both Malcolm and me throughout the three-year endeavor, and Len Levin heroically copyedited nearly every word in this book. After adding the many writers who stepped up late in the game to do a bit more work, this was a true team, just as the 1970 Orioles were.

When the 1970 baseball season played out, I was a nine-year-old fan of the Boston Red Sox. Kids are capable of imagining all sorts of realities, and one of mine was that the Red Sox had a chance to finish ahead of the Orioles. A friend on my street was an Orioles fan, and we would have spirited arguments about our teams every year. I would tout the abilities of Ray Culp and Sonny Siebert, and he would counter with Jim Palmer and Mike Cuellar. I would brag about Tony Conigliaro, and he would calmly mention Frank Robinson. I acted unimpressed, but really, I knew even then it was nothing like a fair fight.

The Baltimore Orioles were the envy of nearly every team in baseball, year after year. They often had the best players, the best manager, the best front office, the best scouts, and the best Minor League teams. They never seemed to make any mistakes on the field. If the Red Sox were lucky enough to have a lead late in the game, the Orioles always had the perfect pinch hitter or relief pitcher to regain the advantage. No matter the situation, manager Earl Weaver always had the perfect card to play.

The Orioles had the best record in the American League in both the 1960s and 1970s, and kept it up through their 1983 World Series victory. But of the many good and great Oriole clubs, the 1970 juggernaut may have been the best. They had Frank Robinson and Boog Powell hitting home runs, Brooks Robinson and Paul Blair making great defensive plays, and Jim Palmer and Dave McNally throwing shutouts. This perfectly balanced team played the game the way every fan wanted their team to play.

This book is a celebration of that great Orioles team, and the men who played the game of baseball so splendidly. Whether you are old enough to remember the events described here, or want to discover these stories for the first time, pull up a chair and start reading. We have a lot of stories to tell.

Chapter 1. The Oriole Way

Warren Corbett

The seed that sprouted into the powerful Baltimore Orioles teams of the 1960s and 1970s was planted by two baseball lifers who despised each other. Together they lifted the once-woeful St. Louis Browns into the ranks of the game's elite.

The Orioles were just one season removed from their sorry history in St. Louis when Paul Richards took over as both general manager and manager in September 1954. He proclaimed, "I'm running the show."[1] A lanky, hard-eyed Texan—a friend's wife described him as "a cold fish"—Richards came from Chicago, where he and general manager Frank Lane had transformed the sagging White Sox into a consistent winner. Wearing his two hats in Baltimore, Richards exercised total control over baseball operations.

The scouting and farm director he inherited, Jim McLaughlin, had come with the franchise from St. Louis. The farm system was a joke; the Browns had been too poor to invest in scouting and player development. But McLaughlin convinced Richards that he could do better with money to spend. It was a marriage made in hell. The two had just one thing in common: each of them got up every morning, looked in the mirror, and thought he saw the smartest man in baseball.

The 1954 Orioles played like the old Browns; they lost 100 games, the same as in their final season in St. Louis. It took Richards and McLaughlin six years to build them into pennant contenders. By 1960, when the Birds flew with the Yankees until the last two weeks of the season, the foundation for future success had been laid.

Recalling the fractious partnership, McLaughlin said, "Where Richards and I saw eye-to-eye

Jim Palmer was the best of the wave of talent that emerged from the Orioles' farm system in the 1960s.

was on pitching, the priority it ought to have in building a farm system."[2] McLaughlin and his scouts found the pitchers; Richards and his coaches molded them. In 1960 the Orioles had grown five pitchers under age twenty-three, called "the Kiddie Korps," who recorded fifty-eight of the club's eighty-nine victories. Baltimore also boasted the American League Rookie of the Year, shortstop Ron Hansen, and twenty-three-year-old third baseman Brooks Robinson, who found his bat and finished third in the Most Valuable Player voting behind Roger Maris and Mickey Mantle.

By then Richards and McLaughlin had created the player development scheme that came to be known as "The Oriole Way." The team established a Minor League spring training base in the piney woods at Thomasville, Georgia, on the grounds of a rest home for war veterans. It had eight military-style barracks with thirty cots in each. Uniform numbers rose into the triple digits—pitcher Steve Barber drew number 285 in his first camp. That was about 100 more players than could fit on the rosters of the eight farm clubs. Minor League managers and coaches graded the prospects and suspects on a scale of 1 (the best) to 4 in hitting, running, throwing, power, and pitching. In the evenings the staff met in a conference room called "The Bird's Nest" to cut the ones who didn't measure up. A thirty-year-old Minor League manager, Earl Weaver, became director of the Thomasville camp in 1961. Of delivering the painful verdicts that often ended a young man's dream, he said, "Some of them cry, others get mad, a few go crazy. One pulled a knife on me."[3]

Richards prepared a small manual for instructors in the Orioles' system explaining how he wanted them to teach the game's fundamentals. It was a condensed version of his 1955 book, *Modern Baseball Strategy*, a catalog of the nitty-gritty: how to execute cutoffs and pick-offs; how to defend against bunts with a runner on first, runner on second, or runners on first and second; how to stop a double steal. Richards once wrote, "The simple things in baseball number into the thousands. The difficult or esoteric? There is none."[4]

Every spring he brought Minor League managers and coaches to the Major League camp and indoctrinated them in his system so the techniques would be taught the same way from the top to the bottom of the organization. Dick Williams, an Orioles utility man and future Hall of Fame manager, recalled how Richards opened spring training by taking players to the on-deck circle: "This is what we do going up to the plate as far as looking at the coaches and getting the sign is concerned."[5] Richards made a circuit of the bases, explaining

offensive and defensive plays at each stop. The lectures went on for about two hours at a time; it took him three days to cover the entire field. Teaching baseball was Richards's passion, "24 hours a day," Orioles scout Jim Russo said.[6]

The Richards-McLaughlin power struggle eventually brought both men down. Richards was forced out of the general manager's job after the 1958 season because the owners had had enough of his free spending and disdain for the chain of command. His successor as GM, Lee MacPhail, soon tired of refereeing between his two lieutenants. MacPhail said, "It got to the point where you were either a 'McLaughlin player' or a 'Richards player' in the organization, and there were decisions made on that basis."[7] Late in 1960 he fired McLaughlin. After leading the Orioles to second place in 1960 and third in 1961, Richards moved on to a new challenge: building the Houston expansion franchise, the first big league team in his home state.

The Orioles won their first pennant in 1966 under Hank Bauer, one of several ex-Yankees MacPhail brought to the club. But after sweeping the favored Dodgers in the World Series, Baltimore slipped to a losing record over the next season and a half. When Bauer was fired in July 1968, Weaver, who was now the first base coach, took over. General manager Harry Dalton had identified the feisty Weaver as a comer soon after the bush league second baseman began managing in the Minors at age twenty-six.

Weaver thought the organization had strayed from the fundamentals of the Oriole Way. With Dalton's support, he brought the philosophy back to the forefront. Richards' little manual had been expanded into a bigger book that told a player what to do from the moment he walked into the clubhouse. "It was a detailed, position-by-position, definitive system of how the game should be taught and played," farm director Lou Gorman said. "Every player in the organization had to read and absorb the manual, at every level, and play the game on the field the Orioles way."[8] There was another manual for instructors and a third one for scouts. This was not an original idea; Branch Rickey had standardized instruction in the Cardinals and Dodgers organizations. But the Orioles stuck with their way through a succession of owners, front-office executives, and managers.

"The Oriole Way was 'never beat yourself,'" catcher Elrod Hendricks said. "And that's why we won so many close games. We let the other team make mistakes and beat themselves, and when the opportunity came we'd jump on it."[9] It was the gospel according to Paul Richards: most games are lost rather than won.

As important as the techniques were the men who did the teaching. Many of the Orioles' instructors were career Minor League players like Weaver, but they made up a roster of future Major League managers: George Bamberger, Billy Hunter, Clyde King, Jim Frey, Darrell Johnson, Joe Altobelli, and Cal Ripken Sr. The front office was a farm system for future general managers: Dalton, Gorman, Frey, Frank Cashen, Hank Peters, John Hart, and John Schuerholz.

The first links in the winning chain were the scouts. Jim McLaughlin was one of the first to insist on using cross-checkers rather than betting on the opinion of a single scout. He devised a circular chart that he labeled "The Whole Ball Player." The top half of the circle covered the player's visible tools: speed, arm strength, hitting. McLaughlin told his scouts to learn about the bottom half, traits that "cannot be seen with the eye": intelligence, teachability, family background, habits. He brought in FBI agents to teach scouts how to conduct a background investigation and sent his Minor League managers to seminars designed by Dale Carnegie, the author of *How to Win Friends and Influence People*, to improve their communications skills. The Orioles were one of the first teams to give players psychological tests.

"The Orioles pay attention to two things when they sign players," said George Bamberger, who worked his way up to become Weaver's pitching coach. "The first is talent. Next is attitude. They are far more aware of a player's attitude than most organizations."[10] After McLaughlin left, Walter Shannon came over from the Cardinals as scouting director. (Shannon had signed seventeen-year-old second baseman Earl Weaver, not the brightest line on his resume.) The eyes and ears of the organization were scouts like Walter Youse, Dee Phillips, Bill Werle—who had the final word on pitchers—and Jim Russo, who was nicknamed "Super Scout."

Building on Richards' and McLaughlin's foundation, the Orioles emphasized signing young pitchers and developing them through consistent instruction as they climbed the ladder. "It begins in rookie ball," one of those pitchers, Dave Ford, said. "The first thing they told me was I didn't have to strike everybody out. The second thing was not to walk anyone. The third thing was learn to throw a changeup."[11]

Throughout the system, instructors taught that the Oriole Way was a winning way. "There are two ways to play," farm director Don Pries said. "One team goes to the park to play the game. The other goes to the park to beat you. We went to the park to beat you, not just play the game."[12] By 1970 the Orioles' farm clubs had recorded eight straight winning seasons.

"We had the right players, no doubt about it, but we stressed those strong fundamentals in our minor league system for years," Weaver said later. "When guys came up they were well-schooled in the Oriole Way. They knew what they had to do."[13] Ron Hansen, Curt Blefary, Al Bumbry, Eddie Murray, and Cal Ripken Jr. were named Rookies of the Year. The prospects graduated to the big club like waves breaking on the shores of the Chesapeake Bay.

Breakout players from the Orioles' farm system, 1957–1970, by first season with significant Major League time

1957	Brooks Robinson
1958	Milt Pappas
1959	Jack Fisher, Jerry Walker
1960	Steve Barber, Marv Breeding, Chuck Estrada, Ron Hansen
1961	Jerry Adair
1962	Boog Powell
1963	Dave McNally
1964	Wally Bunker
1965	Paul Blair, Curt Blefary, John Miller, Jim Palmer
1966	Andy Etchebarren, Davey Johnson, Eddie Watt
1967	Mark Belanger, Larry Haney, Jim Hardin, Curt Motton, Dave May, Tom Phoebus
1968	Elrod Hendricks, Dave Leonhard
1969	Merv Rettenmund
1970	Terry Crowley

Some of the farm system's products were traded in deals that added key pieces to the club. The most famous one sent Pappas to Cincinnati for Frank Robinson. Ron Hansen and Pete Ward brought Luis Aparicio, the shortstop on the 1966 championship team. Mike Epstein, a first baseman blocked behind Boog Powell, was exchanged for reliever Pete Richert; Jack Fisher for reliever Stu Miller; Curt Blefary for Cy Young Award winner Mike Cuellar; Tom Phoebus for twenty-game winner Pat Dobson; Merv Rettenmund for pitcher Ross Grimsley; Rich Coggins for Ken Singleton.

The Oriole Way produced dramatic success. After Weaver became manager in July 1968, the club staged a second-half pennant run before finishing second behind Detroit. The next season Baltimore won 109 games and another pennant. Then another, plus a World Series, in 1970. Previewing the 1971 season, Frank Deford wrote in *Sports Illustrated*, "By consensus, the Orioles are not only the best team, but the best organization—with the best players, the best manager, the best system, the best front office, the best morale and, definitely, the best chances. . . . The team may or may not be a dynasty, but it is accepted as the model of a dynasty, as the Rickey Cardinals and Dodgers were, or the Weiss Yankees."[14] But even after a third straight pennant in 1971, the club was never recognized as a dynasty because it won only one of three World Series.

The next generation—Don Baylor, Bobby Grich, Al Bumbry, Doug DeCinces—was already rising through the farm system. Over two decades, from 1964 through 1983, the Oriole Way produced at least ninety victories sixteen times, with only a single losing season—the best record in the Major Leagues.

WARREN CORBETT

Chapter 2. **Earl Weaver**

Warren Corbett

The colorful Earl Weaver lost a lot of arguments with umpires in his career but won enough ballgames to reach the Hall of Fame.

When introducing the Orioles' new manager in 1968, general manager Harry Dalton said, "In short, I believe Earl Weaver is a winner."[1] Weaver was short. And he was a winner.

For the next 14½ seasons the Orioles won more games than any other team, piling up six division titles, four pennants, and one World Series championship. Weaver, a career Minor League player, became the revered Earl of Baltimore while fighting with umpires, his own players, and English grammar.

Earl Weaver's road to the Hall of Fame started on a laundry truck. His father owned a dry-cleaning shop and took care of the St. Louis Browns'

and Cardinals' uniforms. Young Earl began roaming the clubhouse at Sportsman's Park when he was six years old. Born in St. Louis on August 14, 1930, Weaver showed his shrewdness when he signed his first professional contract at the age of seventeen. Both hometown teams wanted to sign him, but the Browns offered a $2,000 bonus only if he stuck in the Minors; the Cardinals offered $1,500, no strings attached. Weaver became a Cardinal farmhand.

As a five-foot-seven-inch second baseman, he made it to the Cardinals' spring training camp once, but never came close to a big-league at bat. He had a weak arm and little power, plus a belligerent streak that infuriated umpires and opponents. "The only thing I'd ever wanted in my life was to be a major-league ballplayer, but I had to admit to myself that I wasn't good enough," he said. "It broke my heart."[2] By his twenty-sixth birthday the Cardinals had let him go to Knoxville, an independent Class A club. He reluctantly took over as interim manager of the last-place Smokies at midseason in 1956.

That fall Weaver was prepared to leave baseball. He had married Jane Johnston when he was eighteen and they had two children (a third came later). He enjoyed his off-season job with Liberty Loan in St. Louis; the company told him he would soon be managing an office. But an assistant in the Orioles' farm system, Harry Dalton, had met Weaver in Knoxville and was impressed. The Orioles offered him a job as manager of Class D Fitzgerald, Georgia, a one-restaurant town at the bottom level of professional ball. Weaver took the job—and a pay cut.

Under manager and general manager Paul Richards, Baltimore was building one of the strongest farm systems in the Majors. Farm director Jim McLaughlin's scouts signed players by the busloads; Richards trained Minor League managers and instructors to teach the game's fundamentals the same way throughout the organization. Weaver later named Richards and a longtime manager in the Cardinals system, George Kissell, as his most important teachers. After four seasons managing low-level teams, he was put in charge of the Minor League spring camp in Thomasville, Georgia, in 1961.

But the young manager's temper threatened to torpedo his career. His rages at umpires prompted at least two league presidents to call Harry Dalton and demand that he muzzle his wild man. Dalton warned Weaver that his frequent ejections were interfering with his job teaching players. Still, he was a winner, with three pennants and five second-place finishes in eleven years. Starting in 1962

he spent four seasons at Elmira, New York, in the Double-A Eastern League. His first wife left him—her parting words were, "Earl, the only thing worse than you being gone is you being home."[3] In 1964 he married Marianna Osgood, a divorcee with a young daughter. He bought a house in Elmira and was content to make his home there.

The Orioles promoted Weaver to their top farm club in Rochester in 1966. After he led the club to a pennant and a second-place finish, Dalton, now the Orioles' general manager, brought him to Baltimore as a coach in 1968.

The Orioles had fallen from their 1966 championship to sixth place and a losing record the next year. Although injuries to 1966 MVP Frank Robinson, pitcher Jim Palmer, and others could explain the decline, Dalton felt manager Hank Bauer deserved a big share of the blame. Bauer said Dalton invited him to resign after the '67 season, but he would not walk away from the year remaining on his contract. So Dalton replaced most of the Orioles' coaches. Brooks Robinson recalled, "I think everybody knew that sooner or later Weaver would be the manager, simply because Weaver was Dalton's guy."[4]

When Bauer was fired at the All-Star break, the Orioles stood slightly above .500 but far out of the pennant race. Weaver's promotion was no surprise, but he couldn't even take his dream job without a fight. He rejected Dalton's first salary offer and stood firm until the GM agreed to pay him $28,000.

As soon as Weaver took over, the team's unquestioned leader, Frank Robinson, asked what he could do to help. Weaver urged him to autograph baseballs, a chore the players detested. When Robinson began signing, the rest of the club did, too. Robinson's attitude helped Weaver—the bush leaguer—win acceptance in the clubhouse. In addition, he had managed nearly half the Orioles on their way up through the Minors. He put a sign on the clubhouse wall: "It's what you learn after you know it all that counts." Baltimore made a run at the league-leading Tigers but could not catch them. The Orioles, 43-37 when Bauer was fired, went 48-34 under Weaver and finished second.

In 1969, the first year of division play, Baltimore ran away with the American League East title. Frank Robinson returned to superstar form, twenty-three-year-old right-hander Jim Palmer pitched like a budding superstar after two years of arm trouble, and Mike Cuellar, a thirty-two-year-old left-hander acquired from Houston, won twenty-three games. Young lefty Dave McNally won his first fifteen decisions and finished 20-7. The Orioles moved into first place in the season's ninth game and stayed there. Their lead stretched to twenty-two games in mid-September. After a 109-53 regular season, Baltimore swept the Twins in the first American League Championship Series and won the opening game of the World Series against the "Amazing Mets."

That was their last victory of 1969. The Mets won the next four while the Orioles scored only 5 runs. With the championship slipping away, Weaver achieved the distinction of being the first manager ejected from a Series game in thirty-four years. Some critics thought the Orioles were complacent after their easy ride through the American League, but Weaver said, "They just pitched better than us."[5]

The 1970 Orioles' record looks equally impressive at 108-54, as the team spent all but nine days in first place and again allowed the fewest runs in the league, but the race was closer in the first half before Baltimore pulled away. Palmer joined Cuellar and McNally as twenty-game winners, and Boog Powell won the MVP award. The club came from behind to win forty-two times and finished the season with eleven straight victories, then swept the Twins in the playoffs.

"From Opening Day, we were all on the same page as far as not letting what the Mets did to us the year before happen again," Powell remem-

bered.[6] Against Cincinnati's Big Red Machine, winner of 102 regular-season games, the Orioles pounded ten home runs in the World Series' five games, and Brooks Robinson put on a memorable show at third base. Reds manager Sparky Anderson said, "Robinson beat us." He also told the press that Weaver had not gotten enough credit for Baltimore's two pennants.[7] Weaver did not win the Manager of the Year award in 1969 or '70, despite leading his club to the best record in the league. The voters evidently agreed with Weaver's explanation for his success: "My best game plan is to sit on the bench and call out specific instructions like 'C'mon, Boog,' 'Get hold of one, Frank,' or 'Let's go, Brooks.'"[8]

Before the 1971 season opened, *Sports Illustrated* anointed the Orioles "The Best Damn Team in Baseball."[9] This time they had four twenty-game winners, racked up 101 victories, and swept the Oakland A's in the playoffs to claim their third straight pennant. The World Series against the Pirates went the full seven games before Pittsburgh won the championship. It was Roberto Clemente's Series: he batted .414 with 12 hits and 2 homers.

Baltimore had put up a historic run, despite losing two out of three World Series. Only the 1929–31 Philadelphia A's and the Yankees (several times) had won three consecutive AL pennants. But the core of the team was aging. Frank Robinson, now thirty-five, was traded after the 1971 season to make room for young outfielder Don Baylor. Mike Cuellar was also thirty-five, Brooks Robinson and Don Buford, thirty-four. The franchise's strong farm system provided some replacements, but none who could match the two Robinsons.

The Orioles fell to third place in 1972, then rallied to win division titles in '73 (Weaver was named American League Manager of the Year) and '74 before losing in the league playoffs both times. A greater threat emerged when Major League players won free agency in 1976. Even during their best years the Orioles had been laggards at the gate;

the club was embarrassed by empty seats at some playoff games. Owner Jerry Hoffberger didn't have the deep pockets to compete with the free-spending Yankees and Angels. Home-grown stars Wayne Garland and Bobby Grich moved on, along with several lesser players. Don Baylor, a year away from free agency, was traded to Oakland for, among others, Reggie Jackson, who signed with the Yankees after one season in Baltimore. General manager Hank Peters said he had watched an All-Star team walk out the door.

During the long dry spell between pennants, from 1972 until 1979, Weaver's reputation grew as he juggled the turnover on his roster and usually kept the Orioles in contention. He won another Manager of the Year award after a second-place finish with a young team in 1977. Always quotable, he was catnip for sportswriters, and was never shy about saying what he thought.

Weaver preached his prescription for winning: "pitching and three-run homers." He explained, "Pitching keeps you in the games. Home runs win the game."[10] That formula developed with experience; in his first seasons with the Orioles he called for more sacrifice bunts than the average AL manager, but he came to believe that "your most precious possessions on offense are your 27 outs," and "if you play for one run, that's all you'll get."[11]

He was famous for his devotion to statistics, tracking head-to-head matchups between pitchers and hitters, something other managers either claimed to keep in their heads or ignored altogether. His celebrated note cards (actually a combination of cards and loose-leaf notebooks) told him Boog Powell couldn't hit Detroit left-hander Mickey Lolich, so Powell didn't play against Lolich. His good-field, no-hit shortstop, Mark Belanger, turned into a .300 hitter against Nolan Ryan, so Belanger moved up in the lineup when Ryan pitched. He platooned Gary Roenicke and John Lowenstein; combined, they outhit most teams' regular left fielders.

The game's nine innings were Weaver's canvas, the twenty-five-man roster his palette, and he mixed and matched every available hue. He wanted a veteran bench with what he called "deep depth." He maintained, "A manager wins games in the winter when he picks his team."[12] The front office generally tailored the Orioles to the manager's specifications. "If a player is on his team he will use him," GM Peters said. "You can't give him 13 good players and 12 dogs, because Earl will play the dogs. You have to know he likes guys on the bench who can hit. We lose some speed and defense to keep players like Terry Crowley and Jose Morales," two of Weaver's favorite pinch hitters.[13]

Weaver was not a player's manager; he harangued and argued with many of them. He and fiery catcher Rick Dempsey habitually conversed at the top of their lungs and had to be separated in the dugout more than once. "We don't hold back our tempers," Dempsey said. "We say and do things we don't mean. But he won't hold it against me and I don't hold it against him."[14] Even Weaver's detractors acknowledged that, however heated the argument, he forgot about it when he filled out the next day's lineup card. Frank Robinson, who returned to the Orioles as a coach, said, "He does the best job of any manager I've ever known at keeping 25 ballplayers relatively happy. He doesn't do it by being their friend; he does it by never, but never, taking anything personally and by making damn sure nobody else does either."[15]

Pitchers were his particular targets. Dave McNally spoke for most of them when he said, "The only thing Earl knows about pitching is that he couldn't hit it."[16] Weaver's battles with Jim Palmer —elegant ace and world-class worrier—sometimes played out on the mound in view of the fans. When a fading Mike Cuellar complained that Weaver wouldn't give him a chance, Weaver scoffed, "I gave Mike Cuellar more chances than I gave my first wife."[17] He believed rookie pitchers should begin their careers in long relief, where they faced the least pressure. That early coddling may help explain why Orioles pitchers seemed immune to arm injuries. And he stuck with a four-man starting rotation long after almost every other manager had switched to five, reasoning that it was easier to find four reliable starters than five.

He kept his distance from his players, because "you're the person who decides all the worst things in their lives." The manager benches them, sends them to the Minors, and one day has to tell them they're through. "You can't help loving them, yet you can't afford to."[18] He believed his off-season jobs as a loan officer and used-car salesman had taught him to read people. He also believed in hypnotism and recommended it to cure everything from batting slumps to emotional problems.

Weaver reserved his worst tirades for umpires. His confrontations with them were the stuff of legend and low comedy. They said he never stopped agitating from the dugout in a voice raspy from heavy smoking and heavy screaming. His ninety-four ejections rank fourth all-time among managers. Weaver, ever the soul of logic, explained, "You've got to tell a guy when he's wrong."[19]

His feud with flamboyant umpire Ron Luciano began in Elmira and continued for two decades. He didn't exactly get in Luciano's face; the hulking former football lineman jeered, "I have to tell him to get his nose off my kneecap." Once, Luciano publicly proclaimed, "I don't care who wins the pennant as long as it isn't Baltimore." The league office kept him away from the Orioles for a while, but when Luciano and Weaver confronted each other again, Weaver protested the game "on the grounds of the umpire's integrity."[20] That earned the manager a three-game suspension.

On one occasion, umpire Bill Haller was wearing a microphone during a game for a TV show, but Weaver didn't know that when he went out to argue a balk call. Weaver claimed Haller had poked him in the chest, igniting an exchange of views immortalized years later on YouTube:

BILL HALLER: You're lying, Earl. You're lying.
EARL WEAVER: No, you are!
BH: You're lying.
EW: You are a big liar!
BH: You are a liar, Earl.
EW: You are!
BH: No, you are.

In 1978 the Orioles fell to fourth in the seven-team Eastern Division as a new generation of key players matured: first baseman Eddie Murray, third baseman Doug DeCinces, and pitchers Mike Flanagan, Dennis Martinez, and Scott McGregor. But Weaver, like many veteran managers, had become impatient with youngsters. He was so hard on them that anyone who got a kind word was called "Earl's son" by his teammates.

Weaver thought his 1979 club was nowhere near as talented as the 1969–71 juggernaut—"But they won," he said.[21] Jim Palmer gave Weaver his 1,000th career victory on Opening Day. Baltimore charged into first place on May 18 and stayed there despite injuries to Palmer, DeCinces, and several others. As Weaver rotated his role players in and out of the lineup, some observers called them the "Who's That?" team. Weaver won his third Manager of the Year award from the Associated Press. Baltimore rang up 102 victories before beating the Angels in the playoffs. The Orioles set a franchise attendance record, quieting some of the fears that the new owner, Washington lawyer Edward Bennett Williams, planned to move the team to the nation's capital.

In the World Series against the Pirates, Baltimore took a three-games-to-one lead, then it turned into '69 all over again. The Orioles' bats went silent; they scored only two runs in the last three games. In the decisive Game Seven, Weaver used twenty players, including six pitchers and five pinch hitters, but Pittsburgh claimed the championship.

The next year the Orioles won 100 games for

the fifth time in Weaver's tenure (they won at least ninety in seven other seasons), but finished three games behind the Yankees. In 1981 they were in second place when the players went on strike, then fell to a close fourth in the second half. Weaver was arrested for drunk driving on August 31, the second time he had been caught driving while impaired, but that did not seem to hurt his popularity in Baltimore.

Weaver thought his influence in the organization was waning when Peters traded third baseman DeCinces in January 1982 to open the position for rookie Cal Ripken Jr. Weaver, alone among the decision-makers, wanted the six-foot-four Ripken to play shortstop. Although he was only fifty-one, Weaver announced that 1982 would be his last year. Retirement was his own idea, but GM Hank Peters later said he'd thought Weaver was slipping.

It looked as if Weaver's final season would be his worst when the Orioles fell to last place in May. But they rallied with a 15-9 June and began chasing the Milwaukee Brewers, a team built by Weaver's patron, Harry Dalton, and called Harvey's Wallbangers after manager Harvey Kuenn, who took over in June and turned the Brewers' season around. Weaver was juggling an aging lineup with only two rising stars. Eddie Murray put up his first 30-homer, 100-RBI year. The twenty-one-year-old Ripken started the season at third base, but Weaver moved him to shortstop on July 1. Ripken hit twenty-eight homers and won the Rookie of the Year award. No Orioles pitcher had an ERA under 3.00 or won more than sixteen games.

The club's marketing department was touting "Oriole Magic." Baltimore was seven games behind on August 28 when the magic materialized. They won ten in a row, but Milwaukee still led by three with four games left—four games in Baltimore. The Orioles had to sweep to win the division.

The showdown started with a Friday double-header before a frenzied sellout crowd. The Orioles knocked out Milwaukee's ace, Pete Vuckovich, as they piled up 15 hits and won, 8–3. In the nightcap Baltimore's twenty-year-old rookie right-hander Storm Davis pitched his first complete game, backed by Murray's and Ripken's homers, for a 7–1 victory. The next day the Orioles pummeled Brewer pitching for 18 hits and an 11–3 win to tie for first place.

That set up a winner-take-all 162nd game matching Jim Palmer against Don Sutton. Both future Hall of Famers labored. Sutton, shot full of cortisone and penicillin for a sore throat, gave up ten hits and five walks but kept wriggling out of trouble; the Orioles left a dozen runners on base. Robin Yount, who would win the MVP award, touched Palmer for two home runs. Palmer left after Cecil Cooper added another homer in the sixth to give Milwaukee a 4–1 lead. The Brewers tacked on another run, then iced their cake with five in the ninth to deny Weaver his seventh division title.

Weaver's last season was over, but the crowd of 51,642 wouldn't go home. They shouted, "Earl, Earl!" When the little manager finally came back onto the field, he contorted his body to spell "O-R-I-O-L-E-S." The love-fest lasted forty-five minutes, a tribute to the man who had reigned as the pugnacious face of the franchise from the heyday of Brooks Robinson to the coming of Cal Ripken Jr.

Weaver and Marianna moved permanently to their winter home in Miami, where they indulged their love of golf and the horse and dog races. Other teams offered jobs—eleven times, by Weaver's count—but he insisted he was done with managing. It took one of the country's greatest lawyers to argue him out of retirement.

The Orioles won the 1983 pennant and World Series under Weaver's successor, Joe Altobelli, then fell to fifth place in the East the next year (although with a winning record). Owner Williams grew contemptuous of his manager—by one account, referring to Altobelli as Cement Head. When the club fell into a slump early in 1985, Williams began pining for Weaver.

Weaver needed a job. He had given up his part-time consultant's role with the team and had been dropped from ABC's broadcast booth. He said inflation was eating up his retirement nest egg. When Williams dangled a reported $500,000 salary, Weaver jumped at it.

At his first game back on June 14, 1985, a big crowd chanted, "Weaver! Weaver!" But he could barely recognize the club he inherited. While Murray and Ripken were still the anchors, the vaunted farm system appeared to have dried up. Williams had imported several aging free agents who didn't know or care about the "Oriole Way." The team did worse under Weaver (53-52) than it had under Altobelli (29-26).

Weaver said he returned to the dugout again in 1986 because he thought the team could win. On August 5 they were just 2½ games out of first place, despite injuries to Murray, center fielder Fred Lynn, and a dozen others. Then the Orioles collapsed. They went 14-42 the rest of the way to finish last for the first time in their history. Murray asked to be traded after owner Williams insinuated he was out of shape. The clubhouse turned surly. The pitching was awful (tenth in the league in runs allowed) and the defense was worse. By August 21 Weaver told Williams he would not be back. When Weaver's first losing season mercifully ended, there were no curtain calls. Weaver returned home to Miami and made his retirement stick this time.

Weaver was elected to the Baseball Hall of Fame in 1996. Forty years after the Orioles' 1970 World Series victory, surviving members of the team were honored at the Orioles' new ballpark in 2010. When the seventy-nine-year-old Weaver took the lineup card to home plate before the game, umpire Bob Davidson ejected him.

Earl Weaver's Ten Laws of Baseball

1. No one's going to give a damn in July if you lost a game in March.

2. If you don't make any promises to your players, you won't have to break them.

3. The easiest way around the bases is with one swing of the bat.

4. Your most precious possessions on offense are your 27 outs.

5. If you play for one run, that's all you'll get.

6. Don't play for one run unless you know that run will win a ballgame.

7. It's easier to find four good starters than five.

8. The best place for a rookie pitcher is long relief.

9. The key step for an infielder is the first one— left or right—but *before* the ball is hit.

10. The job of arguing with the umpires belongs to the manager, because it won't hurt the team if he gets kicked out of the game.[22]

Chapter 3. **George Bamberger**

Tom Hawthorn

Baltimore left-hander Mike Cuellar pitched a shaky first inning in Game Five of the 1970 World Series. The Cincinnati Reds touched him for three runs on four hits—a single and three doubles. The Orioles bullpen was active as the inning ended. Cuellar came into the dugout, grabbed a towel, wiped his face. His catcher, Andy Etchebarren, took that simple act as a promising sign. "By that time," he said, "he was warmed up."[1]

Despite winning twenty-four games in the regular season, the Cuban-born pitcher had lasted only $4\frac{1}{3}$ innings in the opening game of the American League Championship Series. He was knocked off the mound after just $2\frac{1}{3}$ innings of the second game of the World Series. Another short outing seemed in the works.

The battery huddled in the runway behind the home dugout at Memorial Stadium, where they were joined by pitching coach George Bamberger. Two of the hits, by Johnny Bench and Hal McRae, had come off screwballs high in the strike zone. A decision was made—no more scroogies, a lot more curves.

Cuellar retired the next ten Reds, issued a walk, then stymied six more batters in a row. He gave up a pair of singles in the seventh, but got out of the inning to complete the game, sewing up the World Series in dominating fashion.

Bamberger, a quiet man with some unorthodox ideas about handling hurlers, flourished as pitching coach of the Orioles from 1968 to 1977. A twenty-win season is a standard of excellence for a starting pitcher. Bamberger had eighteen pitchers reach that mark, four of them—Cuellar, Jim Palmer, Pat Dobson, and Dave McNally—doing so in

Legendary pitching coach George Bamberger had a wonderful record of success with players in Baltimore; he saw three become twenty-game winners in 1970 and four more in 1971.

1971, the third consecutive year in which the O's won the pennant.

"He's one of the game's greatest teachers," longtime Orioles manager Earl Weaver once said. "'Throw strikes,' he would say. There is nothing complicated about baseball. Maybe that's what makes George so good—there's nothing complicated about George."[2] Shortly before Bamberger's death in 2004, Weaver said, "If there was a Hall of Fame for pitching coaches, he should be there without a doubt."[3] Frank Cashen, the president of the Orioles during Bamberger's years in Baltimore, said, simply, "He was the best pitching coach I ever saw."[4]

Where Weaver was flamboyant and volatile, Bamberger was calm, unflappable, a pitcher's friend. He was also nearly deaf in his right ear, so he made a point of sitting on Weaver's left in the dugout.

Bamberger's own Major League career was brief and undistinguished. In eighteen seasons in the Minors, he transformed himself from a wild thrower into a control pitcher who set a mark for consecutive innings pitched without issuing a walk. After his time coaching for the Orioles, he had two stints managing the Milwaukee Brewers, who were known as Bambi's Bombers, with an unsuccessful spell as skipper of the New York Mets sandwiched in between the Milwaukee stints.

George Irvin Bamberger was born on August 1, 1923, in Staten Island, New York. He attended McKee High School before entering the U.S. Army in 1943. The 5-foot-11½, 180-pound right-hander signed with the New York Giants as an amateur free agent in 1946, about the time two years were shaved from his age. The official guides always listed his birth year as 1925. He debuted in 1946 with the Class C Erie (Pennsylvania) Sailors of the Middle Atlantic League, going 13-3 with a league-leading earned run average of 1.35. He was then promoted to the Class B Manchester (New Hampshire) Giants and, in 1948, to the Triple-A Jersey City Giants. He led the International League in wild pitches in 1949 with 11, though he also tied for the league lead in shutouts with 5. Pitching for the Oakland Oaks the following season, he led the Pacific Coast League (PBL) in wild pitches with 13.

During the 1950 season Bamberger married Wilma Morrison of New Jersey at First Presbyterian Church in Oakland. The best man was Oaks second baseman Bobby Hofman. The entire ballclub, including president Brick Laws and manager Charlie Dressen, joined the couple afterward for a cocktail hour followed by a buffet dinner.

Bamberger made his Major League debut with the Giants on April 19, 1951, during the second game of a doubleheader at Boston against the Braves. In two innings, he gave up two runs on a walk and three hits, including a home run by Sam Jethroe. In his only other appearance with the Giants that season, he failed to register an out while surrendering two more runs.

Bamberger was soon demoted to play for the Ottawa Giants in the International League. On Father's Day he pitched a no-hitter in a 1–0 victory over the Maple Leafs at Toronto. Not only did Bamberger hold Toronto hitless, but he was responsible for the game's only run, coaxing a bases-loaded walk on four pitches from mound rival Russ Bauers in the second inning. After the game Bamberger lit a fat cigar in celebration, not of his no-hitter, but of the birth of his daughter Judy in New York the night before.

In 1952 Bamberger started the season with the Giants again, appearing in five games and allowing four runs in four innings. In June he was traded back to the Triple-A Oakland Oaks in exchange for pitcher Hal Gregg.

He spent four seasons as a starting pitcher for the Oaks, compiling a 52-44 record. The Oaks moved to Vancouver (and joined the Baltimore system) for the 1956 Pacific Coast League season, and Bamberger went along, spending seven seasons with the Mounties. He went 9-14 his first season in British Columbia, complaining of a sore arm that cost him his fastball. In 1957 new manager Charlie Metro convinced him that the only way to recover was to "throw, throw and throw."[5] It worked. Bamby's exploits at Capilano (now Nat Bailey) Stadium made him a perennial fan favorite. Bamberger carried himself like someone who knew he belonged in The Show and had been left behind by an oversight that would surely soon be corrected.

"Bamberger was a chesty guy with thinning hair," Denny Boyd of the *Vancouver Sun* once wrote, "a nose the size of a wedge of pie and a dimple in which you could catch thrown balls." Boyd dubbed him the Staten Island Stopper. The pitcher's limited repertoire—a so-so fastball, a deceptive changeup, a wicked curve that dipped like the new roller coaster at the city's exhibition grounds—was enhanced by the occasional use of a spitball, an illegal pitch and a scofflaw's best hope. "We all knew he used it," Boyd wrote, "but we could never get him to admit to throwing the wet one."[6] Bamby acknowledged that he had a special pitch that he called the Staten Island Sinker. It certainly was wet like a sink.

In 1958 Bamberger established a league record by pitching 68⅔ consecutive innings—the equivalent of more than seven complete games—without allowing a base on balls. The old mark of 64 innings had been set by Julio Bonetti in 1939. Bamberger's record stood for more than four decades. The streak began on July 10, after he walked a batter in San Diego in the fourth inning. He recorded his hundredth PCL victory in his next start, for which the Mounties held a George Bamberger Day on August 1. The club gave him a hundred Canadian silver dollars. In return, Bamby beat Seattle 6–3, again without walking any batters.

"When you come right down to it, there is no excuse for walking a batter," Bamberger told Boyd in 1958. "It's accepted as normal, but it isn't normal; it's a mistake. If you throw four bad pitches, you have made four mistakes. There is no other sport where you can survive making that many mistakes."[7]

The streak ended on August 14, when a Phoenix pinch hitter walked on four pitches. The record remained unchallenged until bettered by Nashville's Brian Meadows in 2003.

Bamberger's final cup of coffee in the bigs came courtesy of the Orioles, who used him three times in April 1959. His entire Major League career involved pitching just 14⅓ innings for two teams over three seasons spanning eight years. He had no wins or losses and one save in relief, and carries into eternity an inflated ERA of 9.42. He returned to Vancouver and kept pitching.

In a 1962 game in Vancouver, Bamberger took part in a wacky episode. He was outfitted with a radio receiver sewn into an inside pocket of his uniform. It looked as though he had a cardboard pack of cigarettes in his undershirt. Unseen in the Vancouver dugout, manager Jack McKeon barked commands into a transmitter. The skulduggery failed to catch out any opposing base runners, although it did bamboozle fans and the first baseman, who took one unexpected pick-off throw in the chest. Before long, baseball banned the use of radios on the field.

Bamberger added coaching duties to his responsibilities in 1960 while still pitching for the Mounties. After retiring as a player at the end of the 1963 season, which he spent at Dallas–Fort Worth, Bamberger worked for the Orioles as a Minor League pitching instructor. He was hired as the parent club's pitching coach in 1968, replacing Harry Brecheen, who had held the post for fourteen seasons. Manager Hank Bauer complained in spring training that he was tired of having pitchers with sore arms on his roster. Bauer would not last the season, but the Orioles found a solution to the problem in their new pitching coach.

Bamberger's theory was that sore arms and elbows resulted from underwork, not overwork. He insisted that his pitchers run every day, even if tired, even on the road, so he ordered thirty-five minutes of sprints from foul pole to foul pole. "When you pitch, and your legs get tired from lifting them up on every windup, you can lose coordination," he said. A shift in the mechanics could lead to loss of control, which could lead to wildness and sore arms.[8]

He also had his pitchers play catch for fifteen minutes between starts, with twenty minutes of hard throwing the prescription two days after every start. He believed in pitchers throwing many innings and completing as many starts as they could. In 1970 Palmer threw 305 innings, Cuellar 297⅔, and McNally 296.

"My whole idea is to throw the ball over the plate," Bamberger told Dave Anderson of the *New York Times* in 1979. "The most important pitch is a strike. But the trick is to change speeds. Trying to pinpoint a pitch is crazy. Throw the ball down the middle, but don't throw the same pitch twice. Change the speed."[9]

Though regarded by many as solely a pitching specialist, in 1978 Bamberger was hired to manage the Milwaukee Brewers, who had yet to post a winning season in their eight-year history. Remarkably, he turned the perennial also-ran into contenders as Bambi's Bombers posted ninety-three wins in 1978 and ninety-five in 1979. An amiable, happy man, the manager was known to join fans in the parking lot of County Stadium for postgame tailgate parties. After suffering a heart attack during spring training in 1980, he underwent a quintuple bypass. He returned in June but did not last the season.

Two years later, in 1982, Bamberger became the skipper of the New York Mets. The fifty-eight-year-old florid and balding manager was greeted by a memorable description in *New York* magazine: "Bamberger resembles George Kennedy," wrote Vic Ziegel, "but the voice is Art Carney's Ed Norton."[10] The Mets were woeful and could finish only 65-97 during Bamberger's one complete season. "I don't want to suffer anymore," he said after resigning with a 16-30 record early in the 1983 season.[11]

Bamberger returned to manage the Brewers in 1985, but the team was not what it had been. After one poor season and most of a second, he was fired in September 1986 and retired for good.

After baseball Bamberger settled into a life of painting and golf in North Redington Beach, Flor-ida. He died at his home there, after battling colon cancer, on April 4, 2004. He left Wilma, his wife of fifty-three years; three adult daughters; five grandchildren; three great-grandchildren; and a brother.

Sports Illustrated asked Jim Palmer, who won twenty games in seven seasons under Bamberger's tutelage, for his memories: "George had flawless mechanics. If I ever got out of sync, I used to visualize him throwing batting practice. But with us—his 'boys'—he didn't preach mechanics. He had a sixth sense of what a pitcher needed to be better, and he knew it could be different for each guy. There were a few hard rules, but everybody was unique, and he understood that. George's great strength was he didn't overcoach. There's no place for panic on the mound."[12]

Chapter 4. Jim Frey

Adam Ulrey

Many people go through life without having a life-long friend, and even if they do have one, at some point the two will be separated for many years. The friendship of Jim Frey and Don Zimmer not only has endured for many decades since childhood, but the two spent the bulk of their friendship in the game of baseball. They were teammates throughout their childhood, playing high-school and American Legion baseball together. Zimmer went on to play for five Major League teams, coach for eight more, and manage four. Frey had to take the long way into the Majors: despite a career batting average of around .300 for fourteen seasons in the Minors (some records are incomplete), he never made a Major League roster. Eventually he became a Minor League manager and then moved to the big leagues, where he was a scout, coach, manager, and finally a general manager. It all came full circle in 1987 when, as the general manager of the Chicago Cubs, Frey hired his friend Zimmer as manager.

Frey was born on May 26, 1931, in Cleveland, Ohio, and is of German descent. His father, John, who went to law school at night and later became an accountant, stressed the importance of discipline and hard work. "He always felt you had to make things happen in life," Frey said. "He was very strict with my older brother, Don, and me. But we became self-disciplined."[1]

At Western Hills High School Frey earned three letters each in baseball and basketball and graduated in 1949. He (and Zimmer) also played for the Robert E. Bentley American Legion Post team that won the national Legion championship in 1947. Frey drove in the winning run in the eighth inning

Jim Frey finally reached the Major Leagues in 1970, when he worked as the Orioles' bullpen coach. He later managed two teams to the postseason.

of the final game. In 1949 his team won the National Amateur Baseball Federation championship. Frey signed with the Boston Braves after graduating from high school. (He attended Ohio State University in the off-seasons from 1949 through 1951.)

After a brief stay with the Evansville Braves of the Class B Three-I League, Frey was sent to Paducah (Kentucky) in the Class D Mississippi–Ohio Valley League. He hit .325 there, leading the club, then returned to Evansville in 1951 and hit .324.

After another good year in Evansville (.336), he reached Single-A Hartford in late 1952.

In 1953 and '54 Frey played for Jacksonville (Single-A South Atlantic), hitting .317 and .316. He did not have much power, but his 11 home runs in 1954 got him to Triple-A Toledo in 1955. He was twenty-four years old, and his .282 average and 87 walks would appear to have him close to the Major Leagues. Frey split the 1956 season with Austin and Fort Worth in the Texas League, the switch coming on July 4 when the Milwaukee Braves traded him to the Brooklyn Dodgers. In 1957 he moved on to Tulsa in the Philadelphia Phillies' farm system, and he broke out by hitting .336 with 50 doubles and 11 triples, and 74 runs batted in for the Oilers en route to being named the Texas League Most Valuable Player after leading the league in categories.

The next year, 1958, Frey was invited to join the St. Louis Cardinals in spring training. "I hit everything they tossed up that spring," he said, "but I couldn't throw a ball from center to second base. My arm was dead after I banged my shoulder against the fence the year before. Fred Hutchinson [Cardinals manager] gave me a real shot, but he wound up keeping Irv Noren and George Crowe."[2]

That setback all but convinced Frey that he might have more of a future selling real estate than hitting a baseball. He never again had a real shot to join a Major League team. He played through the 1963 season, winning a second batting title in 1960, with the Rochester Red Wings in the International League. Some of the records are incomplete, but it can be verified that Frey ended his Minor League career with at least 1,789 hits.

Just as Frey was about to settle into his new career in real estate, he got a call from Baltimore farm director Harry Dalton asking if he wanted to manage the Orioles' Appalachian League (rookie) team in Bluefield, West Virginia. Frey didn't have to be asked twice. After spending two seasons managing Bluefield to losing records, he served as the Orioles' Midwest scout from 1966 through 1969 before joining Orioles manager Earl Weaver's coaching staff in 1970. Starting as the bullpen and hitting coach that season, he was a member of the team's coaching staff for ten seasons, including six seasons as the first base coach. During his tenure the Orioles won three pennants and the 1970 World Series.

In October 1979 the unheralded Frey was hired to manage the Kansas City Royals, replacing the popular Whitey Herzog. The Royals had won three consecutive division titles from 1976 through 1978, losing to the New York Yankees in the playoffs each time, before a second-place finish just three games behind the California Angels cost Herzog his job. One of the strongest endorsements for Frey came from Earl Weaver. "The Royals couldn't have picked a better man than Jim," said the Birds' peppery little leader. "I know the Orioles will miss his knowledge, his judgment, and his organization ability."[3]

The first person to call the new manager was his old Little League, high school, and Legion teammate Don Zimmer, then the manager of the Boston Red Sox. "Our school was a gold mine for baseball talent," Zimmer told the *Kansas City Star* after Frey was hired. "Besides me and Jim, it sent Clyde Vollmer, Herm Wehmeier, Art Mahaffey, Russ Nixon, Eddie Brinkman, and Pete Rose to the majors."[4]

In an amusing aside, Zimmer told the *Star* how Frey acquired his most prominent facial feature, his nose:

It was all my fault. We were playing our archrivals, Walnut Hills, in basketball. They were always one of the state powers, and this year, they had a real hotshot guard, a left-hander named Don Griewe. He was averaging 20 points a game when most teams didn't score much more than that in a game.

I couldn't shoot worth a darn, but I could play

real tough defense. So naturally, I got to cover Griewe. I held him to a basket and free throw in the first half, and he was really mad. That's when the elbowing started. He gave me a shot to the ribs, and I gave it right back. Soon everyone was running on the court. Jim took one step off the bench to help me, and some big guy from the other team hit him flush on the nose. It hasn't been the same since. But every time Jim looks in the mirror, that big nose reminds him of the one time we beat Walnut Hills in basketball.[5]

It didn't take long for Frey to show he could manage, as he led the Royals to a 97-65 record and the 1980 American League West title. The club's success was aided by future Hall of Famer George Brett, who flirted with a .400 batting average in late summer before finishing at .390. The Royals swept the Yankees in the American League Championship Series and went to their first World Series, where they lost to the Philadelphia Phillies in six games. Frey was criticized for his handling of the Royals' pitching staff, in particular for bypassing fourteen-game winner Paul Splittorff, a left-hander who pitched just once in relief. Frey said he believed that right-handers were more effective against the Phillies, and he started Rich Gale in the third and sixth games.

Still, it was a very good year, and hopes were high for 1981. The season was interrupted by a fifty-day midsummer players strike, at which point the Royals were struggling at 20-30. When they split their first twenty games after play resumed, Frey was abruptly fired by the Royals. He was replaced by Dick Howser, whose Yankees Frey had defeated in the 1980 ALCS.

Frey wasn't out of work long. In November he signed on as hitting coach of the New York Mets, working under manager George Bamberger, with whom he had coached in Baltimore for many years. He coached for the Mets for two seasons.

After the 1983 season Frey was hired to manage the Chicago Cubs, a team that had not had a winning season since 1972. Once again he had immediate success, leading the Cubs to a 96-65 record and a National League East Division title, their first postseason appearance since 1945. The Cubs were led by second baseman Ryne Sandberg, whose .314 average with 19 home runs and 19 triples were enough to get him named the Most Valuable Player, and pitcher Rick Sutcliffe, who was acquired from the Cleveland Indians in June and then rattled off a 16-1 record for the Cubs.

The Cubs faced the San Diego Padres in the playoffs and quickly won the first two games at Wrigley Field, 13–0 (behind Sutcliffe) and 4–2. Chicago needed just one more victory as the series headed to San Diego for the final three games. Shockingly, the Padres won all three, beating Sutcliffe in the final, and headed to the World Series, where they lost to the Detroit Tigers. Despite the playoff loss, Frey was named National League Manager of the Year.

The Cubs started well in 1985, holding first place in mid-June, but then lost 13 straight games and finished 77-84 and in fourth place. After a bad start in 1986 Frey was fired in June. He spent the 1987 season working for Chicago radio station WGN as the color commentator for Cubs games. In December 1987, the Tribune Company, the Chicago-based newspaper chain that owned the Cubs, hired Frey to replace his old boss Dallas Green as general manager of the Cubs. Frey quickly turned to his old friend Don Zimmer to be the new manager.

Frey soon put his imprint on the team by dealing his star relief pitcher, Lee Smith, to the Boston Red Sox for pitchers Al Nipper and Calvin Schiraldi. He then traded popular outfielder Keith Moreland to the Padres for reliever Goose Gossage, who replaced Smith as the closer. None of these moves paid off, as the Cubs finished 77-85 in 1988. Frey made another bold move after the season, trading two youngsters, outfielder Rafael Palmeiro and pitcher Jamie Moyer, to the Texas Rangers for hard-throwing reliever Mitch Williams. The trade worked out in the short term, as Williams saved thirty-six games for the Cubs in 1989, but he had a forgettable season in 1990 and was traded to the Phillies. Meanwhile, Palmeiro and Moyer went on to highly productive careers.

Chicago finished 93-69 in 1989, winning the National League East Division title for the first time since Frey led them in 1984. Once again the club fell in the playoffs, losing four of five games to the San Francisco Giants. After a disappointing 1990 season (77-85), Frey was active in the free-agent market, acquiring outfielder George Bell and pitchers Danny Jackson and Dave Smith. Jackson and Smith flopped in their roles in 1991 and Zimmer was fired in May, apparently on orders from Frey's bosses at the Tribune Company. After the 1991 season Frey was relieved of his general manager duties.

Frey retired after that and split his retirement between Naples, Florida, and Baltimore with his wife, Joan. The Freys raised four children. After almost eighteen years away from the game he was named vice chairman of the Somerset Patriots in the independent Atlantic League, a post he still held in 2010.

Chapter 5. **Billy Hunter**

Michael Huber

Billy Hunter played shortstop with a flashy glove, great team spirit, and a zest for the game. The Brooklyn Dodgers thought he could someday succeed Pee Wee Reese. But as things turned out, they traded Hunter away before he reached the Major Leagues, and by the time Reese retired, Hunter was playing out the string.

Gordon William "Billy" Hunter was born on June 4, 1928, in Punxsutawney, Pennsylvania. His father grew up with Mike Ryba, who spent lots of time with Dodgers boss Branch Rickey in the Cardinals organization in the 1930s and moved to the Red Sox organization in 1941. Shortly after the 1946 World Series, Ryba contacted Hunter and expressed interest in his shortstop abilities. Hunter had accepted a football/baseball scholarship to attend Penn State, beginning in 1947. However, to leave room for servicemen returning from World War II that year, Penn State did not take any freshmen on its State College campus, so Billy attended Indiana State Teachers College in Indiana, Pennsylvania. He then enrolled at Penn State as a sophomore (1948) for spring football practice and played as a T-formation quarterback. However, Hunter's goal was to play professional baseball. When the Brooklyn Dodgers invited him to Vero Beach, Florida, for 1948 spring training, the nineteen-year-old met Mike Ryba again (Ryba was then managing the Red Sox's Scranton club, who were training in Cocoa Beach). Mike had been waiting for Hunter to give him a call, and Billy had been waiting for Ryba's call. Not wanting to wait any longer, Hunter signed a contract with the Dodgers for $2,000. Ryba tried to talk him out of it, saying, "You know what the Dodgers are like?

Billy Hunter spent fourteen years as Baltimore's third base coach before a successful stint as manager of the Texas Rangers.

They have 21 farm clubs." Billy replied, "If I have it, I'll get there. If I don't have it, it wouldn't make any difference whether I was in the Red Sox camp or in the Dodgers camp."[1]

Hunter spent five seasons in the Minors before reaching the Majors in 1953. He played for Three Rivers (in the Canadian-American League) in 1948, for Nashua (New England League) and Newport News (Piedmont League) in 1949, and for Pueblo (Western League) in 1950. In 1951 and 1952 he was with the Fort Worth Cats in the Double-

A Texas League before being sold to the St. Louis Browns in October 1952. The '52 season had been Hunter's best in the Minors, as he sported a .285 batting average with 174 hits in 161 games. He knocked in 75 runs and stole 24 bases.

Hunter's 1952 Texas League MVP season put him at the top of every general manager's wish list. Browns owner Bill Veeck pried Hunter away from the Dodgers in exchange for $95,000 plus three players, Ray Coleman, Stan Rojek, and Bob Mahoney, and made Billy the highest priced rookie in team history. Hunter found out about the trade while reading the *New York Daily News* in Puerto Rico, where he was playing winter ball. He called his wife, who confirmed it by finding a story in the *New York Times*. The league minimum salary was $5,000, and Veeck signed Hunter for a salary of $6,000. According to Hunter, "Veeck apologized for only being able to pay me $6,000. 'Bill, we're bankrupt,' he told me, 'but I'll take care of you next year.' Well, you know what happened next year."[2] The Browns moved to Baltimore under new ownership. The shortstop didn't get the raise.

At the age of twenty-five, Hunter began his Major League career, debuting for the Browns on April 14, 1953, as the team's Opening Day shortstop. He hit his first home run on September 26, the next to last day of the season, off Connie Johnson of the Chicago White Sox. It was the final home run in St. Louis Browns history. In his first season in the Majors, Hunter played in all 154 games (152 at shortstop), garnering 124 hits in 567 at bats (.219) for the Browns, who finished in the American League basement with a 54-100 record. Hunter was hitting well enough at All-Star time to make the American League team for the All-Star Game, representing the Browns along with Satchel Paige. He didn't get to bat in the game, but he pinch-ran for Mickey Mantle. "I was in the top 10 in hitting at the end of June," Hunter later said. "I always joke that I must not have got another hit the rest of the year because I ended up at .219!"[3] His

career average in 630 Major League games also turned out to be .219.

A solid fielding shortstop, Hunter often played deep in the hole. He told *Sports Collectors Digest* in April 1997 that "I could come in on ground balls very well and playing deep gave me more range, so I would have a whole lot of assists."[4] This attitude helped him to save Bobo Holloman's no-hitter on May 6, 1953, with a dazzling defensive gem, a play that Holloman later called the greatest he'd ever seen. The field was wet from an earlier rain, but Hunter snared a line drive up the middle off the bat of Joe Astroth. It should have gone through the middle, as St. Louis's surface was usually "like concrete," but the shortstop dove for the ball, caught it, and threw out Astroth from his knees. Hunter later said, "The funny thing about it was that there were only 2,000-some people there to see Holloman's no-hitter because of the bad weather."[5] The Browns beat the Athletics, 6–0, in the sole no-hitter of that year's Major League season.

Before the next season the Browns became the Baltimore Orioles. Billy noticed right away a change from how things had been done in the Browns organization, later describing the trip from St. Louis to Baltimore in John Eisenberg's *From 33rd Street to Camden Yards*: "When we got to Camden Station, we got into convertibles and made the trip from downtown out to the park. It was unbelievable. There were people everywhere. I was in a car with Vern Stephens and Vinicio Garcia, the three of us in back, up on top, throwing balls or something out to the crowd. People were hanging out of windows. It was a big deal, like we won the war or something. We were thinking, 'What a huge difference from St. Louis.'"[6] The Orioles finished their first season with a 54-100 record, matching that of the '53 Browns, but they drew over a million fans to the park, compared with just under 300,000 for the Browns in 1953. Hunter was third on the team in games played

(125), second in stolen bases (5), and third in triples (5). He had 100 hits in 411 at bats (.243).

After the 1954 season Hunter was part of the massive seventeen-player trade between the Orioles and the New York Yankees. The big names were Hunter and pitchers Don Larsen and Bob Turley, all of whom went to the Yankees. The trade was started on November 17 and completed on December 1. Hunter spent most of 1955 and all of 1956 with the Yankees. After 98 games as the regular shortstop in 1955, he was optioned to Denver in the American Association to make room for Enos Slaughter on New York's active roster. The Yankees brought him back in 1956, but Hunter played in only 39 games behind Gil McDougald, getting 21 hits in 75 at bats. Hunter's biggest disappointment in professional baseball was being on the roster for the 1956 World Series and not getting into a game. The Yankees played seven games while Hunter warmed the bench.

In early 1957 Hunter was involved in a twelve-player deal between the Yankees and Kansas City Athletics. In an interview many years later (in 2003), he remembered hitting two home runs off Hall of Famer Early Wynn in a game on August 17, 1957, then squeezing in the winning run in the bottom of the ninth. But he managed only a .191 average in 116 games for the Athletics, who finished seventh. After batting a disappointing .155 in 22 games in 1958, Hunter was traded to Cleveland, where he played in 76 games and batted .195. After the season the Indians sent him to San Diego of the Pacific Coast League.

In 1959 Hunter smacked 8 home runs, batted .249, and scored 51 runs for the Padres, in what proved to be the end of his playing career. After the season his contract was sold to Toronto in the International League. In a 1992 interview he recalled thinking, "At age 31, if I can't get back to the big leagues after the season I just had, then I might as well retire."[7] He had told Toronto owner Jack Kent Cooke that the only way he would play again in

the Minors would be as a player/manager. Cooke had hired Mel McGaha the day before as manager, so Hunter retired. Hoot Evers was the acting general manager for Cleveland and offered Hunter a part-time job scouting players in the International League. The pay was $3,000 plus expenses. The next year, Evers offered him the same opportunity. In the meantime, Lee MacPhail of the Orioles offered him a full-time scouting position, which Hunter accepted.

In 1962 Hunter managed the Orioles' rookie team in Bluefield, West Virginia, with the understanding that if a coaching opportunity on the Orioles opened up, he would be considered for it. Hunter piloted Bluefield to consecutive Appalachian League pennants. Speaking in 1992, the skipper was extremely proud of the fact that he had managed shortstop Mark Belanger in Bluefield and later Belanger's two sons, Rich and Rob, at Towson State University.

In 1964 Hunter's former Yankee teammate Hank Bauer was named manager of the Orioles, and he hired Hunter as the third base coach and base-running instructor. In 1968, when Bauer was fired, the Orioles hired Earl Weaver to manage. Hunter was clearly disappointed, but Weaver rallied in support of Hunter, telling the press, "I really think I need him."[8] Hunter stayed on for nine years under Weaver. In the not uncommon event of Weaver being ejected from an Orioles game, it was often Hunter who took over the reins for the duration. In fact, Hunter managed the Orioles in the fourth game of the 1969 World Series (a 2–1 loss to Tom Seaver and the Mets), when Weaver became the first manager in thirty-four years to be ejected from a World Series game.

In 1974 Hunter displayed a new gimmick. When an Oriole hit a home run, Billy would unbutton his shirt and display his T-shirt to the crowd. There was only one word on the shirt: ZAP. The *New York Daily News* called the gimmick "bush."[9] In May 1975, the coach fractured his left arm when he was struck by a line drive off the bat of future Hall of Famer Rod Carew. It didn't deter his enthusiasm. Hunter was a loud coach, often described as feisty. In 1975 Jim Martz, a columnist for the *Miami Herald*, called Hunter "a throwback to the days when baseball was peppered with hoot 'n holler guys." Martz quoted Hunter as saying, "'I just wouldn't know how to act if somebody on the center-field wall couldn't hear me.'"[10]

During Hunter's 13½ years as the Orioles' third base coach, Baltimore enjoyed unprecedented success. The Orioles won two World Series titles (1966 and 1970), four American League pennants, and five AL East titles. Frank Robinson, noted as the "judge" in the Orioles' Kangaroo Court (a mock court conducted by Oriole players), credited Hunter with starting the Court "as a way to loosen the club up and point out some mistakes at the same time. Laugh and get a point across in a light atmosphere."[11]

Hunter was named the Texas Rangers' manager on June 28, 1977, the fourth Texas manager of the season, accepting a three-year, $250,000 contract. (The Rangers had fired Frank Lucchesi and replaced him with Eddie Stanky, who quit after two games, claiming homesickness. Connie Ryan managed eight games before Hunter accepted the job.) Bill, as he now became known, guided the Rangers to a second-place finish with a 60-33 record, and the rookie skipper received considerable mention in the Manager of the Year balloting, won by his former boss, Earl Weaver. At the end of the 1977 season, Hunter told reporters that "our crying need is a big RBI man. And we could use a starting pitcher. I'm satisfied with our defense and our bullpen, but we need a man who can drive in 90 to 100 runs."[12]

Texas first baseman Mike Hargrove described playing under Hunter: "He came in here and showed a perfect blend of knowing how to handle people, plus knowing the game. If you took a jar,

put Billy Martin and Frank Lucchesi in that jar, shook it up, then emptied it, out would come Billy Hunter. He combines the best qualities of both our previous managers."[13]

The successful skipper was offered either a three-year or five-year contract in the middle of the 1978 season, but he wanted a one-year contract instead. Hunter had become disenchanted with long-term contracts and didn't see how to motivate players with long contracts. In addition, his wife had no desire to live in Texas. The latter sentiment had a lot to do with his decision to turn down the offers. In a strange turn of events, Hunter was fired on the second-to-last day of the 1978 season, despite a record of 86-75, which had the Rangers in second place. Shocked by his dismissal, Hunter vowed that he would never manage or coach in the Majors again. He called the president at Towson State University, outside Baltimore, and became the head baseball coach, leaving the Major Leagues for a salary of $5,000. The Rangers installed Pat Corrales at the helm.

In 1979, Hunter's first season at Towson State, he guided the Tigers to an 18-10 record. In 1981 he commented that the biggest difference between college and professional ballplayers lay in the fundamentals. "That was the biggest adjustment I had to make," he said. "The players in college aren't as well versed in the fundamentals. I found I was taking a lot for granted. You have to do a lot more teaching."[14] One of the things he liked best about coaching at Towson was that the field was only three miles from his house.

One of Hunter's assistant coaches was Ron Hansen, who left in the middle of the 1980 season to join the Milwaukee Brewers' coaching staff. One of his players at Towson, left-handed pitcher Chris Nabholz, became only the second player in the school's history to make it to the Major Leagues. (The first was Al Rubeling.) Drafted in the second round of the 1988 draft by Montreal, Nabholz pitched in the Majors for six years, compiling a 37-35 record with a 3.95 earned run average.

In 1984 Hunter was named the athletic director at Towson, an NCAA Division I program. He served in the dual role of baseball coach and athletic director for three years before turning the program over to his longtime assistant Mike Gottlieb. Hunter's baseball coaching record at the collegiate level ended at 144-166-3.

Towson enjoyed unprecedented athletic success during Hunter's eleven years as the director of athletics. The Tigers men's basketball team made back-to-back appearances in the NCAA Tournament in 1990 and 1991, and the men's lacrosse team played for the national championship in 1991. The Towson baseball team went to the NCAA Tournament in 1988 and 1991, and the gymnastics team was nationally ranked and finished ninth in the nation in 1991.

Hunter married his wife, Beverly, in 1949. They had two sons (Kevin, born in 1953, and Gregory, born in 1961) and four grandchildren. The Hunters settled in the Baltimore area when Hunter was the Orioles' shortstop in 1954. As of 2010, they had lived in the same home in Lutherville since 1955. Hunter retired as Towson's athletic director in 1995. In 1996 he was inducted into the Baltimore Orioles Hall of Fame. In 1997 he was inducted into the Towson University Athletic Hall of Fame.

Chapter 6. **George Staller**

Malcolm Allen

"His reputation is that of a driving, spirited leader who at all times has evidenced an interest in the boy's future, rather than furthering any ambitions he might have had for himself." With those words in *The Sporting News*, columnist John Steadman introduced George Staller as the latter joined the Baltimore Orioles' coaching staff in 1962.[1] Indeed, Staller spent the bulk of his nearly four decades in professional baseball behind the scenes, managing, coaching, and scouting dozens of young players who eclipsed his own largely unnoticed three-week career as a Major League player.

George Walborn Staller was born on April 1, 1916, in Rutherford Heights, Pennsylvania, part of East Harrisburg in the south central region of the state. No April fool, he nonetheless had a good sense of humor and a knack for the national pastime that he honed in the Keystone State's rugged semipro anthracite leagues. As described by William C. Kashatus in *Diamonds in the Coal Fields*, "Anthracite baseball was an excellent proving ground for the professional game because it taught independence, pride, and above all, a necessary outlook on life as incessant struggle where nobody was going to give you anything—you had to earn it."[2]

One of Staller's opponents in the 1930s who exemplified this spirit was one-armed outfielder Pete Gray, who reached the Majors with the St. Louis Browns during World War II. "Pete was a fierce competitor who used to slide into bases with his spikes high," Staller recalled with admiration. "On one occasion, he almost got into a brawl with one of the coal miners on our team, but he wasn't the one to back away."[3]

The Orioles' longtime first base coach George Staller was well versed in the Oriole Way by 1970.

Like pitchers Charlie Wagner and Ken Raffensberger before him, Staller passed through the semipro Lebanon Valley League as a stepping-stone on his way to the pros. His break came midway through the 1937 season when the business manager of the Elmira Colonels, a Brooklyn Dodgers affiliate, signed him off the central Pennsylvania sandlots. The twenty-one-year-old left-handed outfielder reported to the Class D Beatrice Blues, got some batting tips from manager Leon Riley, and pounded Nebraska State League pitching for a .354 average in 36 games.

The next season the boyish-faced Staller, who had a playing weight of 190 pounds and stood five feet eleven, played briefly with Elmira of the Eastern League, and spent the bulk of the campaign with the Class C Dayton Ducks, earning All-Star honors as the Middle Atlantic League's top right fielder with a .366 batting average and a league-leading 92 RBIs and 43 stolen bases. Southpaw pitchers gave him trouble, but when Staller got to Elmira in 1939, manager Clyde Sukeforth gave him an opportunity to play through his struggles. Staller rewarded his skipper's faith by winning the Eastern League batting title with a .336 mark. Now playing left field because of an arm labeled a liability, Staller improved his defense playing home games in spacious Dunn Field, and led the circuit with 187 hits and 49 doubles batting out of the leadoff spot.

The Dodgers invited Staller to spring training in 1940, and Sukeforth predicted to *The Sporting News* that Brooklyn manager Leo Durocher, "whose plan is merely to look at the boy, won't let Staller out of his sight after he's had a chance to watch him for 20 minutes or so."[4]

Staller wound up in Double-A with the Montreal Royals, where he continued progressing toward the big leagues by hitting .307 with 94 runs scored and 85 RBIs. In addition to legging out a dozen triples and slashing a league-leading 40 doubles, Staller more than quadrupled his previous personal best by hitting 14 home runs. His season ended on September 5 when he caught a spike sliding into second base and fractured his ankle.

He was still limping when spring training rolled around in 1941, and after batting just .263 in 53 games in Montreal, he was dealt away by the Dodgers to the unaffiliated Nashville Vols of the Southern Association, where he hit .287 in 42 games. He helped Nashville sweep the Dallas Rebels in the Dixie Series but found himself out of a job at season's end. Staller wound up signing with

the Baltimore Orioles of the International League, just a ninety-minute drive from his home.

Back in right field in 1942, Staller walloped 20 home runs while batting .283 with 72 RBIs. Feeling even better after an ankle operation, he returned to Baltimore in 1943 and hit .304 with 16 homers and 91 RBIs. That got the attention of Connie Mack's cellar-dwelling Philadelphia Athletics, who brought him up the Majors for the last three weeks of the 1943 season.

Staller debuted on September 14 at Yankee Stadium, notching his first Major League hit, walking twice, and scoring a pair of runs in Philadelphia's 6–5 loss. The Athletics were swept the next day on their way to 105 total losses, but Staller made a nice running catch.

He hit safely in his first eleven games, and saw action in twenty-one contests, twenty of which were starts in right field. He batted .271 with 1 double, 3 triples, and 3 homers in 85 at bats, scoring 14 times and driving in 12 runs. He stole 1 base and committed 1 error, and that was the end of his Major League playing career. Staller spent 1944 and 1945 serving in World War II with the U.S. Marine Corps. The June 14, 1945, issue of *The Sporting News* reported, "Sgt. Willard Marshall, former Giants outfielder, and Pvt. George Staller, late of the Athletics, are members of the same Marine team at a Pacific base."[5]

With the war won, Staller rejoined the International League Orioles on May 30, 1946, and batted .254 in 72 games. He dipped to .251 for Baltimore the following year before moving on, at the age of thirty-one, to the next phase of his baseball career.

Staller returned to the Athletics organization, accepting an offer to be the playing manager of the Portsmouth A's of the Class D Ohio–Indiana League. The club finished second with an 82-58 mark, helped in no small measure by Staller himself. He batted .333 with 13 homers and 98 RBIs, and scored 122 times. In six years managing in the Athletics' system, that was Staller's only winning season. Eighth-place finishes with Martinsville (Virginia) in the Carolina League and Sunbury (Pennsylvania) in the Interstate League came the next two years, followed by three seasons in sixth place.

Staller spent 1951–52 skippering the Class A Savannah (Georgia) Indians of the South Atlantic League. In Augusta, Georgia, on May 20, 1951, he was arrested along with his catcher for interference and abusive language, respectively, after bad feelings erupted midway through the second game of a doubleheader. Augusta started making outs on purpose with a 3–0 lead in an effort to make the contest official, while Staller's club stayed true to his surname by slowing things down. After the ensuing argument, Staller and catcher Al Spaziano were allowed to finish the game, then arrested and held on a fifteen-dollar bond when it was over. Augusta Mayor W. D. Jennings investigated the incident, and then accompanied his city's club on its next trip to Savannah a few weeks later to return the bond money, get an autographed baseball, and allow two Augusta players to be "arrested" as a joke to make amends.

Staller played in less than half of the games in his two seasons at Savannah, which were his last as a player-manager. After batting .338 and .336, he didn't play at all in 1953, when he was granted a request to manage the Single-A Williamsport (Pennsylvania) Eastern League club to be closer to his ailing father. When the St. Louis Browns were moved to Baltimore for the 1954 season, Staller returned to the Baltimore organization (and stayed close to home) by taking over the reins of the York (Pennsylvania) White Roses of the Piedmont League, where he remained for two years.

Hall of Fame third baseman Brooks Robinson began his professional career at York in 1955 as a second baseman, but Staller and Orioles manager Paul Richards shifted him to the hot corner after forty games. Robinson has spoken glowingly about the long hours Staller spent working with him to hone his infield play. Staller, however, humbly insisted during Robinson's MVP season in 1964 that Brooks had always been a great fielder.

Staller moved on to the Aberdeen (South Dakota) Pheasants of the Northern League in 1956, then the Knoxville Smokies of the South Atlantic League for the next two seasons. With a pinch-hit single in the last game of the 1958 season, he closed the books once and for all on a professional playing career that saw him bat .309 with 124 homers and 858 RBIs in 1,526 Minor League contests.

His father, Ervin, died in April 1959 at the age of sixty-nine, and Staller spent that summer managing the Double-A Amarillo Gold Sox of the Texas League. He went north to Canada in 1960 to manage the Vancouver Mounties of the Pacific Coast League, then returned to the Texas League a year later to guide a Victoria (Texas) Rosebuds club that moved to Ardmore, Oklahoma, in late May because of poor attendance. Then, after thirteen "home" cities in sixteen years since he returned from World War II, he came back to the big leagues, when the new Orioles manager Billy Hitchcock hired Staller to be his first base coach in 1962.

The Orioles were a talented bunch seemingly on the verge of challenging the Yankees. Adding Staller to the coaching staff made perfect sense; he had managed a lot of the young Orioles in the eight years he'd spent in the organization. Jerry Adair, Steve Barber, Chuck Estrada, Jack Fisher, Ron Hansen, Dave McNally, Dave Nicholson, Milt Pappas, Brooks Robinson, Wes Stock, and Jerry Walker had all played for Staller.

Staller seemed like a natural fit, but when the Orioles slipped to a disappointing 77-85, seventh-place finish, coaches Cal Ermer and Staller got the ax. Whispers hinted that they were too genial and quiet, and Baltimore replaced them with a pair of "holler guys" in Luke Appling and Hank Bauer. "We wanted to shake things up in view of our disappointing season," said club president Lee MacPhail. "We feel we need coaches with more experience. Cal and George are capable fellows, and we'd like to keep them in the organization."[6] Indeed, both Ermer and Staller had been offered and accepted scouting jobs before other clubs knew they'd been let go. Staller's territory included Pennsylvania and southern New Jersey, and he covered it for more than five years.

The Orioles won the World Series in 1966 under Bauer, who had succeeded Hitchcock as manager, but the front office became disenchanted again when the club fell below .500 the following year. General manager Harry Dalton asked Earl Weaver, then a Minor League manager in the Orioles chain, to recommend some coaches. "I started with George Staller," Weaver recalled in *Weaver on Strategy*:

> He had given me a ton of advice when I was a minor-league manager, and he had been part of the Orioles organization for a long time. George couldn't pitch batting practice, but I told Harry that George would be a fine first-base coach. He got along with everyone, and had a knack for cooling people down in stressful situations, which is a wonderful gift. He had the marvelous ability of getting along with the players, and of having fun with them, yet being able to keep their respect and listen when he did some teaching.[7]

Surely, some of Staller's skills were honed during the dozen off-seasons he spent working as a guard in Pennsylvania prisons. Asked for similarities between his two dissimilar careers, he noted that in both cases you did not want to get too close to the charges. The Orioles made Weaver, not Staller, the first base coach in 1968, but midway through the season, "The Earl of Baltimore" started working on his Hall of Fame plaque by replacing Bauer as manager. One of the first things Weaver did was to appoint Staller his first base coach.

The 1969 Orioles won 109 regular-season games and romped through the inaugural American League Championship Series; a World Series title seemed like a mere formality. However, they were defeated by the upstart New York Mets. The despair surrounding the Orioles when they returned to Baltimore after having lost to the Mets in five games was palpable, the type of thing that could have undermined a lesser team. Staller, however, had other ideas. "It is George Staller trying to overcome unhappiness and cheer everyone up," wrote columnist Doug Brown, describing the trip. "Waiting at the airport for the flight back to Baltimore, Staller crept up behind his wife and gave her a hotfoot [to hotfoot is to set a shoe on fire, via the shoelaces or other means]. On the plane, he gave another wife a hotfoot. It was Joan Cashen, wife of the club's executive VP [Frank Cashen]."[8]

Rather than dwell on their loss, the Orioles were determined to come back better than ever in 1970, and they did just that, earning Staller a World Series ring in the process. Baltimore made it three straight American League pennants in 1971, still the most glorious era in franchise history. Staller did a lot of little things that could easily go unnoticed, like tossing the ball to the Orioles pitcher at the beginning of each inning . . . unless it was Mike Cuellar. Staller knew the superstitious Cuban southpaw wanted the baseball resting in the grass in front of the mound. When Earl Weaver initiated a tomato-growing competition down the left-field line at Memorial Stadium in 1972, Staller was one of the charter participants.

The Sporting News published an anecdote that gave insight into the benefits Baltimore gleaned from Staller's wealth of baseball experience. Early in the 1970 season, Weaver realized he didn't have a scouting report on Detroit Tigers rookie Elliott Maddox, who was in the lineup that day. Maddox had played in the Carolina League, but the Orioles didn't field a team in that circuit. The rookie had also played in the Florida State League,

MALCOLM ALLEN

but nobody connected to Baltimore's FSL outfit was on hand. "'Wait a minute. I'll get something,' first base coach George Staller finally said, heading out of the dugout toward a gent sitting in the front row behind the screen. Three minutes later, Staller was back. 'Likes the ball up and out over the plate,' George said. 'Has a good arm, but it's erratic sometimes. Good man to test on a bunt.'"[9]

Sure enough, when Mike Cuellar left a pitch up and out over the plate, Maddox drove it to the warning track. The Tigers rookie also made a throwing error and was unable to make a play when Baltimore shortstop Mark Belanger bunted for a base hit.

By early 1975, though, it was clear that Staller's days in Baltimore were numbered. Other than an aging Brooks Robinson, the players he'd managed in the Minors were all gone, and there were some in the organization who thought Staller, at fifty-nine years of age, was getting too old. Loyal organization man Cal Ripken Sr. was ready to join the coaching staff, and Staller decided to make 1975 his last season, though he did some scouting work for the expansion Seattle Mariners the following year.

Staller moved smoothly into retirement in Harrisburg, where he remained until his death at the age of seventy-six on July 3, 1992. He was buried at Hershey Cemetery, leaving behind his wife of fifty-two years, Joy, his son, George, and his daughter, Nelda.

Chapter 7. **Looking Ahead to the Season**

Mark Armour

The Baltimore Orioles entered the 1970 season on a mission. Their remarkable 1969 season had come to a rather sudden and shocking end, and the club had no intention of allowing itself another letdown. The 1969 Orioles finished 109-53, winning the new American League East by nineteen games over the Detroit Tigers. After dispatching the Minnesota Twins in three straight games in the League Championship Series, the Orioles were heavily favored to beat the upstart New York Mets, whose storybook season had captured the fancy of much of baseball. The Mets ultimately finished off their "miracle" season by shocking the Orioles in five games.

The Mets' victory was marked by a series of dazzling defensive plays (by players not renowned for their defense), home runs by nonsluggers, bloop hits, and odd umpires' calls. In the end it was the Mets' great pitching and all those great outfield catches that made the difference in the 1970 Series. The Orioles won the first game at home, but lost the next four.

"After the last game, I was in a daze," recalled catcher Elrod Hendricks. "I'm sitting out in the bullpen saying, 'I don't believe this.' Then all of a sudden it sunk in. We lost. Knowing we had a better club, I remember sitting out there and watching the fans jump around, and I left Shea Stadium. Even though I had to go to Puerto Rico and play winter ball, all I could think about was next year."[1] Hendricks's attitude was typical of the Orioles players'—the best team had not won the Series, and they could not wait for April 1970.

The Orioles did not seem to have any weaknesses, and general manager Harry Dalton resisted any

The Orioles entered the 1970 season determined to make up for their disappointing showing in the previous World Series. Especially determined was star third baseman Brooks Robinson, who had hit just .053 in the loss to the Mets.

attempt to "fix" the team. If anything, the team had too many good players, particularly in the outfield. Starters Don Buford, Paul Blair, and Frank Robinson all had had excellent seasons, leaving no room for Curt Motton, Dave May, Merv Rettenmund, and Terry Crowley, all of whom appeared ready for regular duty. There were rumors all fall that Buford would be dealt to make room for one of the youngsters, or a kid would be traded, but none of this happened. The Orioles did not appear to need any players.

Their infield—Brooks Robinson, Mark Belanger, Dave Johnson, and Boog Powell—was the best in baseball defensively, and all but Belanger were productive hitters. Shortstop Bobby Grich was one of the best prospects in baseball. The catching tandem of Hendricks and Andy Etchebarren was well-liked by the pitching staff and by manager Earl Weaver. The Orioles had three great starting pitchers—Jim Palmer, Mike Cuellar, and Dave McNally—and a solid group behind them. Although they were rumored to be looking for a fourth starter, the team that showed up at spring training was basically unchanged from the year before.

In its preview of the 1970 American League season, *Sports Illustrated* said of "the superlative Orioles" that "they won more games than any other team in the American League during the 1960s, and they are expected to win more games than anybody else this year."[2] Joe Trimble called them the best non-Yankee team since before the time of Babe Ruth, and wrote, "Obviously, they are too much for the rest of the league and so Harry Dalton, the young and smart general manager, is keeping the club intact."[3] *The Sporting News* was equally optimistic, picking them to "enjoy themselves another romp" in the American League East. Oddsmakers in Las Vegas made the Orioles the 8–5 favorite to reach the World Series.[4]

Still, there was a season to be played, and twenty-three other teams determined to slay the Oriole juggernaut. The club trained in Miami that spring and finished 9-8 in the Grapefruit League spring-training season, after having gone 18-4 in 1969. Did this spell hope for the rest of the league?

Chapter 8. **Don Buford**

Mark Armour

AGE	G	AB	R	H	2B	3B	HR	TB	RBI	BB	SO	BAV	OBP	SLG	SB	GDP	HBP
33	144	504	99	137	15	2	17	207	66	109	55	.272	.406	.411	16	1	8

The leadoff men of the 1960s were known mainly for slapping singles and stealing bases. Into this game stepped Don Buford, a versatile switch hitter with speed and a little power, and also the ability to draw walks and get on base. He had some success for a few years with the White Sox, but it was not until he joined forces with Earl Weaver in Baltimore that the full measure of his talent was utilized. Weaver wanted his leadoff man to be a productive hitter who could start the offense, and the first thing he did when hired in July 1968 to manage the Baltimore Orioles was to put Buford, a utility player at the time, at the top of the batting order every day. Buford became a star, and, not entirely coincidentally, the Orioles became one of the best teams in baseball history.

Donald Alvin Buford was born on February 2, 1937, in Linden, Texas, a small town in the northeast corner of the state, near the Louisiana border. His father was apparently a pretty good semipro player, but Don never got to know him—he was killed in a shooting accident when Don was about six or seven years old. Soon after, his mother, Sedalia, moved with Don to Southern California to be closer to her own family.

Buford grew up playing sports with his friends, in sandlots and backyards with whatever equipment they could rustle up. He always worked, beginning with a paper route as a boy. He starred in baseball and football for Dorsey High in Los Angeles, but because of his small size (five feet seven, 160 pounds), was not heavily recruited. After his 1955 graduation, he spent three semesters at Los Angeles City College, winning all-conference honors at quarterback in 1955 and at halfback in

The first move Earl Weaver made upon becoming manager in 1968 was installing Don Buford as his lead-off hitter and left fielder.

1956, and earning honorable mention as a junior college All-American. He tried to interest several Pacific Coast Conference schools in his services, and chose the University of Southern California so that he could play baseball as well. He played baseball in the spring of 1957 before his football scholarship started in the fall.

On the baseball diamond Buford played little in 1957 but regularly the next two years. He hit .323 as an outfielder at USC, and his 1958 squad, which also included future Major Leaguer Ron Fairly, won the College World Series, the first of ten won by Rod Dedeaux as head coach. On the gridiron, Buford played defensive and offensive halfback in 1957 and 1958; he led the Trojans in 1958 in interceptions, punt returns, and rushing yardage, and in both seasons in kickoff returns. In the big game against Notre Dame in November 1958, Buford rushed for thirty-four yards, threw a touchdown pass, returned kicks and punts, and made two interceptions. Notre Dame won, 20–13, but all the national stories featured Buford's performance. That year he was named All–Pacific Coast, and was a halfback for the national college all-stars in the Copper Bowl in Tempe, Arizona. In May 1959 he was awarded USC's Jacob Gimbel Athletic Attitude Award, given to the senior athlete with the best attitude.

Still, when Buford graduated there were no professional football offers and few for baseball. Buford later said he spoke with four baseball clubs—the Yankees, Dodgers, Pirates, and White Sox—and it was Chicago that gave him the best deal, a Triple-A contract and a small bonus. He was signed in November 1959 by scout Hollis Thurston.

In the spring of 1960, Buford trained with the Triple-A San Diego Padres (Pacific Coast League) and hit safely in his first twenty-one games before being stopped in the spring-training finale. This earned the twenty-three-year-old a starting outfield position for the Padres to start the season, but after hitting .268 for two weeks, he was sent down to Lincoln, Nebraska, in the Three-I League. There he hit .287 with 91 walks and 36 stolen bases but suffered a knee injury late in the season that required surgery. The knee bothered him the rest of his career, and was operated on three additional times.

Buford recovered in time to play all of 1961 with Charleston in the Sally League, where he hit just .236 in 132 games. He showed signs of progress after the season, hitting .324 playing against many future Major Leaguers in the Florida Instructional League. The next year he began with Triple-A Indianapolis, but after going just 3-for-27, was sent down to Single-A Savannah in the Sally League. He hit .323 there, with 91 walks and 100 runs scored, again showing signs of the great on-base skills that would later mark his Major League career. He shifted to third base in midseason and was named the third baseman on the circuit's all-star team after the season. He was a promising player, but at the age of twenty-five, a bit long in the tooth for Single-A. He played that fall in the Florida Instructional League, then played winter ball in Venezuela.

Buford, though small in stature, developed surprising power from both sides of the plate. With Indianapolis in 1963, he proved himself ready, leading the International League with a .336 batting average, 206 hits, 41 doubles, 114 runs scored, and 42 stolen bases and helping his team capture the league's championship. He was named the league's most valuable player and rookie of the year, and *The Sporting News* chose him as its Minor League player of the year. After the season he joined the White Sox, where he played 12 games and hit .286 in 42 at bats. In his September 14 debut in Washington, Buford finished 1-for-3 with a double off of Bob Baird. He spent the winter playing in Puerto Rico.

With the young star third baseman Pete Ward blocking Buford's path to the Majors, the club played Buford a bit at second base in September and after the season sold longtime second baseman Nellie Fox to Houston, partly to open the job for Buford.

Although it would take another generation before on-base skills became universally valued, Buford's performance in this area was always remarked upon. At Buford's first Major League spring training, Al Lopez raved, "This fellow knows how to get on base."[1] What came more difficult for Buford was his transition from third base, a position he had played only a couple of years, to second base, in particular having to the learn the difficult double-play pivot at age twenty-seven. Although he proved to be sure-handed, most observers felt that he had trouble taking the ball out of his glove fast enough on the pivot. In early April 1964, Buford and the San Francisco Giants' Jesus Alou were named by *The Sporting News* as the rookies most likely to succeed that season.

Buford was not the best rookie in the league, but he did hit .262 with good plate discipline that made up for his erratic glove. Middle infielders in the mid-1960s rarely hit as high as .262, so Buford's job was secure. He improved considerably the next year, up to .283 with 67 walks, which helped him score 93 runs, fourth most in the league. He generally hit second in the batting order, but he defied type by drilling 10 home runs among his 37 extra-base hits.

Nonetheless, Buford's defensive struggles caused the White Sox to play him at third whenever their regular, Pete Ward, needed a rest. In 1966 manager Eddie Stanky moved Ward to the outfield so that Buford could play his "natural" third base, a position he had really not played until his last year in the Minor Leagues. Buford responded by leading league third basemen with 26 errors, mostly on throws. He also fell off at the plate, hitting just .244 while still scoring 85 runs. Stanky also wanted Buford to run more, and offered him a sports coat if he stole 30 bases. In response, Buford stole 51, second in the league, earning himself slacks, a shirt, and tie along with the jacket.

The next season Buford continued to struggle getting hits, dropping to .241, but walked enough to be a valuable offensive player. The White Sox were part of a historic four-team race for the pennant, and Buford epitomized the club—a versatile singles hitter with good speed (34 steals). Stanky moved him back to second base during the pennant race, and he handled himself well enough at second, third, and left field. Nonetheless, after the

season he was traded to the Orioles, going with pitchers Roger Nelson and Bruce Howard for outfielder Russ Snyder, first baseman John Matias, and shortstop Luis Aparicio. The Orioles mainly wanted the pitchers, while the White Sox coveted Aparicio (whom they had traded away five years earlier) and Snyder.

Buford was going to a team one year removed from a championship, and a team that already had an All-Star third baseman (Brooks Robinson), an established second baseman (Dave Johnson), and three outfielders (Curt Blefary, Paul Blair, and Frank Robinson) whom manager Hank Bauer liked. Buford had no place to play. Earl Weaver, who joined the club that year as the first base coach, loved Buford's game, and remembered managing against him when he was a star outfielder in the Minors. He urged Buford to remind Bauer that he could play the outfield, but Buford spent the early part of the 1968 season as a part-time second baseman, when Johnson sat down or moved to shortstop in place of Mark Belanger. At the All-Star break he had started 22 games and played in 26 others, mainly at second, and was hitting .234 with his usual patience. During the break, Bauer was fired and replaced by Weaver.

In Weaver's first game, he played Buford in center field and batted him leadoff. Buford walked and scored in the first, then homered in the fifth, the only runs in Dave McNally's 2–0 shutout over the Minnesota Twins. Buford never left the lineup again that season. Weaver essentially platooned Blair and Blefary, with Buford playing left field when Blair started and center field when Blefary did. Buford hit leadoff the rest of the way, and responded by hitting .298 with 11 home runs and 45 walks in the final 82 games of the season. "Don Buford is the spark plug," said teammate Frank Robinson after the season, "the guy who always gets on base, who doesn't scream or yell, but when you see him out there on a sack, you just have just got to bring him home."[2] Buford scored 45 runs in the second half of the season.

Weaver's 1968 team had a lot of talent, and he helped guide them to a second-place finish behind the Tigers. His key change to the club was his insertion of Buford into the regular lineup, a move that helped spark the team to its three straight pennants. Leadoff men of the 1960s were often little guys who choked up on the bat and hit singles. Weaver loved Buford because he got on base, a skill not universally valued at the time but coveted by the rookie manager.

For Buford, the move to Baltimore was easier on the field than it was off. The Buford family, which included his wife, Alescia, and two sons (soon to be three), had difficulty finding housing in Baltimore, suitable apartments suddenly not available when the renters realized that the interested family was black. Once their plight became publicly known, offers were made, and they rented a place just north of Memorial Stadium in a predominantly black neighborhood. Still, Buford openly wondered how things would have gone were he not a famous baseball player.

Meanwhile, Baltimore's outfield picture was complicated in 1969 by the arrival of Merv Rettenmund, who had hit .331 with 22 home runs at Rochester in 1968, and was ready to break in. Although Buford assumed the regular left-field job on Opening Day, many observers felt that Rettenmund would take over soon enough. Instead, Buford played 144 games, hitting .291 with 11 home runs, 31 doubles, 96 walks, and 99 runs scored. He led off all year and helped spark the great offense and the team to a magnificent 109-53 record. After hitting .286 in the team's playoff sweep of the Twins, he led off the bottom half of the first inning of the World Series with a home run off Tom Seaver, leading the Orioles to a 4–1 victory over the New York Mets. But he hit only 2-for-20 in the Series, which the Orioles lost in five games.

Rettenmund broke through to hit .318 in 1970,

playing part time at all three outfield positions, though mainly in center field. Buford played 144 games again, and the club dominated the division with 108 wins. Though his average dropped to .272, he compensated with 109 walks and 17 home runs, helping epitomize the perfect Weaver leadoff hitter. On April 9 he hit home runs from both sides of the plate, the first Oriole to accomplish the feat. On August 28, after Milwaukee pitcher Dave Baldwin intentionally walked pinch hitter Boog Powell, Buford hit a grand slam to lead the Orioles to an 8–4 victory. He hit .318 in the postseason, with a home run in both the ALCS and the World Series, helping the great club to a dominating World Series title over the Cincinnati Reds.

Buford's final big year came as a thirty-four-year-old in 1971. Weaver brilliantly employed his four outfielders, giving them all between 545 (Robinson) and 589 (Rettenmund) plate appearances. Despite the slightly lessened workload, Buford responded with a .290 average, 89 walks, a career-high 19 home runs, a career-high .413 on-base percentage (fourth in the league), and a league-leading 99 runs. He played in his only All-Star Game, striking out against Don Wilson of Houston in the AL's 6–4 win. He hit .300 in the postseason, including 2 home runs in the World Series, but the Orioles fell to the Pirates in seven games. For his career, Buford hit 5 home runs in 22 postseason games.

In December 1971 the Orioles traded Frank Robinson to the Dodgers to ease the logjam in the outfield, though the holdovers had to contend with another great prospect, Don Baylor. The incumbents all later claimed they tried too hard to adjust to Robinson's departure, and the entire offense collapsed. The Orioles had led the league in runs for the past two seasons but fell to eighth of twelve teams in 1972. Buford, now thirty-five, hit just .206 for the season, and scored just 46 runs.

After the season the Orioles offered Buford a big salary cut, and the sides could not come to terms. Instead Buford signed to play with the Tai-heiyo Club Lions in Japan, doubling his salary and allowing his wife and three sons to enjoy a new culture. He played three years for the Lions, making two All-Star teams, and then in 1976 played with the Nankai Hawks. He finally retired after the 1976 season, after seventeen years in professional baseball.

With his baseball career over, Buford went to work as a personnel manager for Sears (the department store), with whom he had worked over several off-seasons. He kept this job until 1981, when his old friend Frank Robinson, manager of the San Francisco Giants, hired him to coach. Buford worked as the first base coach for four years and later served under Robinson with the Orioles and Washington Nationals. He also served as a Minor League manager several times and worked with the Orioles in player development for a few years in the 1990s.

In 1960 Don married Alescia Jackson, who eventually graduated from UCLA law school and owned her own public-relations firm in Sherman Oaks, California. The couple raised three sons. Donald Jr. played baseball at Stanford and USC, and graduated cum laude in economics from USC. He then played four years in the Orioles' Minor League system before graduating from UCLA medical school. He began a practice as an orthopedic surgeon in Dallas in the mid-1990s. Daryl graduated from UC Berkeley and USC Law School, and became a lawyer and sports agent in Beverly Hills. Damon followed his father to USC and then had a nine-year career in the Major Leagues with the Orioles, Mets, Rangers, Red Sox, and Cubs.

Don and Alescia Buford, rightly proud of the accomplishments of their sons, pointed especially to their educational achievements, which they both had stressed. "I just really have tried to encourage all three of them, and be in their corners," Don told the *Baltimore Sun*. "I always told them that whatever they do, they have to dedicate themselves."[3] Asked by another writer about Damon following in his footsteps as a Major League player, Don said, "Damon wasn't raised to be a baseball player. He decided he wanted to pursue it from the time he was in college. They were kids, not really stressing being professionals but enjoying themselves and having fun."[4]

Buford was elected to the Baltimore Orioles Hall of Fame in 1993 and was hailed as the club's greatest-ever leadoff man. Despite their early difficulties finding a place to live in 1968, the Bufords grew to love the city, and the city them. "That was the time of our lives," Mrs. Buford told the *Sun*. "That was home."[5]

Chapter 9. Dave Leonhard

Thomas Ayers

AGE	W	L	PCT.	ERA	G	GS	GF	CG	SHO	SV	IP	H	BB	SO	HBP	WP
29	0	0	.000	5.08	23	0	4	0	0	1	28.1	32	18	14	0	4

Dave Leonhard had a mediocre high-school and college pitching career. He refused a scout's first offer to sign him, then changed his mind and signed for a nine-dollar bonus. From that humble start, he carved out a six-year career as a pitcher with the Baltimore Orioles.

David Paul Leonhard was born on January 22, 1941, in Arlington, Virginia. His mother, Marion Leonhard, was a civilian clerk for the Navy Department, and his father, Paul Leonhard, worked for the Social Security Administration. Neither knew much about baseball, Leonhard said in an interview, and he learned the game playing with friends and classmates and in Little League and American Legion baseball at various positions. As a youth Dave was nearsighted, and when he batted he had difficulty picking up the trajectory of pitches. Once he realized he wasn't much of a hitter, he concentrated on pitching and stayed at the position even after his vision problem was diagnosed.[1]

Leonhard had what he described as an undistinguished high-school pitching career. Afterward, he attended Washington College in Chestertown, Maryland, where he played baseball and basketball, then transferred to Johns Hopkins University in Baltimore. Sports aren't an emphasis at the heavily postgraduate institute, and it had produced only one alumnus who played Major League baseball, Otis "Old Gray Fox" Stocksdale, who had a four-year career in the 1890s. Leonhard pitched for the university's baseball team but he later told his Orioles teammate Jim Palmer that he didn't pitch particularly well there and didn't seriously entertain thoughts of a professional career.[2] Leonhard graduated with a bachelor's degree in histo-

Pitchers emerging from the Orioles farm system in the late 1960s had a difficult time breaking into the team's great rotation. Such was the fate of Dave Leonhard.

ry in 1962. In his senior year, he won three games and lost two.

A gift from his mother changed his life. "For Christmas in 1962 my mom gave me a pair of baseball shoes for a present," Leonhard said. The shoes didn't quite fit, so he went to exchange them at a sporting goods store in downtown Baltimore. There he ran into Walter Youse, a Baltimore Orioles scout who had seen him pitch the previous summer for Lady of Fatima, a church league team. Youse, who had coached an opposing team, was impressed with Leonhard, and when he saw Leonhard again in the store, he offered the 145-pound pitcher a contract on the spot.[3]

At the time Dave was teaching eleventh grade history at Sparrows Point High School in Sparrows Point, Maryland, outside Baltimore. Believing that he was just a mediocre pitcher, Dave refused the offer. "I had a contract to teach through June and I didn't want to leave," he told the writer of a profile on him in a Johns Hopkins alumni magazine.[4] Youse persisted and offered Leonhard $450 a month to play rookie ball after the school year. Leonhard accepted Youse's offer, figuring it was a much better summer job than anything else he'd find, but said that he "had no intentions of being a professional ballplayer." Meanwhile, since professional teams got a 30 percent discount at the store, Youse got Leonhard a nine-dollar discount on the shoes. Leonhard joked, "My bonus amounted to the discount I got when I paid for the shoes."[5]

Leonhard reported to Bluefield, West Virginia, in June 1963 as an atypical rookie ballplayer. He was twenty-two, and had married his high-school sweetheart, Judy, just after graduating from Johns Hopkins. Their romance had ended when they went away to college, but they reconnected at an alumni football game and rekindled their relationship. "Most of the ballplayers were just kids out of high school. . . . I was like an old man among them," Leonhard recalled of his debut with the Appalachian League team. "Right away, I saw it wasn't going to be a picnic. There were six- to seven-hour bus trips over bumpy mountain roads."[6] His apartment in Bluefield was small and cramped, and he got just three dollars a day in meal money.

But Leonhard quickly impressed, putting up an 0.82 earned run average in eleven innings, and was rapidly promoted to Appleton, Wisconsin, to play for Fox Cities in the Class A Northern League. This was a full-season league and Leonhard immediately noticed a difference as "the kids there had been to spring training, and the caliber of play was better."[7] After two starts and one victory for Fox Cities, he spent a month with Aberdeen, South Dakota, of the Class A Northern League, going 4-2 with a 2.45 ERA. That stretch included the most successful start in Leonhard's Minor League career, a seven-inning no-hitter against Winnipeg on August 29.

Leonhard returned to Aberdeen the following season. Giving up just 135 hits in 181 innings and striking out 143 batters, he posted a 16-4 record with a 2.83 ERA. He led the Northern League in wins in 1964 and was second in complete games, third in strikeouts, and fifth in ERA. In spring training that year, Dave met Jim Palmer, the future Hall of Famer, who became one of his best friends in baseball.

In 1965 Leonhard moved up to Double-A Elmira (Eastern League) and had another excellent season, finishing 20-5 and leading the league in victories and strikeouts (209). He was disappointed when he wasn't promoted by the Orioles in September, believing his small frame and lack of outstanding stuff kept him down. Leonhard recalled, "I knew then that it wasn't going to be easy to crack the big time." Earl Weaver, Leonhard's manager at Elmira and later with the Orioles, expressed the same sentiment: "Other young pitchers with great natural skills didn't have to win like Dave did. Even with losing records, they'd get a longer look on account of having a fastball that really hummed. All Dave could do was to keep proving himself, keep winning."[8]

Weaver believed in Leonhard's talent and sometimes rode the Virginian hard, particularly when Dave grew discouraged or struggled with his concentration. Weaver recalled the time Leonhard lost to Pittsfield in the thirteenth inning by walking the pitcher and then hitting the next batter, Reggie Smith. Leonhard said Weaver was so exasperated with him that he began to cry. Weaver remembered that he "gave [Leonhard] hell for it" as "he had too much control for that." After Weaver's outburst Leonhard won thirteen of his next fourteen decisions. Despite Weaver's fiery personality, Leonhard recalled that the manager knew "how and when to turn it on and off. He knew some guys would respond to screaming and others needed a pat on the back. That was what made him a success as a manager."[9]

Leonhard went to spring training in 1966 believing he had a chance to crack the Baltimore rotation. Instead, he wound up with a minor shoulder injury and followed Weaver to Rochester. The Vietnam War was on, and with the help of the Orioles, Leonhard, rather than wait to be drafted, joined the U.S. Air National Guard. The combination of the nagging shoulder injury and the stress of commuting to Baltimore for regular National Guard meetings led to an off year, as Leonhard finished with 9 victories and 7 defeats and a 3.86 ERA in 30 games with Rochester.

Leonhard returned to Rochester in 1967 and pitched considerably better, finishing 15-3 with a 2.61 ERA. His Minor League record then stood at 66 wins and 21 losses. He was rewarded with a September promotion to the Major Leagues. On September 21 he made his Major League debut, starting against the Washington Senators before a sparse crowd of 1,718 at DC Stadium. He allowed 3 runs, all on a home run by Bob Chance, in 5 innings, as the Senators defeated the Orioles in 11 innings. Manager Hank Bauer presumably saw something he liked, as he tabbed the twenty-six-year-old to start against Washington again four days later at Memorial Stadium in Baltimore. Leonhard fared better in this start, going 7⅓ innings and allowing 2 runs while striking out six batters, although he didn't receive a decision as the Orioles won 3–2 in the bottom of the ninth. He made one more appearance that year, pitching the last two innings in a 4–0 shutout of the Cleveland Indians. He finished with a 3.14 ERA in 14⅓ innings.

While the 1967 season was a good step forward, Leonhard viewed the 1968 season as the one that would determine whether he had a future in the Majors. In November he told a reporter, "Next year will be my last if I don't make it." He saw winter ball as an opportunity to improve his chances, so he played for Santurce in Puerto Rico during the off-season, the first of six seasons in which he would pitch winter ball. Leonhard said he gained more confidence from his performance that winter than he did from the two starts against the Senators, since "they weren't much of a ballclub back then."[10]

Leonhard didn't pitch well in spring training the following year and the Orioles sent him back to Rochester. He was upset, believing he had earned a chance to play in the Majors. In the end the Orioles agreed to pay Dave half of the $5,000 bonus he had been promised if he spent ninety days on the big-league roster. As it turned out, Leonhard never made it to Rochester. After the Rev. Martin Luther King Jr. was assassinated on April 4, Leonhard's Maryland Air National Guard unit was called up for riot prevention patrol in Baltimore. Leonhard spent nine days on active duty.[11] After he was deactivated, he spent a day, April 15, in Baltimore to pitch batting practice for the Orioles. That night Baltimore's traveling secretary Phil Itzoe told Leonhard, "You're coming with us to the West Coast." Orioles pitcher Pete Richert had also been called up to his reserve unit in Washington and was still on duty. The Orioles wanted Leonhard as insurance during an eight-game road trip. Leonhard said, "I assumed I'd only stay until Richert got out."[12]

Despite a rough start against the Angels (four runs in four innings), the Orioles kept Leonhard when Richert returned later in April. He solidified his place on the team with two great starts at home—a one-run, five-hit complete game against the Yankees and a one-hit shutout of the Tigers. He walked thirteen men in the two outings, but with that pair of victories Leonhard began to feel as if he was a member of the Orioles team. "Before I won a game I just got sympathetic smiles from the players. . . . Little things indicate you don't belong. Like card games. Nobody ever invited me to card games. Card games aren't for transients. . . . Now I'm in card games."[13]

Leonhard took two losses in his next three starts, but on May 30 he got his second shutout, against the Chicago White Sox. Earl Weaver replaced the fired Hank Bauer in July and soon announced that Leonhard would be a regular in the pitching rotation. These plans were interrupted when Leonhard was recalled to the National Guard in late July. He pitched as a starter and reliever when he returned, finishing with a 7-7 record and a 3.13 ERA for his rookie season.

The coaches noticed that Leonhard had a lazy, short-arm delivery. He wasn't using the top part of his body, and coach Billy Hunter explained, "Davey . . . doesn't bring his arm way back and fire. It's closer in to his body, which is against the principles of pitching. A pitcher of that sort tends to get sore arms, and doesn't use the arm to full advantage. (Pitching coach) George Bamberger changed him a little." Leonhard described his pitching style: "I had to get by on the life, not the speed, of the ball . . . on how that fastball wiggles. That and two other pitches that broke—a curve and a slider."[14]

Dave got on well with most of his teammates, particularly Jim Palmer and Terry Crowley, as he liked joking around and having a good time. However, he noticed something about Major League players. "Ballplayers are a homogenous group. I don't know why for sure. But as a rule, even if a guy is different, he soon gets molded. Either it happens unconsciously or, if he resists, he'll be kidded to the point where he feels self-conscious."[15]

The 1969 season was Leonhard's most successful, and the one during which he saw the most consistent work. He pitched in Baltimore's first two games of the season and picked up his first vic-

tory of the season in the second, with a scoreless thirteenth inning in a 2–1 victory over the Boston Red Sox. Dave also defeated the Red Sox in relief for his second victory, and picked up his third win with five innings of two-hit relief against the Oakland Athletics on May 23. Leonhard's ability to do both short and long relief stints made him a valuable member of the bullpen.

Leonhard made his first start of the 1969 season on June 22 and shut out the Cleveland Indians on three hits. This effort was noteworthy because he was on weekend leave from his summer military training.[16] On the 29th he got another victory with 6⅓ scoreless innings against Detroit, with six strikeouts, in relief of Tom Phoebus to improve his record to six victories and zero losses. He finished the year with a 7-4 record and a career-low 2.49 ERA in a career-high 37 appearances. He did not pitch in the American League Championship Series, in which the Orioles swept the Minnesota Twins, and appeared in one game in the World Series, which the Orioles lost to the New York Mets. He pitched two innings in Game Three, allowing one run on a home run by Ed Kranepool.

Leonhard often experienced teasing from his teammates about his education. "I try not to make anything out of [Johns] Hopkins," he told the author of the *Johns Hopkins Magazine* article, "but the guys on the team like to kid me about it. They call me Professor or when I make a mistake—and I make my share of them—they ask, 'Didn't they teach you at Hopkins?' . . . The only time my educational background becomes a factor with the players is when somebody needs help with a crossword puzzle."[17]

Leonhard reported to spring training in 1970 with a guaranteed place in the bullpen for the first time in his career. Though the season was a triumph for the Orioles—they won the World Series—it didn't go well for Leonhard. He made 23 appearances, all in relief, and threw 28⅓ innings with a 5.08 ERA. Leonhard struggled with his control as he never had before, walking 18 batters, surrendering 5 home runs and throwing a career-high 4 wild pitches. He had no wins or losses and one save. "I was supposed to be the long man in relief. My job was to come in when McNally or Mike Cuellar got knocked out early. That never happened," he explained. Leonhard did not appear in either the ALCS or the World Series. "I wasn't looking to pitch; my confidence wasn't high and I found it hard to get into a routine with those long stretches of inactivity," he recalled.[18]

Leonhard came to spring training in 1971 and was told he had to pitch his way onto the team, which he thought he accomplished with a 1.20 ERA in six spring appearances. When he was told he had been assigned to Rochester, he said that he would rather retire. "I can't see it. . . . I want to force the team to trade me . . . or I want assurance that if I go to Rochester, I'll be back in a month or so," he told a Baltimore reporter.[19]

Leonhard soon changed his mind and joined Rochester. After winning seven games and losing four with seven complete games in thirteen starts, he was called up to the Orioles on July 6. On July 10 he relieved Grant Jackson against Cleveland in the first inning with 3 runs in and finished the game, pitching 8⅓ innings of shutout relief in picking up the 11–3 victory. The only hit the Indians managed off Leonhard was a leadoff single by Chris Chambliss in the ninth inning. Weaver gave Leonhard his first start of the season on July 22 in Kansas City, and his faith in the right-hander was rewarded as Leonhard threw a five-hit shutout, more than two years after his last Major League start.

Leonhard stuck with the Orioles as a long reliever and spot starter, pitching 54 innings and finishing with a 2-3 record and a 2.83 ERA. His strikeout rate, never high, fell to the lowest in his career as he struck out just eighteen batters, and he walked more than he struck out for the third season in a row. Leonhard didn't pitch in the ALCS

against Oakland but got into Game Five of the World Series against the Pittsburgh Pirates, which the Orioles lost in seven games. He relieved Dave McNally in the fifth inning and pitched a scoreless inning.

After the Series the Orioles went on a tour of Japan, but Leonhard skipped it. He went back to Puerto Rico to play winter ball for the fifth time. It was a time of controversy for Leonhard, fueled by remarks he had made to Baltimore Sun sportswriter Phil Jackman the previous January. As it appeared in the Sun, the article, about his experiences playing in Puerto Rico, was comprehensive, but an excerpt published in Puerto Rico focused on negative things he said.[20] The Spanish-language article was titled, "Leonhard Sees Island as Land of Dead Bugs, Lice and Roaches."[21] The excerpt focused on Leonhard's recollections of the island's problem with cockroaches, including a time that the team bus became roach-infested and some cockroaches literally carried his sandwich off the luggage rack.[22] The excerpt also contained a reference to voodoo, but Leonhard explained that these were written in a joking manner and just included to add some humor to the article. During the season Leonhard received some angry mail from Puerto Ricans, and after the home opener in Puerto Rico he had to get a police escort home. "They booed me for about ten minutes," he recalled. "They threw stuff at me in the bullpen. Their faces were contorted with hatred and I got kind of scared."[23] At another game, fans in the outfield stands unveiled a thirty-foot-long sign that read, "Cucaracha Leonhard Go Home." *Cucaracha* is Spanish for cockroach. Dave, who came to be known as Cucaracha Leonhard on the island, bought the sign from the fans during the game.[24]

The conflict was eventually resolved when Leonhard and the Santurce team's owner, Hiram Quevas, went to see the editor of the *San Juan Star* about the misunderstanding. They explained the confusion, and the owner vouched for the fact that

Leonhard was friendly with Puerto Ricans and had bought an apartment on the island.[25] Leonhard explained that he kept returning to the island for the love of the game and expressed his appreciation for the fans, the island, and his teammates. When Santurce manager Rubén Gómez also expressed his support for Leonhard, the situation seemed to be resolved.[26] The events on the diamond, where Santurce wound up losing to Ponce in the national semifinals, seemed almost secondary that year.

The 1972 season was notable because Baltimore used only eleven pitchers all season, as Weaver depended principally on his four starters. Despite being on the roster all season, Leonhard appeared in only fourteen games, in which Baltimore was 2-12, and he pitched just twenty innings. He finished with no wins or losses, a 4.50 ERA, 12 walks, and 7 strikeouts. Leonhard's most effective appearance of the year was 3⅓ scoreless innings in relief of McNally in a 7–4 victory over Chicago on July 14. His final big-league appearance came on September 20 in Boston when he pitched two scoreless innings in a 9–1 loss.

That winter was also his last in Puerto Rico, where he finished with a career 26-21 record for Santurce with a 3.44 ERA in 406 innings pitched.[27]

Leonhard split 1973 between Rochester and the Salt Lake City Angels as, halfway through the season, he got his wish and was traded to California. Harry Dalton, who was familiar with Leonhard from Baltimore, acquired him for utility man Jim Hutto. Leonhard was never recalled by the Angels and was 6-6 with a 4.08 ERA in 15 appearances for Salt Lake City after going 3-1 with a 4.34 ERA in ten games for Rochester. He split 1974 between Salt Lake City and Wichita in the Chicago Cubs organization.

After the 1974 season, Leonhard was appointed as a pitching coach for the Québec Carnavals, the Expos' affiliate in the Double-A Eastern League. In his two seasons there he found the time to throw sixty-nine innings while tutoring Montre-

al's prospects. Among Leonhard's most famous pupils were Joe Kerrigan, who became a pitching coach himself; Shane Rawley, who won over one hundred games in the Majors; and Dan Schatzeder, who had a fifteen-year big-league career as a reliever. Dave also coached Gerald Hannahs, who, before pitching seventy-one innings in four Major League seasons, went 20-6 for Québec in 1976 to became the Eastern League's first twenty-game winner since Leonhard himself in 1965.

Leonhard said he "loved the life" of coaching, from the camaraderie to the active nature of the job. However, at that time coaches made very little money, even in the Majors, and job security was minimal. He worried about how he was at the mercy of the front office with regard to events that didn't necessarily reflect how well he was doing as a coach. He had offers to keep coaching but decided after two years that he wanted more stable employment.

Dave's marriage to Judy ended in divorce after a few years. During a road trip to Boston in the early 1970s he met Doris, who became his second wife. For a couple of years they ran a Christmas tree stand in the off-season in the Boston area. After Leonhard decided not to continue coaching, he and Doris bought a flower shop in Beverly, Massachusetts, in May 1975 and turned it into a garden center. As of 2010 they owned seven greenhouses and sold flowers, shrubs, and various other garden supplies.[28]

Jim Palmer always said that Leonhard was his best friend during his big-league career.[29] Decades after their careers ended, they still saw each other frequently. Leonhard was invited to speak at Jim Palmer Day in Baltimore in 1985. Known for a good sense of humor, Dave remarked, "It's a grand event befitting a gentleman and a gentle man. But I don't want to give you the idea he's perfect because, number one, he introduced me to my wife, and number two, he introduced me to golf."[30]

Chapter 10. **Curt Motton**

Malcolm Allen

AGE	G	AB	R	H	2B	3B	HR	TB	RBI	BB	SO	BAV	OBP	SLG	SB	GDP	HBP
29	52	84	16	19	3	1	3	33	19	18	20	.226	.369	.393	1	0	1

[Curt] Motton has been Baltimore's best pinch-hitter ever since I've been managing this club. He was an automatic choice in this spot.

—Orioles manager Earl Weaver after Motton's game-tying double helped Baltimore come from behind to beat Oakland's Vida Blue in the 1971 American League Championship Series

Curt Motton grew up in the Oakland, California, housing projects with future Major Leaguers Willie Stargell and Tommy Harper. Stargell became a Hall of Famer and Harper had a fifteen-season big-league career. In Motton's eight Major League seasons he was never a regular, but he found his big-league niche as a pinch hitter.

Curtell Howard Motton was born on September 24, 1940, in Darnell, Louisiana. The eldest son of Robert Motton and the former Mary Lean Coleman, he was the third of nine children born to the couple (four boys and five girls). Motton (pronounced MOE-ton) was a French surname (originally pronounced MOE-tawn); the spelling evolved over the years. His mother was a housewife and homemaker, while his father worked in construction. When Motton was five or six years old, the family moved to Oakland to pursue better job opportunities.

Motton, Stargell, and Harper attended Encinal High School together, and they starred on the gridiron as well as the diamond. Harper quarterbacked the school football team, Stargell played end, and Motton was an electrifying halfback. Though he was only about 5 feet 7½ inches tall and weighed 175 pounds when he reached the Majors, the diminutive Motton was a four-sport ath-

Doomed to play behind three excellent outfielders in Baltimore, Curt Motton had to settle for being Earl Weaver's favorite pinch hitter for a time.

lete at Encinal, also participating in basketball and track. (More recently, the school sent 2003 National League Rookie of the Year Dontrelle Willis and 2007 NL Most Valuable Player Jimmy Rollins to the big leagues.)

Motton admired Milwaukee Braves star Hank Aaron for the way he held and swung his bat, and proved to be a pretty good hitter of his own in helping the team from Hayward, California, reach the Connie Mack World Series in St. Joseph, Missouri, after his high school graduation. Then it was

43

off to the University of California by way of Santa Rosa Community College. When the Chicago Cubs offered him $4,000 to sign in the summer of 1961, the twenty-year-old Motton accepted it and commenced his professional baseball career the following year.

He earned Northern League All-Star recognition for the St. Cloud Rox in 1962, hitting .291 with 13 home runs and 69 RBIS in 125 games. He was honored as the circuit's Player of the Month after batting .347 in May. But despite his auspicious debut, he didn't stay in the Cubs organization for long. The Baltimore Orioles acquired an entire outfield in the first-year player draft in November 1962: future All-Star Paul Blair (from the Mets), Dave May (from the Giants), and Roger Sorenson, who never advanced past Single-A. Baltimore farm director Harry Dalton knew about Motton's questionable throwing arm and wasn't sure he needed to draft a fourth outfielder that day. So Dalton called Billy DeMars, skipper of Baltimore's Northern League affiliate, to get a firsthand opinion. "Good bat and he can run," DeMars assured him. "Go for him."[1]

Motton showed up for work in the Arizona Instructional League only to learn from some teammates that the Orioles had paid $12,000 to select him. "The manager said I couldn't suit up because I was no longer Cubs property," Motton recalled. "I had mixed emotions. I figured it would be easier to break into the Cubs' outfield."[2]

In 1963 Motton batted .333 to finish second in the California League batting race, helping the Stockton Ports win the title. He hit 10 home runs and stole 22 bases, walked 90 times, and notched 90 RBIS. His plan was to continue his development in the Peninsula Winter League, but he ended up being drafted into the U.S. Army. During his two-year hitch, he was mainly stationed in Fairbanks, Alaska.

Disappointed at having to postpone his pursuit of a professional career, Motton nonetheless managed to stay sharp playing a pretty good brand of ball in the service. In the summer of 1964, he joined the Goldpanners of the Alaska Baseball League, a college players' circuit, for 16 games, batting .286. Still, he'd missed almost two seasons by the time the army let him go home early to pursue his career. He joined the Fox Cities (Appleton, Wisconsin) Foxes of the Class A Midwest League late in 1965, making the All-Star team despite his abbreviated stint, with an average of .275 and a 6-homer performance in 44 games. Then he was off to the Florida Instructional League, where his .336 average topped the circuit as the Orioles' entry won the pennant under Vern Hoscheit. Finally, in February, he played for the La Guaira Sharks in the Venezuelan Winter League, helping them win their second consecutive title.

Motton began 1966 with the Double-A Elmira Pioneers. Hitting .287 with 11 home runs and 62 RBIS in 112 games, he was challenging for the Triple Crown before his call-up to the Triple-A Rochester Red Wings in mid-August. Motton hit .337 to help Rochester win the International League pennant on the season's last day. (For his performance at Elmira, he lost Eastern League MVP honors by one vote to Howie Bedell of the York White Roses.)

Motton started the 1967 season with Rochester. He was briefly derailed by a botched hit-and-run play early in the season. He dived head-first into second base and was knocked unconscious when his chin struck the knee of the opposing shortstop. Motton needed eight stitches to close the wound, and he spent two nights in the hospital with a mild concussion. When he returned to the Rochester team he was out of the lineup for six days. "And the first time back I felt a little dizzy," he said. "I was a little gun shy at the plate, afraid I couldn't get out of the way of the ball if I had to. But gradually, the dizziness disappeared."[3]

With his average up to .336 on the Fourth of July, Motton was called up to the Orioles when

MALCOLM ALLEN

they traded pitcher Steve Barber to the Yankees. In a little less than a month with the big club, Motton collected his first big-league hit (off the Chicago White Sox's Jim O'Toole at Comiskey Park) and his first home run (off the Red Sox's Galen Cisco at Fenway Park), and batted .244 in 17 games. After being sent back down to Rochester, he wound up leading the International League in RBIS with 70 and finished second in the batting race at .323. Motton hit 18 home runs and drew 72 walks. Though a 3-for-24 September dropped his Major League average to .200 for 1967, Motton's composite .307 mark in the Minors since turning pro meant he'd hit himself into the big leagues.

"I've always had success in hitting," Motton said. "Mostly it's a matter of concentration. I've maintained the same batting style that I've had since I was 14 and played American Legion ball: closed stance, stand straight up and keep my hands close to my body."[4]

In 1968 Motton made Baltimore's Opening Day roster and got an early-season opportunity when Frank Robinson missed time with the mumps. Motton started eighteen consecutive contests, including all but the first game of a 13-and-2 stretch that lifted Baltimore from fifth place to first. The Birds followed that with seven consecutive losses and never regained the division lead.

Motton's most memorable hits in his rookie campaign came off the bench. On May 15 and 17 he tied a Major League record by hitting home runs in consecutive pinch-hit at-bats. The hits, off Detroit's Jon Warden and Cleveland's Hal Kurtz, both came with two runners on base. In late August Motton went on the disabled list for a few weeks after pulling a hamstring. He finished his freshman season with just a .198 batting average in 83 games but demonstrated good patience at the plate and cracked 8 home runs in 217 at bats.

Elrod Hendricks and Motton were roommates at that time, and when the Orioles catcher looked back on his quarter-century-plus with the Orioles,

he recalled Motton as the worst driver of all. "I remember Luis Tiant telling him, 'Please, Mr. Motton, watch the road. Please, Mr. Motton, you're going to get me keeled,'" Hendricks told the *Baltimore Sun*. "But he drove me around for two years. I can't complain too much."[5]

The Orioles were a dynasty for Earl Weaver's first three full seasons as manager, 1969–71, winning 318 regular-season games and a trio of pennants. For Motton, however, it was something of a bittersweet time, as he started just forty-six games in those three years, after having started fifty-three times as a rookie. "We're winning. That's the only good thing about sitting on the bench here," he observed at the time. "With a club like this, you can make more money because we get in the playoffs and the World Series."[6]

Weaver empathized with Motton's desire to play more and with the difficulties of coming off the bench, but the manager had three very good reasons for his lineup selection. "In left field, we've got Donny [Buford], an outstanding leadoff hitter," Weaver said. "Paulie [Blair] is an outstanding center fielder, and Frank [Robinson] is an outstanding everything in right, so Curt has to settle for being our best pinch-hitter."[7]

For Motton, it wasn't that easy. He confessed feeling depressed about being unable to force his way into the lineup. "I thought maybe they could do as well with 24 men as with 25," he said. "They didn't need me that much. They were winning with the same eight guys."[8] After he managed just one hit in his first ten pinch-hit attempts in 1969, Motton's spot on the roster was in jeopardy. Weaver reminded him, "You're not here on a pass," and Motton got the message. "What it boiled down to was that if I didn't start doing better, Earl was going to make some changes and get another pinch-hitter."[9] Crediting a gradual mental adjustment, Motton batted .389 (7-for-18) as a pinch hitter the rest of the way, including game-winning homers off left-handers Jim Rooker and

Paul Lindblad to beat the Kansas City Royals and Oakland Athletics, respectively, in August. Overall, Motton reached base 13 out of 33 times off the bench to rank as one of the league's best reserves. In 56 games overall, he contributed to Baltimore's first-place finish by hitting .303 with a .398 on-base percentage and a slugging average of .573.

Arguably the biggest hit of Motton's Major League career delivered a crucial victory over the Minnesota Twins in October's inaugural American League Championship Series in 1969. After a thrilling twelve-inning comeback victory in the series opener, Baltimore came precariously close to dropping the second game before the series shifted to Minnesota. Deadlocked in a scoreless tie in the bottom of the eleventh, the Twins called on left-handed relief ace Ron Perranoski to face Elrod Hendricks with two on and two outs. Weaver countered by sending up Motton, who set up the Orioles' eventual sweep with a game-winning single. "The pitch was away on the outer part of the plate," Motton recalled. "And I did something I rarely did—I hit it to right field. I just wanted to make good contact and hoped things would work out."[10]

Motton grounded out in his only World Series plate appearance as Baltimore suffered a stunning upset loss to the New York Mets, and he wasn't surprised at all when neither the Royals nor the Pilots chose him in the expansion draft that offseason. "No one had seen me play enough," he observed.[11]

He went to Puerto Rico that winter to join the Santurce club, managed by Frank Robinson. Motton viewed it as an opportunity to get some opportunities against right-handed pitchers, after just forty such at bats during the 1969 season. He saw enough curves and sliders from right-handers to consider it a worthwhile journey but wound up on the disabled list after straining a tendon in his left hand on a checked swing. The pain was so intense that he couldn't even squeeze a tube of toothpaste.

Santurce dealt him to the Caguas team, but Motton came back home instead and got married. He and his wife, Jackie, moved to Baltimore full time about a year later and welcomed daughter Simone Nicole in early 1971. Motton remained in the area even after the couple divorced.

In 1970 Motton started only five games through the end of July and saw his overall numbers slip to a .226 batting average with a .393 slugging mark. He made the most of his 19 hits though, collecting 19 RBIs thanks to a .346 mark with runners in scoring position. "The thing that kept me keyed up and always ready was the way Earl [Weaver] used me," Motton said. "He almost always used me when it was a close ballgame. If I did my job, I was going to make a positive contribution to the ballclub."[12]

Motton was known as "Cuz" to his teammates owing to his friendly manner. The nickname was also fitting because he'd found his baseball niche with the Orioles in Baltimore. Broadcaster Roy Firestone, who was the Orioles' spring-training batboy in 1970, recalled, "He was country, sweet, so funny, and had a down-home wisdom to him that made everyone around him especially [Paul] Blair, [Don] Buford, and [Dave] May love him to death.[13]

"Guys like Curt made us more of a complete team," recalled Hall of Fame pitcher Jim Palmer.[14] The Orioles romped through October to win the 1970 ALCS over the Twins and the World Series against the Cincinnati Reds with such relative ease that Motton did not see action in a single postseason game. One of his Louisville Sluggers wound up in the Hall of Fame, though, after teammate Dave McNally borrowed it in Game Three and belted the only grand slam hit by a pitcher in the history of the Fall Classic.

Motton's playing time with the Orioles became even scarcer in 1971. It started when he suffered through a difficult spring training after being bothered by a bad heel. Though he insisted he

MALCOLM ALLEN

didn't worry because he knew Weaver remained confident in him, Motton had just fourteen at bats with one hit in the Orioles' first eighty-four games. Finally, on July 10, Weaver started him in both games of a doubleheader against the Cleveland Indians at Memorial Stadium. Motton ripped a grand slam off Sam McDowell in the opener and a two-run homer off Mike Paul for the Orioles' only runs in the nightcap. Nevertheless, he finished the season hitting just .189 in 53 at bats, though he did hammer 4 home runs.

When the Orioles needed him in the playoffs against Oakland, Motton was ready. Baltimore trailed Vida Blue, that year's Most Valuable Player and Cy Young Award winner, by 3–2 with two on and two out in the bottom of the seventh in the ALCS opener. Motton stepped up as a pinch hitter for pitcher Dave McNally, worked the count to three balls and a strike, and ripped a game-tying double to the left-field corner.

Baltimore went on to win the game, sweep the series, and earn a third straight trip to the World Series, but Motton did not get into any games as the Orioles lost a seven-game classic to his old friend Willie Stargell and the Pittsburgh Pirates. After Baltimore dealt right fielder Frank Robinson to the Dodgers in December, Motton figured he'd at least be back again in 1972 as a pinch hitter. However, one week after the Robinson trade, Motton was sent to the Milwaukee Brewers for cash and a player to be named later. The Orioles received hard-throwing reliever Bob Reynolds in spring training.

Milwaukee provided even fewer chances for Motton to strut his stuff. Despite hitting a homer in his first Brewers game, he was traded to the California Angels for reliever Archie Reynolds after getting only seven plate appearances in six games. The Angels sent him down to Triple-A Salt Lake City, where Motton mashed Pacific Coast League pitching for five homers and a .320 batting average

in 26 contests before earning a return ticket to the majors. He got into 42 games with the Angels, but made only forty-four plate appearances as he was often employed as a pinch runner or pinch hitter. He batted just .154.

Motton began the 1973 season back at Salt Lake City, but he didn't hit and was loaned to the Oakland A's Southern League affiliate in Birmingham. The Angels released him in mid-July, and he was re-signed by the Orioles two days later. Baltimore sent him to Rochester to play himself into shape, but Motton continued to struggle. His eyes and reflexes were as good as they had been in 1967, when he played himself into the Majors for the first time, but his timing was off from half a decade of playing so sparingly. In 92 Minor League games in 1973, Motton batted just .199, though he did hit 12 home runs in 236 at bats. The Orioles called him up for the last two weeks of the season and he got into four games, even hitting a three-run homer against the Indians in the season finale.

Motton spent 1974 as a player/coach with Rochester under Joe Altobelli. He batted .300 and drew 58 walks in part-time action for an amazing .462 on-base percentage. The Orioles brought him up late in the year, but he went hitless in the last ten plate appearances of his professional career.

After retiring, Motton got into real estate and insurance sales, but he returned to baseball in 1981 as a Minor League instructor with the San Francisco Giants, where his best friend in baseball, Frank Robinson, was managing. After five years in that position, Motton returned to Rochester and was on the Red Wings' coaching staff from 1986 through 1988, then was Baltimore's first base coach from 1989 through 1991 when Robinson took over as the Orioles' skipper. Motton remained with the organization for more than a decade after that as a special assignment scout, traveling to the Dominican Republic, Venezuela, and across the United States.

Motton remarried in 1993, wedding law-enforcement veteran Marti Franklin, and the couple settled in Parkton, Maryland, in northern Baltimore County. He participated in fantasy camps, became a regular at Orioles Fan Fest, appeared at autograph signings, and taught baseball clinics for youngsters on behalf of Virginia's Diamond Dream Foundation. "People in Baltimore remember me because I was part of those [great] ballclubs," he said.[15]

Motton became a grandfather early in the new millennium when his daughter, Simone Nicole, gave birth to a son, Tyree. In 2006 he was inducted into the Rochester Red Wings Hall of Fame. He was diagnosed with stomach cancer shortly thereafter and died at the age of sixty-nine on January 21, 2010. He is buried in Druid Ridge Cemetery in Pikesville, Maryland.

Chapter 11. **Jim Palmer**

Mark Armour

AGE	W	L	PCT.	ERA	G	GS	GF	CG	SHO	SV	IP	H	BB	SO	HBP	WP
24	20	10	.667	2.71	39	39	0	17	5	0	305	263	100	199	1	10

In an era filled with pitching stars, many of them working for the Baltimore Orioles, it took Jim Palmer a few years to rise to the top of the heap. Once he did, he became the greatest pitcher in his league for a number of seasons, and one of the best pitchers who ever lived. Along the way, he achieved success as a model and as a television broadcaster, becoming one of the sport's most visible and successful figures for several decades.

Jim Palmer was born on October 15, 1945, in New York City. When he was just two days old, he was adopted by Moe Wiesen, a wealthy executive in the garment industry, and his wife, Polly Kiger Wiesen, who owned a dress shop. The newborn was named James Alvin Wiesen, and he was joined by sister Bonnie, who was eighteen months older but adopted about the same time. Moe Wiesen was Jewish and Polly was Catholic, but religion did not play a big role in the children's upbringing. The family lived at first in a large house on New York's Park Avenue, joined by several servants. They later moved north to Westchester County, where Jim attended schools in Rye and White Plains. He and his neighbors had large houses and property large enough to allow the playing of baseball in the front yard.

When Jim was nine years old Moe Wiesen died, and Polly soon moved with her two children first to Whittier, California, and then to Beverly Hills. While in California, Polly married Max Palmer, a character actor who had appeared in *Dragnet*, *Highway Patrol*, *Playhouse 90*, and many other television shows. (There was another Max Palmer in movies at the time—an eight-foot-two-inch man who played monsters in B movies and later became

Though many people had thought his career was over just a year earlier, Jim Palmer won twenty games in 1970, the first of eight times he would reach this milestone.

a professional wrestler. Some websites have conflated the two Max Palmers, even suggesting that Palmer's stepfather was a pro wrestler.) Max Palmer eventually adopted Jim and his sister, and Jim became very close to Max.

The boy who was now Jim Palmer dreamed of becoming a baseball player, and starred in Little League, Pony League, and the Babe Ruth League. Before he started high school the Palmers moved to Scottsdale, Arizona, where Jim earned all-state honors in baseball, football, and basketball, and a 3.4 grade point average in school. On the baseball team he pitched and played center field, both very well, while he was a high-scoring forward in basketball and a receiver in football. He had several college offers, and considered UCLA, USC, and Stanford, and later briefly enrolled at Arizona State in nearby Tempe.

After his high school graduation, Palmer played summer ball for a team in Winner, South Dakota, a team that included future Major Leaguers Jim Lonborg, Merv Rettenmund, Bobby Floyd, and Curt Motton. The club lost in the league finals, but Palmer impressed Baltimore Orioles farm director Harry Dalton, who scouted the series. Some league observers thought the seventeen-year-old Palmer threw harder than anyone they had ever seen.[1] On the 1,200-mile drive home, a friend of Palmer's (driving Palmer's car) fell asleep at the wheel, and the car careened into a ditch and flipped several times. There were no seatbelts in the car, and Palmer escaped with a sore left knee, an injury that eventually required surgery. The Orioles were unaware of the injury when they signed Palmer to a $50,000 contract right after he returned home.

Just before heading to spring training, Palmer married Susan Ryan, whom he had known throughout high school The couple headed to Aberdeen, South Dakota, where the Orioles had a Single-A affiliate in the Northern League. The club was managed by Cal Ripken Sr. and featured several future Major Leaguers, including Mark Belanger and Lou Piniella. Aberdeen ran away with the league pennant, while Palmer finished 11-3 with a 2.51 earned run average, throwing a no-hitter in June. He battled control problems—130 walks in 129 innings—but otherwise kept the opponents off the bases.

The Orioles had seen enough, and the nineteen-year-old Palmer made the big club out of spring training in 1965. The team had a lot of young pitching talent, and Palmer was mainly used as an emergency starter (6 starts) and mop-up reliever, finishing 5-4 with a 3.72 ERA in 92 innings. He later recalled learning a lot that season from his roommate, Robin Roberts, the former Phillies star pitcher, who was near the end of his career. Palmer's first Major League victory came in relief on May 16, 1965, against the Yankees. In the same outing he hit his first home run, a two-run shot off Jim Bouton.

The next season, Palmer had a great spring and made the starting rotation. In the season's second game, in Boston, he took a three-hit shutout into the ninth inning and settled for a 5–1 victory and his first complete game. His best pitch throughout his career was a high fastball, though his first Major League manager, Hank Bauer, told him he couldn't win throwing high. Even by 1966 there were opponents who were impressed. "I think he's the hardest thrower in the league," said Bill Skowron, veteran White Sox first baseman.[2]

For the 1966 season, Palmer finished 15-10 with a 3.46 ERA in 30 starts, leading a deep Baltimore staff in victories. The Orioles won the American League pennant, with Palmer winning the clincher with a five-hitter in Kansas City on September 22. He drew the Game Two World Series start in Dodger Stadium against Sandy Koufax, and the twenty-year-old Palmer came through with a 6–0 four-hitter, besting Koufax in his final career appearance, and the Orioles went on to a 4–0 series sweep. It was during this season that Palmer earned the nickname "Cakes" for his habit of always eating pancakes on the morning of his starts.

Although Palmer seemed on the fast track to stardom, his career hit its biggest obstacle the next season. In fact, Palmer later recalled feeling arm soreness during the 1966 World Series. He began the 1967 season well, throwing a one-hit masterpiece in Yankee Stadium on May 12: a single by Horace Clarke leading off the seventh was the only hit, and Clarke was quickly erased on a double play. Unfortunately, Palmer's shoulder stiffened up in this very game, and after lasting only one inning in his next start, he soon found himself in the Minor Leagues. He pitched seven games for Miami and Rochester before making it back to the Orioles for two starts in September. He finished 3-1, 2.94 for Baltimore, but with an aching shoulder and back. Palmer later believed that his injury started as bicep tendinitis, but his favoring of the arm led to a torn rotator cuff in his shoulder.[3]

The 1968 season was another lost year for Palmer—he started ten total games for Miami, Elmira, and Rochester, losing his only two decisions and throwing just thirty-seven innings. He never made it to Baltimore and was so distressed that he considered attempting a comeback as a position player. Palmer was placed on waivers late in the season and was not protected in that fall's expansion draft to stock the new teams in Seattle and Kansas City. He went unselected, and many feared his career had come to an end.

The Orioles did not believe in pampering sore arms. George Bamberger, the Orioles' pitching coach, wanted his charges to pitch through soreness until it was determined that the injury required surgery. Accordingly, Palmer pitched in the Florida Instructional League in the fall, then for the Santurce Crabbers (managed by Frank Robinson) in the Puerto Rican Winter League. Just as Bamberger had hoped, in Puerto Rico Palmer's pain suddenly went away. He showed up at spring training to give it another shot. "It was a miracle as far as I was concerned," recalled Palmer. "Like getting a new toy."[4]

In mid-1968, while Palmer was in the Minor Leagues, the Orioles hired a new manager, Earl Weaver, with whom Palmer would publicly battle over the next fourteen seasons. Weaver loved Palmer the pitcher, however, and a good spring got Palmer a start in the fifth game of the 1969 season. He responded with a five-hit shutout of the Senators, striking out slugger Frank Howard four times. "I think I'm back in business," said Palmer.[5]

By the end of June he was 9-2 with a 1.96 ERA; his two losses were 2-0 to Detroit's Denny McLain and 1-0 to the White Sox's Joel Horlen. He soon returned to the disabled list with a torn muscle in his lower back, missing six weeks of action, but in the second start after his return he pitched a no-hitter against Oakland, walking six but coasting to the 8-0 win. He finished the season 16-4, and his 6 shutouts and 2.34 ERA were both second best in the league. He easily defeated the Twins in the third game of the playoffs (11–2) to complete a Baltimore sweep but lost to the Mets' Gary Gentry in Game Three of the World Series and watched New York go on to its historic five-game upset.

Palmer's arm troubles were mostly over, and over the next nine seasons he won twenty or more games eight times and captured three Cy Young Awards. In fact, it is hard to separate Palmer's outstanding seasons, as the honors and league-leading seasons piled up. During the Orioles' great run of pennants (1969 to 1971) he was often considered the third starter on the team, behind Dave McNally (who won sixty-five games in the three seasons) and Mike Cuellar (who won sixty-seven), and Palmer pitched the third game in the playoffs in all three seasons. In reality, other than the missed time Palmer had in 1969, he was generally the team's best pitcher, leading the Orioles' great starting staffs in ERA every year between 1969 and 1973, and again between 1975 and 1978—nine times in ten seasons.

Although Palmer and Weaver had many public disagreements—about pitching, where the fielders should play, whether the team should bunt—many observers felt that they were made for each other. Paul Blair, the club's center fielder, felt that the young Palmer would not want to stay in the game if he didn't have his best stuff, and would "invent" a soreness in his arm or something. While Hank Bauer would take him out of the game in these situations, Weaver would not. "So Palmer learned to get his fastball over, his curveball over," recalled

Blair, "and he learned to pitch because he was going nine. Earl made him grow up a little bit."[6]

In 1970 Palmer finished 20-10 with a 2.71 ERA, leading the league with 305 innings pitched and 5 shutouts. Weaver employed a four-man rotation, and Palmer made 39 starts and completed 17 of them. In Game Three of the playoffs he dominated the Twins on a seven-hitter, also racking up twelve strikeouts as the Orioles completed a three-game sweep. In the World Series, against the Cincinnati Reds, Weaver switched up and gave Palmer the Game One start—he fell behind 3–0 early but the Orioles scraped out a 4–3 win for him. He came back in Game Four with a chance to sweep the Reds, and it looked for most of the game that he would succeed. The Orioles led 5–3 going into the eighth inning. After Palmer walked Tony Perez and allowed a single to Johnny Bench, Weaver brought in Eddie Watt to face Lee May. The Reds slugger promptly belted a home run, giving the Reds a 6–5 lead that would hold up. The Orioles won the Series the next day instead.

Palmer and the Orioles stormed back in 1971, this time highlighted by a pitching staff that featured a remarkable four twenty-game winners (Palmer, Cuellar, McNally, and the newly acquired Pat Dobson). Palmer was the fourth to do it, with a 5–0 three-hitter over the Cleveland Indians on September 26. He went on to beat the Oakland Athletics in the playoffs to complete a series sweep for the Orioles, allowing three solo home runs in a 5–3 victory. This marked the fourth time Palmer had clinched a pennant for the Orioles, doing so in the 1966 regular season and all three years since the playoff format began in 1969. He also defeated the Pittsburgh Pirates in Game Two of the World Series, 11–3, then watched the Pirates win three straight to take a 3–2 lead in games. Palmer pitched well in Game Six, leaving after nine innings tied 2–2 in a game the Orioles won. Unfortunately for the Orioles, the Pirates wrapped up the Series the next day.

The Orioles juggernaut took a big step back in 1972, though Palmer kept up his excellent pitching: he finished 21-10 with a 2.07 ERA as the club dropped to third place. In 1973 he did it all again, upping his record to 22-10 with a league-leading 2.40 ERA and capturing his first Cy Young Award, helping the Orioles win another division title. Palmer pitched a five-hit shutout to start off the playoffs against the A's, but he was knocked out early in the Game Four, a game in which the Orioles rallied to keep the series alive. Alas, Oakland wrapped up the pennant the next day. By this time, Palmer had finally moved to the head of the class among Oriole pitchers, though he had been a great pitcher for years. "If you had to pick one guy to win a game," recalled first baseman Boog Powell, "he was my guy. As much as I loved Mike Cuellar, as much as I loved Dave McNally and Pat Dobson . . . if I had one game to win, Palmer was on the mound for me."[7]

Palmer suffered an off season in 1974, plagued by a sore arm and poor team support on both offense and defense. His record was just 7-12, though his ERA of 3.27 was better than the league average. His sore arm kept him out of action for two months. The Orioles staged a big team comeback—they were in fourth place, eight games behind the Red Sox with a 63-65 record on August 28, but finished 28-6 and won the division easily. Palmer threw two shutouts in September to help the cause. In Game Three of the playoffs he lost to Oakland's Catfish Hunter 1–0, allowing only a solo home run to Sal Bando, and the Orioles went down in four games.

Palmer put together what might have been his best season in 1975, finishing 23-11 with a league-leading 10 shutouts and a 2.09 ERA. His next season he went 22-13, leading the league in wins and innings pitched. Though the Orioles finished second in each season, Palmer captured both Cy Young Awards, becoming the first American League pitcher to grab the honor three times.

Palmer was the last star remaining from the great teams of the early 1970s, which gave him the stature to bicker with Weaver. Both men had big egos, and as much as Weaver liked to tell Palmer what pitches to throw, Palmer like to tell Weaver how to manage the game. "He was Mr. Perfection," recalled Weaver. "It had to be perfect. When things don't go right, you've got to accept it. He didn't want to. But he was a good pitcher." As for Palmer, the pitcher allowed: "The bottom line is we were out there trying to do the same thing."[8]

Along with the fame he gathered from being one of baseball's greatest pitchers year after year, Palmer also became a very visible model for Jockey underwear. About 1977, he took part in an ad campaign involving several other athletes, including fellow baseball stars Pete Rose and Steve Carlton, with each man depicted in various styles of underwear in magazine ads. Eventually Jockey built its campaign around Palmer only. Jockey sold a very popular poster of Palmer in a pair of small briefs, and the photogenic Palmer appeared in Jockey ads for twenty years. His face was also used to sell other products nationally and in the Baltimore area.

Meanwhile, the great seasons kept coming. His 20-11, 2.91 campaign in 1977 included league-leading totals of 39 starts, 22 complete games, and 319 innings pitched. He did not win his third straight Cy Young Award, finishing a close second to Yankee relief pitcher Sparky Lyle. Palmer attained twenty wins for the eighth time in 1978— only Warren Spahn (thirteen times) and Lefty Grove (eight times) have matched this feat among post-1920 Major League pitchers. Palmer's 21-12, 2.46 season in 1978 was nothing more than typical for him. He was only thirty-two years old but had racked up 215 lifetime victories against only 116 defeats.

The 1979 Orioles surprised many observers by winning 102 games and easily capturing their first division title in five years. Palmer started typically well, and was 6-2, 2.80 at the end of May. For the rest of the season, however, he battled arm soreness and was on the disabled list twice, limiting him to just 22 starts and a 10-6 final record. Palmer was no longer the best pitcher on the club but a respected leader to several promising young hurlers like Mike Flanagan, Dennis Martinez, and Scott McGregor. His stature helped earn him the Game One start in the playoffs against the California Angels, and he pitched nine strong innings in a game the Orioles won 6–3 in the tenth. In Game Two of the World Series against the Pirates he pitched seven innings and left the game tied 2–2. In Game Six he lost 4–0 to John Candelaria, and the Orioles lost Game Seven the next day.

Palmer came back strong in 1980, finishing 16-10 for a Baltimore team that won 100 games but finished second to the Yankees. No longer as durable as he'd been in his big seasons, Palmer had more no-decision outings. The next season was marred by a fifty-day player strike in midsummer, and Palmer never really got on track, winning just seven games.

After Palmer started poorly in 1982 (1-1 with a 6.84 ERA in five starts), General manager Hank Peters let it be known to the press that Palmer no longer warranted a spot in the team's rotation. Weaver disagreed, though he did briefly put Palmer in the bullpen (where he struggled for four more appearances). Weaver thought that Palmer would turn it around, and once back in the rotation, he did just that. From June to September, Palmer made 24 starts and compiled a 13-1 record with a 2.24 ERA. Weaver had announced early in the season that 1982 would be his final year, and the Orioles spent most of the season seemingly out of contention, finding themselves seven games behind the Brewers in late August. As they had done so often during the Weaver years, the club got red hot in September (19-9), then beat the Brewers three straight games to tie them with one final game to go. The red-hot Palmer faced off against Don Sutton in the finale on October 4, but the Brewers prevailed, hitting three solo homers off Palmer and then pulling away against the bullpen, 10–2.

For the 1982 season Palmer finished 15-5 with a 3.13 ERA (third in the league). This marked the tenth time that he finished in the top five in earned run average, and earned the thirty-six-year-old a second-place finish in the Cy Young balloting.

Jim started well in 1983, allowing no earned runs in either of his first two starts, but he spent two long stretches of the season on the disabled list, ending the season 5-4 in just 11 starts. The Orioles returned to the postseason again, though Palmer did not play a large role in the pennant race or the playoffs. In his one postseason appearance, a relief effort in Game Three of the World Series against the Philadelphia Phillies, Palmer earned his fourth World Series victory; it made him the only pitcher in history to win World Series games in three different decades. His career postseason record was 8-3 with a 2.61 ERA in 17 games, 15 of them starts. His teams won three World Series titles in six tries.

Palmer again made the Orioles rotation in 1984, but after just three starts and two relief stints (0-3, 9.17 ERA), the Orioles gave him his release on May 17. Palmer believed he could still pitch and likely had offers from other teams, but he chose not to pursue them. He made news seven years later when he went to spring training with the Orioles to try a comeback, but he called it off after suffering a hamstring injury during an exhibition game.

Palmer remained visible and active after his retirement. He began working for ABC Sports while still an active player—providing color commentary during several postseasons and the 1981 World Series—and continued this work after he no longer played. He worked five World Series and several All-Star Games for ABC, along with many other sporting events. After ABC lost its national

baseball contract in 1989, Palmer became an announcer for the Orioles, a role he had performed for twenty-three years by 2011. He was a regular presence in documentaries about the game and the world of sports over the years. He published a book on pitching in 1975 (*Pitching*), an exercise book in 1987 (*Jim Palmer's Way to Fitness*), and a humorous memoir largely focused on his relationship with manager Earl Weaver in 1996 (*Together We Were Eleven Foot Nine*).

Palmer's uniform number, 22, was retired by the Orioles, and he was elected to their Hall of Fame in 1986. He made the National Baseball Hall of Fame in 1990, overwhelmingly elected on his first try along with Joe Morgan. Their induction ceremony was rained out, and held the next day in a local high school.

Jim had two daughters (Jamie and Kelly) with his first wife, Susan, and in 2010 was married for the third time, to a woman also named Susan. While the Baltimore franchise has fallen on hard times in the new century, Palmer remains a link to and a visible reminder of the club's long period of success. He conquered the fields of pitching, modeling, and broadcasting, and has shown no signs of slowing down.

Chapter 12. **Dave May**

Charlie Weatherby

AGE	G	AB	R	H	2B	3B	HR	TB	RBI	BB	SO	BAV	OBP	SLG	SB	GDP	HBP
26	25	31	6	6	0	1	1	11	6	4	4	.194	.286	.355	0	3	0

A journeyman outfielder during his twelve Major League seasons, Dave May was called by *The Sporting News* "a good man to have on a team."[1] The stocky 5-foot-10½, 186-pound left-handed hitter played in 1,252 games for Baltimore, Milwaukee, Atlanta, Texas, and Pittsburgh, posting a .251 average with 96 home runs and 422 runs batted in. Best known for once being traded for Hank Aaron, May had experiences most journeymen would envy: playing in a League Championship Series, the World Series, and the All-Star Game. Dave Bristol, who managed him on the Milwaukee Brewers, called him "a big-inning hitter [who has] the power to hit balls out of any park, including Yellowstone."[2] Del Crandall, who also handled him at Milwaukee, said May was "a good defensive outfielder [with the] speed to steal a base now and then. . . . There aren't many better center fielders in the majors."[3]

The *Dallas Morning News* called May "without question one of the friendliest players in the sport."[4] According to *The Great Delaware Sports Book*, "Dave May could always hit."[5] And he could look good doing it; Bobby Grich, his teammate on the Orioles, called Dave "the greatest batting practice hitter ever," adding, "He was awesome . . . He could hit an 80-mile-an-hour fastball better than anyone."[6] For his efforts, Dave May is in two Halls of Fame, though neither is at Cooperstown. That honor is reserved for one of his gloves.

A native of New Castle, Delaware, David LaFrance May was born on December 23, 1943, the fourth of Sylvester and Catherine (Richardson) May's nine children. His father worked for an auto dealership; his mother was a custodian for the lo-

Dave May escaped the logjam of Oriole outfielders in a mid-1970 trade to Milwaukee, where he became an All-Star in 1973.

cal school district. Sports were important in his family. His father was a catcher as a teenager and a boxer as an adult; his mother was a good softball player.

Dave learned baseball from his older brothers, Scrappy and Gilbert. Sylvester "Scrappy" May, the oldest, was one of the all-time great players in the Delaware Semi-Pro League. A seven-time all-star infielder, Scrappy helped his club win seven pennants and had a .330 lifetime average. Gilbert was the best player in the family and was a stand-out shortstop for William Penn High School. His promising career was abruptly ended when a cherry bomb accident blew off the fingers of one of his hands.

The May household on Williams Street was next to a firehouse; Dave threw tennis balls against its sidewall and caught the rebound. "I would do it late at night and my brothers and sisters thought I was crazy," May said. "I always told them what I was going to be and it turned out to be true."[7]

May's first baseball club was Buttonwood of the New Castle Little League; Gilbert played shortstop and Dave pitched and played third. After playing Babe Ruth ball, Dave was a three-sport athlete at William Penn High School, earning All-Blue Hen Conference honors as a third baseman in baseball and as a halfback in football, receiving scholarship offers from Syracuse, Purdue, and Maryland. Dave was scholastically ineligible for sports during 1961–62, his last school year; he began to play semipro ball for Parkway during those summers.

May was only thirteen when he started playing American Legion ball with Lawrence Roberts Post, a club that won a state championship in 1961. Scout Chick Genovese of the San Francisco Giants was impressed with Dave's tape-measure home runs and the way he got the jump on the ball, and often stopped by the May household to talk and conduct a workout. Genovese signed May to a contract with a $15,000 bonus in September 1961. Bob Carpenter and Judy Johnson of the Philadelphia Phillies signed him an to even bigger contract the same day, but he belonged to the Giants because their contract was received first by Organized Baseball.

May began his professional career with the Salem (Virginia) Rebels of the Appalachian League, where the young outfielder won the batting title with a .379 average and was named to the league all-star team. After the season he was selected by Baltimore in the 1962 first-year player draft. As-signed first to the Stockton Ports in the California League, after hitting .250 in 40 games of part-time action, May was sent to Appleton, Wisconsin, to play for the Fox Cities Foxes of the Midwest League. The move was rewarding—Dave hit .310 in 71 games.

May returned to Appleton in 1964 and earned a trip to the league's all-star contest. On September 2, Fox Cities won the league championship by beating Clinton 8–5; Dave had 3 hits, 2 runs, and 2 steals. He also won his second Minor League batting title (.368) and was chosen as the Foxes' MVP.

May's Tri-City Atoms (who played in Kennewick, Washington) won the Northwest League championship in 1965, and his stellar play included setting a Northwest League record for runs scored (129). He hit .335 with 23 home runs and 105 RBIS, and led the league in hits, total bases, and stolen bases. He was named to the Northwest League All-Star team and the Class A West All-Star team. In December the *Tri-City Herald* said May "probably was the most valuable player in the NWL last season."[8]

Promoted to the Triple-A International League's Rochester Red Wings in March 1966, right fielder May hit .274 with 11 home runs as his team won the league pennant. On September 9, May was re-called by the Orioles, to report to camp the following spring. Before that, he traveled to Santurce to play in the Puerto Rican Winter League. Santurce won the championship in February, with May driving in the tying run with a single in the ninth inning of the final game. Dave returned to play for the Crabbers for the next three seasons, and also played a season with Puerto Rico's Ponce Lions in 1970–71 and two in Venezuela with the La Guaira Sharks in 1975–76 and 1976–77.

In mid-1967, back in Rochester, his hot bat (.313 with 56 RBI) earned him a trip to the league's all-star game, but before he could go, he was promoted to the Orioles. On July 28 he started in right field, batted third, and was 1-for-5; his first Major League hit came in the fourth inning, an infield hit off Cleveland's Steve Hargan. May's first Major League homer came two days later, a 2-run shot in the first off Cleveland's Stan Williams, triggering a 4–2 Baltimore victory. He stayed with the club as a reserve, and finished with a .235 average.

He made the club the next year and started most games in April and May, but after hitting .146 into early June, he began wearing glasses. On June 22 he was sent to Rochester. His .315 average during his five weeks there earned him a recall to Baltimore on August 3. Used primarily as a pinch hitter and defensive replacement, he finished the season at .191.

May was a pinch hitter and spot starter for the American League champion Orioles in 1969. Sent to the outfield against the Yankees on May 3, he cracked an eighth-inning home run to give Baltimore a 5–4 win. Dave hit .299 in August and September and added 22 points to his average during six consecutive starts from September 9 through 18. In 78 games, May hit .242 with 3 homers and 10 RBIs. He batted once in the playoffs against the Twins, and twice in the World Series against the Mets, drawing a walk off Gary Gentry in Game Three.

The next year May again struggled for playing time, with four strong outfielders (Don Buford, Paul Blair, Frank Robinson, and Merv Rettenmund) plus pinch hitter Curt Motton ahead of him. After just thirty-one at bats, mainly pinch-hitting, on June 15 May was traded by the Orioles to Milwaukee for two Minor League pitchers. Switching Memorial Stadium clubhouses, May faced his old mates two days later, going 0-for-2 with a walk, a strikeout, and a sacrifice-fly RBI.

"It was tough playing for the Orioles because . . . it was hard to get into a groove," Dave told *The Sporting News*. "You like to be with a winning club, but with them, I was sitting around. With Milwaukee, I'll get a chance to play."[9] Of his time with Baltimore, he said, "You can't help but learn when you're around guys like Brooks Robinson and the guys I got to watch as teammates."[10] Robinson was World Series MVP that year using May's glove, which was sent to the Hall of Fame. Robinson had a habit of trading with teammates, preferring game-used leather. According to May, "Brooks had a deal with Rawlings because he owned a sporting goods store in Baltimore. He liked my glove and said, 'What do you want for the glove?' And I said, 'I'll take five pair of spikes and two gloves.' The next day, all those things were in my locker and he had gotten my glove. I had written my name on it in black marker and he couldn't get it off. He used it that year; the glove went to Cooperstown."[11]

At Milwaukee, May became the starting center fielder. He played in 100 games for the fifth-place Brewers, hitting .240 with 7 home runs and 31 RBIs. His fielding was excellent, prompting manager Dave Bristol to tell *The Sporting News*, "You don't have to worry about balls hit in his direction. He'll get anything that gets up into the air. . . . I'm not looking for a center fielder any more."[12] May's presence lifted a .300 club before his arrival to one that played at .448 afterward. Rusty and overweight, Dave dropped fifteen pounds before the 1971 season. Batting second, he was Milwaukee's hottest hitter in May and June with twelve- and fourteen-game hitting streaks. The next season he finished at .277, the Brewers' leading hitter.

May struggled all year in 1972. "They kept saying that I was in a slump," he told *The Sporting News*. "I was hitting the ball hard, but this year it was at somebody."[13] He also had to deal with the illness and death of his father. By the end of the year, Dave was hitting aggressively and giving the team tremendous defensive play, but he finished with a.238 average and just 9 homers.

In 1973 May enjoyed his finest big-league season. *The Sporting News* said, "May carried the club all year. . . . [He] was instrumental in igniting the Brewers' 10-game winning streak and a 15-out-of-16 victory binge in mid-season."[14]

May hit in twenty-four straight games from July 4 to July 31 and earned a spot on the American League All-Star team, the biggest thrill of his Major League career. He entered the game, a 7–1 National League victory, in the top of the fifth as a replacement for starting center fielder Amos Otis. He popped up to second base in the sixth and again in the bottom of the ninth. A bruised thumb hampered May's swing in the season's final weeks, but he finished his career year among the league leaders in several categories, including batting average (.303), hits (189), home runs (25), and RBIS (93). He led the league with 295 total bases. Milwaukee writers named May and George Scott as the club's co-MVPs.

In 1974 Dave had a bad case of the flu during spring training. Five games into the season, manager Del Crandall moved him from center to right field, leaving May perplexed. "I'm not happy about it at all," he told The Sporting News. "It's going to take time to adjust after being accustomed to playing center field for so long."[15] Weak from the flu and unhappy with the move, May struggled at the plate, finishing the season at .226 with 10 homers.

On November 2, 1974, Milwaukee traded May to the Atlanta Braves for Hank Aaron and Minor League pitcher Roger Alexander. "I didn't ask to be traded," Dave told the Chicago Defender, "but . . . the way I was being played, I felt a trade was necessary and would help me out. Of course, there was an extra thrill involved in being traded for Hank Aaron."[16]

With the Braves May was used as a pinch hitter and was platooned most of 1975, finishing at .276 in 82 games, with 12 home runs and 40 RBIS. His on-base percentage of .361 was the highest of his career. In 1976 Dave Bristol, Atlanta's manager, continued to use May as a platoon outfielder and pinch hitter, and he hit only .215. After the season Atlanta traded May and four others, plus $250,000, to the Texas Rangers in exchange for slugging outfielder Jeff Burroughs. May welcomed the deal. "I feel I can play two more years at least as a regular," he told The Sporting News.[17]

May played sparingly during the early weeks of 1977. In June the Dallas Morning News wrote, "May continues to hit in the clutch while regular outfielders Ken Henderson and Claudell Washington remain out of the lineup with injuries."[18] With his old Orioles coach Billy Hunter managing the team for the season's last three months, May continued to excel on offense.

Nolan Ryan was tough on May, who hit .125 against him. One at bat, however, was memorable. Ryan, then with the California Angels, was pitching against the Rangers in Arlington on September 12. Batting in the sixth inning with a man on base, May swung and one of his contact lenses popped out. Everybody looked for it. Ryan said, "Oh, just forget about it, you're going to strike out anyhow." Riled, May asked the batboy to bring his glasses, then smashed a ball down the left-field line for a double, scoring Willie Horton with the third Texas run in a 3–2 victory. May stood at second base and hollered to Ryan, "Is that a strikeout?" "I'll always remember that one," Dave said, "He didn't like it—he just wants to get back at you."[19] Ten days later, May preserved a no-hitter by Bert Blyleven at Anaheim by charging in on a line drive by Don Baylor in the eighth inning and catching the ball waist-high. Texas won, 6–0.

May (.241, 7 homers, 42 RBIS) was at his best for the second-place Rangers with runners in scoring position, hitting .299. At the annual Dallas–Fort Worth winter baseball banquet on January 20, 1978, he received the Good Guy Award.

May was placed on the disabled list with a sore shoulder on April 22, 1978. He hadn't played yet that season. Sold to the Milwaukee Brewers on May 17, he played in 39 games, 25 as a designated hitter or pinch hitter, all against right-handers. He hit just .195 with 2 home runs and 11 RBIS for the Brewers in 91 plate appearances. On September 13 Milwaukee sold May to the Pittsburgh Pi-

CHARLIE WEATHERBY

rates. With the Pirates, he reached base once in five pinch-hitting appearances; batting for pitcher Clay Carroll on October 1, he drew a walk from Dan Boitano and stole second in a 5–3 Pirates win. It was his last Major League game; he was released by Pittsburgh on November 6.

The Phillies signed May as a free agent in 1979 but released him during spring training. He signed with the Santo Domingo Azucareros of the short-lived Inter-American League, a six-team independent Triple-A circuit. Limited attendance doomed the league after two months, causing a financial nightmare for everyone. Miami (51-21) was declared the champion; Santo Domingo (38-29) finished third. According to May, "It was one of the worst things I ever did."[20]

May returned to Delaware and hooked up with Colonial Wallace, a semipro team run by a furniture-store owner. He sold furniture when he wasn't playing, finishing his five years in the league with a .313 average. In the spring of 1980, May, Chris Short, and Johnny Briggs led Colonial Wallace to Clearwater, Florida, for six exhibition games with the Phillies' Minor League teams, winning four of the contests. Best of all, Dave said, "It was another chance to go to spring training for free."[21]

In 1983 May became a roving hitting instructor for the Atlanta Braves' Minor League teams. During spring training he served as "the hatchet man." "I would tell the guys that Henry [Aaron] wanted to see them to give them their release. They didn't like to see me coming."[22] After camp, May moved on to work with the Anderson and Savannah clubs. His star pupils included Ron Gant and Andres Thomas.

At the end of the season, May returned to furniture and home-appliance sales. He later worked for the county for five years as a recreational sports site director. In 2003, while working as a factory cook, May was diagnosed with diabetes and his right leg was amputated. He also dealt with a heart problem at the same time. "I went through hell that year," Dave recalled.[23] He began kidney dialysis and was forced to use a wheelchair.

The thirty-second Delawarean to play in the Major Leagues, May was inducted into the Delaware Sports Museum and Hall of Fame in 1984. He was inducted into the Delaware Afro-American Sports Hall of Fame in 2004.

May married Maxine Hopkins in 1964; they divorced in 1983. They had three children, David Jr., Derrick, and Denae. David and Derrick played baseball, football, and basketball for Newark High School and were first-team All-State in baseball. David played baseball for Wilmington College and the University of Delaware from 1986 through 1990. In 2000 he became a scout for the Seattle Mariners. Derrick, a former first-round pick of the Chicago Cubs, had a 797-game Major League career (1990–99), primarily with the Cubs and Houston Astros, posting a .271 average with 52 home runs and 310 RBIs. In 2007 he became the hitting coach for the Springfield Cardinals of the Texas League.

Dave's daughter, Denae, an office manager, was a fine softball player and sprinter for Caravel High School. May said her track coach told him, "The best athlete in your family is your daughter."[24]

In 2009 May told an interviewer that he spent much of his time following sports on television. "The Eagles and Phillies have kept me going," he said. "I live for the weekends."[25] He said four of his nine grandchildren (he also had a great-grandson) had potential as ballplayers—perhaps a third generation of Mays will make it to the Majors.

"To have two sons that followed in the profession you were in is very gratifying," May said. He also learned that "the guys I played ball with are happy because I played in the big leagues and that gave them the sense that they are playing in the big leagues because they played with or against me. They say 'I was on the same field that you were on.' I was so happy that they feel that way and that I played as long as I did."[26]

Chapter 13. **April 1970 Timeline**

Malcolm Allen

All headlines below are from the next day's edition of the *Baltimore Sun*.

April 7—BIRDS "WALK" PAST TRIBE IN OPENER—The Orioles opened a season in Cleveland for the first time, on a chilly, forty-two-degree Tuesday afternoon in front of 38,180 spectators. They trailed Indians southpaw "Sudden Sam" McDowell 2–1 through six innings, with eleven Baltimore batters retired by strikeout. The lead changed hands in the seventh, however, when four Cleveland pitchers combined to walk five Orioles. Baltimore broke the game open in the eighth, and Dave McNally struck out a career high thirteen in a complete-game four-hit effort to win 8–2.

The Orioles' starting lineup that day was:

Don Buford	LF
Mark Belanger	SS
Frank Robinson	RF
Boog Powell	1B
Paul Blair	CF
Brooks Robinson	3B
Dave Johnson	2B
Andy Etchebarren	C
Dave McNally	P

April 8—CUELLAR'S 5-HITTER TOPS TRIBE—Baltimore drew eleven more walks—ten from Cleveland starter Barry Moore in the first five innings—and earned the first of a club-record 40 one-run victories in 1970. After Frank Robinson was hit on the right hand by a pitch in the sixth, Dave May replaced him and made a brilliant nosedive catch into the soggy turf in right-center, reminiscent of Ron Swoboda's grab against the Birds in the 1969 World Series. Final score: 3–2.

April 9—BIRDS ROUT TRIBE, 13–1, FOR SWEEP—Switch hitter Don Buford homered from both sides of the plate for the first time as a Major Leaguer and led the Baltimore attack with a career high five RBIS. Pitcher Tom Phoebus knocked in three more, and held Cleveland to a pair of hits by Vada Pinson. Before the game got completely out of hand, Orioles center fielder Paul Blair made a leaping catch in right-center to rob Graig Nettles of a home run.

April 10—BIRDS EDGE DETROIT IN 10TH, 3 TO 2—Thirty-mph wind gusts and an eight-day lay-off contributed to Jim Palmer's career-high eight walks in the home opener at Memorial Stadium. Dave Leonhard and Dick Hall picked him up with scoreless relief work, and Brooks Robinson played hero in the tenth inning. After diving behind the third-base bag to spear a line drive and save a run with the Tigers at bat, number 5 sliced the game-winning hit to right-center with two down in the bottom of the frame.

April 11—BIRDS RALLY IN 8TH NIPS TIGERS, 5–3—A four-run rally in their last at bat spurred the Orioles to their first 5–0 start in club history. Detroit's Bill Freehan nearly tied the game with a drive to left in the top of the ninth but, with a strong wind blowing in, it landed safely in the glove of Don Buford.

April 12—TIGERS SUBDUE ORIOLES, 7–2, AS PITCHER NIEKRO STARS—With two-time Cy Young Award winner Denny McLain suspended by Commissioner Bowie Kuhn for ties to an illegal bookmaking ring, Detroit handed the ball to Joe Niekro, who worked into the ninth inning to hand the Birds their first loss of the season.

April 13—No game scheduled.

April 14—Home game versus Senators rained out and rescheduled as part of a doubleheader on April 15.

April 15—The rain stopped falling in Baltimore by noon, but nearly two inches of precipitation left the grounds at Memorial Stadium too wet for baseball.

April 16—BIRDS FALL ON HOWARD HOMER, 4–2—Earl Weaver could only whisper after a morning surgery on a cyst on his vocal cord, but that didn't stop him from twice coming out to argue with umpires. Jim Palmer went to a three-ball count on eleven of the first fifteen Washington batters, and the damage was done by then on a "wounded quail" double by the opposing pitcher and a prodigious homer by Frank Howard after Palmer thought he'd struck him out. The Senators did not win any of their eight remaining games at Memorial Stadium in 1970.

April 17—BIRDS LOSE ON "BONER" BY JOHNSON—Hours after former Orioles catcher Dick Brown passed away from cancer at the age of thirty-five, rookie Terry Crowley's pinch-hit single in the eighth forced the year's first meeting with the Yankees into extra innings. Davey Johnson forgot to cover second on what should have been an inning-ending force play in the eleventh, and New York took advantage of the extra chance when Danny Cater followed with a three-run triple.

April 18—BIRDS SNAP LOSS SKEIN, WIN BY 5–4—New York's Horace Clarke led off the game with a home run, but the Orioles built a 3–2 lead by the

bottom of the seventh. After a walk, Dave McNally missed a bunt sign, but he doubled on the next pitch just inside the left-field line. The Yankees brought their infield in, and Don Buford punched a single through the right side to drive in a pair of insurance runs that ended up coming in very handy.

April 19—ORIOLES TOP YANKS BUT THEN LOSE—The Orioles wrapped up their first home stand of the season by splitting a Sunday doubleheader on Cap Day. Cuellar won the opener, 4–3, despite 6 walks and 2 wild pitches, but Horace Clarke's 5-for-6 performance led a seventeen-hit Yankee attack as New York took the nightcap, 8–5.

April 20—BIRDS POST 3–2 WIN IN SHORT GAME—The Patriots Day game at Fenway Park in Boston began at 11:00 a.m. in a steady drizzle, and Jim Palmer threw two wild pitches and walked seven from a slippery mound. He also earned his first win of the season, thanks to Boog Powell, who knocked in the tying run with a 400-foot single ("the longest I've ever seen," remarked Red Sox announcer Johnny Pesky[1]). The rain didn't affect the Boston Marathon, but the baseball game was shortened, with Powell hammering what proved to be a game-winning homer in the sixth and final inning. For the eventual 1970 AL MVP, it commenced a stretch of nine long balls in seventeen games.

April 21—No game scheduled.

April 22—BOSOX SHELL MCNALLY TO WIN BY 5–2—Dave McNally started a day early because of Tom Phoebus's blister problems and suffered his first loss, getting pounded for twelve hits. The Orioles dropped a game and a half behind Detroit, the largest deficit they would experience all season.

April 23—No game scheduled. Earl Weaver tells *The Sun*, "I feel bad because we have the best team in baseball and there are seven clubs in the major leagues with better percentages than ours."[2]

April 24—BIRDS BELT 3 HOMERS, WIN 7 TO 5—There had never been more than five home runs hit in a single game in sixteen years of American League baseball played at Municipal Stadium in Kansas City, but seven balls cleared the fence in this one. Reigning Cy Young Award winner Mike Cuellar surrendered four of them, and hit one as well, but the decisive blows came in back-to-back fashion in the seventh. Frank Robinson took Royals reliever Mike Hedlund deep for the tie, Boog Powell followed with a shot off the scoreboard for the lead, and Baltimore prevailed thanks to four scoreless relief innings from Jim Hardin and Pete Richert.

April 25—ORIOLES WHIP ROYALS ON FIVE IN FIRST, 9–3—Maryland-born southpaw Bill Butler was clobbered for a 450-foot bomb by Paul Blair and Brooks Robinson's second homer of the year in the opening inning as the Orioles hit back-to-back blasts for the second straight game.

April 26—ORIOLE BATS OVERCOME ROYALS, 10–9—Dave McNally couldn't complete a single inning after the offense spotted him a five-run lead, and Frank Robinson earned what would be the only ejection of an Orioles player in 1970 by arguing a called third strike. Baltimore trailed by two runs entering the top of the eighth, but Don Buford's three-run homer with two outs lifted the Birds back into first place to stay.

April 27—No game scheduled.

April 28—BOOG STARS AS ORIOLES TOP CHISOX—Powell hit a three-run homer in the first inning at Comiskey Park off Chicago's Jerry Janeski, and drove in all of Baltimore's runs in a 4–2 win. Mike Cuellar went the distance for the win.

April 29—BIRDS RIP CHISOX TO 18-2 SHREDS—Every starting Oriole hit safely as they established a club record for hits (20) in a nine-inning game, in logging what would be their highest scoring output of 1970. Paul Blair became just the third Baltimore player to bash three homers in a single game and notched a career-high six RBIS.

April 30—CHISOX END BIRDS' WIN STREAK, 6–3—The smallest crowd to watch the Orioles all season (1,469) endured a thirty-one-minute delay before winless Tommy John's first pitch, and a seventh-inning stoppage that lasted about an hour. Baltimore was leading until the bottom of the sixth, but catcher Andy Etchebarren bounced a throw past Boog Powell that led to four unearned runs and a defeat witnessed by few.

AL East Standings, April 30:

Team	W	L	GB
Baltimore	13	6	—
Detroit	12	6	0.5
Boston	11	8	2.0
Washington	11	8	2.0
New York	9	12	5.0
Cleveland	7	11	5.5

Chapter 14. **Tom Phoebus**

John Stahl

AGE	W	L	PCT.	ERA	G	GS	GF	CG	SHO	SV	IP	H	BB	SO	HBP	WP
28	5	5	.500	3.07	27	21	2	3	0	0	135	106	62	72	6	7

American League batters in the late 1960s often cited the five-foot-eight, 185-pound Tom Phoebus as one of the toughest pitchers to hit against. According to *The Sporting News*, Phoebus possessed an imposing arsenal of pitches: a good fastball, a slider with the break of a curveball, and a "ridiculous" curveball. Phoebus's primary pitching challenge was consistent control; he was characterized as sometimes having "too much stuff."[1] He pitched professionally from 1960 to 1973, winning fifty-six Major League games, including fifty for his hometown Baltimore Orioles. In 1970 he had a 5-5 record and won the second game of the World Series for the Orioles in relief.

Born in Baltimore on April 7, 1942, Thomas Harold Phoebus grew up on Fawcett Street within two miles of the site of Memorial Stadium, which was completed in 1950. As a child, he played baseball in his neighborhood Catholic Youth Organization League.[2] From 1956 to 1959, Phoebus attended Mount Saint Joseph High School, playing fullback on the football team and pitching for the baseball team. As a senior he pitched a no-hitter, striking out fifteen hitters.[3] (In 1985 Phoebus was inducted into the Mount Saint Joseph Hall of Fame.)

After graduating in 1960, the eighteen-year-old Phoebus signed with the Baltimore Orioles for a $10,000 bonus. He had been recommended to the Orioles by scouts Arthur Ehlers, Fritz Maisel, and Walter Youse. For Orioles fan Phoebus, playing for his hometown team was the realization of a childhood dream. "As kids," he later reflected, "we would go to the (Orioles) games, sit in the bleach-

Tom Phoebus entered the 1970 season as the Orioles' fourth starter, but he had fallen out of favor by the end of the season.

ers for 50 cents and ride the right fielder for the opposing team."[4]

With the Bluefield (West Virginia) Orioles in the rookie Appalachian League in 1960, Phoebus pitched 91 innings in 18 games and compiled a 6-5 record. In 1961 he pitched for Leesburg (Florida) in the Florida State League (Class D). He suffered the worst year of his professional career, pitching in 34 games and compiling a 1-12 record for the

63

last-place team with a 5.56 earned run average (he walked 98 batters in 81 innings). Despite this setback, the Orioles pushed the twenty-year-old up to Aberdeen (South Dakota) in the Class C Northern League, and the results were much better. For the Pheasants, Phoebus finished 13-10 with a 4.47 ERA and a league-leading 195 strikeouts. His 152 walks in 167 innings suggest that he did not always know where the ball was going.

In 1963 Phoebus pitched for the Elmira (New York) Pioneers in the Double-A Eastern League. In this advanced league, he pitched in 29 games and 175 innings, and posted a 12-7 record with a 3.03 ERA. He walked 124 and struck out 212, which broke the club record for strikeouts. At Elmira Tom pitched for Earl Weaver, for whom he would pitch in the Major Leagues. After the season, the Maryland Professional Baseball Players Association selected Phoebus as Maryland's "star of the future."[5] He later called the award one of the highlights of his early professional career.

For the next three seasons, beginning in 1964, Phoebus pitched for the Orioles' highest affiliate, the Rochester (New York) Red Wings of the International League. In 1964 he pitched in 30 games, finishing 11-9 with a 3.39 ERA. Rochester finished fourth in the regular season, but won two rounds of playoffs to capture the league title. Phoebus started and won a game in each playoff round.[6] The next season he slipped to 8-8 in 23 games for a fifth-place club. "He's the kind of kid who gives you ulcers," said George Sisler, then the Rochester general manager. "He's always in and out of hot water. You always have the impression it'll be a tough game. Then you look up in the seventh inning and Tom is still out there pumping and we're usually ahead."[7]

Phoebus had high expectations for his 1966 season going into spring training. "I wanted to make (the Orioles) more than anything in the world," he remembered.[8] His hope turned to disappointment; he had a good spring training only to be reassigned again to the Red Wings. The Orioles had continu-

ing concerns about his control, particularly his ability to keep the ball down. Phoebus regrouped and finished 13-9 while posting career bests in complete games (14), shutouts (5), innings pitched (200), strikeouts (a league-leading 208), and ERA (3.02), and pitched a no-hitter. With Weaver at the helm, the 1966 Red Wings won the regular-season title but lost in the first round of the playoffs.

Phoebus's no-hitter, on August 15, was a 1–0 gem in seven innings, the first game of a double-header at home against Buffalo. Phoebus struck out seven and walked two. He helped save his no-hitter by knocking down a potential ground-ball hit barehanded and throwing the batter out. The only other potential hit was an infield slow roller that resulted in a close, disputed out at first base. Phoebus relied on his curve and slider through most of the game, using the fastball only to complement his breaking pitches. Manager Earl Weaver was impressed. "It's a beautiful thing to watch when the curve and the slider are working for him," said Weaver.[9]

In late August, after the no-hitter, the Tom Phoebus Fan Club conducted a friendly protest in his old Baltimore neighborhood, urging the Orioles to call him up immediately. Primarily composed of his friends and neighbors and their young children, the small crowd carried signs with slogans such as "Give Tom Phoebus a Chance to Pitch." In early September, Weaver summed up Phoebus's status to *The Sporting News*. "He has major-league pitches. Everybody in the organization knows this. It's just that he must prove that he can throw strikes consistently. . . . Tom has a major-league fastball and slider right now. It's his curve that he has trouble controlling. . . . I think he has an excellent chance to pitch for Baltimore next year"[10]

Phoebus and several other Red Wings players joined the Orioles in mid-September. The 1966 Orioles were destined to be the world champions but were currently on a four-game losing streak. "(There's) nothing wrong with us that a few well-pitched games wouldn't fix," grumbled manager Hank Bauer. When Phoebus arrived, Bauer decided to start him immediately, telling him, "Just pitch like you did in Rochester."[11] For Phoebus it was his "homecoming," his first opportunity to pitch for his childhood heroes.

After rain postponed his start for two days, Phoebus started the first game of a doubleheader against the California Angels on September 15 in front of 7,617 customers on a damp, chilly evening. Among the crowd were his mother, his younger brother, about fourteen aunts, uncles, and other relatives, and many of his neighbors. Phoebus responded by pitching a complete-game shutout, beating Dean Chance, 2–0. He struck out eight, walked two, and allowed only four hits. As he fanned the last hitter, the fans gave him a standing ovation. After his triumph, Phoebus was immediately hailed by the Baltimore press as the new hometown hero. Phoebus was ecstatic. "If Tom's post-game grin would have been any wider," reported the *Baltimore Sun*, "it would have swallowed his ears." Asked if the postponements had made him nervous, Phoebus responded, "I'll say I was nervous. I've been nervous since Tuesday." How did he deal with his nerves? "I just tried to relax around the house, listening to my brother's stereo. Mostly, I listened to rock 'n' roll." He credited his defense with preserving his shutout. "They made some great plays. They were terrific behind me," said Phoebus. "I just tried to throw strikes." Orioles general manager Harry Dalton, manager Hank Bauer, pitching coach Harry Brecheen, and catcher Andy Etchebarren all gave Phoebus the credit.[12]

Five days later Phoebus got his second start and pitched his second shutout. Pitching against Catfish Hunter in Kansas City, he blanked the Athletics 4–0. Phoebus became only the seventh pitcher since 1900 to pitch shutouts in his first two games.[13] The streak ended in his next start, on September 26, when the Angels tagged Phoebus for seven hits and three runs in four innings and won,

6–1.[14] Ineligible for the World Series, Phoebus watched from the dugout as the Orioles swept the Los Angeles Dodgers. In his brief debut he posted a record of 2-1 in 22 innings with a 1.23 ERA, striking out 17 and walking only 6.

Phoebus's Maryland roots quickly made him a fan favorite. During the offseason, he reportedly filled nearly thirty speaking appearance requests, working them in around his offseason job as a draftsman. Convinced that his control problems were behind him, the Orioles began the 1967 season with Phoebus in their starting rotation. It was a bad season for the Orioles: a 76-85 record and a sixth-place finish. But Phoebus sparkled. He posted a 14-9 record with a 3.33 ERA. He started 33 games and pitched 208 innings. He led the pitching staff in innings pitched, games started, strikeouts, and victories. In late May and early June he pitched three consecutive shutouts, against New York, Boston, and Washington, equaling the achievement of an earlier Orioles pitcher, Milt Pappas. *The Sporting News* picked Phoebus as the 1967 American League Rookie Pitcher of the Year. After a courtship of three months, Phoebus married his wife, Susan, a Baltimore native.[15]

The 1968 season was a year of major transition for the Orioles. Although they finished second to the Tigers, with a 91-71 record, manager Hank Bauer was fired in midseason and Earl Weaver succeeded him. Phoebus posted a 15-15 record with career bests in games started (36), strikeouts (193), innings pitched (240⅔), and ERA (2.61). He also pitched a no-hitter against the defending American League champion Boston Red Sox at Memorial Stadium on April 27. The night before, he had left the ballpark early with a sore throat. He talked with Bauer the next morning and they decided he would pitch as scheduled. Rain delayed the start of the game about ninety minutes. The contest began in a light drizzle in front of a small crowd of 3,147 paying customers and 11,568 scholastic safety-patrol youngsters. Phoebus struck out nine and walked three in the 6–0 victory. Two defensive plays saved the no-hitter. In the third inning Phoebus deflected a chopper off the tip of his glove. Shortstop Mark Belanger charged in, scooped the ball up, and threw the batter out. In the eighth, third baseman Brooks Robinson lunged to his left and speared a line drive. For his achievement, the Orioles rewarded Phoebus with a $1,000 bonus.[16]

Phoebus started strongly in 1969, beginning with two shutouts. By the end of May, his record stood at 5-1 with a 3.79 ERA in 10 starts, and he settled in to finish 14-7 with a 3.52 ERA in 202 innings. With the acquisition of Mike Cuellar from Houston and the comeback from injury from Jim Palmer, Phoebus was no longer one of the top starters on the club. In fact, although he won the pennant-clinching game by beating the Cleveland Indians on September 13, he did not appear in either the playoff series against the Minnesota Twins or the World Series loss to the New York Mets.

For 1970 Phoebus faced stiff competition (Jim Hardin) for the fourth starting pitcher position, which they wound up sharing. Through July 27 Phoebus appeared 18 times, starting 14 games and relieving 4 times. He slumped in August and pitched infrequently but rebounded to win a couple of September starts to finish 5-5 with a 3.07 ERA. In Game Two of the World Series, in Cincinnati, Phoebus relieved Mike Cuellar in the third inning with the Orioles losing 4–0. He got Lee May to ground into a double play to end the inning, then pitched a scoreless fourth. The Orioles scored five times in the top of the fifth to take the lead and won 6–5, making Phoebus the winner in his only World Series appearance.

In December 1970 the Orioles traded Phoebus and three other players to the San Diego Padres for pitchers Pat Dobson and Tom Dukes.[17] Phoebus and his wife greeted the news with mixed emotions as both were Baltimore natives and had many friends and family members in the area. However, he soon realized the opportunity he had to resurrect his career in San Diego. "I couldn't adjust to spot starting with the Orioles," he said. "I want to start every day." As for moving from a world championship team to the Padres, he remained positive. "It's the desire to win that overcomes everything," he said. "I believe it's the biggest factor to be successful in the majors. And you have to have it every day."[18]

But 1971 turned out to be Phoebus's worst year in the Major Leagues. He appeared in 29 games (21 starts) and posted a 3-11 record. He pitched 133 innings, allowing 144 hits and finishing with a 4.47 ERA. After July San Diego used Phoebus exclusively as a reliever. In April 1972 he was traded to the Chicago Cubs for cash and a player to be named later. For Chicago he appeared in 37 games (just one as a starter), finishing 3-3 with a 3.78 ERA.

In November 1972 the Cubs traded Phoebus to the Atlanta Braves for struggling infielder Tony La Russa, later to win fame as a Major League manager. Phoebus spent the 1973 season with the Braves' Richmond club in the International League. He pitched 125 innings and posted a 7-11 record with a 3.38 ERA, not enough to earn him another chance in the Major Leagues. After the season he retired from baseball. He was thirty-one years old.

After baseball Phoebus moved to Florida, working first for a liquor distributor and then for Tropicana, the orange juice manufacturer. At the age of thirty-nine he enrolled at Manatee Community College, and then at the University of South Florida, graduating with a degree in education. He spent nearly two decades as a physical education instructor in three Florida grade schools before retiring. In 1991 Phoebus was inducted into the Maryland State Athletic Hall of Fame.

As of 2010 he was living in Palm City, Florida, the father of two sons: Thomas, a high school teacher, and Joseph, a computer graphic artist. Phoebus played golf regularly but reported that his fastball has lost its "oomph." "I can't crank it up to 94 [miles per hour] anymore," he lamented.[19]

Chapter 15. **Dave Johnson**

Mark Armour

AGE	G	AB	R	H	2B	3B	HR	TB	RBI	BB	SO	BAV	OBP	SLG	SB	GDP	HBP
27	149	530	68	149	27	1	10	208	53	66	68	.281	.360	.392	2	11	0

After a highly successful career as both a slick-fielding infielder and a slugger, Davey Johnson went on to an even more decorated career as a manager. As of 2010, his winning percentage of .564 was tenth all-time among managers with 1,000 victories, and is surpassed by only Earl Weaver among pilots who began their career after 1960. But it was while playing for Weaver in Baltimore that Johnson first became a prominent name in baseball, as the valuable second baseman for four pennant winners and the 1966 and 1970 champions. Four men share the record for starting twenty-one World Series games for the Orioles: Brooks Robinson, Frank Robinson, Boog Powell, and Dave Johnson.

David Allen Johnson was born in Orlando, Florida, on January 30, 1943. Johnson's father, Frederick, was a highly decorated World War II tank commander, who eventually rose to the rank of lieutenant colonel. Frederick left for the war just as Dave was born and later spent time in an Italian prisoner-of-war camp, where he had his teeth pulled without an anesthetic. He later escaped and lived with members of the Italian resistance. The stories of his wartime life were never discussed in the Johnson home—Dave did not learn of them until he was an adult himself. All he knew was that his father was deeply respected by other military men the family associated with. "Dad was very tough, a stubborn Swede on the outside but very caring down deep," recalled Johnson decades later. "I'm stubborn, too. Yet even if he was hard, you still knew he was always thinking about his family, his soldiers, that he'd try to move mountains for them."[1]

Slick-fielding Dave Johnson also provided a good bat for the Orioles during four pennant-winning seasons.

As the child of a U.S. Army officer, Johnson lived on army bases in Germany, Georgia, Texas, and Wyoming. The family eventually settled in San Antonio, Texas, where Johnson first attracted baseball scouts at Alamo Heights High School. Johnson first went to Texas A&M, where he played shortstop for "the greatest coach in the world, Tom Chandler, a real classic who taught me real respect for the game, and gave me an opportunity to show what I could do."[2] After two years in College Station, where he also played guard for the varsity basketball team, Johnson entertained suitors from several Major League teams before signing with the Orioles. Scouts Dee Phillips and Jim Russo visited Johnson right after his last college game, and made a deal for a $25,000 bonus.[3]

After signing with the Orioles, Johnson joined the Stockton club in the California League. As a nineteen-year-old in 1962, he hit .309 as the club's shortstop, and became one of the best prospects in a system loaded with young talent. The next year he played under Earl Weaver at Elmira (Eastern League) and hit .326 before earning a promotion to Triple-A Rochester in July. The International League proved a bit tougher (.246 in 63 games), and the move also required him to shift to second base, a position he took to very well. He returned to Rochester in 1964 and hit .264 with 19 home runs, playing both middle infield positions, and developing into one of the more promising infielders in the Minor Leagues. Baltimore was a fine team, and Johnson's path was blocked by shortstop Luis Aparicio and second baseman Jerry Adair, both defensive stalwarts. Johnson made the club in 1965 and backed up at second, short, and third (manned by Brooks Robinson) for half a season before the Orioles decided to send him back to Rochester. He hit just .170 in 47 at bats in the big time, but .301 back in Triple-A.

In the spring of 1966 Orioles manager Hank Bauer turned the second-base job over to Johnson, bypassing the incumbent Adair, who had held the job for five years. The promotion could have been temporary, but Adair complained enough to cause the Orioles to deal him to the White Sox in June. Johnson played in 131 games in 1966 and hit .257 with 7 home runs. He drew raves for his defense and provided hope for his offense. "We feel," said general manager Harry Dalton, "that this boy is going to be a big hitter among big-league second basemen. He has done everything now that we have asked him to do. He has the intelligence to apply himself."[4] The Orioles also won the pennant in 1966, and Johnson's .286 average in the World

Series contributed to the sweep of the Los Angeles Dodgers. Johnson earned the distinction of being the batter who got the final hit off Sandy Koufax, a single in Game Three.

Johnson built on his fine rookie year with excellent defense and more power (10 home runs and 30 doubles) in 1967, though the Orioles fell to sixth place. After the season the Orioles traded Luis Aparicio to the Chicago White Sox, and the ascension of shortstop Mark Belanger completed the great infield (along with Johnson, third baseman Brooks Robinson, and first baseman Boog Powell) that helped define the great Orioles of the coming years. In the club's climb back to second place in 1968, Johnson hit .242 and made his first All-Star team, striking out against Ron Reed in his only plate appearance.

Johnson battled back woes in 1969, but he still hit .280 with 34 doubles, his best offensive season to date. He was selected to another All-Star Game, though he did not play, and won his first Gold Glove for his defensive play. He did all this despite regular visits to the chiropractor and enough discomfort that he often could not sit down. He hit just .231 in the playoff series with the Twins, and was just 1-for-16 in the World Series loss to the Mets. "I'm still flabbergasted we lost," remembered Johnson decades later, "that destiny made all sorts of funky things happen. Gusts of wind blowing balls back to their outfielders, [Ron] Swoboda's diving catch, Al Weis hitting a home run; our winning just wasn't meant to be."[5]

Even early in his career Johnson's intellect was commented upon in the press. In 1969 he fed various batting orders into a computer at Trinity College, where he took classes, to see what the optimal Baltimore lineup would be. Pitcher Dave McNally, a longtime teammate, recalled a time Johnson visited him on the pitcher's mound, in order to explain to him about "unfavorable change deviation theory." McNally was wild that day, and Johnson was suggesting that he aim for the middle of the plate so that he would miss his spot and hit a corner.[6]

Johnson had another excellent year in 1970, hitting .281 with 38 extra-base hits. He started the All-Star Game (replacing the injured Rod Carew), going 1-for-5, and won his second Gold Glove award. He also starred in the postseason, hitting .364 with 2 home runs in the playoff series, then .313 in the Orioles' victorious World Series.

In early 1970 Johnson spoke out about his annual contract hassles, and announced that he had asked the club to trade him. "It's not the city," he said. "I like Baltimore. I like the players, the coaches, and the manager. I don't like management."[7] In the spring he even suggested he might retire and go sell real estate—he had recently earned his license. After his fine 1970 season, and the Orioles' championship, he signed for $50,000 early in the off-season and declared himself happy the following spring. He came through in 1971 with his best year yet, .282 with 18 home runs and 72 runs batted in and a third Gold Glove, helping the Orioles to a third straight league pennant. In the end, the club lost the World Series to the Pirates.

In 1972 Johnson battled shoulder and back woes and hit just .221 in 118 games, part of a season-long offensive malaise for the Orioles, who fell to third place. Johnson was also affected by the emergence of twenty-three-year-old infielder Bobby Grich, who played 133 games mainly at shortstop and second base. Grich quickly became a star both at bat and in the field, making the twenty-nine-year-old Johnson expendable. On November 30, he was traded to the Atlanta Braves in a six-player deal. "I wanted to be traded to the National League," said Johnson, "and I'm happy to be coming to a good club."[8]

In 1973 Johnson made the most of his new league, belting 43 home runs and driving in 99 runs for the Braves. He joined with Darrell Evans (41) and Henry Aaron (40) to be the first set of three teammates to hit 40 home runs in a season.

"It was the greatest thing that ever happened to me in baseball," Johnson said of the trade, "and the big reason was joining Aaron. He helped make me a better hitter." Aaron refused to take any credit, saying only, "Dave's a smart hitter. He knows what he's doing up there."[9] Aaron's chase of Babe Ruth's career record of 714 home runs captivated the baseball public, and he ultimately ended the season one short at 713.

Aside from the home-run barrage, Johnson's error total increased from 6 to a league-leading 30 in 1973. The next season he shifted between first base and second base in deference to Marty Perez. For the season Johnson started 70 games at first and 62 at second, and hit just .251 with 15 home runs. The next season he was tapped as a platoon first baseman, but after a single at bat (a pinch-hit double), he signed with the Yomiuri Giants of the Japan Central League. He joined teammate Sadaharu Oh, who that same season hit his 715th home run, passing Babe Ruth's mark just as Henry Aaron had done the previous year.

The Giants were the most dominant and storied team in Japanese baseball, having won fifteen Japan Series titles in the previous twenty-four seasons, featuring both Oh and Shigeo Nagashima. The immensely popular Nagashima had retired at the end of the 1974 season, and immediately was named manager. One of his first acts was to recruit Johnson as his replacement, making Johnson the first foreign-born player on the Giants in nearly twenty years and the first American star player to play in Japan. His 1975 season was a disaster—he hit just .197 with 13 home runs, he was heavily criticized by the press, the fans laughed at him, and he lost twenty-five pounds. "I swear," recalled Johnson, "I would go to bed sometimes and hear bells. I thought I was losing it there for a while."[10]

The next year he came back determined to make good. He reported for volunteer winter training in January and regained his starting job. He hit .268 with 26 home runs, was named the league's top fielding second baseman, made the postseason All-Star team, and helped lead the Giants to a league pennant. His tenure ended badly, however, as he clashed with Nagashima over a midseason arm injury and a late-season illness—in both cases his manager did not believe he was hurt, and publicly humiliated Johnson in front of the team. After his excellent season the Giants tried to get him to return, but Johnson would do so only if Nagashima apologized for his treatment. He would not, so Johnson returned to the United States.

Now thirty-four years old, Johnson signed with Philadelphia in February 1977. For the Phillies, he served as a reserve infielder, playing mostly first base. He hit well, batting .321 with 8 home runs in 156 at bats. He also returned to the postseason, and played in the first game of the playoffs against the Dodgers at first base, going 1-for-4 at the plate. In 1977 Johnson returned in the same role, but as he was hitting only .191 in August, the Phillies traded him to the Cubs for relief pitcher Larry Anderson on August 8. He hit better in Chicago, .306 in 49 at bats. Interestingly, Johnson's poor season with the Phillies included a historic accomplishment. Though he hit just two home runs for the club, he became the first Major League player to hit two pinch-hit grand slams in one year. After the season, Johnson decided to retire as a player.

Johnson had studied to be a veterinarian at Texas A&M, but he continued his education in the off-season and earned a mathematics degree at Trinity College in San Antonio. Despite his success in baseball, he continued to learn new things. He became a licensed pilot, a scratch golfer, a talented fisherman, and a scuba instructor. He also became adroit at using a computer long before many people owned one, taking graduate classes at Johns Hopkins University while with the Orioles. With all of these hobbies and skills, Johnson knew what he wanted to do—stay in baseball as an instructor or manager.

Over the next five years Johnson managed three seasons in the Minor Leagues (taking one season off and working the other as an instructor) and won three league championships. His final Minor League season was in 1983 with Tidewater, the New York Mets' Triple-A affiliate, and it was a surprise to no one when in 1984 Johnson was promoted to manage the parent club, which had been floundering for many years. Johnson was forty-one years old.

Johnson's boss in New York was general manager Frank Cashen, who had held the same position with the Orioles when Johnson played there. Johnson's first successful move was to persuade Cashen to promote the nineteen-year-old pitcher Dwight Gooden, whom Johnson had managed at the tail end of the 1983 season. Gooden won 17 games and the Rookie of the Year Award. This fit a pattern with Johnson, who favored several young players from the system over the mediocre veterans the Mets had been playing. The club won 90 games in 1984, the second best record the club had achieved in its twenty-three-year existence.

The Mets won 98 games in 1985, then 108 and the World Series in 1986. The latter club was remarkably balanced, with league-leading pitching (Bobby Ojeda, Ron Darling, Gooden, Sid Fernandez, and Jesse Orosco) and hitting (Keith Hernandez, Gary Carter, Darryl Strawberry, Lenny Dykstra, and Mookie Wilson). The team was also very deep, and Johnson used his roster fully, as Earl Weaver had done with Johnson's Orioles clubs.

Although the Mets won 92 games in 1987, and 100 games and the division title in 1988, many observers considered the club a disappointment for reaching only a single World Series. Johnson had become the only manager in big-league history to win 90 games in each of his first five seasons, but his legacy in New York is marred by the team's reputation as a traveling frat party. Strawberry and Gooden both spent years battling cocaine addiction and other problems, Dykstra led a wild lifestyle, Hernandez battled drug issues—

several books have been written about this club's off-field antics. Johnson was not directly involved, but he has been criticized for allowing it to go on. After two second-place finishes in 1989 and 1990, a slow start in 1991 (20-22) led Cashen to fire Johnson in May.

Johnson spent the next three years out of baseball, managing some property in Florida when he wasn't fishing, flying, or golfing. Johnson had married Mary Nan in the early days of his baseball career, and the couple raised three children—David Jr., Dawn, and Andrea. The Johnsons' marriage ended in the late 1980s, and Johnson admitted that he developed a bit of a problem with alcohol in subsequent years.

Although his name often surfaced when there were job openings, his reputation as a strong and opinionated manager might have scared some teams off. Johnson had battled with Cashen constantly in New York. Finally, in May 1993 Johnson became manager of the Cincinnati Reds, working for their controversial owner Marge Schott. Johnson's hiring was not popular because the Reds had fired local favorite Tony Perez just 44 games into his first managerial season. The previous manager, Lou Piniella, had resigned in the off-season because of Schott's meddling.

The Reds finished just 53-65 under Johnson in 1993, but the next year they had the best record in the National League West (66-48) when the season was ended by the players strike in August. The 1995 season was delayed by the same strike, but once things got going, Johnson brought the club home in first place in the new NL Central Division. The Reds swept the Dodgers in three straight in the first round of the playoffs, before falling to eventual champion Atlanta in the National League Championship Series.

Johnson began dating Susan Allen in the early 1990s, and it was their cohabitation that first earned him the wrath of Reds owner Schott. The couple married in 1994, but his relationship with Schott, who had her own off-field problems, did not improve. Despite two first-place finishes in his two full seasons, he was fired after the season.

Johnson was not unemployed for long, signing on to manage the Baltimore Orioles, the organization for which he had played for eleven years. In Baltimore he worked for Pat Gillick, who had been his teammate in Elmira in 1963. As he had done everywhere, Johnson continued to win—88 games and a wild-card berth in 1996, then 98 and a division title in 1997. In each season the Orioles won a division series before falling short in the League Championship Series. His most challenging personnel decision was his move of Cal Ripken from shortstop to third base—briefly in 1996, then permanently to start the 1997 season. Ripken had not missed a game at shortstop in fourteen years, but Johnson felt the thirty-seven-year-old would be more valuable and effective at a less demanding position. Ripken was cool to the idea, but adjusted and played every day at third base for two more seasons before ending his consecutive-game streak at 2,632 in September 1998.

Along with winning, Johnson's two years in Baltimore were marked by occasional public spats with owner Peter Angelos, who resented Johnson's "swagger."[11] After the 1997 season Johnson, who had not spoken to Angelos in six months, faxed a letter demanding either a contract extension or a buyout. Angelos considered the action yet another sign of insubordination. He accepted the resignation on November 5, 1997, the same day that Johnson was named Manager of the Year.

Johnson's next Major League assignment, with the Los Angeles Dodgers in 1999 and 2000, saw his team win 77 and 86 games. Johnson was let go with little fanfare after the latter season.

The ensuing years were a struggle for Johnson. In 2005 he suffered the tragic loss of his thirty-two-year-old daughter, Andrea. She had once been a world-class surfer, but had suffered through years of depression and schizophrenia.

Soon after her death Johnson developed stomach problems, eventually diagnosed at the Mayo Clinic as a ruptured appendix that cost him half his stomach and more than fifty pounds.

In 2003 he managed the Netherlands to a European championship, and in 2008 he skippered the United States team to a Bronze Medal in the Olympic Games in Beijing. He also led the American team in the 2009 World Baseball Classic.

As of 2010, Johnson and Susan lived in Winter Park, Florida. He was an adviser for the Washington Nationals, and had spent two seasons coaching in the Florida Collegiate Summer League. "If you're a baseball person, and love it, it's what we do," he said.[12] In 2010 he was named to the New York Mets Hall of Fame, along with his former players Dwight Gooden and Darryl Strawberry, and his former boss, Frank Cashen.

Johnson was often rumored to be available for the latest managerial opening, and in July 2011 he was hired to manage the Nationals after Jim Riggleman's abrupt resignation. It was unclear whether Johnson would return in 2012.

Chapter 16. **Jim Hardin**

Malcolm Allen

AGE	W	L	PCT.	ERA	G	GS	GF	CG	SHO	SV	IP	H	BB	SO	HBP	WP
26	6	5	.545	3.53	36	19	4	3	2	1	145.1	150	26	78	1	3

In 1969 the *Oriole News* stated: "[Jim] Hardin is one of those pitchers who doesn't have an overpowering fastball or an outstanding breaking pitch. But his physical ability is of major-league caliber, make no mistake about it, and he's the type who squeezes every ounce out of what he has."[1]

Jim Hardin began his baseball life as a catcher, but made a 180-degree turn to find his future in the sport on the pitcher's mound. Born on August 6, 1943, in Morris Chapel, Tennessee, near Memphis, he had been a catcher since the sixth grade, and a pretty good one at that. As a high school sophomore he earned second team All-Memphis honors behind future twenty-one-year big leaguer Tim McCarver (even though Hardin outhit his rival backstop, .475 to .470).

But one day when Hardin was a senior, the team ran out of pitchers. "Here, you pitch," his coach told him.[2] Jim took the mound and stayed there. He nearly went undefeated as a high school pitcher save for some extra-inning defeats. Hardin impressed on the hill in American Legion ball too, and professional contract offers started coming in. After enrolling at the University of Memphis, he turned down higher offers and, still having pitched in only fourteen games, he signed a contract with a $10,000 bonus from the New York Mets, figuring the expansion franchise would provide the shortest route to the Majors.

Though he had a strong right arm, Hardin had difficulty throwing strikes. With the New York–Penn League Auburn Mets in 1962 and the Quincy Jets of the Midwest League in '63, he walked 184 batters in 184 innings and finished a combined

In his only season as a full-time starter Jim Hardin won eighteen games. By 1970 he was a valuable spot starter and long reliever for the Orioles.

8-13 with a 4.79 earned run average. He improved just slightly in 1964 after going back to Auburn to start the season. He walked 50 in 60 innings there but went 4-1, earning a promotion at midseason to the Double-A Williamsport Mets of the Eastern League, where he walked 48 in 63 innings. "I didn't have a winning season until I got married in January 1964," Hardin quipped about his combined 7-4 won-lost mark that year. "Donna deserves all the credit."[3] However, he still walked more than seven men per nine innings, and regressed to 5-10 back at Williamsport in 1965 despite improving his control even further (58 walks in 124 innings).

In November 1965 the Mets lost Hardin to the Baltimore Orioles in the Minor League draft for $12,000. Years later, Hardin still wasn't sure what prompted the Orioles to take a flyer on a pitcher who'd yet to make it through a single season without getting sent to the bullpen. "We just went by the reports we got from [Earl] Weaver," Lou Gorman, then the Orioles' director of Minor League clubs, told Hardin. "The only times he saw you were when you faced his [Eastern League Elmira] club."[4]

Hardin met pitching instructor George Bamberger for the first time in the Orioles' Minor League camp in 1966, and Bamberger told him, "Don't nibble around the plate. You've got good enough stuff to challenge them. Even the good hitters only get three hits in 10 tries."[5] Hardin joined the Elmira Pioneers for his third straight year in the Eastern League, and fired an early-season no-hitter against his old mates in Williamsport. He wound up making the bulk of his appearances in relief for the fifth straight year, though, finishing 8-2 with a 3.44 ERA.

Hardin was one of eight Baltimore pitchers sent to the Florida Instructional League after the 1966 season, and he worked with Bamberger every day. "He kept saying if you don't walk anybody, and put the ball over with something on it, you'll get the hitters out," Hardin recalled.[6] The right-hander went undefeated in seven decisions that fall before heading off to Mexico to reinforce his lessons. But Hardin's winter-league season was cut short on Christmas Eve by a case of "turista" (the Mexican colloquial name for the diarrhea that strikes tourists because of changes in food and water). Unable to locate the one local doctor who spoke English, Hardin tried in vain to get medical personnel to insert a glucose treatment into his left arm, not

his right. The vein in his pitching arm swelled up, leaving him sore and unable to pitch, so he went home.

Hardin attended his first Major League spring training in 1967. Though he was a long shot to make the Opening Day roster of the World Series champion Orioles, any chance he may have had was ruined when he went looking for bonefish off Key Biscayne on an off day. Wading into murky waters in his canvas sneakers, Hardin startled a stingray nearly two feet in diameter, and was slashed by the creature's sharp, poisonous tail through the top of his shoe. He was taken to a hospital to have the half-inch wound cleaned and received three shots. His foot swelled up so much that more than a week went by before he could put on a shoe, and the Orioles sent him back to their Minor League camp in the first round of cuts. "You spend five years in the minors, and you step on a stingray just as you're about to get a chance?" scolded his wife.[7]

The setback proved only temporary as Hardin excelled after finally making it to Triple-A. With Rochester of the International League, the one-time wildman walked only 14 batters in 53 innings, and had a 2.04 ERA and a 5-3 record after hurling a shutout in Columbus with Orioles general manager Harry Dalton and superscout Jim Russo in the stands. Dalton and Russo had arrived to check out tall right-hander Gene Brabender for a possible Major League call-up, but Hardin forced his way to the front of the line. After missing his next start because of a bout of food poisoning, Hardin was called up to the big leagues a few days later. Jim Palmer described the twenty-three-year-old pitcher as "promising, but not overflowing with confidence."[8]

The six-foot, 175-pound right-hander debuted with two scoreless innings in Washington on June 23 and compiled a 0.82 ERA in a handful of relief outings over the next three weeks. Most impressively, he walked only one in eleven innings.

He surrendered a three-run homer in the first inning of his first start, on July 23, but won eight of his first ten decisions before a poor final outing. Overall, he won 8 and lost 3, limiting opponents to 85 hits and 27 walks in 111 innings and pitching to a 2.27 ERA, including shutouts against the Kansas City Athletics and the pennant-winning Boston Red Sox. It was a wonderful year for the Hardins, as Donna gave birth to their first child, Gina Michelle, in November. In 1971 they added son James, and Michael came along in 1989.

Hardin was a fine golfer, having won the Minor League portion of a tournament for ballplayers the previous off-season. After he helped Earl Weaver's Santurce club to the Puerto Rican league finals in the fall, he returned to the States just in time to win the first round of the National Baseball Players Golf Tournament in February. With spring training in full swing on March 16, Hardin recorded his first hole in one, on the sixth hole of Miami's Kendall Golf Course.

By late June of 1968 Hardin's pitching had earned him the cover of *The Sporting News*. "I'm basically a very uncomplicated pitcher," he said. "My pattern is to throw fastballs and breaking pitches and just keep moving the ball in and out, up and down. I'd say I pitch just about the same way to everybody."[9]

"For some reason, he's not particularly liked by some of the guys," Jim Palmer recalled in his autobiography. "But Brooks Robinson, Davey Leonhard, and me, we think he's a decent guy if you get to know him, which most of the others didn't do."[10]

The quick-working Hardin won his first four decisions in 1968. By the time he notched his only career ten-strikeout performance, on May 25 against the Washington Senators, he'd won 6 out of 7, which grew to 8 of 10. He strained his back in a complete-game victory in Detroit on July 21 that improved his record to 12-5 with a 2.13 ERA, and lost ten pounds from an intestinal infection shortly thereafter, but came back strong to pitch a pair of shutouts in August and run his record to 17-8 with five weeks remaining in the season.

"He could flat-out pitch," Jim Palmer recalled. "He learned self-hypnosis. He had his mantra—jam, J-A-M, and he had learned down in Puerto Rico to put himself under self-hypnosis. He put himself in a trance. He had great stuff, great command, great change-up, good fastball."[11]

Hardin's bid for a twenty-win season went up in smoke when he lost five of his last six decisions, though three of the defeats came by scores of 2–0, 2–1, and 3–2. He finished the season fifth in the American League in wins (18) and complete games (16). "He was making $14,000 a year," Palmer recalled. "They said if you had a good year—18-13 with a 2.51 ERA apparently wasn't a good year—we'll give you a raise. Well, he didn't get a raise, so he came down to the Instructional League in Clearwater, Florida, for like the last two weeks, then went down to Puerto Rico."[12]

Hardin pitched a 5–0 shutout at Caguas in his first outing of the winter, an effort Palmer described as "one of the best games I ever saw pitched,"[13] but more than six weeks had passed since his previous game action and he emerged feeling stiffness in the large muscle behind his right shoulder. Later, he admitted that the shoulder had begun feeling sore when he favored a bum ankle late in the '68 season.

It didn't help at all that Major League Baseball tried to increase offense by lowering the pitcher's mound in 1969. "They're liable to hurt some arms," Hardin warned. "The pitcher has to drive off the rubber harder and open up his body quicker to get the same results as before. This is going to tell on the arm."[14] Regardless on the exact cause of Hardin's woes, it quickly became clear that he was out of step as the Orioles began their march to three straight American League pennants. After a winless April with a bloated 5.48 ERA, he spent the season bouncing back and forth between the rotation and the bullpen. "I'm not myself. I'm not throwing the same," he said. "Whether it's rhythm, or the arm or the back—I'm just not sure. I'm not 100 percent. This game is tough enough when you're 100 percent."[15]

Two of Hardin's season highlights actually came with a bat in his hands. The .103 lifetime hitter's first Major League homer was a game-ending blast off former Oriole Moe Drabowsky to beat the Kansas City Royals on May 10, and he also connected for a 3-run shot against the Chicago White Sox in the most lopsided shutout win in Orioles history, a 17–0, 2-hit win in July. (Of Hardin's 24 Major League hits, 3 were home runs, 3 were triples, and 1 was a double.) Overall in 1969 Hardin averaged fewer than six innings per start, saw his won-lost mark dip to 6-7, and watched his ERA soar more than a run per game higher, to 3.60. At one point, he used an analogy from a different sport to describe his situation: "The difference between this year and last is like the difference between hitting a 50-cent golf ball and a $1.25 golf ball."[16]

Hardin and his wife purchased a home that fall in Miami just a few blocks from the home of Orioles first baseman Boog Powell. The pitcher worked out daily at a junior college trying to recapture his peak form, but treaded water in 1970, finishing 6-5 with a 3.53 ERA. After making 11 of his first 15 appearances in relief, he got an opportunity to start for a few months but got no-decisions in eight consecutive games. By season's end, he'd won only 3 of 19 starts for a Baltimore club that went all the way to a World Series triumph. Hardin didn't pitch a single inning in the playoffs for the second straight year, but still reveled in being a champion.

But Hardin's right arm wasn't going to keep him in Baltimore much longer. It started bothering him in 1970 after a September start in Cleveland when "the temperature had dropped 12 to 15 degrees" between innings, and had gotten progres-

sively worse. He didn't pick up a baseball all winter, and opened the 1971 season on the disabled list.

Hardin allowed 12 hits in just 5⅔ innings after being activated in late April, and the Orioles traded him to the Yankees for right-handed pitcher Bill Burbach on May 28. Burbach never made it to Baltimore at all (going straight to Triple-A), and Hardin was probably cursing New York before putting on pinstripes for the first time. After tossing five garment bags in his car and leaving Baltimore in a rainstorm after learning about the deal, Hardin reached the Big Apple after midnight and stopped for about forty-five minutes to eat. When he returned to his car, all of his belongings had been stolen from his vehicle and he was left with only a shaving kit and the clothes on his back.

Plagued by a stiff shoulder and an arm that pained him all year, Hardin missed all of August and got into only a dozen games with the Yankees, going 0-2 with a 5.08 ERA. The league batted .343 against him in 1971, and New York released him shortly before Opening Day of 1972.

For weeks, Hardin called teams looking for a new employer, but without success. Finally, he reached Paul Richards, general manager of the Atlanta Braves, and offered to pay his own travel expenses if the National League club would just take a look at him. "I don't throw quite as hard as I used to," Hardin told Richards. "But I'd hate to think I didn't learn anything in all these years in baseball."[17]

The Braves signed Hardin on April 28 and brought him back to the Majors just over two weeks later after a trio of decent outings for Triple-A Richmond. Hardin made 26 appearances for the Braves, including 9 starts, and finished 5-2 with 2 saves and a 4.41 ERA in what proved to be his final season in professional baseball. His six-year Major League career ended with a 43-32 record and a 3.18 ERA.

Out of baseball at the age of twenty-nine, Hardin embraced his new life with gusto. He became a star commercial account representative with the Xerox Corporation in Miami, parlayed his usual 70s golf game into club champion status at the Mayacoo Lakes Country Club in West Palm Beach, and became an award-winning fisherman, earning the coveted Master Angler Trophy in the Metropolitan Miami Fishing Tournament. Kite-fishing was his favorite method, and Hardin kept his own boat in Key West and obtained his skipper's license. He also learned to fly and bought a single-engine Beechcraft airplane.

On March 8, 1991, Hardin and two friends flew to Key West to use his boat, caught a cooler full of fresh fish, and got back on the plane intending to make it back to West Palm Beach in time for a golf tournament. It was a trip he'd been making regularly for about three years. This time, tragically, less than two minutes after takeoff from Key West International Airport, Hardin made a "very panicky"[18] radio call in the words of the National Transportation Safety Board investigator. His engine had stalled in strong, gusting winds, causing his propeller to fail, and he tried to return to the airport for an emergency landing.

It was impossible. All three men died when Hardin's plane crashed into a shopping center parking lot after what the *Miami Herald* termed "a valiant effort to miss a baseball park filled with youth league players." "He didn't have a whole lot of control from what we're hearing," said fellow pilot Bill Kieldsen, who'd known Hardin for two decades. "He probably saw the baseball field and made an abrupt maneuver to keep it from coming down there."[19] Jim Hardin was forty-seven years old.

Chapter 17. **Elrod Hendricks**

Rory Costello

AGE	G	AB	R	H	2B	3B	HR	TB	RBI	BB	SO	BAV	OBP	SLG	SB	GDP	HBP
29	106	322	32	78	9	0	12	123	41	33	44	.242	.317	.382	1	4	4

Perhaps no Virgin Islander made a greater lifetime contribution to baseball than Elrod Hendricks (1940–2005). The native of St. Thomas also embodied Baltimore Orioles tradition; only Brooks Robinson wore the orange and black for even half as many games. Ellie's Major League career spanned twelve seasons from 1968 to 1979, but he also spent a remarkable twenty-eight years as the Orioles' bullpen coach from 1978 through 2005. In addition, he played in sixteen Puerto Rican winter seasons and earned the nickname "the Babe Ruth of Mexico" while playing there.

Yet one must look beyond the field to get the full measure of this giving man. He was warm-hearted, always beaming, with a rumbling (often colorfully profane) voice and laugh. Ellie made a personal connection with thousands of fans—especially the young.

Elrod Jerome Hendricks was born in Charlotte Amalie, Virgin Islands, on December 22, 1940. His parents were Arthur Hendricks and Berecia Callendar. He had three brothers, Volmie, Arthur, and Morse. A childhood accident slowed the youth's athletic development—his father's car rolled over his feet, crushing his insteps, which had to be rebuilt.[1] Thus, he did not come to baseball until he was thirteen.

Hendricks explained: "I was introduced [to the game] by my uncle, Wilburn Smith, who at the time was one of the star players, shortstop, second base. He was well established in the islands." Ellie played in the local men's league, thanks to his uncle and a mainstay of St. Thomas baseball, Lealdo Victoria. "Lealdo and I became very, very close friends—he was more of a father figure to me. The

Elrod Hendricks was one half of a valuable catching platoon during the Orioles' three straight pennant-winning seasons.

Texaco Stars were a club, you had to be a member. They ushered me in and nurtured me. It was probably the best thing that happened, because I matured fast and I learned the game playing with those guys."

About five years later, on March 1, 1959, the eighteen-year-old Hendricks signed to play pro ball. No less a figure than Hank Aaron was instrumental.[2] "Hank came down on a tour after the 1958 World Series, a hitting exhibition. Bill Steinecke, who was then a scout/manager in the

Braves' Minor League system, him and Luis Olmo, they all came with Hank. On Friday afternoon, I was asked by my principal, would I be willing to go catch the exhibition? I said, 'When!?'

"There was supposed to be a clinic that Saturday, and I didn't go because I had my chores to do around the house. That Sunday, I knew there were two games, it was in all the papers. But since I did not go to the clinic, I decided I was not going to go to the games. But I went to church that morning, and after church I went out to the ballgame, just to see it, because it was against St. Croix, sort of an all-star thing. And while I was there, Hank saw me sitting in the stands.

"Everyone in the stands was asking 'Why aren't you down there?' because Hank was a big name. We were not used to seeing Major Leaguers, professionals for that matter, spending time with us. So he saw me and said, 'Why aren't you out here?' and I told him, 'I didn't go to the workout yesterday, so it's not fair to the guys who went and were chosen.' He said 'Well, I want you. So go and get your uniform. It's across the street [with Ellie's grandmother, who lived right by Lionel Roberts Stadium]. I read about that!'

"So I put on my uniform, and still sat in the stands. In the seventh inning, we had the bases loaded, and Mr. Steinecke called me in to pinch-hit for my cousin, Gene Francis, and he was leading the league in hitting! But as fate would have it, I hit a double and drove in three runs. After the game, they asked me to sign a contract. I said, 'I couldn't, my mom'll kill me,' but my uncle said, 'Go ahead, I'll sign for you.'"

At Class D McCook (Nebraska State League) in 1959, Ellie had a dismaying early experience—his first exposure to the knuckleball, courtesy of twenty-year-old Phil Niekro. "Oh God, yes. Poor Knucksie, he held his heart, he was more worried about me than I was about myself. I had a brand-new catcher's mitt, the first one I ever owned, and I was there trying to break it in. I just tried to keep

the ball in front of me, but it was bouncing off every part of my body." Manager Bill Steinecke had to come for Hendricks in the sixth inning.

Also on that squad was future author Pat Jordan (*A False Spring*). Bonus boy Jordan had a brief punch-up with the "very black, very limber" Elrod, who "spoke a rhythmic calypso English that amused most of the American players."[3] Still, the smile never left Ellie's face.

The Braves released Hendricks in December 1960, but the Puerto Rican Winter League became his safety valve during his career's bleakest period. Ellie did not play summer ball in 1961, working at a car rental in St. Thomas instead. However, help came from Luis Olmo, a teammate of Alfonso Gerard, a St. Croix native who played in the Negro Leagues and with a very young Roberto Clemente for the Santurce Cangrejeros (Crabbers). Olmo, the Crabbers' manager when Ellie first turned pro, offered an invitation. His successor, Vern Benson, wanted to get a longer look. Benson was also a coach with the Cardinals' farm club at Tulsa, and the organization needed catchers.

In Santurce Hendricks backed up Valmy Thomas, another St. Croix ballplayer, and then shared the job with him during the next two seasons before the veteran retired. "When I joined Santurce, it was good to see someone from home," said Ellie. "Valmy may not know how much he helped me as a player. I would ask him certain things about catching, and he would never answer me, but I watched him and I learned from him. At first I thought, maybe it's that St. Croix–St. Thomas rivalry, maybe you don't want to talk to me! But invariably, he would do something and he would look over my way, as if to say, 'I hope you got that.'"

Ellie roomed for a couple of winters with still another Virgin Islands player, Horace Clarke.[4] "There was that rivalry with St. Croix, I even had people asking me, 'How can you room with him, you're a traitor!' I said, 'Hey, he's a nice guy,

I played against him in high school.'" Although they were rarely around at the same time, owing to the schedule, they still became close. Hendricks remembered that the musically inclined Horace, "who hardly said anything," played vibraphone and xylophone.

He also recalled the generosity of Sandy Alomar Sr.'s brother, Tony, and Juan "Terín" Pizarro. "They took me under their wings, drove me anywhere I wanted to go, wouldn't let me spend my money." Ellie remained lifelong friends with Pizarro and also learned more craft from catching him and Rubén Gómez. Other cagey vets like Canena Márquez and Ozzie Virgil Sr. taught him a further trick or two. "They would look terrible swinging at a breaking ball early in the game and then look back at me. When I got in a tight situation, I'd call for that breaking ball and they would rifle it to right-center, and when they got to second, they would look back at me again. Pizarro would say, 'You big dummy, don't you know they're good breaking-ball hitters who can't catch up to the fastball anymore?' I learned after being burned a couple of times!"

The Crabbers connection again kept Ellie's career alive at a low point, as the Cardinals cut him in 1963. However, his closest friend with the Crabbers, pitcher William de Jesús, was playing with Jalisco of the Mexican League. De Jesús recommended Hendricks to Jalisco's manager, Major League and Puerto Rico veteran Jungle Jim Rivera.[5] From 1964 through 1967, Ellie put up very potent if not quite Ruthian numbers for the Charros, including 41 home runs, 112 runs batted in, and a .316 batting average in his last year.

Hendricks caught the eye of Earl Weaver, who was managing Santurce. When Baltimore prospect Larry Haney got hurt, Ellie also became a regular in Puerto Rico, and Weaver insisted that the Orioles should draft him in 1966. The Angels had a working agreement with Jalisco at that time, so they had his rights. After the extra endorsement of

Orioles scout Trader Frank Lane, Baltimore selected Hendricks in the Rule 5 draft in 1967. He finally made the Majors in 1968.

"Hank Bauer was the manager at that time. And naturally anything that Earl brought to the table he was against, because he knew Earl [then the first base coach] was there to take his job! No matter what I did, I was wrong; he even changed my stance. Charlie Lau, who was our hitting coach, just closed his eyes. He said, 'Hank, I saw this kid hit in Puerto Rico that way, and he hit against Major League pitching.' Earl was cringing, and he finally just said, 'I know you hate doing it, but just do it for me, please.' By then I knew exactly what was going on, because I'd heard some stories." Earl's epoch began halfway through the 1968 season.

Hendricks—the lefty-swinging half of a catching platoon with Andy Etchebarren—was a lesser but still vital cog in Weaver's superb Orioles teams of 1969–71. He was involved in some memorable World Series moments, including two in 1969: Tommie Agee robbed him of a likely triple in Game Three, and Pete Richert ran him off J. C. Martin's bunt in Game Four. Game One in 1970 featured the pileup at home plate with Bernie Carbo and umpire Ken Burkhart; Hendricks also hit a homer to back Brooks Robinson's fielding.

Ellie's outstanding attribute as a player was handling the pitchers on the Orioles' first-rate staff—especially Jim Palmer, a cerebral power pitcher, and Mike Cuellar, a most crafty junk-baller who had to outthink hitters after hurting his arm.

"They had a mental toughness. Palmer was probably the toughest of all to catch because he knew so much about the game. He knew himself, he knew every hitter, he knew every pitch that he threw. He knew what got hit and what didn't get hit. Basically, he was going to throw 85 to 90 percent fastballs, you knew that as a catcher. But he would battle you the whole game, so that's why he was tough to catch, because mentally you'd be ex-

RORY COSTELLO

hausted when the game was over. But the days that he had great stuff, it was so easy."

In 2001 Jim Palmer reciprocated: "He was the perfect receiver. If I told him to sit on the corner, he sat on the corner. If I got the ball there on time, he could throw the runner out. And between him and Andy Etchebarren, we'd get 20 homers. He caught my no-hitter [on August 13, 1969, vs. Oakland]. I had the utmost confidence in him.

"Ellie paid his dues—after nine years in the Minors, coming out of the Mexican League, he was in a position to subjugate his ego and do what was good for the club and the staff. He was and is a good communicator. Here he is thirty-three years later still doing the same thing.

"Sure, we'd battle mentally. But he would come out there to the mound with that smile on his face, and he'd know where to give. Some catchers would think they know better—and maybe they do—but there was that special knowledge with Ellie. He knows the game of baseball."

Although Ellie's arm was not very strong, it was highly accurate. He nailed 38 percent of opposing base stealers during his career—42 percent if one includes runners he picked off. While Hendricks batted only .220 lifetime in the Majors, never climbing above .250, he did have some power. He exemplified the Oriole Way of playing baseball: smarts, sound fundamentals, and a roster full of useful role players.

In *The Umpire Strikes Back*, the late Ron Luciano told how much he liked having Ellie behind the plate. He was a buffer between the perennially feuding Luciano and Weaver, he had "the nicest way of arguing of anyone in baseball," and was even trusted to call balls and strikes if the ump was "having a bad day."[6]

Except for the Orioles' postseason trip to Japan in 1972, Ellie always wintered in Puerto Rico, his secure place.[7] There they called him El Madamo, a reference to his African-Caribbean origin. His

peak there was 1968–69, when he won the MVP award.

Hendricks spent two stretches away from Baltimore, which he regarded as the low points of his career. In 1972 he suffered partial paralysis in his right hand and arm, owing to a calcium deposit at the base of his neck.[8] That August he was traded to the Chicago Cubs while his second wife, Merle, was recovering from childbirth complications. Ellie later said, "It's a funny thing, not even being able to button your shirt. . . . I couldn't even hold my car keys to open the door last summer. I couldn't hold a cigarette to my mouth. I had numbness in all my fingers. Last year was a complete waste."[9]

What was the real cause? In 2001 Hendricks said "there's some validity" to the belief that his career-threatening injury arose when he got hit by a backswing after defying superstition by knocking a cross made of sticks (or, in the tale's embroidered version, chicken bones) off second base in a winter-league game against Caguas in 1968–69.[10]

However, fellow Virgin Islander Joe Christopher (a great believer in numerology) said, "Elrod was born lucky because of his birthdate!" Indeed, things turned up. With the encouragement of Frank Robinson, Ellie decided to keep playing at Santurce. Crabbers trainer Nick Acosta, a masseur "who was a magician with those fingers," brought back the lost sensation. In 1972–73 he tied his Puerto Rico Winter League personal best with 12 homers and was the All-Star catcher once again.

Even when Ellie left the Orioles he paid dividends. The 1972 waiver deal with the Cubs brought Tommy Davis, who gave Baltimore three productive years as a designated hitter. That October the club got Hendricks back for Francisco Estrada, a one-game Major Leaguer.

Then in June 1976, Hendricks was part of the big ten-player deal with the Yankees that brought Baltimore Scott McGregor, Rick Dempsey, and Tippy Martínez. Under Billy Martin, he appeared in his fourth World Series but wound up going to Triple-A in 1977. Still, Hendricks thought highly of the other scrappy little bastard ex-second baseman for whom he played.

"Billy was so much like Earl. Anyone that wanted to win, I wanted to play for, because you learn an awful lot. Even though I had been on successful teams in the Minors, I didn't know how to play until I got under Weaver's tutelage. And then when I left Baltimore to come to New York, it was like looking at the same guy in the mirror. Billy wanted to win more than anything else. You sit and listen to them, they rant and rave, but you pick up an awful lot about the game.

"They hated each other's guts, but they were so much alike, and I think that was one of the reasons." If anything, Ellie thought Billy wanted to beat Earl even more because Earl had the upper hand more often. But he stressed how both were masters of roster management, player positioning, and all forms of in-game strategy. "Their teams were built around pitching and defense. That's the one thing they did not tolerate, not being able to do the little things. Bunt the guy over, make the routine play, don't beat yourself, let the other team beat themselves. That's the way they played the game and that's the way they managed the game."

In November 1977 "big-league daddy"[11] Weaver rescued Hendricks again; Ellie succeeded Cal Ripken Sr. as bullpen coach. The winter of 1977–78 was also his last with the Crabbers. His 105 career homers in Puerto Rico rank third on the all-time list, and he played on five league champions.

Hendricks, Baltimore's most loyal lieutenant, endured eleven manager changes as a coach. He appeared in thirteen games as a player-coach during 1978, including one as a pitcher during a 24–10 blowout.[12] When the rosters expanded in September 1979, he was activated for one last go behind the plate.

Although there was talk that Ellie might become a manager at some point, especially in the 1980s, he put those ambitions on the back burner. He remained a popular institution as bullpen coach. He had no retirement date in mind, but after he survived testicular cancer in 2003 and a mild stroke in April 2005, the Orioles did not allow him to exit on his own terms. He was "reassigned" after the 2005 season. Ellie's position with the organization was still "under review" when he succumbed to a sudden fatal heart attack a day short of his sixty-fifth birthday. Only two days before, he had played Santa to 100 underprivileged children.

Elrod Hendricks was survived by Merle, their sons, Ryan and Ian (who both played in the Minor Leagues), and two sons and two daughters from his first marriage (Elrod Jr. also played briefly in the Minors). Yet his legacy has also endured in other ways—his magic lay in how he reached out to fans and brought them inside the game.

Chapter 18. **Chico Salmon**

Russell Wolinsky

AGE	G	AB	R	H	2B	3B	HR	TB	RBI	BB	SO	BAV	OBP	SLG	SB	GDP	HBP
29	63	172	19	43	4	0	7	68	22	8	30	.250	.287	.395	2	3	1

When Ruthford Eduardo "Chico" Salmon stepped up as a pinch hitter in the fifth inning of Game Two of the 1970 World Series, Baltimore was trailing Cincinnati, 4–1. Salmon was batting for Tom Phoebus, already the second pitcher used by Earl Weaver. "I got the greatest thrill of my life just walking up to the plate," Chico told the *Baltimore Sun*'s Jim Elliot. But just moments later, the man dubbed "Supersub," often to his distaste, was to receive an even greater thrill. Taking advantage of Riverfront Stadium's artificial turf, Salmon ripped a sharp grounder up the middle beyond the outstretched glove of shortstop Woody Woodward. "When I got the hit and [was] standing on first base, I thought I was the king of the world," he recalled.[1] Don Buford and Paul Blair quickly followed with base hits of their own, the latter scoring Salmon. By the time the O's were done batting in their half of the frame, they led 6–4. It ended 6–5. For Salmon, that hit represented his lone World Series at bat. He retired with a 1.000 batting average in Fall Classic play.

And that was often the way it would be for the colorful, quotable, versatile Salmon—particularly in 1970, his second season with the Birds. After sharing the utility infielder role with Bobby Floyd in 1969—Weaver figuring his regular shortstop, Mark Belanger, would often be pinch-hit for—Chico served as the lone spare in 1970. Kansas City Royals outfielder Lou Piniella needled Salmon one evening: "I've been in this league only two years, but I've never seen you play, Chico. What do you do for a living?"[2] Such was the life of a utility infielder on a great team.

The funny and popular Chico Salmon provided versatility, and seven home runs, to the Orioles' cause in 1970.

Born in Colon, Panama, on December 3, 1940, Salmon graduated from Abel Bravo High School, where he lettered in baseball, basketball, and track. He later attended Abel Bravo College, where he also played baseball. It was as a college student that Salmon played for the Panamanian baseball team during the 1959 Pan-American Games in Venezuela. Shortly after playing in that tournament, Chico was signed by the Pacific Coast League's Denver club of the Milwaukee Braves organization. As far as a bonus was concerned, "Not even a penny," he later complained. "Not even a

83

steak. But I think I would have got one if I waited longer. Right after I signed, a scout from Kansas City [Athletics] talked to my mother, but it was too late."[3]

Salmon had some fine years in the Minor Leagues. In 1960, at age nineteen, he hit .345 for Pocatello in the Pioneer League, then hit .292 with the Durham Bulls (Carolina League) the next year. He played third base his first two seasons in the Minors, then played both outfield and first base in 1962 for Knoxville (Sally League), for whom he hit .330 with 16 home runs before earning a late season recall to Denver of the American Association. He stayed with Denver the next season, and won the PBL (Denver had switched leagues) batting crown with a .325 average.

Salmon did not make the Cleveland Indians out of spring training in 1964, reporting instead to Portland, Oregon, which had become the Indians' PBL affiliate. Although slumping to a career-low .234 with the Portland in 71 games, he was recalled on June 27 when Cleveland third baseman Max Alvis was stricken with spinal meningitis. In his first start, at first base on June 29, he got his first two big-league hits—both singles off Chicago's Gary Peters. On August 5, he got his first home run, off Washington's Alan Koch. He hit well all season, finishing at .307 (leading the team) with 23 extra base hits. He played 86 games, including 70 starts at second base, first base, and right field.

Salmon played seven of the nine fielding positions in his nine-year Major League career with Baltimore and the Cleveland Indians, but never more than 164 games at any one spot (second base). Opinion varied widely as to Salmon's ability in the field. "They said I had bad hands," Chico said of his time at shortstop with the Pioneer League's Pocatello Giants in 1960, his first professional season. "They changed me to second base, then third base, then the outfield, then first base. I guess they thought my hands were real bad."[4] Late

in Salmon's career, an Orioles teammate quipped, "If Chico's hands get any worse, we'll have to amputate."[5]

Any defensive deficiencies on Salmon's part were not for a lack of effort or hustle. Regis McAuley of the *Cleveland Press* recalled a defensive gem of Chico's from spring training of 1964. In pursuit of a Red Sox batter's foul fly at Tucson's Hi Corbett Field, Salmon ran toward a low barrier in left field and "somersaulted head over heels into the crowd. All you could see of Chico was his long arm sticking up out of the crowd with the baseball clutched tightly in the center of his glove." An impressed manager Tebbetts, seated beside McAuley, announced, "That kid just made this ballclub."[6] He did not, but returned in June.

If Chico Salmon is in any way remembered by baseball fans, it is more likely than not to be for his fear of ghosts and, later, snakes. Early in his career, Salmon slept with the lights on, and stuffed towels under doors and chewing gum in keyholes. "When I was young," he said, "I heard talk about evil spirits and I started to believe it. I still do believe it, but I've never seen one." A six-month stint in the U.S. Army Reserve during the winter of 1964 somewhat cured Chico of his fear of ghosts, but substituted a fear of snakes:

> I tell them when I get in that I afraid of ghosts all my life and they tell me, "KP or guard duty." . . . The Army scare me more than any old ghost. But now I'm scared of snakes. They everywhere down here [Company B, 4th Battalion, 3rd Training Regiment, Fort Polk, Louisiana]. Before you put your foot down someplace, you got to look to see if there's anything under it. We go in the woods and sleep at night. . . . I don't sleep. . . . There are snakes down here that crawl in the water.[7]

Salmon did not play baseball on the post team because he was not a permanent member of the post. He kept in shape by playing pickup ball with the men in his barracks and "sawing potatoes every other day." He served six months, and did not return to the Indians until May of 1965.

During the remainder of his career with the Indians, his versatility seemed to keep him from gaining a regular starting spot. "(Salmon) was our leading hitter last year," manager Birdie Tebbetts noted. However, "I can't get him in our lineup regularly." He played little for the Tribe that year though (parts of 79 games). Chico began the season 0-for-12 and never saw his batting average rise above .250, ending 1965 at .242.

After raving about Salmon's talents a couple of years later, Cleveland coach George Strickland was asked why he thought Chico was not a regular in the Indians' lineup. "He just can't seem to keep up at his top-level ability for any extended time," the coach replied. "Chico seems to run out of gas if you play him every day."[8]

In May 1966 regular Indians second baseman Larry Brown was injured in a harrowing collision with left fielder Leon Wagner, suffering a fractured skull, broken cheekbone, and broken nose. He was knocked unconscious and was taken off the field on a stretcher, bleeding profusely. There was considerable doubt he would play again that season and his baseball future appeared grim.

Salmon took over the position on May 22, and from then until July 5 Chico hit at a .313 clip (60-for-192). Indians beat writer Russell Schneider called the utility man's performance "positively amazing." Tebbetts nominated his man as the AL All-Star shortstop. "Are you kidding me?" the ebullient Panamanian wanted to know. "Man, what a thrill that would be. Why, I'd be the biggest man in Panama. Everyone would want to talk to me. The first boy from Panama to make the All-Star team. My mother would be amazed. . . . I mean, happy."[9] Alas, Boston's Rico Petrocelli and Jim Fregosi of the Angels were selected as the shortstops for the American League team. Salmon slumped in the second half of the season, finishing at just .256.

Defying his reputation on defense, Salmon's fielding gem helped preserve Sonny Siebert's June 10 no-hitter against Washington. With two out in the Senators' sixth, Salmon raced in on Don Blasingame's chopper up the middle. The shortstop "made a quick grab and caught the runner by a full step," keeping the Cleveland right-hander's no-no intact.[10] (As a rookie playing first base, Chico helped preserve a Siebert shutout against Minnesota when his backhanded stab of Don Mincher's bases-loaded drive robbed the Twins' slugger of a potential extra-base hit.)

But when Salmon was asked what he thought was his best position, he answered without hesitation, "At-bat."[11] Standing around the hitting cage watching Tony Oliva take batting practice before an Indians-Twins series in Cleveland during the 1966 season, Salmon remarked, "Man, he's a great hitter, just great." "Better than you?" the man dubbed Supersub was asked. "Oh, I don't know about that," he replied.[12] Positioning himself deep in the batter's box, so deep that his back foot rested outside the box—"It takes the ball longer to get to me," he reasoned, "[b]ut umpires make me move up"[13]—Salmon hit out of a crouch, chin extended out nearly to the strike zone, bat held high, wrapped behind his head. He was an aggressive hitter who seldom walked (.290 career OBP) and was often pitched inside. Jack Hamilton, the pitcher who beaned the Red Sox's Tony Conigliaro in 1967, caught Chico in the jaw with a pitch in 1964, briefly knocking him out. Nevertheless, Salmon was back in the starting lineup for that afternoon's nightcap and maintained the same batting stance throughout his big-league career.

Even after rising to the Major League level, Salmon still returned home annually to play ball in the Panama Winter League. Salmon was the leadoff hitter for the Marlboro Smokers (at one time managed by longtime Minor League pitcher Winston Brown). During the winter of 1966–67, Chico ran off an eighteen-game hitting streak for the

Smokers, including a run of five consecutive singles. Salmon played winter ball in Panama in every season the country could field enough teams for a league until knee surgery in 1968 forced him to remain idle.

The following March, in an exhibition game played in Mexico City, Salmon "twisted his left knee in [an] aborted steal attempt."[14] The knee continued to bother him, but not enough to keep him out of the lineup. He was ready for the regular season, but totaled just 203 at bats on the season, batting a career-low .227. Stationed in left field in the eleventh inning of a June 13, 1968, contest against Oakland, played at Cleveland Stadium, Salmon reinjured the knee, this time more seriously. In pursuit of "a lollipop to left" hit by the A's Sal Bando, "Chico's left knee collapsed under him just as he thought he was about to catch [it]." The runner on first, Danny Cater, was off with the crack of the bat and scored the game's only run as the ball fell untouched. "I musta stepped in a hole or something," Salmon said, sitting on the trainer's table, his knee packed in ice. "All I know is I stepped and it just twisted over. Then I couldn't get up. My kneecap was out and [Cleveland trainer] Wally [Bock] pushed it back in place."[15] Chico was immediately placed on the disabled list. Dr. Vic Ippolito described the injury as a "derangement of the internal left knee."

Salmon returned to the Cleveland lineup on July 6, limping his way to a meager .185 batting average with only three extra-base hits the rest of the way. Chico underwent surgery on the balky knee immediately after the season and began his rehabilitation program less than two weeks later. Despite the operation, he was still much in demand by rival American League clubs, primarily for his versatility. The thought was that Cleveland would now be more willing to deal Salmon, figuring that he'd be selected in the coming expansion draft. But at the time of the 1968 World Series, "the Indians appeared reluctant to trade Salmon."[16]

As it happened, Salmon was selected by the brand new Seattle Pilots in the expansion draft in November 1968. Salmon saw it as an opportunity to become a starting player again. It was not to be. Tommy Harper established himself as the Pilots' starting second baseman, Chico became expendable, and on March 31, 1969, Seattle dealt him to Baltimore for pitcher Gene Brabender and utility man Gordie Lund. "[Salmon will] give [manager Earl] Weaver more mobility and flexibility," said Orioles general manager Harry Dalton. "[A]nd give the club better balance. Chico is not just a body. We can use him, and we will use him."[17]

Arguably his finest Major League offensive performance came as a member of the Orioles on August 16, 1969, at Seattle's Sicks' Stadium. In a 15–3 Baltimore romp over the Pilots, Salmon went 4-for-4 at the plate with a pair of home runs and 6 RBIs. The following afternoon, the Orioles team bus pulled up at Sicks' to find a queue waiting to purchase tickets for the game. "They coming out to catch my act again," Chico explained to his teammates.[18] Nonetheless, the Orioles were set at every position, and Salmon had no chance of breaking in. He hit .297 for the season, but in just 91 at bats spread over 52 games.

In 1970 he held the same role, and he excelled in the early going. At the end of May he was hitting .483, highlighted by a four-hit game against the Indians on May 26. He struggled the rest of the way, dropping below .300 for the first time on July 27 and ending at .250, but with 7 home runs. In late June Chico reinjured his left knee and missed nearly three weeks of action. He finished the year with his big hit in the World Series, and his first and only championship team.

And still, like any utility man, despite his heroics of the previous season and a .385 spring batting average, Salmon worried about making the club in 1971. Challenges from young infielders Bobby Grich and Jerry DaVanon in training camp worried him. "I decided to go to a movie, instead of

RUSSELL WOLINSKY

the park," the personable sub said after finding out that twenty-one-year-old Don Baylor had already been sent down to Triple-A Rochester. "Maybe they got something to tell me."[19]

Beginning the year in a 1-for-17 slump, through the Orioles' first sixty-seven games played Chico appeared in but fourteen, with 4 singles in 25 at bats (.160). Through 112 games, the former Super-sub had a mere 59 at bats. His speed almost totally gone after the knee surgery, Chico did not attempt a single steal. His 3 RBIs on September 28 helped spur Baltimore to a 5–4 decision over Boston, a victory that marked the third consecutive 100-win campaign for the Birds. Salmon did not make a single appearance in either the ALCS or World Series that year.

Chico accompanied the Birds on a postseason exhibition junket to Japan but immediately expressed concern regarding his future with Baltimore. "With [Bobby] Grich around now, there may be no place for me. I just hope if I'm not in Baltimore this year, I'm playing somewhere."[20]

Despite a team-leading .360 batting average in spring training, Chico played even less in 1972. Into mid-August he had 1 hit in 16 at bats. On August 18 Baltimore acquired Tommy Davis to shore up its slumping offensive attack. Salmon was placed on waivers for the purpose of giving him his unconditional release.[21] There were no takers for the thirty-one-year-old gimpy utility man. He signed with the Triple-A Charleston Charlies, but retired from the game shortly after.

Returning to Cleveland, Salmon went to work for the Lincoln Recreation Center. During his years with the Tribe, Chico had worked with troubled youngsters during the off-season. He also was involved in the center's drug abuse program. But no more baseball: "I leave it for the young kids, except for the Sunday Morning Softball League." The former Indian piloted East Cleveland's El Patio Lounge softball team.[22] In 1979 Chico briefly managed the Panama Bangueros of the Triple-A Inter-American League (piloting them to a league-worst 15-36 mark before being replaced by Willie Miranda). He also scouted and managed the Panama entry of the World Amateur Baseball Series. Salmon continued working with youth teams in and around his native Bocas del Toro until his death in 2000.

Eventually, Salmon made it back to Bocas del Toro, Panama, where he worked with youth teams for several years. Although he had married Easterlene Jackson in 1967, the couple eventually divorced. He was living with his mother on September 20, 2000, when he suffered a heart attack and died. He was fifty-nine years old.

In looking back at his former Baltimore teammates, catcher Elrod Hendricks listed Salmon as one of the three funniest (along with Frank Robinson and Boog Powell). "Chico Salmon," the receiver reminisced, "just some of the phrases he used made him funny."[23] Chico Salmon's gift to baseball consisted of more than just his performance on the field.

Chapter 19. **May 1970 Timeline**

Malcolm Allen

All headlines below are from the next day's edition of the *Baltimore Sun*.

May 1—BIRDS DRUB TWINS, 9–3, IN OPENER—Terry Crowley smacked his first Major League homer with two aboard to give the Orioles a lead they wouldn't lose against Baltimore native Dave Boswell.

May 2—TWINS BEAT ORIOLES AND CUELLAR, 4 TO 2—On Bat Day at Memorial Stadium, Minnesota's Harmon Killebrew decided a pitcher's duel between Mike Cuellar and Jim Perry with a two-out, two-run double in the eighth. The winning rally started with the first Major League hit by thirty-six-year-old rookie Minnie Mendoza, who, like Cuellar, was born in Cuba.

May 3—TWINS NIP ORIOLES IN 9TH, 4–3—Jim Palmer struck out a season-high eleven batters on a cool, cloudy afternoon, but suffered a 4–3 defeat in the ninth after Killebrew clobbered a two-run homer off the roof of the visitors' bullpen shanty in right-center. Minnesota's only other runs scored when Davey Johnson made two errors on the same play in the sixth. That gave Johnson four miscues in the last fifteen games, but he would make only four more in his last 127 contests to earn his second of three consecutive Gold Gloves.

May 4—The Orioles' exhibition game against the Midshipmen at the Naval Academy in Annapolis was rained out.

May 5—ORIOLES HIT 4 HOMERS, TOP ROYALS—Davey Johnson's fourth-inning homer off the right-field foul pole at Memorial Stadium tied the score. After the ball bounced back into the field of play and was returned to Royals pitcher Dick Drago, Elrod Hendricks whacked the same baseball 400 feet into the right-field seats to give Baltimore a lead it wouldn't lose. It was the tenth consecutive game with at least one long ball for the Birds, and they hit 21 during this stretch.

May 6—BIRDS KEEP ROYAL HEX ON K.C., 3–1—Brooks Robinson went 4-4 and Dave McNally whiffed eleven Royals and carried a shutout into the ninth. After Kansas City finally got on the scoreboard, southpaw reliever Pete Richert came on to record the last two outs with the tying runners in scoring position. Richert was in the midst of one of two stretches of pitching hitless ball for 8⅔ innings that he would log in 1970.

May 7—BIRDS DOWN ROYALS ON FRANK'S HIT—In the series finale, the Royals came within one out of beating Baltimore for just the second time in franchise history, but Frank Robinson hammered the first pitch from former Oriole Moe Drabowsky over the center-field fence with two aboard to give the Birds a thrilling 7–6 victory.

May 8—BOOG RAPS 9TH HOMER AS ORIOLES WIN, 6–1—Boog Powell walloped a first-inning three-run homer off White Sox rookie Jerry Janeski for the second time in ten days, and Jim Palmer went the distance for the victory. Chicago lost slugging third baseman Bill Melton in the sixth inning when he failed to catch a foul pop-up and it hit him in the nose.

May 9—ORIOLES GET THREE HITS BUT WIN, 4–3—After being held hitless for five innings by Chicago's Tommy John, the Birds drew even and surged ahead on Brooks Robinson's 200th career home run in the sixth. Eddie Watt got the last two outs with the tying runner aboard to save Tom Phoebus's victory.

May 10—BIRDS SWEEP WHITE SOX 7–2 AND 4–2—The Orioles won their sixth and seventh straight to wrap up an 8–2 home stand with a Mother's Day doubleheader sweep. Dave McNally became the AL's first six-game winner with a complete game in the opener, while Marcelino Lopez and Dick Hall supplied 4⅔ innings of shutout relief work in the nightcap.

May 11—No game scheduled.

May 12—BIRDS EDGE TWINS FOR 8TH IN ROW—Elrod Hendricks gunned down Rod Carew on an attempted steal of second to complete a game-ending strike 'em out, throw 'em out double play. Hendricks also matched his career high with four hits in Baltimore's 5–4 victory at Minnesota.

May 13—TWINS BEAT BIRDS ON HIT BY REESE—The Orioles stranded ten base runners—seven of them in scoring position—and had their eight-game winning streak snapped when Eddie Watt surrendered doubles to Tony Oliva and Rich Reese with two down in the bottom of the tenth.

May 14—No game scheduled.

May 15—BIRDS EDGE NATS, 4–3, ON RUN IN 11TH—Boog Powell grounded into an apparent game-ending double play in Washington, but Frank Robinson slid hard into Dave Nelson and the Senators' second baseman bounced his throw to first. Washington first baseman Mike Epstein juggled the ball, and umpire Bill Kunkel changed his initial out call to safe. Given new life, Baltimore prevailed in the eleventh on successful pinch hits by Merv Rettenmund and Curt Motton off former Oriole Darold Knowles.

May 16—ORIOLES HOLD OFF SENATORS AS MC-NALLY WINS NO. 7, 4–3—On Preakness day, Brook Robinson delivered the Orioles' biggest hit with a three-run homer that caromed off the facing of the balcony façade in left-center at RFK Stadium. As reliever Eddie Watt warmed up to face Frank Howard with the tying run aboard in the eighth, he took exception to Senators' on-deck hitter Rick Reichardt coming too close to the plate to observe him. Watt nearly drilled Reichardt with a wild delivery, prompting Washington skipper Ted Williams to race out of the dugout to complain. When order was restored, Watt got Howard to ground into an inning-ending double play, and took care of Reichardt and the Nats in the ninth to record the save.

May 17—Rained out in Washington DC.

May 18—YANKS RIP ORIOLES ON BIG INNING—Reigning Cy Young winner Mike Cuellar saw his ERA soar to 5.20 after an embarrassing seven-run third inning at Yankee Stadium. The avalanche began with New York pitcher Fritz Peterson's two-run homer off the foul pole, and the Yankees became the first club to score double digits against the 1970 Orioles with a 10–4 victory. Second-place New York moved within five games of Baltimore for the AL East lead.

May 19—BIRDS DOWN YANKS, 5–1, FOR PALMER—Jim Palmer hurled a complete-game four-hitter to get the Orioles back on track. After New York reliever Gary Waslewski knocked down Frank Robinson in the seventh, the Baltimore right fielder stepped back in the box and doubled for his third hit of the game, raising his average to a league-leading .395.

May 20—TIGERS TOP BIRDS, 4–0, ON 3-HITTER— The Orioles were shut out for the first time in 1970, managing just three singles against Detroit lefty Mickey Lolich. More than one Baltimore hitter heatedly objected to the ball-strike calls of home plate umpire Ed Runge.

May 21—BIRDS SPLIT TWINBILL WITH TIGERS—A five-run seventh inning off Dave McNally led to a 6–4 loss in the opener and dropped McNally's record to 7-2. Earl Weaver couldn't contain his frustration with the crew of umpires. While he made it clear that he wasn't blaming the men in blue for the Orioles' losses, or questioning their integrity, he warned that he was going to get thrown out of a game soon if things didn't improve. "Some of the calls have been brutal," complained the Baltimore skipper. "It's unbelievable."[1] Mike Cuellar pitched brilliantly for seven innings in the second game, but got no decision as Merv Rettenmund's decisive two-run homer in the Birds' 3–1 victory didn't come until the ninth.

May 22—BIRDS SCORE 4 IN FIRST, TOP RED SOX— Back in Baltimore, the Orioles raced out to a 4–0 first-inning lead against the Red Sox. After Boston fought back to pull even, Boog Powell regained a share of the league lead in long balls with a sixth-inning blast to put Baltimore back on top. Frank Robinson was hurt chasing Rico Petrocelli's eighth-inning foul fly in vain, tearing a spike loose from his left shoe and bruising the knuckles on his left hand. Dick Hall secured the Birds' 7–4 victory with four innings of excellent relief.

May 23—BIRDS BLANK BOSOX, 3–0, for palmer— On Banner Day at Memorial Stadium, Jim Palmer fired the Orioles' first shutout of 1970, a seven-hitter to outduel Boston's Ray Culp. Subbing for injured Frank Robinson, rookie Terry Crowley pulled a two-out, two-run double in the fifth to break a scoreless tie, and helped keep the Red Sox off the scoreboard with an excellent running grab.

May 24—BIRDS WIN, THEN LOSE TO RED SOX— Mike Cuellar hurled nine innings of two-hit ball on two days' rest, but nearly suffered a 1–0 defeat until Curt Motton's pinch-hit single in the bottom of the ninth forced extra innings in the opener of a doubleheader. Brooks Robinson was beaned in the sixth inning when Mike Nagy's pitch glanced off the earflap of his helmet and caromed into the seats to the right of the backstop. Number 5 got up and remained in the game, though, and crashed a 400-foot game-winning homer off Sparky Lyle in the bottom of the tenth. American League ERA leader Tom Phoebus worked into the ninth inning of a 3–3 tie in game two, but Boston rallied for its only victory of the season at Memorial Stadium after a leadoff walk.

May 25—ORIOLES WIN AS MCNALLY TAKES 8TH— The Orioles scored six times in the first two frames against veteran right-hander Bob Miller, and Dave McNally shut out the Indians into the ninth before settling for a 6–2 complete-game six-hitter and the AL lead in victories.

May 26—HARDIN'S 5-HITTER TOPS TRIBE—Jim Hardin held Cleveland to five singles for his first shutout of 1970, winning 7–0 with Chico Salmon matching his career high of four hits to lead the attack.

May 27—BUFORD HIT GIVES BIRDS 5–4 VICTORY —Cleveland, led by five hits by Ted Uhlaender, seized the lead and knocked Jim Palmer out of the box in the top of the seventh, but Don Buford punched a two-run single through the right side in the bottom of the inning and put the Orioles back on top. The come-from-behind win completed a sweep and a 6–1 home stand.

May 28—No game scheduled.

May 29—CUELLAR AND POWELL HALT ANGELS, 2 TO 0—After no Baltimore pitcher threw a shutout in the first thirty-nine games of the season, Mike Cuellar became the third to toss one in the week. Not only did the Cuban lefty whiff a season-high ten batters, he tied a Major League record by notching four strikeouts in the fourth inning. The Orioles' first West Coast game of the season was a scoreless affair into the eighth, but Boog Powell made it a success with his league-leading fourteenth homer, a two-out, two-run blast off Andy Messersmith.

May 30—In a game that went too late to make the morning papers back in Baltimore, the Orioles suffered a 3–2 defeat when Angels left-fielder Alex Johnson, the eventual 1970 AL batting champ, whacked a tie-breaking homer off Dick Hall with two outs in the bottom of the seventh.

May 31—BLAIR HURT AS ORIOLES LOSE, 6 TO 1— The Orioles dropped a 6–1 decision to Angels ace Clyde Wright with Dave McNally lasting only three innings, but Baltimore's biggest loss came courtesy of California reliever Ken Tatum in the eighth inning. After he hit Boog Powell (who was fine), Tatum's next pitch caused Paul Blair to leave the field on a stretcher. The Orioles' Gold Glove center fielder had double vision, broken bones below his left eye, a broken nose, and a broken cheekbone after being hit in the face. After 3½ hours of emergency surgery, he would miss three weeks of action.

AL East Standings, May 31:

Team	W	L	GB
Baltimore	33	15	—
New York	26	23	7.5
Washington	22	24	10.0
Detroit	21	23	10.0
Boston	20	25	11.5
Cleveland	16	27	14.5

Chapter 20. **Boog Powell**

Joe Wancho

AGE	G	AB	R	H	2B	3B	HR	TB	RBI	BB	SO	BAV	OBP	SLG	SB	GDP	HBP
28	154	526	82	156	28	0	35	289	114	104	80	.297	.412	.549	1	14	5

On a crisp, sunny autumn afternoon, the 1970 World Series began in Cincinnati's brand-new Riverfront Stadium. The Reds and the Baltimore Orioles had breezed through their respective League Championship Series to meet at the apex of the baseball season. For the visiting Orioles, the taste of bitter disappointment lingered like castor oil on their tongues from the previous year's defeat at the hands of the New York Mets. Baltimore had been heavy favorites in the 1969 Series, but lost in five games to the "Amazing Mets." The goal in 1970 had been to avenge their frustration.

As Game One moved along, it was the Reds who jumped out to a 3–0 lead after three innings. But in the top of the fourth, with one out, center fielder Paul Blair beat out a grounder down the third-base line. First baseman Boog Powell strode to the plate to face Reds starter Gary Nolan. The left-handed-swinging Powell had been receiving a steady diet of breaking balls from Nolan. "But he fooled me—or tried to," Powell later recalled. "He threw me a fastball. Expecting a breaking ball, I got the bat around a little late. But even though I hit it to the opposite field, it went over the left-field wall for my first Series homer and cut the Reds' lead to 3–2."[1]

Elrod Hendricks homered in the fifth inning to tie the game. In the bottom of the sixth, Reds first baseman Lee May sent a grounder down the third base line that just crossed over the bag. Brooks Robinson fielded the ball, and with his momentum carrying him into foul territory, stopped and threw the ball off balance to first base. First baseman Powell stretched to catch the one-hopper and nipped May in the spectacular—at both ends—

Boog Powell had many fine seasons for the Orioles, none better than his MVP campaign in 1970.

fielding play. The next two Reds hitters reached base, so a potentially disastrous inning was avoided. Brooks Robinson's seventh-inning home run gave the Orioles their first lead, and eventually a 4–3 victory in Game One, and they took the Series four games to one.

The man who got the Orioles' offense going in that first game, John Wesley Powell, was born on August 17, 1941, in Lakeland, Florida, the oldest of three sons (followed by Charles and Richard) born to Mr. and Mrs. Charles Powell. Charles Powell worked as a car salesman. "My mother died when I was 9," said Powell. "My father married again when Charles was 7, and my stepmother had a 7-year-old son,—Carl (Taylor)."[2]

Powell said he received his odd nickname, Boog, from his father. "In the South they call little kids who are often getting into mischief buggers, and my dad shortened it to Boog. Hardly anybody ever calls me John. I don't know if I'd even turn around if someone called me that."[3]

When Powell was twelve he pitched for the Lakeland Little League team that made it to the Little League World Series in Williamsport, Pennsylvania. Carl was the catcher and Charlie played in the outfield. The team's run was short-lived; it lost to Schenectady, New York, 16–0, in its first game. Carl Taylor went on to a six-year Major League career (1968–73), mostly with Pittsburgh and Kansas City. Charlie spent a couple of years (1962–63) with the Baltimore organization in the lower Minor Leagues.

When Boog was a teenager the Powells relocated to Key West, Florida, where he was a three-sport star (football, basketball, baseball) at Key West High School. He had several college football scholarships but favored baseball over going to college. Based on scout Fred Hofmann's glowing reports on the six-foot-three, 235-pound prospect, Baltimore farm director Jim McLaughlin offered Powell a $35,000 bonus.

At the age of seventeen, fresh out of high school, Powell started his climb through the Baltimore chain at Class D Bluefield (West Virginia) of the short-season Appalachian League. Playing in 56 games, Powell slammed 14 home runs, drove in 59 runs, and batted .351. Clearly, he was on his way. Although Baltimore signed Powell as an outfielder, when he moved over to Clearwater in the Florida State winter league, he was given endless instruction in how to play first base. Orioles field director Eddie Robinson, a former Major League first baseman, worked with Powell on the intricacies of the position. Powell credited Robinson with help-

ing him at the plate as well. "I like the way Robinson talked to me," he said. "He didn't order that I try to hit with his stance. He just suggested what he thought I should do."[4]

Boog was promoted in 1960 to play at the Class B level with Fox Cities of the Three-I League. He was stationed at first base for the season, fielding at a .983 clip, showing that the work he put in with Robinson was paying off. But it was at the plate that he really excelled. He hit 13 home runs and 23 doubles, and had 100 RBIs as the Foxes, under manager Earl Weaver, won the league pennant. General manager Bob Willis later told visitors to the Foxes' ballpark to look at the clock high above the right-center-field fence. In batting practice one time, Powell hit a smash that ripped through a protective wire screen, broke the glass facing, and stopped the clock at 10 minutes after 7. "We've had numerous hitters drive the ball against the clock, but until Boog came along, nobody ever broke it," Willis recalled.[5]

Powell made the jump to Rochester of the Triple-A International League in 1961 and led the league with 32 home runs while hitting .320 with 92 RBIs. He was called up to the Orioles late in the season and made his Major League debut on September 26 at Yankee Stadium in New York. He collected his first Major League hit the next day, a single off Bill Stafford in the third inning. His Minor League numbers made Powell the most anticipated hitting prospect in Baltimore since the Orioles relocated from St. Louis in 1954.

Baltimore manager Billy Hitchcock put Powell in left field in 1962, scrapping the plan to play the prized prospect at first base. Veteran Jim Gentile played first and was one of the team's few long-distance threats. "Jim Gentile would be a tough man to move," said Powell. "I like to swing a bat, so it doesn't matter where I play."[6]

On May 2, 1962, at Metropolitan Stadium in Bloomington, Minnesota, playing left field against the Minnesota Twins and batting fifth, Powell hit his first two Major League home runs, a two-run shot off Jim Kaat in the third inning and another two-run homer off Ted Sadowski in the fifth. Powell's promising rookie campaign was affected by injuries. On May 29 he suffered a deep muscle bruise above his left knee when he ran into the left-field fence in Detroit. He returned to the lineup on June 7 and was hit in the head by a pitch from New York's Bud Daley on June 13, being taken off the field on a stretcher. Powell still managed to play in 124 games and hit .243, with 15 home runs and 53 runs batted in.

On July 9, during the All-Star break, Powell and Janet Swinton of Rochester, New York, were married. She was a psychology major at Kent State University in Ohio. They would have three children.

Powell spent part of the off-season playing winter ball for Mayaguez in the Puerto Rico League. The extra work seemed to help, as he led the Orioles with 25 home runs and 82 RBIs in 1963 while lifting his average to .265. "I worked on spreading my feet a little more in Puerto Rico to keep from lunging. I was getting way out in front of pitches," he said.[7] On August 10 at Washington, Powell became the first Oriole to hit three home runs in a game. On August 17 and 18 in Kansas City, he went 7-for-9 at the plate in two games, with three runs scored and three RBIs. "He's swinging at fewer bad balls, he's got more confidence and he knows the pitchers and how they're going to pitch to him," said Hitchcock.[8]

For 1964 Hank Bauer replaced Hitchcock as the Orioles' manager. Toward the end of the season Bauer, who had played for several championship Yankees teams, found himself chasing his old club. On September 23 the Orioles were tied with the Chicago White Sox four games behind New York. From then until the end of the season, the White Sox went 8-0 and the Orioles 7-1, but they couldn't catch the Yankees, who went 6-4 in their last ten games. Baltimore finished the year at 97-65, in third place, two games behind the Yankees.

That season Boog showed the power output the Orioles faithful were waiting to see. He drilled 39 home runs, drove in 99 runs, and led the league with a .606 slugging percentage. On June 27 he victimized the Senators again, connecting for three homers in Washington. He was zeroing in on Gentile's single-season Orioles home run record of forty-six. But a series of injuries, notably a sprained wrist suffered in Boston on August 20, caused him to miss twenty-eight games. In 1965 Bauer moved Boog to first base but the big lefty slumped. His home-run total dropped to 17 and he hit just .248. During the season Bauer fined Powell for being overweight; Boog battled to keep his weight down throughout his career.

After the 1965 season the Orioles acquired Frank Robinson, relieving Powell of some of the pressure of being the team's main power source (Gentile had been traded after the 1963 season). Although Powell started the 1966 season 1-for-34 at the plate, he rallied to hit .384 in June and went on to a fine season. He hit three home runs on August 15 against the Boston Red Sox at Fenway Park. He finished with 34 home runs and 109 runs batted in, and was named the American League Comeback Player of the Year as well as the American League first baseman on *The Sporting News*' all-star team. As expected, the trade for Frank Robinson proved fruitful for the Orioles. He won the American League Triple Crown and Most Valuable Player award, and led the Orioles to the pennant. In the World Series Powell batted .357, but it was the Orioles' pitching that grabbed the headlines. Led by consecutive shutouts by Jim Palmer, Wally Bunker, and Dave McNally in the last three games, Baltimore swept the Los Angeles Dodgers.

The Orioles slipped to sixth place in 1967, hobbled by injuries to several players (Palmer, McNally, and Frank Robinson among them) and a few down seasons. Powell had a dismal year, hitting .234 with only 13 home runs. He was benched for much of the second half of the season as Bauer played Curt Blefary at first base. The next year the Orioles fired Bauer in midseason. Under his replacement, Earl Weaver, they finished in second place. Powell led the team in home runs (22) and runs batted in (85), and made the first of his three All-Star Game appearances. He struck out twice in two plate appearances during a 1–0 defeat at the Houston Astrodome. After the season, *The Sporting News* named him to its league all-star team.

Powell had a great season in 1969, smacking 37 home runs and 25 doubles, and setting career marks in RBIS (121) and batting average (.304). He was the American League's starting first baseman in the All-Star Game. He had an eighteen-game hitting streak from May 9 to May 30, falling two short of the club record set by Bob Nieman in 1956. On August 16 at Sicks' Stadium in Seattle, he hit an inside-the-park home run off former teammate Steve Barber. He made only seven errors at first base. "Boog has come so far in the last couple of years," said second baseman Dave Johnson. "He used to hug the line and just cover the bag four or five years ago, playing every hitter the same. Now he'll come off, allowing me to shade second."[9]

After sweeping the Twins in the playoffs, the Orioles fell flat in the 1969 World Series, losing to the underdog New York Mets in five games. Powell had a disappointing Series, hitting .263 with no extra-base hits and four strikeouts.

Baltimore faced little resistance repeating as division champs in 1970, finishing ahead of New York by 15 games. Again it was Powell who led the offensive attack with 37 home runs, 104 runs batted in, 28 doubles, 104 walks, a .297 batting average, and a .549 slugging percentage. He again started at first base in the All-Star Game. He was the overwhelming choice as the American League's Most Valuable Player, after having finished second in 1969. "It's about time the Booger won it," said

Detroit pitcher Denny McLain. "He's been doing it for Baltimore for a long time. You, know, without him, I regard the Orioles as just another team because you can pitch around Frank Robinson. With Powell behind him, though, you've got to throw strikes and everybody knows what those guys can do to pitches over the plate."[10]

After sweeping Minnesota again in the ALCS, the Orioles faced Cincinnati in the World Series and disposed of the Big Red Machine in five games. In Game Four, Johnny Bench lifted a high pop toward the first-base dugout. As Powell drifted over, he leaned over the dugout to catch the ball, but it hit his glove and popped out. Showing tremendous reflexes, he caught the ball barehanded to get the put-out. Boog hit .294 in the Series with 2 home runs and 5 runs batted in.

The Orioles went into the World Series again in 1971 after cruising through the pennant race and sweeping Oakland in the ALCS. Powell fell off from his 1970 MVP season, and he was hitting below .200 into late June. Weaver issued a "hit-or-sit" ultimatum to Powell and he improved, but just when he was coming out of his slump, he suffered a hairline fracture of his right wrist. He was out of action for two weeks. He finished the year with a .256 batting average, 22 home runs, and 92 RBIS. In the second game of the ALCS Powell hit two homers off Oakland's Catfish Hunter. But Baltimore lost the World Series to the Pittsburgh Pirates in seven games. Powell had a dismal Series, posting a .111 batting average with only 3 singles in 27 at bats.

In 1972 Detroit snapped Baltimore's stranglehold on the American League East Division, taking advantage of the Orioles' dramatic offensive drop-off. Powell did not climb over .200 until mid-July. He tried wearing glasses in June in an effort to better see the pitches. "Glasses are worth a try," he said when word got out that he would try them. "I'm not expecting them to be a cure-all. These things do sharpen things up a bit, though. They can't hurt anything. I've got to get all the advantages I can."[11] But he quickly discarded them, and discontinued trying different stances at the plate. "I've come a long way, I'll tell you that," said Powell. "I'm just seeing the ball and swinging the bat better. That's all."[12] He batted .252 for the season. In the last three months of the season, Powell collected 17 of his 21 home runs and 61 of his 81 RBIS.

The Orioles regained the top spot in the American League East Division in 1973 and 1974, although they lost in the ALCS to Oakland in both years. Powell hit .265 both seasons, but a sore shoulder cut into his playing time in 1973. In 1974 the Orioles were in a close division race as the season came to a close. Powell was benched in late August in favor of Enos Cabell. "Originally I intended to keep him out of the lineup only three or four days," Weaver said. "But when we went on a winning streak with Enos playing, I wasn't going to change anything."[13] Inserted back into the lineup on September 13, Boog hit four home runs and drove in eight runs to help the team post a 15-2 record the rest of the season and wrap up the division.

The Orioles had tried to trade Powell at the end of the 1973 season and again during spring training in 1974 but found no takers. Frank Robinson had been traded to Los Angeles after the 1971 season, and had subsequently moved to California and then Cleveland. In December 1974 the Orioles acquired slugging first baseman Lee May from Houston. Seemingly, Powell was going to be shown the door, one way or the other. When Indians general manager Phil Seghi told Frank Robinson, now the Indians' manager, that his old friend Boog Powell could be had for catcher Dave Duncan, Robinson replied "Yes, yes, yes."[14] On February 25, 1975, Duncan and Al McGraw, a career Minor Leaguer, were sent to Baltimore for Powell and left-handed pitcher Don Hood.

Cleveland opened its season at home against New York on April 8. Robinson directed the team as a player-manager that season and inserted himself into the lineup as the designated hitter. Robinson hit a first-inning home run off the Yankees' Doc Medich. But it was Powell who delivered the heroics in his Tribe debut. He went 3-for-3 with three RBIS, three runs scored and a home run off Medich in the fourth inning. Robinson said his homer was "the single most satisfying thing that happened at the game, aside from winning. And close to that was Boog getting off to a good start."[15]

Satisfying may be the word to describe Boog's 1975 season in a nutshell. He batted .297, hit 27 home runs, and drove in 85 runs. Just as impressive was his work at first base: he committed only three errors. Boog was voted the 1975 American League Comeback Player of the Year. "His batting average has been a pleasant surprise," said Robinson. "We expected him to hit 20 to 25 home runs and knock in 70 to 80 runs, but the batting average has been an extra. We knew what he could do, and we knew he was better than those last two years in Baltimore."[16]

After his sparkling 1975 campaign, Powell's 1976 season was hampered by a torn thigh muscle in his right leg. For the first time in his Major League career, he played in fewer than 100 games, only 89 of them at first base, and he hit just .209 with nine home runs. He was released at the end of spring training in 1977, and signed with the Los Angeles Dodgers. He was to give the Dodgers insurance against an injury to starter Steve Garvey. But he had only 53 plate appearances, hit .222, almost all as a pinch hitter, and was released on August 31. At the age of thirty-five, he called it a career.

In retirement, Powell made a series of commercials for the Miller Brewing Company and operated a marina in Key West, called Boog Powell's Anglers. In 1979 he was inducted into the Baltimore Orioles Hall of Fame. As of 2010 he ranked among the franchise leaders in many categories: third in home runs (303), fourth in runs batted in (1,063), fourth in walks (889), fifth in games played (1,763), and fifth in total bases (2,698). After the Orioles opened Camden Yards, their new ballpark, in 1992, Powell became a big hit with fans, operating Boog's Corner, a barbecue stand at the ballpark. Powell credited his wife for his successful transition to life after baseball. "Without Jan, I would have done something, but not been nearly as successful," he said.[17] In 1997 Powell underwent surgery to have a tumor removed from his colon and had successful chemotherapy treatment.

On April 9, 2010, Powell and Brooks Robinson threw out the ceremonial Opening Day pitches in the celebration of the fortieth anniversary of the 1970 world championship team. "I don't care how old you are or what you're doing, you know when Opening Day is," he said then. "It's a special feeling. Gets your heart pumping. Anything is possible."[18]

Chapter 21. Clay Dalrymple

Rory Costello

AGE	G	AB	R	H	2B	3B	HR	TB	RBI	BB	SO	BAV	OBP	SLG	SB	GDP	HBP
33	13	32	4	7	1	0	1	11	3	7	4	.219	.350	.344	0	0	0

"I place a premium on a thinking catcher," said Gene Mauch,[1] who managed Clay Dalrymple for eight-plus seasons in Philadelphia. Mauch and Earl Weaver both stressed pitching and defense. Thus, while Dalrymple's hitting declined, his skills behind the plate kept him employed. The Californian handled pitchers deftly and threw out a superior 49 percent of the runners who tried to steal against him during his career. Clay adjusted to Mauch's platoons and then fit in well as a role player for Weaver from 1969 to 1971.

Dalrymple was sidelined when the Orioles won the 1970 World Series. That June, he had suffered a broken ankle in a home-plate collision with Mike Epstein of the Washington Senators. Clay watched the Series from the bullpen and was on hand for the victory celebration. "Yeah, I wear the ring. I really felt like I was a part of that team," he said many years later.[2]

Clayton Dalrymple was born on December 3, 1936. His father, Lyndon (they shared the middle name Errol), grew up in the Dakotas. Lyndon met his wife, Elsie Mae Henderson, in Alberta, Canada. The couple wanted to live in a warmer place, though, so they moved to Chico, California. During the Depression, Lyndon was an iceman. He then recapped tires for a service station and drove a truck for Butte County. He and Elsie had three children before Clay: sons Leslie and Melvin and daughter Lois.

Chico, ninety miles north of Sacramento, is today a city of about 85,000. In 1940, though, it was just a town with only two or three thousand in the center, as Clay recalls. In author Debra Moon's words, "Chico was a fun place. It had an ideal lo-

After several years as a starting catcher for the Phillies, Clay Dalrymple cashed three World Series checks as the Orioles' third-string backstop.

cation for raising food and families." Baseball was also popular: "The Chico Colts [semipro] baseball team drew a big crowd every Sunday afternoon for years. . . . They had some good players. Gordon Slade, a third baseman, later played with the St. Louis Cardinals and Cincinnati Reds [in the 1930s]."[3]

Dalrymple's older brothers Les and Mel both played for the Colts and in the Minors. Les, also a catcher, played Class B ball in 1947 and 1948.

Mel, nicknamed Bush, was a left-handed pitcher. He set records at Chico State College, later named Cal State–Chico. In 1950 Bush played Class C ball. Later, as head baseball coach at both Chico and Pleasant Valley High Schools, he instructed future big-league pitchers Nelson Briles and Pat Clements.

When Clay was a boy, "Chico was just forming Little Leagues at the time. The problem was getting enough kids together for teams in a small town—there were just enough for one." He then followed his brothers to Chico High, the Colts, and Chico State. In his own view, he "was not way out in front of the other kids. My ability grew from year to year on a steady scale. I wasn't one of those players who could have made it to the Majors out of high school."

Dalrymple joined the Colts in 1954 as a high-school senior. Les stepped aside for his seventeen-year-old brother and became manager. Clay remained with the Colts during his first two years at Chico State (1955–56). Back then, "we didn't have the scale or the coaching that they do now." Yet while Cal State–Chico is a good-quality program, as of 2010 Clay was the Wildcats' only Major League alumnus.

Clay had good size (six feet and 200 pounds) and also played football. "It was always interesting, and I enjoyed it. But baseball was far and away my favorite." His other sport was boxing. With an 11-1 record, he became heavyweight champion of the Far Western Conference.

In August 1956 Dalrymple made his pro debut with the Sacramento Solons of the Pacific Coast League. At that time, the Solons were not affiliated with any Major League club. "Don Masterson was a bird dog for Sacramento. He got into pro ball but had an accident. A ball got through his catcher's mask and broke some bones, and then he got a settlement. He told Sacramento I was a good prospect. But they couldn't approach me, they would

have gotten fined. So I called the general manager, Dave Kelley."

From the beginning, Clay established a work ethic. "I had to do a lot of things for the organization to have them be pleased with my progress," he said. In 1957 Dalrymple was assigned to the Amarillo Gold Sox, a team in the Class A Western League that had a working agreement with Sacramento. The left-handed dead pull hitter made the Western League's All-Star team, hitting 17 homers and driving in 81 runs with a .298 average. He said of the city, "I like it fine. These are the friendliest people I've ever met." A day after the season ended, on September 16, Clay married the one he found friendliest of all, Celia Faye Creamer.[4]

During the off-season, Clay went back to Chico State for more classes. (Teaching and coaching was his backup plan, though he never did get his degree.) Meanwhile, the Solons reportedly turned down an offer of $50,000 for their prospect—which the financially strapped club could have used. In August 1958, *The Sporting News* noted, "Although Dalrymple has been hitting only around .190, Dave Kelley says he wouldn't take $90,000 for him now."[5]

After that season, Clay went to Venezuela and Cuba (he brought back colorful memories of both places), but "that was the end of my winter ball experience. It was mainly family reasons, but I found other jobs. I drove a cement truck one year, and I was also with the Southern Pacific Railroad."

Despite his weak batting in 1958, Dalrymple had impressed veteran baseball men such as Phoenix manager Red Davis. The Milwaukee Braves, who now had a working agreement with the Solons, invited Dalrymple to spring training in 1959. After one more summer in Sacramento, the Phillies selected Clay in the Minor League draft that November, thanks to Dave Kelley, who had become their Far West supervisor of scouts. Although viewed as "strictly [a] gamble,"[6] Dalrymple made the Majors in spring training of 1960. He made his mark as a pinch-hitter, but his pitch-calling impressed Phillies ace Robin Roberts. By August, he was the team's regular catcher.[7]

In 1961 Gene Mauch observed, "Dalrymple has sure improved. . . . He gained confidence in his ability to handle a game."[8] Clay (already balding in his mid-twenties) had his best hitting year in 1962. The next year he posted career highs in games and at bats. In 1964, though, Mauch decided to platoon him with Gus Triandos. Clay went into a funk with the bat and never recovered. Nonetheless, he remained a key contributor to the club that looked certain to win the National League pennant. Commenting on the many ingredients that went into the Phillies' notorious "September Swoon" that season, Dalrymple recognized Mauch's strength—"Gene manipulated his players on the field better than anyone I ever played for"[9]—and its flip side, his micromanaging.

From 1965 through 1968, Dalrymple remained in a platoon with various other catchers, none of whom hit well. Yet the notoriously harsh Philly boo-birds piled on him. "Eventually I told the Phils, 'You should trade me. I'm not doing you any good here.'"[10]

Clay's wish was granted—he went to the Orioles in January 1969. Earl Weaver—"a good manager and a good man, though his personality left something to be desired"—already had a catching platoon with right-handed hitter Andy Etchebarren and lefty swinger Elrod Hendricks. However, Earl typically carried three catchers on his roster. Dalrymple was another lefty bat; he added maneuverability and insurance against injury.

At that time Ellie Hendricks was still viewed as more of a hitter and a "project" behind the plate.[11] As he worked to smooth off his rough edges as a catcher, Clay did not mentor him. "I did not feel it was my duty," he said. "[Hendricks] was the number-one catcher. Weaver wanted to write his name in the lineup. It would piss Earl off when pitchers would ask for me." Still, Dalrymple and the good-humored Hendricks got along well, exchanging locker-room banter.

"Etchebarren and I were pretty close," Dalrymple observed. "He had a history of breaking a hand [broken right metacarpals in both 1966 and '68]. You should have seen the mitt he had, it was tiny and thin with a little pocket—such a miserable piece of equipment. I told him, 'That thing must date back to 1912.' It was his right hand that would get broken because he'd have to reach in there with it. I got him to switch, and no more broken hands."

As a backstop, Clay upheld the classic fundamentals. "The mitts you see today, that are more like a first baseman's glove—they lead to backhanding, rather than shifting your weight and receiving the ball. Elrod was a snagging-type catcher." The cost is framing pitches and getting borderline ball-and-strike calls. "The mitt I have bronzed today, it was one of the first from Rawlings that had the cross-webbing. I used that for plays at the plate. For pitches, I formed a big round pocket, a nice target that the pitcher could see."

The mental game was a major dimension for the Baltimore pitchers, notably Jim Palmer and Mike Cuellar. Palmer often battled his catchers, but Clay's flexible approach avoided this. "I would find out how a pitcher's mind works. You call a game according to how the pitcher wanted, not how you wanted."

Playing time was scarce for Dalrymple, though he had a case for more, and he noted that this made it more difficult to stay sharp.[12] He did not appear in the playoffs against the Twins, but in the World Series, he went 2-for-2 as a pinch hitter. "You can win a bar bet with that," he laughed.

In 1989 Clay recalled that as the '69 season began, he said to Andy Etchebarren, "If we were allowed to bet, I'd put every nickel on this ballclub. It was the best team I'd ever, ever seen."[13] He echoed that view in a more recent interview, noting the strength of the pitching. Yet after the Amazing

Mets pulled off their upset, that winter he noted that while the Mets had gathered momentum late, the Orioles were flat. "We played our best earlier. The second half was like a cakewalk. . . . There's no doubt that the reason was lack of excitement."[14]

During the first few months of the 1970 season, Dalrymple's action was even more limited. On June 27, however, he got one of his infrequent starts, in a Saturday night game at Robert F. Kennedy Stadium in Washington. "Palmer insisted that I catch him. In the third or fourth inning, I could see he wasn't on his game—I was nursing him along." Then in the bottom of the seventh, Frank Howard and Mike Epstein singled. Aurelio Rodríguez followed with a double to left. "It was in the gap, and the relay came from Blair to Belanger to me. The throw bounced high off the grass, and when I turned around, Epstein's eyes were barely two feet away from my chest.

"I had put my left foot in front of the plate. I gave him the back edge to slide to. But Epstein, who was a fullback in college football, decided to take me out. My right ankle popped—it was dislocated and broken in two places.

"There was no pain in the ankle at the time—it was really gathering in the knee. The pain was too great for the ankle to register, so it went to the next place, the doctor said." Clay was taken off the field on a stretcher, yet he never lost consciousness. The great play held a 3–2 lead for the Orioles, but Palmer lost it in the eighth inning.

"To show you the camaraderie and the sick humor we had on that team, let me tell you about my friend Merv Rettenmund. Merv's the kind of guy who would joke, even though he's been married to the same woman all his life, 'Why is it that when I come home from a road trip, I always hear the back door slam?' Well, I was there in the hospital with my foot so badly deformed that my toes were pointing in different directions. Merv brought in a card that said, 'Best wishes from your last team.'

But I didn't get pissed off. . . . I laughed my ass off."

The cast came off three months later, just before the World Series. "I tried to do a little bit of jogging, but it was really sore and there were adhesions." Thus, Dalrymple remained inactive for the Series. Also, though he was able to rejoice with his teammates, his wife, Celia, had been diagnosed with the cancer that would eventually claim her life two years later. Her Christian Scientist beliefs dissuaded her from the minor surgery that might have caught the disease early.

Clay was able to come back in 1971. Again he played sparingly, but he did make the postseason roster. However, he did not appear in either the playoffs or the World Series (though he did provide some scouting reports on Pittsburgh batters). "I was in the on-deck circle one time against the Pirates, but the hitter before me made the last out." Tongue in cheek, he added, "I think Weaver wanted me to put my 1.000 lifetime [World Series] average in jeopardy!"

Later that October, the Orioles left on one of the periodic American postseason tours to Japan, but Clay had to cut it short because Celia was ill again. The team also sent him a message by leaving him off the forty-man roster and assigning him to Triple-A Rochester. So that December, he retired after twelve seasons in the majors. "I've fulfilled my baseball dreams," he said.[15]

It's worth reiterating his most impressive big-league stat, though: 306 runners caught stealing against 320 successful. Even as the third-string catcher with the Orioles, each year there he nailed more than 50 percent (25 out of 44 total). Analyst Chuck Rosciam compiled this statistic across the Majors from 1956 through 2007. Over more than half a century, Dalrymple ranked second only to Roy Campanella (whose entire career was available for study).[16]

Clay credited his quick release more than his arm strength. "Every instant, every split-second counted. Facing somebody like Maury Wills, I thought, what do I have to do to cut him down? It was always going to be a bang-bang play anyway. Grab the ball and don't look for the seam—get rid of it. It was almost a side-arm throw sometimes."

Celia Dalrymple, aged only 34, died in November 1972. Dallas Green had offered Clay a job with the Phillies, but he felt compelled to stay with their three daughters, Dawn, April, and Autumn (whom they had adopted eight years after April was born). "I would probably have started managing in the minors. I could have gone into the front office," he said.

During 1976 and 1977, Dalrymple served as a color man on Orioles TV broadcasts. "Bill O'Donnell and Chuck Thompson got me in. They would alternate between radio and TV, and I would join whoever was on TV. I did it for two years, right at the end of Brooks Robinson's career. Then when he retired, I interviewed him and found out he was going to take my job! But Brooks is an Orioles legend and a great guy."

Around 1982 Clay returned home to Chico. He worked in food distribution before retiring in 1998. In 2001 he moved to Gold Beach, Oregon. After his second divorce and losing another wife to sudden death, he said, "I'm very happy now" with his fifth wife, Teresa.

For a couple of years, he helped coach the local high-school baseball team, "but I found there was too big an age gap, I wasn't communicating properly. I don't have the patience any more. I know things about catching that I can't teach. You have to experience it."

In his 70s, Dalrymple said, "I'm starting to feel that old broken ankle now." In Gold Beach he became a commissioner for the local port district, but his most avid pursuit ran in a different direction. "I'm a news junkie," he said. "I follow politics very closely. I write articles, I'm a conservative. I enjoy writing about politics more than anything."

Dalrymple saw his old champion Oriole team-mates—"those of us who are still here"—at a March 2008 autograph show in the Baltimore-Washington Airport. Among the other guests was Reggie Jackson. Once he realized who Clay was, Reggie recalled with pleasure how, as a teenager growing up just north of Philadelphia, he had watched the catcher at Connie Mack Stadium. The show also gave Clay, who used to speak at banquets in the '60s, a chance to flash his relaxed, self-deprecating sense of humor.

"The line for Frank Robinson was snaking all the way around the place when they announced me. About ten minutes went by. . . . I had nobody. I looked at the guy at my table with all the different kinds and colors of pens and I said, 'Watch this.' I stood up and made an announcement. 'Can I have your attention, please?' There was silence. I said, 'I know it's crowded over here, and you're gonna have to be patient—but if you bear with me, I just might be able to squeeze you in!'

"The place broke up laughing. Then I got a nice group of people and we talked about baseball."

Neither a star nor a "character," Clay Dalrymple still struck a chord with many fans. If you appreciate honest artisans and the game's subtle nuances, you could be one of them.

Chapter 22. **Mike Cuellar**

Adam Ulrey

AGE	W	L	PCT.	ERA	G	GS	GF	CG	SHO	SV	IP	H	BB	SO	HBP	WP
33	24	8	.750	3.48	40	40	0	21	4	0	297.2	273	69	190	1	6

Unwanted in Houston, Mike Cuellar averaged twenty-one wins per season his first six years in Baltimore, including twenty-four in 1970.

Mike Cuellar was a four-time twenty-game winner for the Baltimore Orioles, and the winner of 185 Major League games. He could also lay claim to being the one of the most superstitious players in baseball history. "He had a routine and please don't interfere with it," remembered a teammate, Paul Blair.

> He would walk to the mound the same way, same steps. Step on the mound. Go to the front of the mound, and the rosin bag couldn't be on there. Somebody had to come and kick the rosin to the back of the mound or he wouldn't get on the mound. Then he'd walk off the mound the same way. He would come in the dugout the same way; make the same number of steps to the water cooler. Everything had to be the same every time he went out there.[1]

Before taking the field, Cuellar sat on the "lucky end" of the training table, wearing a gold-chain medallion, while the trainer massaged his arm. He took batting practice on the day he pitched even after the designated hitter rule was in place. When the team traveled, he wore a blue suit. Whether his superstitions helped his pitching can be debated. But there is no doubt that for most of his eight years with the Orioles, Cuellar was one of the most effective pitchers in the Major Leagues. A nasty screwball, developed mostly in winter baseball in the Caribbean, saw to that.

Miguel Angel Cuellar Santana was born on May 8, 1937, in Santa Clara, Las Villas province, Cuba. His family, including four boys, worked in the sugar mills. Cuellar did not want to follow in his family's footsteps and enlisted in the Cuban army for 70 pesos a month because he knew he could play baseball on Saturdays and Sundays. He pitched for Cuban dictator Fulgencio Batista's army team in the winter of 1954–55. He hurled a no-hitter that season and was heavily followed by Cuban and American scouts.

After his discharge, the thin (six feet, 165 pounds) left-hander pitched in the summer of 1956 with a Nicaragua Independent League team, finishing 10-3 with a 2.95 earned run average. His manager, Emilio Cabrera, immediately brought him to his Almendares team in Cuba for the 1956–57 winter league season. He pitched in relief (1-1, 0.61 ERA). Before the 1957 season, he was signed by the Cincinnati Reds, who optioned him to their Cuban Sugar Kings (often called the Havan Sugar Kings) affiliate in the International League. He impressed Sugar Kings manager Nap Reyes, who said, "I have coached a lot of pitchers, here in Cuba and in the US, but none so quick to learn as this boy. I have put him in the toughest spots in relief to test him out. He has a good curve but he doesn't have to vary much. He makes the left-handed batters look pretty bad when he does."[2]

Cuellar made a sensational pro debut with Havana in 1957 against Montreal, striking out seven men in a row in 2⅔ innings of no-hit relief. He led the league with a 2.44 earned run average and posted an 8-7 record in 44 games, 16 of them starts. After another winter with Almendares (4-5 with a 3.03 ERA), he returned to Havana in 1958 and pitched 220 innings, with a 13-12 record and a fine 2.77 ERA. That winter he pitched again for Almendares, which won the Caribbean Series title. Cuellar was 5-7 with a 3.79 ERA.

In 1959 Cuellar began the season with the Reds but was ineffective in two relief appearances: four innings, seven earned runs on seven hits, for a 15.75 ERA. He was returned to Havana and did not see the big leagues again for five years.

He found the International League much more to his liking, and he hurled 212 innings, finishing with a 10-11 record but a 2.80 ERA. The Sugar Kings wound up the regular season in third place but upset Columbus and Richmond to win the International League championship, and then captured the Junior World Series title by defeating the Minneapolis Millers of the American Association in seven games. (The decisive seventh game was decided in the bottom of the ninth inning.)

The Junior World Series was notable for more than baseball. In Cuba, Batista had just been overthrown by Fidel Castro's forces, and the games in Havana were played in a fortress-like atmosphere. Because of winter-like weather in Minneapolis, the last five games were all played at Havana's Gran Stadium. Nearly 3,000 soldiers were at the stadium for the seventh and deciding game, many lining the field and others stationing themselves in the dugouts, their rifles and bayonets clearly evident. "Young people not more than 14 or 15 years old were in the dugout with us, waving their guns around like toys," recalled Millers pitcher Ted Bowsfield. "Every once in a while, we could hear shots being fired outside the stadium, and we never knew what was going on."[3] Mauch reported that the soldiers were not above trying to intimidate the Minneapolis players. "Our players were truly fearful of what might happen if we won," said Mauch. "But we still tried our hardest, figuring we'd take our chances."[4] Cuellar started Game Two and pitched 7⅓ innings, giving up four earned runs in a no-decision. He pitched in relief in the next two games, picking up a win in Game Four, before getting knocked out early in a Game Six loss. He did not pitch in the final, won 3–2 by the Sugar Kings.

From 1960 through 1963, Cuellar bounced around the Minor Leagues and the Mexican League, playing for six different teams with not a lot of success. After Castro began tightening travel into and out of Cuba, Cuellar chose to play winter ball in Venezuela or Nicaragua rather than return to his native land. By 1964, his contract had been passed from Cincinnati to Detroit to Cleveland to

St. Louis, but the twenty-seven-year-old seemed no closer to a return to the Major Leagues.

After five consecutive seasons in the high Minors with won-lost records below .500, Cuellar turned things around in 1964. Ruben Gomez, a winter league teammate, persuaded him to start throwing a screwball, the pitch that changed Cuellar's life. He practiced the pitch all winter and spring, and during the 1964 season he threw it 30 percent of the time. For Triple-A Jacksonville, Cuellar logged a 6-1 record and a 1.78 ERA into mid-June. The St. Louis Cardinals called him up to the Majors on June 15, and he got into thirty-two games the rest of the season, starting seven. The August 26 game was special for Mike. When hitless Gene Freese popped weakly to shortstop for the last out, Cuellar finally had his revenge after 5½ seasons. "I hit a pinch-hit home run with the bases loaded off Cuellar in 1959 and that blow sent him back to the minors for five years," Freese said. "He's a lot faster and has come with quite a scroogie."[5] Cuellar finished 5-5 but did not see action in the 1964 World Series, in which the Cardinals defeated the New York Yankees.

Cuellar went to Puerto Rico to pitch that winter, and he finished 12-4 with a 2.06 ERA for Arecibo. At one point he had a stretch of twenty-seven scoreless innings and threw four shutouts. He went to spring training hoping to land in the Cardinals rotation but instead was optioned back to Jacksonville after Opening Day. After dominating the International League for ten weeks (9-1 with a 2.51 ERA), he was traded in an all-pitchers deal on June 15 to the Houston Astros with Ron Taylor for Hal Woodeshick and Chuck Taylor. He spent the rest of 1965 with the Astros, finishing 1-4 with a 3.54 ERA in 25 appearances.

At nearly twenty-nine years old, Mike had finally reached the Major Leagues to stay. By 1966, he was using his screwball between 50 and 60 percent of the time and had added a curveball that

made his fastball appear even sharper. Astros pitching coach Gordon Jones taught Cuellar the curve. Cuellar had been releasing his curve with almost a slider motion but without the good slider break. Jones showed him how to get rotation on the ball by bending the wrist in toward himself and popping the ball loose with the overhand motion.

On June 25, 1966, Cuellar beat the Cardinals and recorded a team-record 15 strikeouts, running his record to 6-0 with a 1.73 ERA. He ended the season by throwing six complete games in a row, including his first Major League shutout, a 2–0 victory over the Pirates on August 29. He finished 12-10 with a 2.22 ERA that was second best in the National League behind Sandy Koufax.

The next season, 1967, Cuellar did it all again, this time with better luck in run support. His ERA rose to 3.03 but he finished 16-11 in 246 innings, including 16 complete games. He pitched two shutout innings in the All-Star Game in Anaheim. After the season the Astros told Cuellar he couldn't pitch winter ball, which did not sit well with the star. At the time many Major League players played in the winter, and to the Latin players in particular it was an important part of their culture. Cuellar blamed his arm trouble the following season to his not playing in the winter. In 1968 he was just 8-11 (for a last-place team), though with a fine 2.74 ERA in 170 innings.

Apparently overreacting to his won-loss record, the Astros traded Cuellar after the season to the Orioles for infielder-outfielder Curt Blefary and Minor Leaguer John Mason. Cuellar was having some off-field difficulties, mainly a struggling marriage and related financial problems. Baltimore general manager Harry Dalton's scouts told him that the pitcher's off-field issues could be rectified. Scout Jim Russo raved about Cuellar and recommended his acquisition. When Cuellar came to Baltimore the Orioles helped him get rid of his debt, and Cuellar was soon divorced and remarried. He became immensely popular with his Baltimore teammates. "Cuellar was a wonderful person," remembered manager Earl Weaver.[6]

With the Orioles, the combination of his great left arm and the tremendous Orioles team made Cuellar one of baseball's biggest pitching stars. In his first year with Baltimore, 1969, he put up a 23-11 record with a 2.38 ERA, and he shared the Cy Young Award with Denny McLain of the Tigers. Cuellar set Orioles pitching records for wins and innings pitched (291) and tied the club mark with eighteen complete games. He threw five shutouts. In the first game of the American League Championship Series against the Minnesota Twins, Cuellar allowed two earned runs in eight innings in a game the Orioles won in the twelfth. In the World Series, he outdueled the New York Mets' Tom Seaver to win the first game, 4–1, but his seven-inning, one-run performance was not enough in Game Four, which the Mets won in the tenth. The Mets won the Series in five games but Cuellar had a stellar 1.12 ERA in 16 innings.

Cuellar's Baltimore teammates called him Chief Crazy Horse for his weird sense of humor and especially his strange superstitions. Since he had pitched well in 1969 spring training with coach Jim Frey warming him up, only Frey was permitted to catch the Cuban southpaw's pregame tosses the rest of the year. Elrod Hendricks—nobody else—must stand at the plate for part of that period, simulating a batter. Cuellar would not finish warming up until the opposing starter had finished. He never stepped on the foul line when he took the field; he always picked the ball up from the ground near the mound himself. He would not warm up before an inning with a reserve while his catcher got his gear on—Cuellar waited for the catcher to get behind the plate. As he kept winning, the importance of ritual only grew.

Cuellar's ERA rose to 3.48 in 1970, but his run support and his remarkable durability allowed him to finish 24-8, with 297⅔ innings pitched and 21 complete games. He typically started slowly, and posted a record of 8-5 with a 4.34 ERA through the end of June. As the weather heated up Cuellar caught fire; in the final three months he went 16-3 with a 2.78 ERA, completing 14 of his 21 starts. Cuellar was joined in a great rotation by Dave McNally (24-9) and Jim Palmer (20-10) The trio made 119 starts and pitched 899 innings. Their 68 victories are the most by three teammates since the 1944 Tigers (also 68).

Paul Blair later said,

With Cuellar, McNally, and Palmer, you could almost ring up 60 wins for us when the season started because each of them was going to win 20. And with Cuellar and McNally, you never knew if they were winning 10–0 or losing 0–10. They were the same guys. They were two really great left-handers, and the reason they were so great was they didn't have the talent Palmer had. They didn't have the 95-mile-per-hour fastball Palmer had. They had to learn to pitch, know the hitters, hit corners, and they did it. And they never complained. Those kind of guys, you just die for. You break your neck to go out there and win for them.[7]

In the first game of the 1970 ALCS against the Minnesota Twins, the Orioles gave Cuellar a 9–1 lead, but he failed to finish the fifth, though he left the game with a 9–6 lead. Reliever Dick Hall shut down the Twins the rest of the way, beginning an Orioles sweep. Cuellar next got the ball in Game Two of the World Series but could not survive the third inning in a game the Orioles pulled out with a five-run fifth inning over Cincinnati. In Game Five he allowed three hits and three runs in the first before shutting the door, going all the way in a 9–3 victory for his only World Series title, the second for Baltimore.

Cuellar again won twenty games in 1971, finishing 20-9 with a 2.08 ERA. This time he, McNally, and Palmer were joined by a fourth twenty-game-winner, Pat Dobson. The Orioles thus became the second team to have four twenty-game winners, joining the 1920 Chicago White Sox. Cuellar was 12–1 with a 2.93 ERA at the All-Star break, and pitched two shutout innings for the American League in the All-Star Game. It was the third of his four All-Star selections. Cuellar cooled off in the second half of the season, but the Orioles easily won their third consecutive division title. He defeated Oakland's Catfish Hunter with a Game Two 5–1 six-hitter as the Orioles swept the ALCS. He lost his two World Series starts against the Pirates, allowing all five runs in a 5–1 loss in Game Three and then falling short in a tough 2–1 loss to Steve Blass in the final. For his career, Cuellar was 2-2 with a 2.61 ERA in five World Series starts.

In 1972 the Orioles' run of championships ended, though it was mostly the offense that fell off. Cuellar pitched 257 innings with a 2.57 ERA but slipped to 18-12. After a slow start, he finished 16-7 after June 1, with 15 complete games, including 6 straight at one point. The Orioles finished third in a tight American League East.

During a May 26 game with the Indians, Cuellar's superstitious behavior was on full display. After Cleveland left fielder Alex Johnson caught Boog Powell's fly ball to end the third inning, he slowly jogged the ball back to the infield. Timing his pace with Cuellar's approach to the mound, Johnson tossed the ball to the pitcher, but Cuellar ducked just in time, and the ball rolled free. Helpfully, the batboy retrieved the ball and threw it to Cuellar. Once more he dodged the ball, which dribbled toward first baseman Boog Powell. Momentarily forgetting his teammate's habits, Powell threw it squarely at Cuellar, who had no choice but to catch the ball in self-defense. Disgusted but undeterred, Cuellar tossed it to the umpire and asked for a new ball. The umpire obliged, and Cuellar again sidestepped the ball, which trickled passed him and stopped right at the feet of his second baseman, Bobby Grich. At long last Grich rolled the ball to the mound, and Cuellar picked it up,

satisfied now that no evil spirits had invaded his place of business.

Cuellar started slowly again in 1973 (4-9 with a 4.09 ERA through July 7) before again turning it on in the second half of the season (14-4, 2.64 the rest of the way). He was now thirty-six years old, and there were concerns that perhaps his days as an elite pitcher were behind him. Not yet, as manager Earl Weaver again got 267 innings out of Cuellar, including 17 complete games, en route to his 18-13 final record as the Orioles returned to the postseason. In Game Three of the ALCS against the Oakland A's, Cuellar hooked up with Ken Holtzman in a great pitching duel. Through ten innings, Cuellar allowed just three hits and one run, but he gave up a game-winning home run to Bert Campaneris in the bottom of the eleventh inning to lose 2–1. Holtzman pitched all eleven innings for Oakland and tossed a three-hitter. The Athletics prevailed in the series, 3 games to 2, and went on to win the World Series over the Mets.

Cuellar returned to the twenty-game circle in 1974, finishing 22-10 with a 3.11 ERA, 20 complete games, and five shutouts. He was now thirty-seven but showed no signs of aging. His performance earned him the Game One assignment against the A's in the ALCS, and he pitched eight strong innings to earn the 6–3 victory. His next start, in the fourth game, was not nearly as successful—he had to be relieved in the fifth after allowing just one hit but walking nine. After walking in a run, the first run of the game, he was relieved, and the Athletics won the game, 2–1, to capture the series. It was Cuellar's twelfth and final postseason start, finishing his log at 4-4 with a 2.85 ERA.

Cuellar finally began showing his age in 1975, dropping to 14-12 with a 3.66 ERA, his highest since 1964. He still threw 17 complete games and had 5 shutouts but did not have the consistency that had been his hallmark during his best Oriole years. After seven years with the Orioles he had 139 victories, just shy of a twenty-win average. The following season, the thirty-nine-year-old finally imploded, finishing just 4-13 with an ERA of 4.96. Earl Weaver was used to Cuellar's slow starts, in a season and also in a game, and he was patient with the pitcher long after others thought he needed to make a change. He finally pulled his beloved left-hander at the beginning of August and put him in the bullpen.[8]

Cuellar was released in December 1976 and was picked up a month later by the Angels, whose general manager was old friend Harry Dalton. But after a terrible spring training and two forgettable regular-season appearances (3⅓ innings, seven runs), he was released by the Angels. Cuellar's Major League career had come to an end, just shy of his fortieth birthday. He continued to pitch in the Mexican League and in winter ball before finally calling it quits after the 1982–83 winter league season. He was a few months short of his forty-fifth birthday.

Cuellar remained occasionally active in baseball, serving as a pitching coach in the independent leagues and for many years in Puerto Rico. He was an instructor with the Orioles during the last years of his life, and he showed up often for team functions and reunions.

Cuellar was a healthy man for many years when he was suddenly diagnosed with stomach cancer in early 2010. He died on April 2 in Orlando, Florida, where he had lived for several years. He was survived by his wife, Myriam; his daughter, Lydia; and his son, Mike Jr. The latter pitched for five years in the Toronto Blue Jays farm system, but did not rise past Double-A ball.

"He was like an artist," Palmer said after Cuellar died. "He could paint a different picture every time he went out there. He could finesse you. He could curveball you to death or screwball you to death. From 1969 to '74, he was probably the best left-hander in the American League."[9]

ADAM ULREY

Chapter 23. **Eddie Watt**

Malcolm Allen

AGE	W	L	PCT.	ERA	G	GS	GF	CG	SHO	SV	IP	H	BB	SO	HBP	WP
29	7	7	.500	3.25	53	0	35	0	0	12	55.1	44	29	33	5	2

When the Baltimore Orioles won four American League pennants in six seasons (1966–71), no Baltimore pitcher earned more saves or appeared in more games than right-hander Eddie Watt. A short, chunky Midwesterner, usually with a pronounced wad of Red Man chewing tobacco bulging in his left cheek, Watt held right-handed hitters to a .200 batting average during his decade-long big-league career and earned two World Series rings.

Eddie Dean Watt was born on April 4, 1941, in Lamoni, Iowa, not far from the Missouri border. He was the youngest of four children born to Lawrence Watt and the former Bonnie Leigh, who married after their high school graduations in the midst of the Great Depression. The family wasn't well off by any measure, and the children all worked paper routes to help make ends meet. The Watts enjoyed playing cards together, always had food on the table, and had plenty to read thanks to their mother.

The family moved to West Branch, Iowa, by the end of 1940s, then to Iowa City when Watt was a teen. That was where he played his first organized baseball game, in the Babe Ruth League. The self-described "short, pudgy thirteen-year-old kid"[1] played a variety of positions, and his strong throwing arm earned him a spot on the pitching staff. His father was working three jobs at the time, and Watt helped him pick up *Des Moines Register* newspapers, wrap them, and distribute them to street-corner paperboys. A University of Iowa pitcher named Ron Schaeffer worked the other side of the Iowa River. Watt's father figured that if his son was going to pitch, he'd bet-

One half of Baltimore's fine short-reliever tandem in 1970, Eddie Watt was a valuable part of the Orioles staff for many years.

ter learn how, so he arranged to pay Schaeffer two dollars a lesson to become Eddie's personal pitching instructor.

"Five or six or eight lessons, or whatever it was," Watt recalled. "That was when I was fourteen years old, and I actually learned how to throw a curve ball, and learned control, and learned how to conduct [myself] as a pitcher."[2]

Watt played American Legion ball, and later a serious brand of semipro against older men when he was seventeen and eighteen. "I mean 25-, 30-,

35-year-old guys that had played a lot of professional baseball and lived in Cedar Rapids; which seemed to be home to a lot of ex–Double-A and Triple-A players." he recalled. He played third base and some outfield, and hit well enough to hire himself out for various Fourth of July and semipro tournaments. "But pitching was where I knew I was going to end up," Watt said.[3]

He became the first member of his family to attend college when he enrolled at Iowa State Teachers College (later the University of Northern Iowa) in the fall of 1959. The baseball coach had a good friend named Phil Gallivan who scouted for the Orioles. That relationship led to perhaps the first scouting report on Watt. Then, when Watt's team played in the NCAA regional finals in Oklahoma during his sophomore season, another Orioles scout, Byron Humphrey, saw him pitch. That summer Watt went to South Dakota to play in the Basin League, and other scouts got a look at him, including Baltimore superscout Jim Russo.

Watt let it be known that he was ready to play for pay. The St. Louis Cardinals and Chicago White Sox offered him deals that would pay him $350 a month to turn pro, but the Orioles offered $400. "So I signed with Baltimore, and it turned out to be one of the best moves I ever made," he said.[4]

Watt needed his parents' permission to sign the contract, and his mother was disappointed that he'd be leaving college when he was on course to graduate in eight semesters. He'd pay to attend class during the off-season instead, since turning pro meant he'd have to forfeit his basketball scholarship. After getting his feet wet in the Instructional League, in the spring of 1962, Watt reported to the Class D Appleton (Wisconsin) Foxes of the Midwest League. He struck out more than a batter per inning, and his 2.19 earned run average was among the circuit's best, but he finished with a pedestrian 11-11 record. Seven of the wins came in July, when he won a Topps pitcher-of-the-

month award. After the season the Orioles added him to their forty-man roster. Though Baltimore lost a whopping twenty-eight players in the Minor League draft that winter, Farm Director Harry Dalton expressed confidence that he'd been able to protect his most prized five, and named Watt among them. Watt also married his college sweetheart, Iva, so 1962 was a pretty good year for him.

In 1963 he took a line drive off his leg on the last pitch he threw in spring training, and lost his first six decisions for the Class C Aberdeen (South Dakota) Pheasants of the Northern League, where he played for manager Cal Ripken Sr. and threw mostly to Andy Etchebarren. But Watt came on strong to finish 10-12 with a 3.14 ERA. The Orioles sent him back to Aberdeen again in 1964. That's when I realized that being pretty good wasn't good enough," he recalled.[5] On a loaded Aberdeen pitching staff featuring future big leaguers Jim Palmer, Tom Fisher, and Dave Leonard, Watt corralled another Topps pitcher-of-the-month award and finished 14-1 with a 1.77 ERA. He added three wins in four decisions after joining Earl Weaver's Double-A Elmira Pioneers (Eastern League) late in the season to finish the year 17-2. "After that, I had the feeling something good may happen," he said. "Before, I guess I wished."[6] Also that year, his daughter, Gina, was born.

After a tremendous spring training in 1965 in which everything seemed to go right, Watt pitched a no-hitter against Williamsport on opening day at Dunn Field in Elmira, striking out 10. He got a no-decision after hurling ten scoreless innings in his second outing, then became the first Eastern League pitcher to hurl a pair of nine-inning no-hitters in the same season when lightning struck again in start number three. Watt's wife was enduring a difficult pregnancy, so the Orioles kept him in Elmira to be near the doctor who was monitoring her. After she gave birth to a son, named Edward, Watt moved up to the Triple-A Rochester Red Wings. (His success in Elmira in 1964 and '65 earned him a selection to the franchise's fiftieth-anniversary all-star squad in 1972.) Watt continued to pitch effectively with Rochester, and could boast of a dazzling 30-8 mark with a 2.34 ERA for Aberdeen, Elmira, and Rochester in 1964–65.

Even so, Watt knew he remained a long shot to crack the Orioles pitching staff in 1966. But Baltimore manager Hank Bauer gave the five-foot-ten, 183-pound right-hander a bona fide chance to earn a spot, and the Iowan responded. Watt saw his first Major League game on Opening Day at Fenway Park, wore a number 39 Baltimore jersey, and saved a marathon come-from-behind victory for the Orioles. "Jim Lonborg balked in the winning run in the top of the thirteenth inning," he remembered of his Major League baptism in Boston.[7]

Watt struck out slugger George "Boomer" Scott, who was also making his Major League debut, and got a couple of groundouts to finish the Orioles' victory. "That was the highlight of my career," he said forty-two years later. "That was the culmination of all my childhood dreams and wildest expectations, and they all came true on that one particular day."[8]

The Orioles seized control of the American League pennant race in July. When All-Star left-hander Steve Barber was hit by elbow tendinitis that limited him to just five innings pitched for more than two months, Watt replaced him in the starting rotation and did a solid job early on, sporting a 9-3 record and 3.26 ERA by mid-August when Baltimore's lead grew to 13 games. Watt began to experience swelling in his left knee, however, and he didn't retire a batter in his next start and lost his final four decisions. He finished the season back in the bullpen. Nevertheless, players polled selected Watt the second-best rookie hurler in the league in 1966, trailing only Kansas City's Jim Nash, who went 12-1 in half a season. The 97-win Orioles were headed to the first World Series in the team's history, and Watt and his fellow relievers were a big reason why. "[Manager Hank

Bauer] was very, very pleased with his bullpen. We had an excellent bullpen," Watt said. "We had Stu Miller, Eddie Fisher—both of whom were vastly experienced—Moe Drabowsky."[9]

Baltimore shocked much of the baseball world by sweeping the favored Dodgers to win the World Series. Orioles starting pitchers hurled three consecutive shutouts. Watt did not get into a game, but he and Miller warmed up a dozen times apiece during the Series. Watt's winner's share was $11,683.04. He returned home to Iowa and capped the year by finishing up his degree in education. He also earned teaching certificates for math and physical education, and helped prospective Baltimore police recruits for civil service exams they'd need to pass to enter the police academy.

Watt knew he would be a full-time reliever in 1967; Hank Bauer had made that perfectly clear when asked about it at an Orioles winter caravan. "As long as he had anything to do with the Baltimore Orioles, I would never start another game," Watt recalled. "That would have made some people unhappy, but it made me very, very happy."[10] Bauer was fired midway through the 1968 season, but Watt never started another game in the Majors.

In the first week of spring training in 1967, Watt suffered an eye hemorrhage and several broken facial bones when a ball struck him as he slid into third during a base-running drill. The prognosis was a six- to eight-week recovery when he finally went home after eight days in the hospital, unsure whether he'd be plagued by double vision or blurred version. Though sunlight continued to bother the eye, and exertion would occasionally lead to a nosebleed, Watt raced back and made his 1967 debut in the second week of the season. He insisted that his vision was okay, and if anybody doubted him, his 0.57 ERA in his first 14 appearances was reassuring. The Orioles slipped to a sixth-place finish after a series of injuries to their starting staff, but Watt held hitters to a .183 batting average in nearly 104 innings and led Baltimore pitchers in appearances (49) despite his late beginning.

Orioles shortstop Luis Aparicio managed the La Guaira Sharks in the Venezuelan League in the winter of 1967–68, and he invited Watt to make some money by pitching for him. With two young children, a mortgage on a Baltimore-area house that had belonged to former teammate Jerry Adair, and no World Series share that year, Watt agreed to go. Aparicio got a bargain. The pitcher who was content to work out of the Baltimore bullpen worked nearly 180 innings as a starting pitcher in Venezuela, going 12-1 with a 1.62 ERA to match Kansas City Athletics right-hander Diego Segui for the best mark in the league. Watt lost a playoff duel to Segui when outfielder Angel Bravo misjudged a line drive.

Back in the United States, Watt made a career-high 59 appearances in 1968, earning 11 saves with his 2.27 ERA, and allowing just one home run. Baltimore won 91 games but never made a serious charge, and after Bauer was fired, Earl Weaver took over the managerial reins at the All-Star break. Watt stayed in the Baltimore area that winter, making sixteen public relations speeches per month on the Orioles' behalf and working out twice a week at a local YMCA with coach Billy Hunter and some other players. Early in 1969 his third child, Tammy, was born.

Weaver admitted some concern when Watt reported to 1969 spring training late and battled control problems, but Watt soon assumed an important role on one of the strongest Major League teams ever. In the first season of divisional play, the Orioles went 109-53 and ran away with the first American League East crown, as Watt chipped in with a 1.65 ERA, 16 saves, and a 5-2 won-lost mark. Right-handed hitters batted a near helpless .140 against him in the regular season, but in the fifth and final game of the World Series a pair of

them, Cleon Jones and Ron Swoboda, doubled off him to produce the go-ahead run for the New York Mets. Swoboda scored another run when Baltimore first baseman Boog Powell fumbled a hard smash and Watt dropped his throw while covering first base. The Mets upset the Orioles' juggernaut in one of the most celebrated surprises in sports history.

The Orioles redeemed themselves, and earned their second World Series title in five years, by beating the Cincinnati Reds in 1970 after another dominant regular season. Watt led the pitching staff in appearances for the fourth straight year, and had a chance to close out another Orioles World Series sweep when Weaver called on him to protect a 5–3 eighth-inning lead in Game Four. Jim Palmer had put the tying runners aboard and catcher Elrod Hendricks called for a Watt sinker in hopes of inducing a double play. Instead, Watt, who hadn't pitched in two weeks, got the ball up. Lee May hit a three-run home run to give the Reds their only victory in the Series. Though the Orioles won the Series the next day, some Baltimore fans never forgave Watt for squandering Baltimore's chance to sweep the Big Red Machine. He heard boos while participating in a halftime contest at a Baltimore Bullets game shortly afterward, and some people never let up on him for the rest of his time in Baltimore.

Watt went to Vietnam in November 1970 for a USO tour with fellow Major Leaguers Willie Stargell and Jim "Mudcat" Grant and Pirates announcer Bob Prince. In 1971 he missed a month in midsummer after breaking his hand tagging Mickey Rivers at home plate, but he helped the Orioles win their third consecutive pennant by pacing Baltimore relievers in saves (11) and chalking up a 1.82 ERA. He saved Game One of the American League Championship Series against the Oakland Athletics and appeared twice in a seven-game World Series loss to the Pirates, getting tagged with the Game Four defeat in Pittsburgh. During

MALCOLM ALLEN

the off-season, he hurt his hand during an Orioles' goodwill exhibition tour of Japan.

By 1972 Watt was the elder statesman of the Baltimore relief corps, and he pitched in with a 2.17 ERA for a team undermined by a lack of offense after dealing away Frank Robinson. In July he married for the second time, to Betty Widhelm of Omaha, Nebraska. After the season he returned to Venezuela to serve as a pitching coach for the Aragua Tigers. Orioles coach Jim Frey managed the team, and he ended up using Watt on the mound often.

The next year began with a jolt when Watt's mother died of a heart attack during spring training. Though Watt pitched effectively and the Orioles made it back to the playoffs, he battled an infection near his thumbnail and lost his status as Earl Weaver's most trusted right-handed reliever to Bob Reynolds. Boos rained down when Watt struggled, sometimes with his wife and children in attendance, as some fans reminded him that one of his pitches had cost the Birds a chance to sweep the 1970 World Series. "May's homer ruined that," Watt acknowledged. "But it beats me why it continued. Maybe people thought booing me the thing to do."[11]

After the season he had surgery to remove cartilage and spurs from his troublesome left knee. On December 7, 1973, the Orioles sold Watt to the Phillies for a reported $70,000. Despite leading Philadelphia relievers with six saves in 1974, he struggled to get left-handers out and uncharacteristically had trouble throwing strikes. He pitched well in spring training the next season, but was unconditionally released the day before Opening Day, too late to catch on with another Major League club.

By now thirty-four years old, Watt was well aware that the end of his playing career was near. He called numerous teams and expressed his desire to remain in the game in some capacity even if he could no longer pitch. The Chicago Cubs found him a job on the mound with the Triple-A Wichita Aeros of the American Association. "There are 24 teams I'd rather be playing for," Watt said at the time. "And they all happen to be in the major leagues."[12]

He was the Aeros' top right-handed reliever in the first couple of months of 1975, and after a good start was back in the big leagues in early June. But Watt was scored on in five of six appearances for the Cubs, in what proved to be the final appearances of his Major League career. He was soon returned to Wichita.

He pitched again in Venezuela the next two winters and spent the next two summers in the bullpen for the Hawaii Islanders, going 10-7 in 68 games for the San Diego Padres' Triple-A affiliate in the Pacific Coast League. Watt kept going for two reasons: "One, I really enjoyed playing. Two, I thought that was the best way that I could stay in the game of baseball."[13] The Islanders finished first both years, but seemed to be falling out of the race late in 1977 until the day Watt threw the rosin bag to the plate instead of the baseball in the midst of a lengthy losing stretch. His teammates, all of them younger, spontaneously laughed at Watt's absurd delivery, and heated up to defend their division crown as well.

In 1978 the Padres made Watt manager of their Single-A Reno Silver Sox club in the California League, and save for a pair of appearances in blowouts that season, he became a full-time skipper for the next four seasons. After finishing twenty-three games behind the leader as a rookie manager, Watt led the Silver Sox to a first-place finish in 1979. He went away to winter ball then finished first again in 1980 when the Padres moved him up to manage the Amarillo Gold Sox, their Double-A Texas League entry. Watt missed a third straight division title when Amarillo finished a half-game back the following year.

He got out of managing and spent the rest of the 1980s working for the Phillies and the Houston Astros, before concluding his career with thirteen seasons in the Atlanta Braves organization during their lengthy run of playoff appearances. In all, Watt spent forty-one years in professional baseball, and estimated that he had dressed for as many as 280 games a year in some of the years in which he also went to winter ball.

"I truly enjoyed playing baseball. I truly enjoyed coaching baseball," he said. "I truly enjoyed being around it, and being around the young people that I was coaching and tried to develop. But the day I retired, which was January of 2003, I had no problem retiring, and have been very, very content."[14]

Watt and his wife Betty settled in North Bend, Nebraska, along the Platte River about fifty miles from either Lincoln or Omaha.

Chapter 24. **Merv Rettenmund**

Jacob Pomrenke

AGE	G	AB	R	H	2B	3B	HR	TB	RBI	BB	SO	BAV	OBP	SLG	SB	GDP	HBP
27	106	338	60	109	17	2	18	184	58	38	59	.322	.394	.544	13	8	3

Merv Rettenmund broke into the seemingly uncrackable Orioles outfield in 1970, hitting .322 in 106 games.

By his own account, Merv Rettenmund was a "scuffler" more than a ballplayer. He never found his niche as a regular starter with the Baltimore Orioles, but he starred as a supersub and was a key cog for the Orioles as they won three consecutive American League pennants, from 1969 to 1971. He twice led the team in batting average in those years while playing all three outfield positions. More than that, Rettenmund always seemed to find himself as part of a winner—the teams he was on, as a player and a coach, reached the postseason in 13 of his 33 seasons in Major League baseball (through 2008). He played in four World Series, winning championships in 1970 with the Orioles and in 1975 with the Cin-

cinnati Reds. Later, he became one of the game's top pinch-hitters with the San Diego Padres and California Angels.

After he retired, Rettenmund became one of the most respected hitting coaches in baseball, and he was on staff for three more World Series—with the Oakland Athletics in 1989 and 1990 and the San Diego Padres in 1998. He once called his job as a hitting coach "50 percent comedian, 25 percent psychologist, and 25 percent teacher," but his methods worked.[1] Led by Hall of Famer Tony Gwynn, who won half of his eight batting titles under the tutelage of Rettenmund, the Padres set franchise records in nearly every offensive category in the 1990s. In a rare move for a coach,

Rettenmund remained with the team through three managerial changes.

Mervin Weldon Rettenmund was born on June 6, 1943, in Flint, Michigan. His father, Weldon, worked for many years with General Motors, as did his uncle and Swiss-born grandfather. His mother, Dolores (nee Tucker), was from Carsonville, a small village in eastern Michigan. Dolores's grandfather had emigrated from England.[2]

Merv came from an athletic family. His mother and sister Susan both played softball. "There was always an opportunity to play," he recalled.[3] In his spare time, Weldon played baseball in semi-pro leagues around Flint, and he was good enough to earn a tryout with the Detroit Tigers. He turned down their contract offer, however, and "always regretted it." When Merv had his own chance to sign with the Tigers after high school, Weldon urged his son not to pass it up. But Merv opted for college instead.[4]

Baseball was always Merv's ambition. "I'd go to games at Tiger Stadium all the time, see those guys in their uniforms and watch them play," he recalled. "I thought, 'Gosh, I'd love to do that.'"[5] In addition to baseball, the speedy teenager also starred as a halfback in football at Southwestern High School in Flint.

After graduating from Southwestern in 1961, he spent the summer as a hard-hitting catcher on Michigan's top American Legion team, the Buick Colts. The Colts won city and state championships—Rettenmund hit .588 to earn the Kiki Cuyler Award as the state tournament MVP—and went on to play at a regional tournament in Princeton, Indiana. "That's the summer Merv really developed," said Legion teammate Wayne Schmitz, who later played in the Atlanta Braves organization. "Scouts wanted to sign him right then."[6]

During the Princeton tournament, Rettenmund was approached by Ray Louthen, the baseball and football coach at Ball State University in Muncie, Indiana. As Merv recalled: "I had been con-sidering Western Michigan or Michigan State—I was looking at them, but I don't know if they were looking at me, you know? . . . Ray Louthen came up to me [at Princeton] and said, 'If you'll come play for us, I'll give a scholarship to your cousin and to your friend.'" It was a football scholarship, Rettenmund said, "so they could bring more players in."[7] Merv took it.

At Ball State, Rettenmund broke the school's single-season rushing record held by Timmy Brown, who played for the Philadelphia Eagles and Baltimore Colts. Rettenmund was good enough to get drafted by the Dallas Cowboys—much to his surprise, because he had played just three games as a senior because of injuries. In baseball, he was a two-time All-Indiana Collegiate Conference first-team selection, hitting .321 in his career. He later became a charter member of the Ball State Athletics Hall of Fame.[8] In 1966, two years into his professional career, he earned his bachelor's degree in education.

Merv also met his wife, the former Susan Clark, at Ball State. She was from Findlay, Ohio, a Spanish major who would later accompany him on trips to Latin America and South America for winter ball when he was in the Minor Leagues. Travel always plays a major role in the life of a ballplayer, and Merv and Susan loved it. In the off-seasons, they began taking trips around the world—including a cruise to Antarctica. "The Red Sea, Jordan, Israel, Ireland . . . pretty much anywhere you can think of, we've been there," he said. The Rettenmunds married in 1964 and had their first child, Cyndi, in 1965. In 1970 they welcomed their second daughter, Christy.[9]

In November 1964, just a few weeks after Merv and Susan were married, Baltimore Orioles scout Jim Terrell signed Rettenmund as an amateur free agent, with a reported $15,000 bonus. He played two full seasons for Stockton of the Single-A California League. In 1966 he hit .307 with 21 home runs in 127 games to earn a spot on the California

League All-Star team. In 1967 he continued his ascent up the Minor League ladder by hitting .286 before a shoulder separation sidelined him late in the summer. That winter, he played in Venezuela and hit .313 for manager Luis Aparicio. Because of the injury, he said, "I couldn't lift my arm. But the one thing it did was it cut my swing down. I think it was the turning point of my career. I really became a good hitter."[10]

As a result, Rettenmund made the 1968 Orioles roster out of spring training. His Major League debut came on April 14, when he struck out as a pinch-hitter against the Angels' Clyde Wright to end the game. He made three more appearances that week, getting two hits and walking once, before being sent down to Triple-A Rochester when pitcher Pete Richert was activated from National Guard duty. In Rochester, the sweet-swinging right-hander flourished, hitting .331 with 22 home runs to earn International League MVP and Rookie of the Year honors, as well as *The Sporting News'* Minor League Player of the Year award. When outfielder Curt Motton was injured in late August, Rettenmund was called up to Baltimore for good.

Three days after Rettenmund's call-up, he was sent in to pinch-hit for Ellie Hendricks in the bottom of the ninth inning. He homered on the first pitch he saw from Oakland reliever Warren Bogle to beat the A's, 5–3.[11] Rettenmund batted .265 in the final month as manager Earl Weaver moved him up and down the lineup. He was a valuable utility man for the Orioles in their championship years, but he never settled into a regular position.

There was no room for a rookie outfielder to break into Baltimore's lineup. Future Hall of Famer Frank Robinson, who had won the American League's Triple Crown in 1966, held down the fort in right field, while Paul Blair was considered the game's best defensive center fielder and Don Buford was a solid starter in left field. In the 1969 World Series against the upstart New York Mets, Rettenmund made his only appearance as a pinch-

runner in a Game Two loss. The Orioles lost the Series in five games, in one of baseball's biggest postseason upsets.

By 1970, Rettenmund's ability was getting hard to ignore. Preseason work with batting coach Jim Frey turned him into a stronger hitter to the opposite field, and he got off to a hot start, hitting .333 in April. But he still couldn't break into the lineup as an everyday starter. So Rettenmund became the Orioles' "noble substitute," spelling the regular outfielders when they were tired or slumping. It took an injury to Paul Blair, who was hit in the face by a pitch on May 31, to finally give Rettenmund the chance to start. He did not take it lightly. "We expected to win every game," he recalled. "It was not a showcase [for prospects]. You were expected to produce."[12]

Rettenmund did. During the second half of the season, he batted a blazing .373, hitting safely in 16 of 17 games between July 26 and August 15. He had three four-hit games in a five-week span, finishing the year with 18 home runs and a team-high .322 average. In the league playoff with the Twins he started the second game and played well—he walked twice, stole a base, and had an RBI single in the ninth inning of a tight game, and the Orioles swept the series. In the World Series, he did not get a chance to start until Game Five, and he did not learn of this until late in the Orioles' Game Four loss.

"I was sitting in the manager's office during that [eighth] inning," he recalled. "You can see the game better that way, you can get a better view on TV than you can from the dugout. I watched [Lee] May hit his home run and Earl comes running in. Boy, is he pissed. He starts yelling. 'Get your feet off that damn desk! Get your ass out of this office! . . . Oh, and by the way, you're starting tomorrow!' That's how I found out I was playing.'"[13]

Rettenmund made the most of his opportunity. In the third inning, after the Orioles had taken a 4–3 lead, he singled home Boog Powell and then scored on Dave Johnson's RBI single with one out. In the fifth, he capped off the Orioles' World Series–clinching victory with a long home run down the right-field line off Tony Cloninger. The Orioles cruised from there, winning 9–3, and celebrated the franchise's second championship deep into the night. "It's a moment you'd like to have kept the rest of your career," Rettenmund recalled. "You think it'll never end. . . . I was thinking, after winning all those pennants, that in spring training what we were doing was getting our pitchers ready for the playoffs, you know? We thought that's how it would always be."[14]

Rettenmund's confidence was sky-high. Teammate Mark Belanger liked to say then, "Merv always says two things in life are certain: There will be snow in the winter and I'll get my two hits." Second baseman Dave Johnson recalled the quote a little differently: "Death, taxes and my three hits."[15]

Whatever the case, the twenty-eight-year-old Rettenmund continued to hit like a machine in 1971—leading the team again with a .318 average, good for third in the American League behind Tony Oliva and Bobby Murcer—no doubt helped by the fact that he finally was receiving steady playing time in the Orioles' lineup, even if he was never sure which position he would play until he got to the ballpark. Rettenmund started 58 games in right field, 38 in left field, and 37 in center field, but logged more innings (1,170) than any other Orioles outfielder. At the plate, he set career highs with 75 RBIS, 81 runs, 15 stolen bases, and 491 at bats in 141 games. His performance earned him a few MVP votes at the end of the year as the Orioles swept the Oakland A's to clinch the AL pennant.

In the 1971 World Series, Rettenmund earned a spot in the Orioles' lineup as Baltimore prepared to defend its title against the Pittsburgh Pirates. His three-run home run off Dock Ellis in the third inning of Game One proved to be just enough of a margin for Dave McNally, who shut down the Pirates on three hits, but the Orioles ultimately fell in seven games.

Surprisingly, the Orioles relieved the crowded outfield by dealing Frank Robinson, their biggest star and leader, to the Los Angeles Dodgers in November. With Robinson gone, Rettenmund inherited the starting job in right field and got the chance to play regularly. But injuries plagued him from the beginning. During a four-hit day in Detroit, he dove for a ball and landed awkwardly on his right shoulder. The next day, he couldn't lift his arm. In August, he suffered a torn abdominal muscle and was placed on the disabled list.[16] In between, he suddenly, inexplicably lost the ability to hit.

His batting average fell below .300 on the season's second day, and it never returned. By the end of the year, Rettenmund was hitting .233— an 89-point drop from his team-leading average in 1969. He couldn't figure it out. One theory suggested that Weaver put extra pressure on Rettenmund to supply the Orioles' power with Boog Powell and Brooks Robinson getting older and Frank Robinson no longer around. So Rettenmund tried to change his stance to pull the ball and hit more home runs—then made other variations such as keeping his bat still and holding his hands lower— and all the adjustments disrupted his swing. Years later, Rettenmund explained his slump this way: "I had a weird swing. And when it was broke, I knew what was wrong and everybody could tell me how to fix it, but I just couldn't fix it."[17]

He dismissed the idea that Weaver played a role in the slump, explaining that he was too easily satisfied as a young player: "You cause these things yourself. I had two goals when I started playing. One, to be a .300 hitter in the Major Leagues, and two, to make X number of dollars. . . . That's all I wanted to do. And after two years in the Majors, I had been doing everything I wanted to do. I didn't have any more goals and I didn't know how to set any more goals. I got myself in a mental rut."[18]

Rettenmund got off to a poor start in 1973, hitting .230 before the All-Star break, and after severely bruising his chest crashing into the outfield wall in Kansas City in May, he lost his job in right field. After a one-year hiatus from the postseason, the Orioles were rolling along to another division title. The club benefited from a powerful farm system that continued to produce strong outfield prospects—before, it had been Blair, Buford, and Rettenmund; now, Don Baylor, Al Bumbry, and Rich Coggins were muscling in for more playing time. When Rettenmund's slump continued in the playoffs, in which he hit .091 in a losing effort against the Oakland A's, he too was deemed expendable.

Rettenmund was given a fresh start with the Cincinnati Reds, who traded for the thirty-year-old in a five-player deal that sent pitcher Ross Grimsley to Baltimore in December 1973. Merv seemed pleased to go from one winning franchise to another, but moving to the National League did not help his hitting get back on track.

In two seasons with the Reds, he batted just .227 and drove himself deeper into despair at the plate. He later said the slump also carried over to his outfield play—"I got to dropping fly balls, which I never did"—and it even affected him driving to the ballpark. "I put so much pressure on myself in Cincinnati," Rettenmund said, adding that it got so bad that he took to swinging at the first pitch in nearly every at bat "so they wouldn't have time to put my average on the scoreboard!" After making three pinch-hit appearances in the 1975 World Series, he was dumped to San Diego in a trade during spring training the following year. He and Terry Crowley, his old friend and teammate who was sent to the Atlanta Braves the same week, celebrated by taking a joyride all around the Reds' practice field in Tampa, Florida.[19]

In the sunny climate of Southern California, and no longer fighting to start every day, Rettenmund began to relax and enjoy the game. And just as suddenly as it began, his debilitating slump seemed to be far behind him. "I could hit fine," he said. "I could hit the curve ball. I was pinch-hitting and having success at it. . . . I started having fun again." In 1977 he became one of the league's top specialists—setting a Padres franchise record with 21 pinch-hits in 67 at bats and setting two National League records as a pinch hitter, by walking 16 times and appearing in 86 games.[20]

Rettenmund signed as a free agent with the California Angels in 1978 and was an asset off the bench, hitting the first pinch-hit grand slam in team history on May 6. In 1979 he helped the Angels to their first postseason appearance by hitting .263 in 76 at-bats. In the ALCS that year, he returned to Baltimore along with three other former Orioles—Don Baylor, Bobby Grich, and Larry Harlow—to face their old team, still piloted by Earl Weaver, whom Rettenmund has called the smartest manager he knew in baseball. "The only way to measure a manager is by how his guys produced for him, and guys *played* for Weav," he recalled.[21] Weaver's players outperformed Rettenmund's Angel teammates in the playoffs, winning Baltimore's fourth and final pennant for the Hall of Fame manager. Rettenmund was limited to just four plate appearances in the ALCS.

That offseason, Rettenmund began to consider life after playing baseball. His education degree made him well-suited for teaching, and coaching was the next best thing. For years, he had helped his teammates—many of them among the best in the game—tinker with their swings, observing what worked and what didn't to develop his own philosophies on hitting.

More than most coaches, hitting coaches work in almost total obscurity. Rettenmund often said that his work ended when the game began, having spent most of his day under the stands in the batting cages or the video room tutoring players.[22] But his reputation as a hitting coach over three decades did not escape notice.

After retiring as a player in 1980, Rettenmund joined the Angels' coaching staff under manager Jim Fregosi. With California—and later the Texas Rangers and the Oakland A's in the 1980s—his primary responsibility was to work in the farm system, teaching young prospects in the Minor Leagues how to improve their focus and discipline at the plate. But when his old teammate Don Baylor was in a 3-for-65 slump in 1981, Rettenmund was asked to help. Said manager Gene Mauch, "Merv came in . . . and both [Bobby] Grich and Baylor went crazy with the bat. If there's any connection to having him here and what we did . . . he's got to be the greatest hitting instructor there is."[23]

In 1989, after serving three years as Oakland's roving hitting instructor, he moved up to become Tony La Russa's hitting coach with the A's, who won pennants in both years Rettenmund was on the coaching staff. Rettenmund maintained that the 1989 A's were the best team he'd ever seen, better even than the two championship teams he played on, the 1970 Orioles and the 1975 Reds.

"That team had thunder, and tons of speed. Oh man, they were loaded," he said of the A's dynasty. "The Orioles had pitching and defense, but they didn't have the thunder. The Reds had thunder and they had the speed. . . . The difference is, the A's had four quality starters and [Dennis] Eckersley waiting in the bullpen. The Reds always worried about pitching."[24]

Rettenmund's third World Series ring, he said, was more satisfying than the two he had earned as a player. "That's when you finally realize how difficult it is," he said. "[As a player], the game was easy. But [winning], it's not always going to happen like that."[25]

In 1991 Rettenmund returned to San Diego—the city he and Susan had made their permanent home since he was traded there more than a decade earlier—as a hitting coach with the Padres. He began working with then four-time batting champi-

on Tony Gwynn, or, as Merv liked to call him: "the 'man with the little hands,' the greatest hitter I've ever seen."[26]

It was a match made in hitting heaven. Gwynn had battled injuries on the field and dissension off it to hit for one of the lowest averages of his career, .309, in 1990. Rettenmund, a gregarious personality who was easy to talk to and loved to discuss hitting as much as Gwynn did, helped the pudgy outfielder reach new heights for the rest of the decade. The future Hall of Famer never hit below .317 again and won four consecutive batting titles from 1994 through 1997 to tie Honus Wagner's National League record with eight in his career.

Rettenmund said the most amazing quality about Gwynn was his consistency: "We'd hit off the tee every day. I think there were years when he hit off the tee 365 times. . . . And he never ducked a pitcher. Some guys will take a day off against a Randy Johnson. Tony would be in there every time." He added that he rarely discussed mechanics with Gwynn, knowing full well that the only time Gwynn stopped hitting was when his knee was hurting.[27]

Other Padres also benefited from the new hitting coach, among them Steve Finley, Ken Caminiti, and Gary Sheffield, the latter of whom made a run at the Triple Crown in 1992 (he won his only batting title, but finished third and fifth, respectively, in home runs and RBIs). Rettenmund said the nine years he spent with San Diego were the best times of his career.[28]

After leaving the Padres in 1999, he bounced around with three organizations (Atlanta, Detroit, and Toronto) before returning to the San Diego coaching staff in mid-2006. Instantly, the Padres—who ranked last in hitting, runs, and home runs at the time—began a surge to the NL West division title. "That was one of the most gratifying years I've ever had," Rettenmund said. "And I know better than to think it was just because of my presence. But that was very gratifying."[29]

Rettenmund was fired partway through the 2007 season, and, after more than four decades in baseball and in his mid-sixties, he said he didn't plan to get back into full-time coaching again. In between trips around the world with his wife and spending time with his grandchildren, he offered private hitting instruction to youths in the San Diego area. He occasionally attended Padres games at nearby Petco Park—"I like to watch. But I like it more when they score some runs!" he said of his offensively challenged former team.[30]

He said he has as much energy as ever. "I feel great, I'm exercising a lot," Rettenmund said. "I might get back in one day, but not at the big-league level. . . . I'd go help out at spring training, evaluate some guys in camp, something like that. I still love it."[31]

Chapter 25. **June 1970 Timeline**

Malcolm Allen

All headlines below are from the next day's edition of the *Baltimore Sun*.

June 1—No game scheduled.

June 2—ORIOLES DEFEAT A'S BEHIND PALMER, 5–1—Jim Palmer stroked three hits to match his career high and held the A's to just five hits in a complete game, nine-strikeout performance in the series opener at Oakland.

June 3—A'S DEFEAT ORIOLES ON BANDO'S HOMER—Frank Robinson blasted his first homer in 3½ weeks, off Rollie Fingers, to tie the game in the seventh, but the outcome was determined an inning later when Sal Bando drove a Mike Cuellar offering over the center-field fence with two aboard to provide Oakland's final 4–1 margin.

June 4—HOME RUNS HELP A'S BEAT ORIOLES, 4 TO 2—The Orioles lost consecutive series for the first time all season by dropping a 4–2 decision to Catfish Hunter. Frank Fernandez and Sal Bando took Baltimore pitchers deep for the second straight game, and Tom Phoebus lost his status as the AL ERA leader in addition to the game.

June 5—ORIOLES NIP BREWERS WITH HOMERS, 3–2—With Paul Blair still in the hospital recuperating from his beaning, the Orioles were infuriated by Milwaukee pitcher Bobby Bolin's brushback pitches. Frank Robinson was nearly hit in the head before getting drilled in the body, Davey Johnson was spun by a pitch behind his back, Don Buford was decked, and Brooks Robinson saw a pitch sail over his head. Nevertheless, the Orioles won their first-ever game at County Stadium in Milwaukee thanks to homers from Elrod Hendricks and Merv Rettenmund and some outstanding relief work from Eddie Watt.

June 6—BREWERS SPILL ORIOLES BY 6–4—On a sunny, 68-degree day described as "perfect baseball weather,"[1] Baltimore dropped the only game they'd lose at County Stadium all year. Jim Palmer failed to last at least five innings for the only time all season, and the Birds lost to former Oriole Gene Brabender.

June 7—BIRDS EDGE MILWAUKEE ON HOMERS—On a humid, 83-degree day when Mike Cuellar served up two more dingers to take over the league lead in that dubious category, the Orioles wrapped up their road trip on a winning note. Boog Powell completed back-to-back homers with Frank Robinson in the fourth with a 450-foot blast that was caught cleanly by backup catcher Clay Dalrymple in the Baltimore bullpen. In the ninth Powell's diving stop to corral an errant relay from Davey Johnson helped Eddie Watt preserve a 7–6 lead.

June 8—While Earl Weaver attended the funeral of his mother-in-law, Billy Hunter managed the Orioles to a 7–4 triumph in an exhibition game at Connie Mack Stadium in Philadelphia to benefit sandlot baseball.

June 9—ANGEL BATS CLIP BIRDS IN 11TH, 7–5—Baltimore coughed up leads in the seventh and eighth innings in their first home game in nearly two weeks but forced the game into extra innings on Elrod Hendricks's two-run double off ex-Oriole Eddie Fisher in the bottom of the ninth. Fisher got credit for a win, however, when Angels third baseman Ken McMullen took Dick Hall deep in extra innings.

June 10—JIM PALMER HURLS BIRDS TO 2–1 WIN —Jim Palmer hurled his eighth complete game of the season to tie for the Major League lead, earning his eighth win by outpitching California's Clyde Wright. After the Angels' Jay Johnstone tied the game at 1–1 with a two-out homer in the top of the seventh, Merv Rettenmund tripled home Don Buford with the game-winner in the bottom of the inning.

June 11—BIRDS BANG 4 HOMERS TO ROUT ANGELS —Mike Cuellar held California to two hits and an unearned run by getting thirteen ground-ball outs, and four of the six hits by the Orioles' offense went over the fence. There was plenty to cheer about in a 9–1 Orioles victory at Memorial Stadium, but a second-inning single by Mark Belanger to snap a 0-for-33 drought brought the fans to their feet as much as anything.

June 12—BIRDS DROP 4-2 VERDICT TO A'S IN 11— After a nineteen-minute rain delay before the first pitch, Tom Phoebus surrendered a pair of home runs in the opening inning, including one by Oakland's leadoff man, Bert Campaneris. Baltimore came back to force extra innings but lost when Campy and Reggie Jackson stroked run-scoring doubles off Eddie Watt.

June 13—A'S WALLOP ORIOLES ON 5 HOMERS— Considering that starting pitchers Dave McNally and Catfish Hunter were tied for the league lead in wins, this hardly seemed like the night two teams would tie the record for homers in a game at Memorial Stadium, but that's exactly what happened.

Unfortunately for the Orioles, they hit only two of the seven long balls in the contest, and Hunter earned his tenth win, 10–7, as Oakland beat the Orioles for the fourth time in five tries.

June 14—BIRDS EDGE A'S, 4–2, ON MAY HOMER— Jim Palmer worked all ten innings on a Sunday afternoon to salvage a game in the series. Palmer's RBI single in the second appeared to be the game-winning hit until he allowed a pair of two-out runs in the eighth, but Dave May (who didn't even start) made him a victor with a two-run walk-off blast to right against Fred Talbot in the bottom of the tenth.

June 15—BIRDS DROP 9–6 CONTEST TO BREWERS —Milwaukee's Bobby Bolin continued to use Baltimore hitters for target practice, knocking down Frank Robinson and Davey Johnson, but Merv Rettenmund exacted a measure of revenge with a first-inning grand slam. The Orioles made the early lead stand up until the eighth, but four Baltimore pitchers flushed it away in a six-run inning for the Brewers. Roberto Pena's three-run double off Pete Richert did most of the damage. Johnson's thirteen-game hitting streak came to an end when he left the game after just one inning with a sprained index finger on his throwing hand. No Oriole would record a longer streak in 1970.

June 16—The game against the Brewers was rained out in Baltimore, but the Orioles made two trades. Right-hander Moe Drabowsky was reacquired from the Royals for infielder Bobby Floyd, while Dave May was shipped over to the visiting clubhouse to join the Brewers in exchange for right-handed pitchers Dick Baney and Buzz Stephen. Neither Baney nor Stephen ever got into a game for Baltimore, but Drabowsky would go 4-2 with a save in twenty-one relief appearances the rest of the way.

June 17—MILWAUKEE WINS BY 5–1 FROM BIRDS—
Ex-Oriole Gene Brabender improved to 2-0
against Baltimore (versus 1-8 against the rest of the
league) in a 5–1 win for the Brewers. The game-
winning RBI came on Dave May's sixth-inning
sacrifice fly, and Mike Hegan put the game out of
reach an inning later with a three-run homer off
Dave McNally.

June 18—No game scheduled for the Orioles,
but Baltimore's division lead decreased to just 1½
games when the Yankees edged Boston 3–2.

June 19—13TH INNING TALLY GIVES BIRDS PAIR—
Boog Powell had four hits and stole his only base
of 1970 as the O's roared out to a 12-4 lead in
the opener of a doubleheader against the Senators. Baltimore held on to win 12–10, despite an
eight-RBI performance from former Oriole Mike
Epstein. In the nightcap, Jim Hardin was one out
from a complete-game victory when a homer by
the Senators' Bernie Allen sent the game into extra innings. Just a few minutes before midnight, in
the bottom of the thirteenth, Merv Rettenmund's
two-out single up the middle caromed off the glove
of diving Senators shortstop Eddie Brinkman, and
Davey Johnson raced home with the winning run.
Rettenmund rapped five homers and drove in sixteen runs in the eighteen games he started in center after Paul Blair was beaned.

June 20—ROBINSON'S 2,000TH HIT BEATS NATS—
Boog Powell powered a two-run homer off Washington's Joe Coleman in the opening inning, and
Brooks Robinson added a three-run shot off the
son of the 1954 Oriole of the same name four innings later. Brooksie's blast was the 2,000th hit of
his illustrious career. Five runs were just enough
for Mike Cuellar, who pitched into the ninth before Pete Richert came on to get the last out of Baltimore's 5–4 win.

June 21—BIRDS WIN, 4-2, SWEEP SENATORS—
Dave McNally's 100th career win, his tenth of
the season, came courtesy of a trio of looping pop
singles to shallow right that drove in runs. Davey Johnson lined up behind the second-base bag
to defend Frank Howard with two aboard in the
Senators' fifth, and it proved to be perfect position
to start an inning-ending double play. Perhaps the
best news of all was the return of Paul Blair as a
pinch-hitter in the sixth, three weeks to the day after his frightening beaning.

June 22—BIRD RALLY IN 9TH NIPS BOSOX, 9–8—
Paul Blair returned to the starting lineup in a nationally televised affair at Fenway Park with three
hits and an outstanding catch against the wall in
left-center. Baltimore fell behind 6–0 in the first
when errors by both Brooks and Frank Robinson
led to four unearned runs, but the team fought
back to tie on homers by Curt Motton and Chico
Salmon in the seventh. The Red Sox regained the
lead entering the ninth, but reliever Cal Koonce
made the mistake of walking Brooks to load the
bases for Frank Robinson. Frank pulled a two-run
double into left to make it 9–8 Orioles, and that's
just how it ended when Eddie Watt caught George
Scott looking at a called third strike with the tying run in scoring position. The Birds won despite
leaving sixteen runners stranded, a season high for
a nine-inning game.

June 23—CULP STOPS ORIOLES ON 3-HITTER—
Jim Palmer had already beaten Ray Culp twice in
1970, but this time the Red Sox righty held the upper hand as Boston won 5–1. Baltimore managed
just three singles and one unearned run, while
Palmer was pounded for a season-high twelve hits,
including back-to-back homers by Tony Conigliar-
o and Rico Petrocelli.

June 24—bosox edge orioles on 5-run rally—The
Orioles hit three homers in a span of four hitters—

MALCOLM ALLEN

including back-to-back blasts by Paul Blair and Frank Robinson—and carried a 5–1 lead into the bottom of the seventh inning. Four pitchers combined to turn the lead into a deficit, with Dick Schofield's three-run triple off Eddie Watt proving most costly. Schofield was in the lineup because regular starter Mike Andrews suffered back spasms while picking his kids up from school earlier in the day.

June 25—ORIOLES COME FROM BEHIND, SUBDUE BOSOX IN 14 INNINGS—Five innings into the series finale at Fenway, the Birds trailed 7–0 and had little to cheer about beyond Don Buford's record-tying two outfield assists in the same inning. Frank Robinson and Davey Johnson homered in the sixth, though, Merv Rettenmund added another in the ninth, and suddenly the game was tied on Andy Etchebarren's two-out double. The Red Sox nearly prevailed in the bottom of the thirteenth, but Frank Robinson made a leaping, game-saving catch down the right-field line to rob Reggie Smith of a homer. "It's just such plays that give you an idea what being super is all about," marveled Earl Weaver.[2] Robinson got back up after a few minutes, but could barely swing a bat due to back spasms after painfully bruising himself along the beltline. So he bunted for a base hit with the bases loaded as part of Baltimore's six-run rally in the fourteenth. The final score was 13–8. The Orioles utilized twenty-two players, pounded a season-high twenty-one hits, and helped establish a club record with thirty-nine hits between the two teams. Moe Drabowsky pitched the last five innings for his first victory since rejoining the Birds.

June 26—FRANK'S BAT LIFTS BIRDS TO 12–2 WIN—After staying up until 4 A.M. taking care of his seven-year-old son's fever, Frank Robinson sure didn't look like a tired man with a bad back. At RFK Stadium in Washington, he hammered his first and second grand slams as an Oriole, becom-

ing just the seventh Major Leaguer with two in a game and the third to do it in consecutive innings. His fifth-inning shot off Joe Coleman went 390 feet to the base of the scoreboard, and his bomb off Joe Grzenda in the sixth went 462 feet into the upper deck in left-center.

June 27—SENATORS END ORIOLES 7-GAME DOMINATION, 5–3, WITH RALLY IN 8TH—Jim Palmer walked six and surrendered nine hits in 7⅓ innings but still handed off a one-run lead to the Baltimore bullpen. Washington nearly tied the game on Aurelio Rodriguez's double in the seventh, but Baltimore catcher Clay Dalrymple stood his ground against an incoming Mike Epstein to catch the relay from shortstop Mark Belanger and apply the tag. Dalrymple was lost for the season after breaking his ankle in the ensuing collision, but incredibly, he held on to the ball. Manager Earl Weaver called it one of the best plays he'd ever seen a catcher make. The Senators loaded the bases in the eighth, though, and pinch-hitter Wayne Comer greeted Eddie Watt with a three-run double down the right-field line to lead the Senators to victory.

June 28—REICHARDT'S HOMER NIPS BIRDS, 4–3—The Orioles and Senators remained tied through eleven innings on a Sunday afternoon, thanks to some nifty relief work by Moe Drabowsky to escape a pair of bases-loaded jams. Paul Blair raced home from second base to break the deadlock in the top of the twelfth when Washington first baseman Mike Epstein dropped what should've been the final out of the inning, and it seemed as if Baltimore had caught a lucky break. Their fortunes reversed quickly in the bottom of the frame, however. After Dick Hall issued only his second unintentional walk of the season to start the inning, Eddie Watt came on with one out and surrendered his first long ball of the season, a two-run, game-winning blast by Rick Reichardt.

June 29—RODRIGUEZ BELT BEATS BIRDS, 5–3—
In the makeup game for the rainout of May 17, the
Orioles blew a lead for the third straight day and
suffered their first three-game losing streak since
the middle of April. Mike Cuellar pitched well other than a pair of pitches, but Frank Howard's two-
run homer in the first and Aurelio Rodriguez's
three-run blast with two outs in the eighth were
enough to beat him, 5–3.

June 30—TWO POWELL HOMERS FEATURE ORI-
OLE WIN—The Orioles returned home after a 3-5
road trip with their American League East lead
over the Yankees down to two games. Baltimore
bombed Indians rookie Steve Dunning for three
home runs—two of them off the bat of Boog Powell—and Dave McNally went the distance for his
league-leading twelfth win as the Birds won 4–2
to finish June with a winning record (14-13). International League batting leader Bobby Grich, recalled the previous day after Clay Dalrymple's injury and Chico Salmon having twisted his left knee
in Boston, lined a single to right for his first Major League hit.

AL East Standings, June 30:

Team	W	L	GB
Baltimore	47	28	—
New York	43	30	3.0
Detroit	38	33	7.0
Boston	34	36	10.5
Washington	34	40	12.5
Cleveland	32	39	13.0

Chapter 26. **Frank Robinson**

Maxwell Kates

AGE	G	AB	R	H	2B	3B	HR	TB	RBI	BB	SO	BAV	OBP	SLG	SB	GDP	HBP
34	132	471	88	144	24	1	25	245	78	69	70	.306	.398	.520	2	13	7

Frank Robinson would not want to be remembered as a racial pioneer. He would prefer to be immortalized as a baseball player who practiced his craft to the best of his ability in the field and at the plate. Robinson knew from a young age that he would face his share of obstacles in life. Rather than allow them to define him, he channeled his frustrations to improve his playing abilities and develop his character as a leader of men. Robinson earned the respect of teammates, opponents, and spectators alike. Jim Palmer described him as "the best player I ever saw"; to Duane Kuiper, he was "the best manager I ever played for"; Jim Kaat, who surrendered Robinson's 400th home run in 1967, recalled that "if you got him out with a pitch, he'd eventually hit that pitch, so you had to constantly change your pattern with him"; and finally, as Orioles historian Ted Patterson remembered, "the Orioles rarely lost with [Robinson] out there"[1]

The youngest of Ruth Shaw's ten children, Frank Robinson entered the world on August 31, 1935, in a Beaumont, Texas, hospital. Though named after his father, he saw little of the elder Frank Robinson. After young Frank's parents divorced in his infancy, his mother moved the family to California. The family settled first in Alameda, then in West Oakland. From his absentee father, Robinson received a sense of determination that would shape his career. When he told Frank's brothers that Frank "will never make a big-league baseball player," the future outfielder became determined to prove his father wrong.[2]

Robinson was raised in ethnically diverse tenement dwellings.[3] Though he never felt deprived, he later lamented that "all got along [but] few got

Twice the league MVP, Frank Robinson was still a dangerous hitter in 1970 for the Orioles.

ahead."[4] The most direct ticket from West Oakland to the American Dream was by staying out of trouble, which for Robinson meant sports. He spent virtually every spare moment of his childhood playing baseball, football, or basketball. It was a competitive atmosphere that also developed Vada Pinson, Curt Flood, and basketball legend Bill Russell.

In 1949 Robinson met George Powles, a legendary local baseball and basketball coach. Although he had yet to turn fourteen, Robinson earned a spot on Powles's American Legion team, the Bill

Erwin Post 237. Through Powles's instruction on "how to think baseball," Robinson overcame his shyness with an instilled sense of confidence. In 1950 he contributed to the local championship with a clutch triple only days after his fifteenth birthday. After graduating from McClymonds High School in 1953, Robinson was signed to a $3,500 contract by Cincinnati Reds superscout Bobby Mattick.

Robinson began his professional career as a seventeen-year-old at Class C Ogden (Utah), where he first experienced institutionalized racism. In a state where "the Mormon religion insisted that Negroes were inferior human beings," no restaurant or movie house allowed black patronage.[5] After driving in 83 runs in 72 games and batting .348 for Ogden, Robinson was promoted to Tulsa (Oklahoma) in 1954 before accepting a reassignment to Single-A Columbia. Although life in the capital of South Carolina was segregated, Robinson remembered it to have been "much better than in Ogden."[6] Road trips in the Deep South offered racial jeering on the field and trying travel conditions away from the ballpark. Robinson hit .336 with 25 home runs for Columbia in 1954, not enough to avoid a return to the city in 1955. A shoulder injury slowed his progress (.263 in 80 games), but he recovered and earned a promotion to Cincinnati in 1956.

In 1956 the Redlegs awoke from eleven consecutive losing seasons by clobbering the opposition with 221 home runs en route to a sterling 91-63 record. Leading the way with 38 homers was Robinson, the rookie left fielder. At age twenty, Robinson also drove in 83 runs while batting .290, earning a ticket to the All-Star Game and the Rookie of the Year Award. Shaking off the sophomore jinx, he improved his batting average to .322 in 1957. In 1958 he slipped to .269, but in 1959 he drove in 125 runs with 36 homers while batting .311.

As Earl Weaver described years later, "Nobody had more guts at the plate than Frank. . . . He actually curled his upper body and head over the plate and dared pitchers to hit him."[7] National League pitchers, particularly Don Drysdale, were only too glad to oblige. In ten years with Cincinnati, Robinson was hit by a pitch 118 times. On the other hand, his slides into bases were "deliberately vicious," and he often spiked infielders to break up the double play.[8] One notorious incident occurred on August 15, 1960. Tagged out by Milwaukee's Eddie Mathews, Robinson slid hard into third base, prompting a gruesome fistfight between the future Hall of Famers.[9]

By 1961 Robinson had moved to right field. It was a surprising season as the Reds propelled themselves to a National League championship. Robinson produced typical offensive numbers for him, batting .323 while hitting 37 home runs and driving in 124 runs. For his efforts, he was named the National League Most Valuable Player. It was a monumental year for Robinson off the field as well, as he met Barbara Ann Cole on a road trip to Los Angeles in August. Two months later, on October 28, 1961, the two were married. Robinson improved on his numbers in 1962, hitting a career-high .342 as he belted an eye-catching 51 doubles and drove in 136 runs with 39 homers.

Robinson rounded out his decade as Cincinnati's franchise player in 1965 with 33 home runs to match his 33 doubles and 113 runs batted in, good for a respectable batting average of .296. Despite Robinson's record as the best run-producer in Cincinnati's history, owner Bill DeWitt perceived him as "a fading talent increasingly hobbled by leg injuries."[10] In addition, a 1961 incident at a Cincinnati diner resonated only too clearly in DeWitt's memory. When taunted by a short-order cook, Robinson brandished a .25 caliber Baretta in his direction; unbeknownst to Robinson, two policemen witnessed the altercation from across the street and promptly arrested the outfielder.[11] In words he would come to regret, Dewitt described Robinson as "an old 30."[12] On December 9, 1965, Robinson was traded to the Orioles for pitchers Milt Pappas and Jack Baldschun, and outfielder Dick Simpson.

"My mind went blank when the trade was announced," recalled Robinson. "But when I thought about it, I changed my thinking. . . . I did not feel I had anything to prove, yet I wanted to prove to Bill DeWitt that I was not done at age 30."[13] Any misgivings about the trade dissipated when one Baltimore player, a white man from Little Rock, Arkansas, welcomed their new teammate to the ballclub. "Frank," exclaimed Brooks Robinson, "you're exactly what we need." Dave McNally later described his initial impression to John Eisenberg: "As good as Frank was, it was how hard he played that really made an impact. . . . The intensity the man had was just incredible." The Orioles had a lot of talent, but to manager Hank Bauer, "Robinson was "the missing cog" who "helped the young players just by talking to them."[14]

The Robinson family, which now included son Kevin and daughter Nichelle, received a rude welcome to Baltimore on a house-hunting trip early in the season. A university professor had been enthusiastic to sublet his house until he met Barbara. As she recounted years later, "He must have thought I was Mrs. *Brooks* Robinson." After days of discouragement, the Robinsons finally rented a home—"grimy and infested with bugs, its floors covered with dog [mess]." Frank was not without a sense of humor on the racial situation. When a reporter could not distinguish him from Brooks, he chided, "Can't you see we wear different numbers?"[15]

Although the Orioles steamrolled to win twelve of their first fifteen games, they found themselves in second place behind the surprising Cleveland Indians. When the Tribe visited Baltimore in early May, they split the first two games before the Orioles won the opener of a Sunday doubleheader. In the second game of that May 8 twin bill, Robinson rose to the occasion. His opponent was Cleveland's Luis Tiant, fresh off three consecutive shutouts. Battling a chronic shoulder injury, Robinson kept his arms high and swung his bat on a first-pitch fastball, crushing the ball 540 feet, the only fair ball ever hit out of Memorial Stadium. A crowd of 49,516 serenaded Robinson with an ovation; as he later told Al Silverman, "I felt I was at home." The Orioles won the contest, 8–3, and had tied the Indians for first place. Moe Drabowsky described the homer as "the big one in the season" as "it galvanized the whole team."[16]

Harmony nearly bred calamity as Robinson averted drowning at a private party in August. Perhaps as a byproduct of institutionalized racism in Oakland to which he was oblivious, Robinson never learned to swim. When the director of a local funeral home invited the Orioles team to his suburban home, many players delighted at throwing each other in the swimming pool. Despite Robinson's protest that he did not swim, his teammates insisted that "you're going in anyway." To them it appeared unfathomable that a gifted athlete like Robinson did not swim. They learned quickly as they watched their fearless leader slouch to the deep end with barely enough air in his lungs to cry for help. Even so, his teammates did not believe he was drowning—the Orioles were, after all, a team of practical jokers. Only when Andy Etchebarren dove in to save Robinson were his teammates convinced. Etchebarren required the help of two attendants to elevate Robinson from the water; coughing water, Robinson required "a little bit of work." Characteristically, after five minutes of lying on the deck, he picked himself up unscathed.[17]

Robinson finished his magnificent Triple Crown season with 49 home runs, 122 runs batted in, and a .316 batting average as the Orioles cruised to the American League pennant. Arriving in Los Angeles for the World Series, the Orioles were greeted by an unwelcoming billboard proclaiming, "Would you believe . . . four straight?" For Robinson and his teammates, it was the latest in a series of opportunities to prove the opposition wrong.[18]

They did so by sweeping the Dodgers, with Robinson hitting home runs in the first and fourth games. Already the World Series Most Valuable Player, Robinson also won the Hickok Belt and the American League Most Valuable Player Award for 1966.

Still, his uncompromising style of play continued. On June 27, 1967, it cost Robinson dearly. Trying to break up a double play against Chicago, he collided with Al Weis. After banging his head against the infielder's knee, Robinson was diagnosed with a concussion and suffered prolonged double vision. Although he missed only thirty-two games and recovered to hit .311, Robinson claimed the injury stunted his career: "I don't know how much I left at second base. . . . I haven't been the same hitter since." Injuries continued to hamper Robinson's progress in 1968, and he began to consider his life after baseball. Two years earlier, he had told Edgar Munzel of the *Chicago Herald Examiner* that "if I play seven or eight more years, then I think I'd have sufficient baseball knowledge to step directly into managing." While still an active player, Robinson accepted his first managerial assignment in 1968 as he piloted the Santurce Crabbers of the Puerto Rican Winter League. It was the encouragement of his new manager in Baltimore, Earl Weaver, that pushed Robinson's plans into action.[19]

As the Orioles were poised for greatness in 1969, their catalyst was once again Frank Robinson. Proving himself as a comeback player, he batted .308 while driving in 100 runs and hitting 32 homers, including twelve in April. Off the field Robinson developed a way to perpetuate team chemistry while keeping his teammates relaxed. Capitalizing on the television success of *Laugh-In*, Robinson established a clubhouse kangaroo court, proclaiming himself "da Judge." Wearing a robe and a mop for a wig, Robinson levied fines for "crimes" such as missing the team bus, missing the cutoff man, or wearing running shoes in public. As

writer Ted Patterson remembered, only Robinson could have got away with saying, "Stand up, Earl. Oh, you are standing." The Orioles donated the proceeds of the 1969 kangaroo court fines to Cincinnati catcher Pat Corrales, whose wife had died that summer giving birth to her fourth child.[20]

Despite 109 regular-season wins and Robinson's home run in the fifth game, Baltimore lost the 1969 World Series to the New York Mets. In 1970 Robinson missed thirty games but hit .306 with 25 home runs and 78 RBIs. On June 25 in Boston, he again demonstrated his all-around abilities. After trailing the Red Sox, 7–0, in Fenway Park, the Orioles tied the score in the ninth inning. As Peter Gammons chronicled in the *Boston Globe*, "Frank made a game-saving catch in the 13th, robbing Reggie Smith of a home run with the bases loaded. But he cracked a rib on the fence railing and couldn't swing the bat properly. Without tipping off the Red Sox fielders in the top of the 14th, he crossed up everybody by laying down a bunt with a runner on third and beating it out, driving in a run. He couldn't swing a bat so he found another way to win."[21] The next night in Washington, he hit two grand slams in a single game.

When Curt Blefary's Yankees were visiting Baltimore that year, he remarked that his former teammates could be overtaken because "they don't have a big red S on their shirts." The next day, Robinson, with Mike Cuellar, Paul Blair, and Moe Drabowsky, swarmed Blefary at the batting cage—all wearing Superman shirts. When the season ended, the Yankees found themselves fifteen games behind the Orioles. Already winners of 108 regular-season games, the Orioles quickly disposed of the Minnesota Twins in three games in the ALCS and the Cincinnati Reds in five games in the World Series.

Robinson had another fine year in 1971, which included three personal achievements. On July 8 he connected for a home run off Washington's Horacio Pina for his 2,500th hit. A week later at the

All-Star Game in Detroit, Robinson hit a two-run blast off Dock Ellis to put the American League ahead, 4-3, and earned the Most Valuable Player Award for the game. Finally, on September 13, he touched Detroit's Fred Scherman for his 500th career home run. Ellis and his Pittsburgh teammates defeated the Orioles in a thrilling seven-game World Series. Robinson hit two home runs, giving him a total of eight in four World Series.

After he had led Baltimore to four pennants in six years, Robinson's tenure with the Orioles came to a sudden and surprising end. With Don Baylor waiting in the wings, the Orioles found Robinson and his $130,000 salary expendable. The thirty-six-year-old was sent to the Los Angeles Dodgers in a six-player deal on December 2. He hit 19 home runs and batted .251 in his only season hitting in the challenging Dodger Stadium.

After a year in LA, Robinson was dealt again, this time just down the road to the California Angels. Harry Dalton, who had been the Orioles GM for many years, acquiring Robinson from the Reds in 1965, was now the general manager of the Angels and wanted Frank's leadership and bat.

Robinson came through, leading the Angels with 30 home runs and 97 runs batted in. However, he clashed repeatedly with manager Bobby Winkles. As batboy Robert Goldman remembered, the former head coach at Arizona State University experienced difficulty persuading Robinson to "buy into his program." Nolan Ryan agreed that Robinson and Winkles were "not a good match. . . . We were in a rebuilding mode and at that point in Frank's career, he would have been better someplace else competing for a pennant."[22] By this point Robinson had made it clear that he wanted to manage a big-league team someday, and he had his own ideas about how it should be done. The close relationship he had with Harry Dalton fueled speculation that he might get the job. Robinson hit 30 home runs in 1973 and another 20 for the Angels in 1974, a season in which Winkles was

fired in June and Robinson himself, now thirty-eight years old, was sold to the Indians on waivers in early September.

After a September collapse following a surprise run at the pennant in 1974, Cleveland manager Ken Aspromonte was fired. On October 3, general manager Phil Seghi announced to more than 100 reporters the selection of Frank Robinson as Aspromonte's replacement. He would be, famously, the first African-American manager in Major League history. He had managed in Puerto Rico for a few years, and his eventual ascension to big-league skipper was considered inevitable.

Robinson stressed the importance of physical conditioning, a quality that did not endear him to all his players. "I'm nobody's slave," exclaimed Gaylord Perry in defiance. Robinson made another enemy in John Ellis when he fined the Indians' catcher $100 for missing the hit-and-run signal. Rico Carty grieved that "he wants [us] to play exactly like he used to." The skipper was disinterested in earning the friendship of his players.[23]

Though relegated to the bench as a designated hitter, Robinson's bat and ageing legs were not fully amortized, as he proved on April 8, 1975. Using himself as a pinch-hitter in his first game as manager, he fell behind the count 0-2 before belting a George Medich fastball into the left-field bleachers. The Indians drew 56,715 to Municipal Stadium on Opening Day, but to Robinson, something made one spectator different from any other: "I was very proud that [Rachel Robinson] would make the trip over there. . . . I hoped and wished that Jackie could have been there. The next best thing was having her there. . . . because it kept me focused."[24] On October 15, 1972, Jackie Robinson had told a sellout crowd before a World Series game in Cincinnati that he hoped to see a black manager in the imminent future. Although Number 42 died nine days later, his namesake was carrying his legacy. Robinson's Indians ended the 1975 season with a respectable record of 79-80, in fourth place behind the Boston Red Sox. With Perry and Ellis traded to the Texas Rangers, the Indians broke the .500 mark in 1976. After having just 185 at bats over the two seasons, Robinson chose after the season to retire as a player.

After a slow start in 1977, however, Robinson was fired as the Indians' manager. He resurfaced as a coach for the Angels before returning to the Orioles organization in 1978. Beginning the season as Earl Weaver's outfield coach, Robinson was reassigned in May to replace Ken Boyer as manager of the Rochester Red Wings. He returned to Baltimore in 1979, coaching for two years before accepting an offer in 1981 to manage the struggling San Francisco Giants.

The Giants had posted seven losing records in the previous nine seasons, had a divided team, and struggled with poor attendance. In a season marred by a midseason strike, the Giants under Robinson's stewardship posted a winning record of 56-55 in 1981. They were even better in 1982, the year of Robinson's induction into the Baseball Hall of Fame. Despite being outscored by their opponents, a lineup featuring Joe Morgan, Reggie Smith, Darrell Evans, and Jack Clark kept the Giants in the pennant race until the final weekend of the season. Despite winning 20 of 27 September contests, the Giants had to settle for third place. However, their fans derived some satisfaction when Joe Morgan homered to knock the Dodgers out of the pennant race before a packed house in the season finale. After dealing Morgan and losing Smith to free agency, San Francisco regressed to a pedestrian 79-83 in 1983. With the club mired in the division cellar with a 42-64 record the next July, Robinson was fired for the second time.

Robinson spent three seasons as an Orioles coach before ascending to the front office in October 1987. On April 9, 1988, after the Orioles opened their season with a six-game losing streak, Robinson returned to the dugout as Baltimore's manager, succeeding Cal Ripken Sr. The Orioles lost another fifteen before earning their first victory of the season. After an abysmal record of 54-107, the Orioles rose meteorically in 1989 to finish 87-75, good for second place behind the Toronto Blue Jays. Robinson was named American League Manager of the Year by the baseball writers. The Orioles' young players disappointed in 1990 as they won only 76 games while losing 85. After they won only 13 of their first 37 in 1991, Robinson returned to the front office.

Although he had had three opportunities as manager, he had always taken over lowly franchises and produced winning teams within two seasons. Robinson's greatest challenge as a manager presented itself in 2002 when he was hired to run the Montreal Expos. Despite a lack of ownership (Major League Baseball had taken over ownership of the team), he kept the Expos in the pennant race in both 2002 and 2003, winning 83 games each year. Finishing in last place (67-95) in 2004, the Expos became the Washington Nationals and finished 81-81 in 2005. After a disappointing 71-91 campaign in 2006, Robinson retired from baseball altogether.

Frank Robinson accomplished as much in baseball as anyone ever had: Rookie of the Year; MVP of each league; MVP of the World Series; MVP of the All-Star Game; Gold Glove winner; Manager of the Year; Triple Crown winner. He was also one of the smartest and toughest players of his time, and one of its most renowned leaders. He earned the respect and admiration of his teammates wherever he traveled, and this was most evident during his time in Baltimore, when he led his team to four World Series in his six years.

Chapter 27. **Don Baylor**

Alfonso L. Tusa C. and Malcolm Allen

AGE	G	AB	R	H	2B	3B	HR	TB	RBI	BB	SO	BAV	OBP	SLG	SB	GDP	HBP
21	8	17	4	4	0	0	0	4	4	2	3	.235	.300	.235	1	0	0

Don Baylor was a hustling player who ran the bases aggressively and stood fearlessly close to home plate as if he were daring the pitcher to hit him. Quite often they did, as Baylor was plunked by more pitches (267) than any other player in the twentieth century, leading the American League eight times in that department and retiring as the category's modern record-holder (though he's since been passed by Craig Biggio). Notoriously tough, Baylor wouldn't even acknowledge the pain of being hit, refusing to rub his bruises when he took his base. "Getting hit is my way of saying I'm not going to back off," he explained. "My first goal when I go to the plate is to get a hit. My second goal is to get hit."[1]

Baylor played for seven first-place teams in his nineteen seasons and was a respected clubhouse leader, earning Manager-of-the-Year recognition following his playing career. The powerfully built six-foot-one, 195-pounder hit 338 home runs and drove in 1,276 runs, and clicked on all cylinders when he claimed the AL Most Valuable Player award in 1979. Not only did he lead the California Angels to their first-ever playoff appearance by pacing both leagues in both runs scored and RBIs, he proved unafraid to kick thirty or so reporters out of the clubhouse. After a critical loss in Kansas City late in that season's pennant race, the press corps made the mistake of asking losing pitcher Chris Knapp about a "choke" within earshot of Baylor, who promptly ordered them to leave.

Baylor broke into the Majors with the Baltimore Orioles when the Birds were in the midst of winning three straight pennants. The Baltimore players policed their own clubhouse with a "kangaroo

The twenty-year-old Don Baylor was coming off a terrific Minor League season for the Orioles in 1969, but he would need two more like it before he managed to force himself into the team's crowded outfield.

court" that handed down a stinging but good-natured brand of justice for a variety of on- and off-field infractions. Before he'd even played in the Majors, a twenty-year-old Baylor ran afoul of the court by predicting—even though the Orioles had a trio of All-Star outfielders plus skilled reserve Merv Rettenmund—"If I get into my groove, I'm gonna play every day." Court leader Frank Robinson read the quote aloud in the Baltimore clubhouse, and shortstop Mark Belanger warned

Baylor, "That's going to stick for a long time." Indeed, Baylor was known as Groove in baseball circles even after he retired.[2]

Don Edward Baylor was born on June 28, 1949, in the Clarksville section of Austin, Texas. His father, George Baylor, worked as a baggage handler for the Missouri Pacific Railroad for twenty-five years, and his mother, Lillian, was a pastry cook at a local white high school. Don had two siblings, Doug and Connie, and going to church on Sundays was a must in the Baylor family.

Baylor was one of just three African American students enrolled at O. Henry Junior High School when Austin's public schools integrated in 1962. One of the friends he made was Sharon Connally, the daughter of Governor John Connally, and Baylor would never forget hearing her screams from two classrooms away when Sharon learned over the school's public-address system that her father had been shot along with President John F. Kennedy on November 22, 1963.

At Stephen F. Austin High School, Baylor had to ask the football coach three times for a tryout, but by his senior year he had made honorable mention all-state and got a half-dozen scholarship offers, including ones from powerhouses like Texas and Oklahoma. Baylor also played baseball, as a sophomore becoming the first African American to wear the school's uniform, and being named team captain for his senior season. After a tough first year under a coach who wasn't accustomed to dealing with blacks, Baylor benefited when a strict disciplinarian named Frank Seale, who believed in playing the game the right way, took over the program for his last two seasons. "Frank was not only my coach, but my friend," said Baylor. "He looked after me and made me feel like I was part of his family."[3] When Baylor finally got to the World Series two decades later, Frank Seale was there.

After suffering a shoulder injury serious enough to inhibit his throwing for the rest of his career, Baylor decided to spurn the gridiron scholarship

offers and pursue a career in professional baseball. Some teams, like the Houston Astros (who opted to draft John Mayberry instead), were scared off by Baylor's bum shoulder, but the Baltimore Orioles selected him with their second choice in the 1967 amateur draft. Scout Dee Phillips signed Baylor for $7,500.

Baylor reported immediately to Bluefield, West Virginia, where he wasted no time earning Appalachian League Player of the Year honors after leading the circuit in hitting (.346), runs, stolen bases, and triples under manager Joe Altobelli. "Alto taught me the importance of good work habits," Baylor recalled. "He was a tireless worker himself, serving as manager, batting-practice pitcher, third-base coach, and, when you got right down to it, a baby sitter."[4]

The 1968 season started with a lot of promise. In 68 games for the Class A Stockton Ports, Baylor smashed California League pitching at a .369 clip to earn a promotion to the Double-A Elmira Pioneers of the Eastern League. He stayed there only six games, batting .333, before moving up to the Triple-A Rochester Red Wings. In 15 games against International League pitchers, Baylor batted only .217 and was benched for the first time in his life by manager Billy DeMars. "I felt frustration for the first time in my career," Baylor admitted. "Maybe DeMars hated young players, period. I also noticed that his favorite targets were blacks like Chet Trail, Mickey McGuire, and a guy from Puerto Rico named Rick Delgado. I felt that DeMars did not have my best interests at heart. I was trying very hard to learn, but I got nothing from him."[5]

Nonetheless, the Orioles invited Baylor to his first big-league spring training in 1969, and he got to meet his role model, Frank Robinson. Soon, Baylor was even using the same R161 bat (taking its model number from Robinson's first MVP season in 1961) that the Orioles right fielder did so much damage with. With it, Baylor began the season by hitting .375 in 17 games for the Class A Florida Marlins of the Florida State League. He spent the bulk of the year with the Double-A Dallas–Fort Worth Spurs, hitting .300 in 109 games to earn a Texas League All-Star selection.

After a strong spring training with the Orioles in 1970, Baylor returned to Rochester to bat third and play center field every day. Midway through the season, he reluctantly moved to left field because Red Wings manager Cal Ripken didn't believe Baylor's weak arm would allow him to play center in the big leagues. "Don's our triple threat," teammate Merv Rettenmund quipped. "He can hit, run, and lob." Pretty much everything else that happened that season, however, couldn't have been scripted more perfectly for Baylor. He was married before a summer doubleheader and tore through the International League by leading all players in runs, doubles, triples, and total bases. *The Sporting News* recognized Baylor as its Minor League Player of the Year. He batted .327 with 22 home runs and 107 RBIs, and was called up to the Orioles on September 8. Ten days later, Baylor made his Major League debut at Memorial Stadium in Baltimore, batting fifth and playing center field against the Cleveland Indians. The bases were loaded for his first at bat, against right-hander Steve Hargan, and Baylor admitted feeling "scared to death."[6] He didn't show it, though, driving the first pitch into right field for a two-run single. In 17 at-bats over 8 games, Baylor batted .235.

After the 1970 season Baylor went to Puerto Rico to play for the Santurce Crabbers in the Winter League. The manager was Frank Robinson. "There I would get to know Frank even better because he was my manager and hitting guru," Baylor remembered. "Mostly he taught me to think while hitting. He would say, 'A guy pitches inside, hit that ball right down the line. Look for certain pitches on certain counts.' Frank also wanted me to start using my strength more. Frank knew there was a pull hitter buried somewhere inside me and fought to develop that power. In Santurce, Frank worked with me to strengthen my defense and throwing. I wound up hitting .290."[7]

With nothing left to prove in Triple-A but no room on the star-studded Orioles roster, Baylor returned to Rochester in 1971 and made another International League All-Star team. He put up strong all-around numbers, hitting .313 with 31 doubles, 10 triples, 20 homers, 95 RBIs, 104 runs scored, 79 walks, and 25 steals as the Red Wings won the Little World Series. The Triple-A playoffs went on so long that Baylor got into just one Major League game after they finished.

He returned to Santurce with the island still celebrating Roberto Clemente's MVP performance in the 1971 World Series, in which he helped the Pittsburgh Pirates dethrone the Orioles. "When Roberto played in Puerto Rico that winter I got a chance to witness up close what a great player he was," Baylor recalled. "In a game against Roberto's San Juan team, I tried to score from second base on a hit to right. I know I had the play beat. I ran the bases the right way; made the proper turn, cut the corner well. But by the time I started my fadeaway slide catcher Manny Sanguillén had the ball. I couldn't believe it. I was out."[8]

Baylor wound up hitting .329 to win the Puerto Rican League batting title. He was confident that he'd be on some team's Major League roster in 1972, but was shocked when the Orioles cleared a spot for him by dealing away Frank Robinson before Baylor returned from Latin America. The Orioles effectively had four regular outfielders in 1971 (Robinson, Merv Rettenmund, Paul Blair, and Don Buford), so Baylor still had some competition in front of him.

Baylor got into 102 games with an Orioles team that missed the playoffs for the first time in four years. By hitting .253 with 11 home runs and 24 steals, he was named to the Topps Rookie Major League All-Star team. He became a father when Don Jr. was born shortly after the season ended.

Baylor came back from Puerto Rico to get his son, before the family returned to the island together to help him get ready for the next season.

Much like the Orioles, Baylor started slowly in 1973, but heated up when it mattered most. Baltimore was in third place in mid-July, and Baylor was hitting under .240 with four homers. Starting on July 17, though, he mashed at a .366 clip the rest of the way, contributing seven home runs and 30 RBIS as the Orioles played .658 ball and won the American League East title going away. Baylor batted .273 in his first taste of playoff action before sitting out a shutout loss to Catfish Hunter in the Series' decisive Game Five.

He played enough to qualify for the batting title for the first time in 1974, batting a solid .272 when the average American Leaguer hit 14 points less. The Orioles were eight games out on August 28, in fourth place, when Baylor and the team caught fire again for another furious finish. Baylor batted .381 as the Birds went 28-6 to finish two games ahead of the Yankees before getting swept by the Oakland A's in the American League Championship Series.

Baylor joined the Venezuelan League Magallanes Navigators that winter, displaying good patience and power with 7 homers, 32 RBIS, and 29 walks in 56 games while batting .271. When Major League action got underway in 1975, Baylor's talents continued to blossom. He hammered three home runs in a game at Detroit on July 2 and smacked twenty-five overall. That made the league's top ten, and his .489 slugging percentage was also among the leaders. With 32 stolen bases, Baylor cracked the AL leader board for the fourth of what would eventually be six consecutive seasons. Though the Orioles finished second to the Red Sox, Baylor's name appeared toward the bottom of some writers' MVP ballots. He was only twenty-six and going places, just not where he imagined.

Just a week before Opening Day in 1976, Ori-oles manager Earl Weaver pulled Baylor out of an exhibition game unexpectedly. "When he told me to sit beside him I knew something was wrong, Baylor recalled. "'I hate to tell you this,' Earl said quietly, 'but we just traded you to Oakland for Reggie Jackson.' I looked at Earl but he couldn't look at me. I was stunned. I started to cry right there on the bench. 'Earl,' I sobbed. 'I don't want to go anywhere.'"[9] Weaver believed Groove would one day be an MVP, but the Orioles sent him packing in a six-player deal to land a guy who'd already won the trophy. Other than a career-high four stolen bases on May 17, and his best season overall for swipes with 52, the highlights were few and far between for Baylor in 1976. He didn't hit well at the Oakland Coliseum, and batted just .247 with 15 homers overall. On November 1, Baylor became part of the first class of free agents after the arbitrator's landmark decision invalidated baseball's reserve clause.

Just over two weeks later, Baylor signed a six-year, $1.6 million deal with the California Angels, but he struggled to justify his salary for the first half of 1977. When manager Norm Sherry got the axe midway through the season, Baylor was hitting a paltry .223 with 9 home runs and 30 RBIS. Dave Garcia took over as skipper and hired Baylor's ex-teammate Frank Robinson as his hitting instructor. Under the Hall of Famer's tutelage, Baylor broke out to bat .281 with 16 homers and 75 RBIS the rest of the way. He never looked back.

Baylor finished seventh in American League MVP voting in 1978 after a breakout season that saw him smash 34 home runs, drive in 99 runs, and score 103. The surprising Angels logged their first winning season in eight years and remained in the West Division hunt until the final week, but Baylor will always remember that September for one of his saddest days as a ballplayer. Teammate Lyman Bostock made the last out of a critical one-run loss on September 23 in Chicago, then stormed by Baylor ranting and raving before ex-

ALFONSO L. TUSA C. AND MALCOLM ALLEN

iting the clubhouse after a fast shower. "Veterans know enough to leave other veterans alone," Baylor said. "So when Lyman walked by, I didn't say a thing. I didn't know there would be no next time for him."[10] Bostock was shot to death that night in Gary, Indiana. The career .311 hitter was only twenty-seven.

Baylor propelled the Angels to their first playoff appearance in franchise history in 1979, batting cleanup in all 162 games and earning twenty of a possible twenty-eight first-place votes to claim MVP honors. His totals of 139 RBIs and 120 runs scored led the Major Leagues, and he added career bests in home runs (36), on-base percentage (.371), slugging percentage (.530), and walks (71) while striking out just 51 times. He batted .330 with runners in scoring position. Baylor struggled while battling tendinitis in his left wrist in June, but sandwiched that down spell with player-of-the-month performances in May and July. He earned his only All-Star selection, starting in left field, batting third, and getting two hits with a pair of runs scored. In his first at bat, he pulled a run-scoring double off Phillies southpaw Steve Carlton. On August 25 at Toronto, Baylor logged a personal-best eight RBIs in one game as the Angels romped, 24–2.

In the 1979 playoffs, Baylor and the Angels met the same Baltimore Orioles club that had developed him, but a storybook ending was not in the cards. Though Baylor went deep against Dennis Martinez in California's Game Three victory, he batted just .188 as the Angels lost three games to one.

As wonderful as 1979 played out, the 1980 season was a nightmare. The Angels started slowly and were buried by a 12-28 stretch during which Baylor missed nearly seven weeks with an injured left wrist. He struggled mightily when he returned, batted just .250 with 5 homers in 90 games, and missed most of the last month with an injured right foot. The Angels went from division cham-

pions to losers of ninety-five games. The next season, 1981, Baylor became almost exclusively a designated hitter and remained one for the balance of his career. Though he batted a career-low (to that point) .239, his totals of 17 homers and 66 RBIs each cracked the American League's top ten in the strike-shortened season.

In 1982 Baylor homered 24 times and drove in 93 runs as the Angels made their second postseason appearance in what proved to be his last season with California. After beating the Brewers in the first two games of the best-of-five Championship Series, the Angels dropped three straight and were eliminated. It certainly wasn't Baylor's fault; he batted .294 and knocked in 10 runs in the series.

Baylor became a free agent for the second time in November 1982, and signed a lucrative deal to join the New York Yankees. In three seasons with the Bronx Bombers, he was twice named the designated hitter on *The Sporting News*' Silver Slugger team (1983 and 1985), and averaged 24 home runs and 88 RBIs. His batting average declined from a career-best .303 to .262 to .231, however, and these were not particularly happy years as Baylor feuded with Yankees owner George Steinbrenner. In 1985 Baylor was selected as the winner of the prestigious Roberto Clemente Award, presented annually to a Major Leaguer of exceptional character who contributes a lot to his community. He was recognized for his work with the Cystic Fibrosis Foundation and the 65 Roses (so-named for the way one child pronounced Cystic Fibrosis) club.

The Yankees traded Baylor to the Boston Red Sox shortly before Opening Day in 1986 for left-handed-hitting designated hitter Mike Easler. Though Baylor struck out a career-high 111 times and managed to bat just .238 in '86, his 31 home runs and 94 RBIs were his best since his MVP year. He also established a single-season AL record by getting hit by pitches thirty-five times. The Red Sox won 95 games to beat out the New York for the American League East title, with Baylor operating a kangaroo court as his mentor Frank Robinson had done in Baltimore. On the night Roger Clemens set a Major League record by striking out twenty Seattle Mariners, Baylor fined him five dollars for giving up a single to light-hitting Spike Owen on an 0-2 pitch. In the American League Championship Series, against the Angels, Boston was two outs from elimination in Game Five when Baylor smashed a game-tying, two-run home run off eighteen-game winner Mike Witt to spark an amazing comeback. Baylor batted .346 in the seven ALCS games, but started only three of seven World Series contests against the New York Mets as designated hitters were not used in the National League ballpark. This time the Red Sox let a Series clincher slip away, losing to New York in seven games.

Baylor turned thirty-eight in 1987, and he posted the lowest power totals since his injury-plagued 1980 campaign, declining to 16 homers and 63 RBIS. He did reach a milestone on June 28, his thirty-eighth birthday, when he was hit by a pitch for a record 244th time. "Change-ups and slow curves feel like a butterfly, a light sting," he said. "Fastballs and sliders feel like piercing bullets, like they're going to come out the other side."[11] He added that getting hit in the wrist by a Nolan Ryan heater in 1973 was the worst feeling of all.

The Minnesota Twins, making a surprising playoff run, craved Baylor's right-handed bat and presence and acquired him from the Red Sox for the final month of the 1987 season. Baylor batted .286 to help Minnesota reach the postseason for the first time in seventeen years, and his eighth-inning pinch-hit single drove in the go-ahead run in Game One of the ALCS against the Tigers. Baylor batted .385 in the World Series against the St. Louis Cardinals, including a game-tying two-run homer off John Tudor in Game Six, helping the Twins to a comeback victory en route to the title.

Baylor wrapped up his playing career with a re-turn to the Oakland Athletics in 1988. Though he batted just .220 in 92 games, the club won 104 regular-season contests and became the third American League pennant winner in a row to feature Baylor on its roster. Oakland defeated the Red Sox in the ALCS but lost the World Series to the Los Angeles Dodgers in an upset, and Baylor struck out against National League Cy Young winner Orel Hershiser in his only at-bat. In the off-season Baylor called it a career after 2,135 hits with a .260 batting average, 338 home runs, and 1,276 RBIS. He stole 285 bases and was hit by a pitch 267 times.

Baylor returned to the big leagues for a two-year stint as the Milwaukee Brewers' hitting coach beginning in 1990 and spent 1992 in the same role with the Cardinals. In 1993 he was named the inaugural manager of the expansion Colorado Rockies, and earned Manager of the Year honors in 1995 when he led the third-year club to a playoff berth faster than any previous expansion club. Pitching coach Larry Bearnarth observed, "He doesn't lose his cool very often. On the other hand, he can be intolerant sometimes of people who don't give their best. He is very direct and he never varies from that, so players are never surprised. If he has something to say, he just says it like he's still a player, like players used to do to each other."[12]

Baylor's Rockies played winning baseball for two more years, but he was fired after the club fell under .500 and slipped to fourth place in the five-team division in 1998. He turned down an offer to become a club vice president, instead opting to become a hitting coach again with the Atlanta Braves. After earning rave reviews for helping Chipper Jones develop into an MVP candidate, Baylor got another chance to manage in 2000 with the Chicago Cubs. Despite eighty-eight wins and a surprising third-place finish in his second year in Chicago, Baylor was fired after a Fourth of July loss in 2002 with a disappointing, highly-paid club sputtering in fifth place. Overall, he went 627-689 as a Major League manager.

Baylor resurfaced with the Mets the next two seasons, serving as a bench coach and hitting instructor under Art Howe, while battling a diagnosis of multiple myeloma. When the Mets changed managers, Baylor moved to Seattle in 2005 to work with Mariners batters. In 2007 he worked part time as an analyst on Washington Nationals telecasts. After three years out of a Major League uniform, Baylor returned to the Rockies in 2009 as their hitting coach. In 2010 Baylor lived with his wife, Rebecca, a former flight attendant.

Chapter 28. **Marcelino Lopez**

Malcolm Allen

AGE	W	L	PCT.	ERA	G	GS	GF	CG	SHO	SV	IP	H	BB	SO	HBP	WP
26	1	1	.500	2.08	25	3	4	0	0	0	60.2	47	37	49	0	0

As of 2010 Marcelino Lopez had won more Major League games than all but one left-hander born in his native Cuba, but when considering that he had fourteen victories by the end of August as a twenty-one-year-old rookie, his 31-40 career mark could be seen as a disappointment. Though he did not establish himself further as a starter, he did play a valuable role as a reliever of the champion Baltimore Orioles of 1970.

Marcelino Pons Lopez was born on September 23, 1943, in Havana, Cuba. "He told me he knew [Fidel] Castro and even played ball against him," said Roy Firestone, who served as the Orioles' spring-training batboy when he was a child. "He told me Castro was a huge baseball fan, but a lousy player."[1] Lopez initially appeared to be on the fast track, signing with the Philadelphia Phillies in the fall of 1959 just ten days after his sixteenth birthday and leading the Florida State League with a 2.35 earned run average a year later. Just five feet eleven and weighing 160 pounds at the time, he struck out 231 batters in 199 innings and earned a spot on the Phillies roster after the season.

Unwilling to rush Lopez, in 1961 the Phillies sent the seventeen-year-old to the Williamsport Grays of the Eastern League (Single-A), where he caught the eyes of the big-league brass again when the Phillies visited for an exhibition. Lopez went 10-5 before a blister ended his season after 22 starts. When he returned to action that winter in the Venezuelan League, *Sports Illustrated* reported that he "handled major-league hitters with ease."[2]

Lopez and his fiancée, Zoraida, were married in January 1962, and he became the father of a

The lefty Marcelino Lopez gave the Orioles some valuable work out of the bullpen in 1970.

son, Eduardo, in October; but most of the news concerning him that year was not good. His arrival two weeks late to spring training because of visa problems was just the beginning of his troubles. A tender elbow prevented Lopez from letting loose, and though he impressed anyway, more elbow soreness contributed to a disappointing performance at Triple-A Buffalo (3-7, 5.57 ERA) as his walk total soared to 95 in 126 innings.

Wildness continued to plague Lopez that winter in Venezuela, but he went 9-6 for La Guaira and hurled 10 complete games, including a fifteen-inning masterpiece in stifling heat to beat Caracas 2–1.

By 1963 a more mature (and on-time) Lopez showed up in spring training. Physically, he'd grown to six feet three and 195 pounds, and his ability to speak English had come a long way since his first pro season in Tampa. He had an opening to make the team after fellow southpaw Dennis Bennett fractured an ankle in an automobile accident in Puerto Rico in January, and Lopez seemed ready to take advantage of it. He was so impressive that a poll of National League writers named him Philadelphia's Most Improved Pitcher, Best Young Pitcher, and Likeliest to Improve.

With his elbow problems behind him for the time being, Lopez made a believer out of Phillies manager Gene Mauch and opened the 1963 season in the big leagues. "Whenever I saw him before, he never threw hard. This spring, he's been throwing bullets," Mauch observed. "He's got a good curve, and a change, too. He's a natural athlete. He can hit, and he's one of the fastest runners on our squad. He can field his position, too. Lopez has a lot of poise for a kid of 19."[3]

Lopez's Major League debut, against the St. Louis Cardinals at Busch Stadium on April 14, was hardly memorable. He started the game and was taken out in the first inning after walking the first two batters and giving up a double to Ken Boyer. He escaped being saddled with the loss when the Phillies scored five runs in the last four innings and won the game. He pitched briefly in relief on April 16, then on the 20th he started against the Cardinals again, at Shibe Park, and pitched five innings to get his first Major League victory, 6–2. He pitched briefly on the 27th before suffering an elbow injury and was sent to Triple-A Arkansas at the end of the month. Two months went by before Lopez was able to pitch, and he was generally ineffective in 69 innings, going 3-5 with a 5.74 ERA in 17 appearances (12 starts). It was a frustrating season, as evidenced by Lopez's reaction to being yanked in the second inning of a start against Jacksonville in August. Rather than hand the baseball to manager Frank Lucchesi, Lopez fired it over the stands, earning a $27.50 fine. "$25 for the throw, and $2.50 for the ball," explained Lucchesi.[4]

Lopez's elbow woes continued to cause him control problems that winter for La Guaira, but he rebounded in 1964 to have a solid season for a bad Double-A Chattanooga team. Though he had a decent 3.77 ERA and struck out 115 in 136 innings, his won-lost record was an unimpressive 6-10. "I pitched well but have the bad record because we have a bad club," Lopez explained. "Our best hitter only hit .270."[5]

Hard luck followed Lopez to the Caguas Criollos in Puerto Rico that winter, where he lost a trio of duels to Los Angeles Angels left-hander George Brunet by scores of 1-0, 2–1, and 3-2. Brunet and Lopez would be teammates come springtime, though, because on October 24 he was traded to the Angels in a complicated deal in which the Phillies, who were in a late-season pennant race, in effect "rented" Angels first baseman Vic Power for the last three weeks of the season, then sent him back to the Angels after the season, throwing in Lopez as a dividend for the rental.

Lopez wrapped up a busy winter by heading to the Dominican Republic to pitch in that league's playoffs, and reported to spring training with no hard feelings towards the Phillies. "I didn't get mad at Philadelphia because they have two good southpaws [Bennett, Short], and they need more right-handers because of the short fence in left," he said.[6]

For a young pitcher with only six innings of big-league experience, Lopez seemed keenly aware of what the deal could mean for him. The Angels needed help in both their rotation and bullpen, and Brunet and Bo Belinsky were the only left-handers on the roster. Besides, Lopez said, "I also hear that LA park [Dodger Stadium, where the Angels were then playing] is good for pitchers. If you get the ball over, you win."[7]

Lopez drew raves from teammates and opponents alike during spring training, and pitching coach Marv Grissom said he had winning stuff if he could get it over the plate, but cautioned, "Unless he develops a curve, he [can't] stay in the big leagues. He was choking the ball as he threw the curve. I told him to move it out onto his fingers where he could manufacture greater spin." Grissom called Lopez "a quick and willing student," and said he worked on the grip after practice every day.[8]

Lopez accepted the challenge and tightened up his self-described "lazy curve." By the end of April, Grissom called him "a cinch to win 15 games."[9] By August 23 he was 14-10, and he took a no-hitter into the bottom of the seventh two weeks later at Chicago. But he wound up 14-13 after missing the last two weeks of the season with a pulled rib muscle. If he had been able to pitch more at home (where he was 10-3), or less against the Yankees (who won all five decisions against him), he would have made good on his pitching coach's prediction. Nevertheless, he took home Rookie Pitcher of the Year honors from *The Sporting News*, and finished second to Orioles outfielder Curt Blefary for overall freshman honors.

Lopez's 2.93 ERA and winning record for a 75-87 team were impressive accomplishments for a twenty-one-year-old, but he was even better when he returned to Venezuela to pitch for La Guaira in the winter. Things started out badly. Lopez's wife was among a group of four players' spouses forced to disrobe during a robbery while they were grocery shopping, and he lost his first two decisions. After that, though, Lopez reeled off 12 straight wins and hurled 51⅔ consecutive scoreless innings at one point. By the end of the winter campaign, he was 12-3 with a 1.57 ERA, 5 shutouts, and nearly 150 innings pitched.[10]

The heavy workload caught up with Lopez in 1966. After a complete-game victory in Chicago in his season debut, Lopez won just six of twenty decisions the rest of the way to finish 7-14 with his ERA increasing by a full run to 3.93. A pair of blisters on his pitching hand prevented him from gripping the ball tightly early in the season, but Lopez had no trouble pinpointing the source of his struggles. "I left my best stuff in Venezuela. I didn't fool myself," he said. "I picked up a million bad habits because I am tired. I don't even know where the ball is going. I don't stride properly, my arm dips down and I don't get my breaking stuff over."[11] Hitters started laying off his hard slider, and his ERA away from Anaheim Stadium was a miserable 5.31. The Angels offered Lopez an off-season job in their ticket department if he'd stay away from pitching winter ball, and he agreed. "It will cost me $4,000 not to go to Venezuela," Lopez said. "But I have the chance to make $30,000, even $40,000, pitching for the Angels."[12]

In the spring of 1967 Angels manager Bill Rigney told reporters he was building his pitching staff around Lopez, but the southpaw lasted only nine innings in his first three starts before heading to the disabled list with tendinitis. "I went to a doctor, and he said the worst thing I can do is rest the arm. My muscles are tight, and just need to be stretched," Lopez said. "He said maybe my arm just got used to pitching after six straight winters, and tightened up when I did nothing. He give me some exercises, and said to throw every other day."[13]

Six weeks later, Lopez returned to the mound and failed to retire any of the five Baltimore Orioles hitters he faced in relief, walking four of them. Nine days later, on June 15, he was dealt to Baltimore with another Minor Leaguer for utility man Woody Held. Lopez returned from a second trip to the disabled list to make his Orioles debut on July 30, then went back on the DL again a week later after failing to get past three innings or display much zip on his fastball in a pair of starts. He was a little better when he returned in late September. The season was a lost cause for Lopez; he pitched just 26⅔ innings, going 1-2 with a 4.72 ERA.

In 1968 Lopez was given a cortisone shot, and the Orioles sent him down to the Miami Marlins of the Single-A Florida State League so that he could pitch himself back into shape. After posting a 3.50 ERA in 11 starts, he moved up to Double-A Elmira (3-2, 5.33 in nine starts), where arm woes bothered him again. In September, he finally had a breakthrough of sorts after having his tonsils removed. "It was real bad. I lost 30 pounds in three days. When they took them out later, I saw the worst tonsil on the left side," Lopez said. "Three weeks later, I threw for 20 minutes. My shoulder felt good. Maybe it was my tonsils."[14]

Flashing improved velocity, even if it wasn't up to his 1965 level, Lopez went 5-3 that winter, again pitching for La Guaira in the Venezuelan League. He was not selected in the October 1968 expansion draft to stock the new teams in Seattle and Kansas City. He acquitted himself well in 1969 spring training with the Orioles but was the last man cut before Opening Day as Baltimore opted to go with right-hander Mike Adamson. A devastated Lopez couldn't hold back the tears, but he went to Minor League camp with the right attitude.

"Instead of grumbling, he did more than he was expected to," said Baltimore executive vice president Frank Cashen. "He helped the manager run the pitchers. He coached third base. He even collected bats. Do you know, he was the fastest player in our entire minor-league camp?"[15]

Lopez went to Triple-A Rochester and pitched well in five starts. After he fired a seven-inning no-hitter at Richmond on May 4, the Orioles brought him back to the Majors. Four times in his first six appearances, he hurled at least three scoreless innings out of the bullpen, earning victories on two occasions. Though he tailed off after a strong start, Lopez went 5-3 with a 4.41 ERA in 4 starts and 23 relief appearances for a Baltimore team that won 109 regular-season games. The club's leading winner was off-season acquisition Mike Cuellar, the only left-handed Cuban-born pitcher to win more Major League games than Lopez. "Marcelino knew Mike Cuellar really well," recalled Roy Firestone. "They grew up together in Cuba and ended up as teammates with a couple of teams."[16] Lopez appeared in the twelfth inning of the first American League Championship Series game ever played, retiring another outstanding Cuban player, Tony Oliva of the Minnesota Twins. Then he made way for Dick Hall, who got the victory when the Orioles defeated Minnesota in the bottom of the inning. Lopez didn't pitch in the World Series as the Orioles were upended by the New York Mets.

Lopez shed twenty pounds over the winter and spent the entire 1970 season with an Orioles team that won another American League pennant en route to the second World Series victory in the franchise's history. In 3 starts and 22 relief outings, he posted a 2.08 ERA and held left-handed hitters to a .136 average. He helped Baltimore preserve a one-run lead in the bottom of the seventh inning of World Series Game Two by getting Cincinnati's Bobby Tolan to pop up with two runners aboard. After the Orioles won the Series in five games, Orioles play-by-play announcer Chuck Thompson interviewed them one after another in the joyous clubhouse. "I just want to say I haven't seen my mother in 10 years, and she's probably watching me on TV now," Lopez told him. "I'd like to say hello, and I'm all right. This is the greatest moment of my life, and I hope next year we can do it again."[17]

Bases on balls were a problematic in an otherwise strong 1970 campaign for Lopez, as he issued 37 free passes in 60⅔ innings, which drove Orioles manager Earl Weaver crazy. "I used to sit next to Earl Weaver in the Miami Stadium dugout and he was brutal with Marcelino," Roy Firestone remembered. "He would scream and humiliate Marcelino for his inability to throw strikes . . . and this was still during spring training!"[18]

Lopez arrived at spring training in 1971 with a chance to compete for a spot in the starting rotation, and his spot on the team appeared secure when Jim Hardin was placed on the disabled list and Dave Leonhard was sent to the Minor League camp. Two days before Opening Day, however, Lopez was dealt to the Milwaukee Brewers for right-hander Roric Harrison and a Minor Leaguer. "We've been after Lopez for a long time, and I don't buy that stuff that the Orioles felt he had a sore arm," said Milwaukee's director of baseball operations, Frank Lane, a former Orioles super-scout. "I know at least three or four other clubs that would like to have his sore arm."[19]

The Brewers tried Lopez in the bullpen, then moved him into the rotation in late June, but his control problems worsened. He walked 60 in 67⅔ innings and finished 2-7 with a 4.66 ERA. Late in 1972 spring training the Brewers sold him to the Indians, and he wound up starting the opener for Cleveland's Triple-A team, the Portland Beavers of the Pacific Coast League. He struggled to throw strikes and finished 8-13 at Portland. In two starts and two relief appearances for the Indians in September, he walked ten batters in 8⅓ innings and had just one strikeout. The Indians released him after the season. His Major League career was over with a 31-40 record and 3.62 ERA in 653 innings.

Lopez struggled through an 0-6 Triple-A season in 1973 for Hawaii and Oklahoma City, and wound up with Veracruz in the Mexican League in 1974. He resurfaced with the Triple-A Charleston Charlies in August of that season, posting a 1.73 ERA in 26 innings for the Pittsburgh Pirates affiliate, but walked 17. His last chance came in 1976 with the Double-A Columbus (Georgia) Astros of the Southern League, but he lasted only four appearances after walking seven in three innings.

Lopez died on November 29, 2001, in Hialeah, Florida. "Sadly," Roy Firestone reported, "Marcelino died penniless."[20]

Chapter 29. **Mark Belanger**

Frank Vaccaro

AGE	G	AB	R	H	2B	3B	HR	TB	RBI	BB	SO	BAV	OBP	SLG	SB	GDP	HBP
26	145	459	53	100	6	5	1	119	36	52	65	.218	.303	.259	13	4	5

One of history's great defensive shortstops, Mark Belanger helped anchor the Orioles infield for many years.

The most electrifying defensive shortstop of his generation, Mark Belanger set the standard by anchoring a great Baltimore Orioles infield for most of fourteen seasons. During this stretch, Baltimore won ninety or more games twelve times with seven postseason appearances capped by the 1970 world championship. Belanger and Ozzie Smith are the only shortstops to retire with fielding averages over .975 while averaging more than five fielding chances per game.

Belanger used two tiny black gloves per season and broke them in with spit and coffee. He got upset if anybody touched them. Watching him have a catch with a teammate on the sidelines was striking. He never seemed to actually catch a ball; rather he redirected them into his throwing hand. *Sports Illustrated* once wrote: "Belanger would glide effortlessly after a grounder and welcome it into loving arms; scooping the ball up with a single easy motion, and bringing it to his chest for a moment's caress before making his throw."[1]

Belanger's fielding prowess was due to the start-and-stop speed of an All-American high school basketball star, his lightning-quick hands, and what scouts called Belanger's First Step. A student of pitch counts, locations, and batter tendencies, Belanger sprinted at odd angles for the big hop and is best appreciated in slow-motion video. His small glove transferred the ball to his right hand—the seams of the ball always aligned the same way—enabling him to uncoil a strong throw on his next left step. In eighteen years, he never dove for a ball, insisting that an all-out sprint was faster and maintained the mechanics of the play. And he was supremely confident: he never wore a protective cup.

Belanger's father, Edward, was of French-Canadian descent and worked as a maintenance man in Cheshire, a town in the Berkshires of western Massachusetts. His mother, Marie, was a first-generation Italian American. Mark, the third of four children (he had an older brother, Al, and two sisters, Jeanne and Linda), learned how to field playing with his siblings on a cow pasture. Born on June 8, 1944, in Pittsfield, Massachusetts, he played basketball and baseball at Pittsfield High School. On the hardwood, he was a six-foot-two forward who jumped center, compiling 1,455 points in three years, a school record until 2003. In baseball, he starred for both the high school squad and the local American Legion Post 68 team. On August 24, 1960, Belanger ripped a fourteenth-inning 340-foot game-winning double off the left-field fence at Alumni Field in Keene, New Hampshire, to earn Pittsfield Post a trip to Hastings, Nebraska, for the American Legion national championship. Scouts for the Orioles noted that Belanger "looks like he's playing on roller skates to the accompaniment of music."[2] Based on scout Joe Cusick's reports, after Belanger graduated from high school Baltimore offered him $35,000 to sign a contract. Belanger signed on June 19. That summer he played in forty-seven games for the Bluefield Orioles in the short-season Appalachian League and eight games with the Single-A Elmira Pioneers of the Eastern League. He hit .298 for Bluefield but was just 1-for-22 at Elmira.

Belanger went to spring training with the Orioles in 1963. Ron Hansen, whom the Orioles had just traded to the Chicago White Sox, approached the rookie with this advice: "Learn to rock forward as the pitcher delivers the ball instead of starting from zero."[3] Belanger took it to heart. Over the years he not only leaned forward but anticipated left or right based on batter tendencies and pitch location. Sometimes Belanger would break right and then correct himself and break left—all before the crack of the bat on the ball. Before the 1963 season began, Belanger entered the U.S. Air National Guard for a year of active duty, completing his basic training at Fort Dix, New Jersey, and playing on the camp baseball squad. Returning the next season with the Northern League's Aberdeen (South Dakota) Pheasants, he hit just .226, but one scouting report enthused about his fielding: "Belanger could be a major-league shortstop if he never got another hit in his life."[4] He was far from perfect in the field, having made 20 errors in 44 games with Bluefield in 1962 and 23 errors with Aberdeen in 117 games in 1964, but talent evaluators had no doubt as to the shortstop's potential.

Belanger played for Earl Weaver at three levels along the way, and Weaver told him, "You're my shortstop if you hit .001."[5] In midseason 1965, Belanger's year at Elmira was interrupted by his first call-up to the Majors when Luis Aparicio caught the mumps. In Kansas City, a gaggle of sportswriters converged on batting practice to find out who Belanger was. A's coach Whitey Herzog said: "I saw him play in the Northern League. During the seven games I watched him, Belanger was the best shortstop I ever saw in my life."[6]

Belanger debuted as a pinch runner on August 7. In Fenway Park on August 10 he fielded his first ground ball. It came off the bat of Felix Mantilla, and Belanger started a double play with the graceful second baseman Jerry Adair. Belanger appeared in eleven games but had only three at-bats, with one hit, a single off Kansas City's Don Mossi on September 10.

Listed as "needs hitting experience" in the spring of 1966,[7] Belanger was one of five Elmira regulars who followed Earl Weaver to Triple-A

Rochester. Belanger did not hit well in the first half and, feeling the pressure to succeed, began smoking cigarettes. Belanger asked Weaver to bench him but Weaver refused, and Belanger responded by outhitting league MVP Mike Epstein the second half, finishing at .262 for the season. The Rochester press called him Remarkable Mark. Called up at the end of the year, he appeared in just eight more games, but was there to join in the wild celebration when Baltimore clinched the pennant on September 22.

Called "the greatest shortstop prospect in baseball history," Belanger drew offers from many clubs but General Manager Harry Dalton was adamant: "I will never trade Belanger."[8] Playing behind Aparicio, a seven-time All-Star and seven-time Gold Glove winner in his career thus far, Belanger showed uneven play in his rookie year of 1967. On April 30, playing second base, he dropped Aparicio's feed and allowed an unearned run to score to give Steve Barber a loss in what ended as a no-hit game. (Barber threw 8⅔ no-hit innings and Stu Miller ⅓ in the loss.) The Orioles' manager, Hank Bauer, still said Belanger "sparkled,"[9] and Bauer liked the fact that Belanger hit well when given consecutive starts. Aparicio had an off-year, and Belanger became his late-inning replacement. In the same May 14 game in which Mickey Mantle hit his 500th home run, Belanger hit one off Yankee Stadium's left-field pole, victimizing the Yankees' Mel Stottlemyre.

Belanger married the former Daryl Apple on November 25, 1967, and the couple honeymooned at Mount Airy Lodge in the Poconos. On their fourth night together, Belanger heard the news that Baltimore had traded Aparicio to the White Sox, opening up the shortstop job. Back home in Pittsfield, Belanger was employed selling sporting goods in the Besse-Clarke department store. To get ready for the season, he squeezed lacrosse balls to build up his wrists.

Belanger almost saw his season derailed when the Air National Guard ordered him to report to the 175th Fighter Group at Middle River, Maryland, just before the season. He missed Baltimore's Opening Day but joined the squad in time for the first Opening Day ever in Oakland, California, the new home of the Athletics, who had moved from Kansas City. California governor Ronald Reagan threw out the first pitch in front of 50,000 fans, and Belanger hit his second career home run. On July 10, Hank Bauer was deposed as O's manager in favor of first-base coach Earl Weaver, who said, "Mark can be a star. A fifty-thousand-dollar player."[10] Perhaps, but he hit just .208 in his first year as a starting player.

The next spring, bullpen coach Charlie Lau approached Belanger to offer batting tips. Lau kept track of every pitch Belanger saw that year, sending him up to bat with instructions to take and swing on specific counts, and encouraging him to expect certain pitches in certain spots based on previous batter-pitcher matchups. Belanger responded with his best batting season ever, won his first of eight Gold Gloves, and earned the nickname Blade for his silhouette as Baltimore rolled to a team record 109 wins. He hit for a .287 average with 50 RBIs.

Belanger became a respected member of the team, offering an articulate clubhouse interview and buffering Earl Weaver's rants. Between the foul lines he was no-joke, all business, directing fielders to shade right or left and approaching rookies and new players with the abrupt "We don't do it that way"—a line he even used on Jim Palmer in 1978.[11] Backed by veterans Brooks Robinson and Frank Robinson, Belanger became a leader on the team, replacing Davey Johnson as assistant player representative. Even in the loose clubhouse atmosphere after wins, Belanger elevated small talk into something relevant without being called a clubhouse lawyer. Late after games, Belanger was still in his canvas chair by his locker talking baseball through a haze of Marlboro cigarette smoke and sips of National Bohemian beer.

Detroit manager Mayo Smith declared that trying to get a hit through the left side of the Baltimore infield was like "trying to throw a hamburger through a brick wall."[12] But in the 1969 World Series the New York Mets did just that, rolling seeing-eye hits between Mark and Brooks—back-to-back no less—in the top of the ninth inning of Game Two en route to a five-game upset. When left fielder Don Buford lost Jerry Grote's double in the sun in the tenth inning of Game Four, and Belanger almost caught the ball, color commentator Lou Boudreau said he "never saw a shortstop go that far." Broadcaster Tony Kubek called him a fourth outfielder.[13]

In 1970 Charlie Lau signed with Oakland, and Belanger jammed his thumb in March. He was described as lost at the plate, batting "all-arm"[14] without a clue. He developed "projection room eyes" from looking at so much film, but all he got for it was a .218 average and a mountain of broken bats.[15] He did hit .333 in the American League Championship Series—in the opener against Minnesota, Belanger's soft liner off pitcher Jim Perry's glove was called the turning point, loading the bases for Mike Cuellar's fourth-inning grand slam. Belanger hit just .105 in the World Series, but celebrated the Orioles' victory anyway. The next year he rebounded to a more respectable .266 and captured his second Gold Glove.

In 1972 Weaver gave a lot of middle-infield at bats to newcomer Bobby Grich, causing Belanger's playing time to be cut in half (he hit just .186), and Baltimore suffered its worst record during Belanger's career. After the season the Orioles traded away Davey Johnson and installed Grich at second base, giving Belanger his full-time job back. The next two seasons were remarkably similar for Belanger and the Orioles. He hit .226 and .225 and captured a Gold Glove award after each season.

The Orioles had second-half surges each season to come from behind to win the division title, before dropping the League Championship Series to the Athletics each season.

The trade-off between Belanger's lousy offense and great defense was usually one Weaver was willing to make, but he was not above trying to gain an edge. In September of 1975, Weaver often used Royle Stillman as the shortstop high in the starting lineup in road games, allowing rookie Stillman to bat in the first inning and Belanger to replace him in the bottom of the first. Stillman was an outfielder, and never played an inning of shortstop in his career, despite his six "starts" there in 1975. He hit 3-for-6 in these games.

Belanger holds the American League career record for being pinch-hit for—333 times. And if he wasn't being pinch-hit for, he was sacrificing; his league-leading 23 sacrifices in 1975 were an Oriole record at least through 2009. In 1976 Belanger carried a .300 average into June and earned over a million votes in the All-Star balloting, making the team as a backup. When Peter Gammons wrote, "Belanger could be the first 140 lb. weakling to win the MVP award," Belanger sought him out at Fenway Park and confronted him: "I'm 170 pounds, and I'm not a weakling."[16] The next year, writing for *Sports Illustrated*, Gammons called Belanger "the leader of the club."[17] One of the last players to represent himself and not use an agent, Belanger signed after 1976 for $60,000, a contract that was later extended through the end of the 1981 season.

On July 28, 1977, even though he was going for his fiftieth consecutive errorless game, he was benched by Weaver and watched his replacement, Kiko Garcia, drop a first-inning pop-up that led to a big loss. Belanger's streak ended on August 20 at 62 games, 48 of them starts. When the team contended in late September, the *Baltimore Sun* called Belanger the "blood and guts of the team."[18] But Belanger went beyond the established bounds of team leadership. He and his wife, Daryl "Dee" Belanger, hosted teammates for baseball talk and home cooking at his residences in Timonium, Maryland, and Key Biscayne, Florida. Pitcher Steve Stone credited one such evening with making him feel comfortable with the team and for his subsequent 1979 success. In 1975 Mark and Dee even suggested that the Orioles play John Denver's "Thank God I'm a Country Boy" during the seventh-inning stretch, the start of a tradition that has spread today to many sports in many cities.

Belanger spent countless hours tutoring young infielders Doug DeCinces, Rich Dauer, Kiko Garcia, and Billy Smith, and the rookies helped him set the Baltimore record for double plays in 1977. When second baseman Dauer set a record by playing in seventy-four consecutive games without an error, he thanked Belanger. "He taught me how to play every hitter . . . and taught me our pitching staff," Dauer said.[19]

In 1980 a two-error game in July was noted to be his first in six years, and Major League shortstops surveyed by *Sport* magazine voted Belanger the best at the position. On September 4, 1981, Weaver benched Belanger, batting .165, for Lenny Sakata amid a team batting slump. Belanger, complaining about a sore shoulder, never started again. Sakata popped a grand slam two days later, coming out twice for curtain calls, and Weaver chortled, "He's been keeping rallies going for us since he's been in there,"[20] a remark poignant for the punchless Belanger, who wasn't even subbing in the late innings any more. Belanger's last game with the Orioles was on October 4, but he asked Weaver not to play him, saying, "I haven't been playing, and I'm not sharp."[21] Public-address announcer Rex Barney thanked Belanger in the top of the eighth inning for the privilege of watching him play. Applause built until Belanger appeared on the top step of the dugout and tipped his cap, an act that only made the stadium roar, delaying the game. The Orioles released him on November 13.

Reflecting on the Orioles without Belanger, catcher Rick Dempsey said, "I feel like we lost half the club."[22]

Belanger signed with the Los Angeles Dodgers for $250,000 on December 11, 1981, to play one last season. Along with his utility-infielder duties, he handed lineup cards to umpires and pitched batting practice. Walking by manager Tommy Lasorda's office in March, Belanger cringed when Lasorda yelled out: "Belanger!" Expecting Weaverlike browbeating, Belanger entered the office only to be told Lasorda wanted a hug.[23] He got a key hit in a Dodgers win on July 31, and walked twice in a final start against fireballer Nolan Ryan. The last grounder he fielded was from Tony Gwynn on September 21.

For many, the close of Mark Belanger's playing days only heralded the beginnings of his real contributions to baseball. The assistant player representative for Baltimore since 1971, Belanger rose to player representative in 1977 when Brooks Robinson retired and took pains to make sure Donald Fehr, then the chief counsel of the Major League Players Association, understood the rank-and-file's concerns. Belanger was tested as the players' front man in the fifty-day strike of 1981 and fought for bargaining benefits that he himself would probably never collect. Belanger's pro-union stance contrasted with that of big earners like Reggie Jackson, who seemed ready to cave in.

Upon Belanger's retirement, player reps demanded that a spot be created for him right under Ken Moffett, the executive director of the players union. Belanger turned down a lucrative offer from Personal Management Associates, a Baltimore player agency headed by Ron Shapiro, and became a tireless "special assistant" to Moffett and later Don Fehr. The partnership with Fehr was fruitful. Belanger brought credibility to executive-board sessions and acted as Fehr's personal bellwether for player opinion. Fehr himself claimed he didn't feel comfortable in the job until 1986.

Until then, Belanger stood behind him at nearly every public appearance, arms folded, repeating key words, and interrupting Fehr's legalese at least once with: "Don. You lost them."[24] Eventually, Belanger's own earnings topped $400,000 annually, yet he still took a personal interest in nearly every player grievance that came across his desk, helping the union move to Midtown Manhattan and to computerize member data. Still making time to play golf with his brother, Al, at the Berkshire Hills Country Club on Saturday mornings, Belanger saw the median Major League salary top $1,000,000 in 1992.

A skiing accident at Lake Tahoe, Nevada, early in January 1997 led to lingering discomfort and a diagnosis of lung cancer that April. Belanger, who had quit smoking in 1991, took the challenge in an upbeat, optimistic mood. He married his second wife, Virginia French, three months later, and worked for the MLPA while an outpatient until he died shortly after the 1998 regular season ended, on October 6, at the age of fifty-four. Besides his wife, he was survived by two sons, Richard and Robert.

Chapter 30. Dick Hall

Chip Greene

AGE	W	L	PCT.	ERA	G	GS	GF	CG	SHO	SV	IP	H	BB	SO	HBP	WP
39	10	5	.667	3.08	32	0	17	0	0	3	61.1	51	6	30	0	0

In June 1970 Ted Williams, then managing the Washington Senators, reminisced for a reporter about the first time Williams had ever seen Dick Hall pitch. Hall, Williams recalled, "was taking his warmup throws, having come in to relieve somebody. I was kneeling in the on-deck circle and I thought to myself, 'Oh, boy, he'll be nice to hit. But was I wrong! He's a pinpointer. He's here and he's there—never throwing in the same spot twice. You never get a fat pitch to hit."

By 1970, Williams had lost none of his appreciation for the tall (6 feet 6½), right-handed reliever. If anything, Williams concluded, "his control is sharper. You can't wait around for him to walk you. You'd better go up there swinging."[1]

Indeed, Williams wouldn't be the only hitter left with that impression. In his fourteen Major League seasons as a pitcher, Richard Wallace Hall displayed remarkable control, and even into his forties proved a durable and effective relief pitcher. He was the consummate control artist, who seemed to get better with age. Asked in retirement to what he attributed his uncanny ability to avoid issuing bases on balls, Hall responded: "Partly it's concentration; partly I was just born that way; and partly I just played a lot."[2] Whatever the explanation, as former Major League pitcher and longtime Baltimore Orioles announcer Rex Barney wrote, "It looked like anybody in the world could hit him, but he knew where to throw the ball. Location, location."[3] As Barney and countless others for so long admired, Dick Hall threw "nothing but strikes."[4] Over the final seven years of his career, a period that spanned 462 innings, Dick Hall issued a total of only 23 unintentional walks.

The oldest American League player in 1970, Dick Hall was an outstanding asset to the Orioles' deep bullpen.

Hall didn't begin his Major League career as a pitcher. At Swarthmore College, a prestigious private university in Swarthmore, Pennsylvania, Hall majored in economics (graduating with a bachelor's degree in January 1953) and minored in history and political science. He also earned eleven athletic letters in five sports. In basketball, Hall was twice named All Conference; in football, he won honorable mention Little All-America after catching 24 passes and scoring 9 touchdowns in 1948; and in track, for many years Hall held the

151

school broad jump record, at 23 feet one-half inch. He also scored a goal as a substitute on the soccer team.

Hall's greatest athletic success, however, was on the baseball diamond. By the time he began his college career, he hadn't played the game very long. Born in St. Louis, Missouri, on September 27, 1930, Hall lived there only five months before his family relocated for five years to Albany, New York, and then for ten years to Bergen County, New Jersey. In New Jersey, he attended Tenafly High School for a year and a half, then for the next two and a half years attended Mount Hermon School, in Massachusetts, from which he graduated. Growing up, Hall didn't play a lot of baseball: "I always played softball as a kid," he said. It wasn't until he was sixteen years old, by which time the family had relocated to the Baltimore area, that Hall began to play baseball. He was a member of a sixteen-year-old team that won the Cardinal Gibbons championship, and that, he said, "was my first taste of baseball."[5]

At Mount Hermon School (now Northfield Mount Hermon School), Hall was a versatile athlete, participating in baseball, football, and basketball. That experience prepared him for athletics at Swarthmore, where he became a baseball star. Pitching and moving to center field when he was not on the mound, in three years Hall batted an impressive .464. Swarthmore played a schedule of only thirteen games, Hall later remembered, but in that time he stroked seven home runs. As a pitcher, Hall averaged 15 strikeouts per game and posted an earned run average of 0.67 in his junior year. He also played summer baseball for two seasons in the Susquehanna League, and semipro ball for East Douglas, Massachusetts, in the Blackstone Valley League.

By Hall's junior year at Swarthmore, Major League scouts were showing up to watch him play, and all sixteen teams expressed interest in signing him. Fifteen of the teams were interested in him

as a pitcher, but the Pittsburgh Pirates and their general manager, the legendary Branch Rickey, were interested in Hall as a hitter. In September 1951, after an impressive late-summer tryout before Rickey at Forbes Field, Hall signed for a bonus of $25,000.[6]

In 1960, when Hall was pitching for the Kansas City Athletics, the scout Jocko Collins recounted how he had scouted Hall at Swarthmore. "I saw him pitch and play the outfield often," Collins recalled:

> The difference is that he has learned how to pitch. . . . I liked Dick a lot and recommended him highly [to the Phillies]. I liked him as an outfielder. He had size, power, speed, and a big-league arm that was something extra. . . . He hit the fastball good, but was a little weak on the curve. . . . His running, throwing, and fielding certainly were good enough for the majors. To be a real good major leaguer he had to improve his hitting. If he had stayed in center, I think he would have done much better.[7]

Phillies owner Bob Carpenter considered making an offer to Hall but eventually declined because, as he put it, "How can you pay that much for a guy when you don't even know what position he plays?"[8]

For three years the Pirates struggled to find a position for Hall. They tried him variously at shortstop, first base, third base, and the outfield, without success. He never developed into a Major League hitter, although Pittsburgh made every effort to improve his skills. One day in August 1955, after Hall had switched from hitter to pitcher, he was sitting in the dugout at Philadelphia's Connie Mack Stadium when a reporter asked him what had prompted his change from the batter's box to the mound. "Simple," Hall responded, "I couldn't hit."[9]

Rickey, who loved Hall's arm and speed, considered the collegian a "can't-miss" prospect and thought he'd eventually develop into a fine hitter. Yet after making the team in spring training of 1952, Hall ended that season hitting just .138, with 17 strikeouts in 80 at bats. Optioned on May 7 to Class B Burlington, he played 101 games there, mostly at shortstop, and batted .242. In 1953, after starting the season with a handful of games at Burlington, Hall was sent to Waco, Texas, in the Class B Big State League, where he batted .246 and hit 6 home runs in 95 games. Recalled again to Pittsburgh on September 1, he appeared in just seven games for the Pirates, this time at second base, and managed just 4 singles in 24 at bats, a .167 batting average. Finally, in 1954, Hall spent the entire season with Pittsburgh, yet hit just .239 in 112 games before the Pirates decided he would never be able to hit at the Major League level.

The seeds for the decision to make Hall a pitcher had been planted in Mexico. Beginning in the winter of 1953–54, the Pirates sent Hall south each year to work on his hitting. He played winter ball there for four years and fell in love with the country and its people. "There isn't enough I can say about Mexico and the people there," Hall later related. "Playing ball there was pure heaven. Four games a week in a semitropical paradise—how could you beat it?"[10]

He played in Mazatlan, in the Mexican Pacific Coast League. "We'd play four games every weekend, including Sunday mornings," he recalled. "That was when you hit the home runs, before the afternoon winds came up."[11] He began the winter of 1953-54 as an outfielder but ended at second base. That winter, in an 80-game season, Hall hit 20 home runs, a league record that was tied by Luke Easter the following winter.

He also found there the love of his life in Mexico. During that first winter he met Maria Elena Nieto; they were married on December 31, 1955, and would ultimately produce three daughters and a son.

"She was queen of the Mazatlan ballclub," Hall said. "She participated in the opening-day ritual. At the time she didn't speak English, so it was up to me to speak Spanish. I learned more in Mexico than I did in college."[12] Ultimately, Hall learned to speak the language fluently, and for the rest of his career would always engage his Latin teammates in conversation in their native language. (Brooks Robinson, who became one of Hall's closest friends, related that during the 1970 World Series, when the American players were asked by the Latin press for interviews, "we grabbed Dick Hall to serve as interpreter. He's married to a beautiful gal from Mexico and speaks Spanish like Juan Valdez."[13])

Hall began to pitch in the winter of 1954. At Mazatlan, the team was managed by a man named Memo Garibay, and in a 1970 interview Hall credited Garibay with getting him "interested in pitching." Hall elaborated: "In the winter of 1954–55 Mr. Rickey sent me down to Mexico . . . to work on my hitting, and I told Memo I had done some pitching in college and could help out in the pinch. We got in a bind one day and he called me in from center field. I pitched two scoreless innings, I think it was, and ended up winning the game. Memo said, 'I think your future is on the mound.'"[14] (In Hall's last season in the Mexican League, he set a league ERA record of 1.20.)

Hall, the Pirates decided, would become a pitcher.

In April 1955, in what was meant to be a developmental period, Hall was optioned to Lincoln, Nebraska, the Pirates' entry in the Single-A Western League, and was sensational. Playing alternately at both pitcher and left field, in two months Hall won 12 games and led the league in winning percentage (.706) and ERA (2.24); he also led the club with a .302 batting average. So good was he that on July 21 the Pirates recalled Hall and inserted him into their starting rotation.

He made his first start on July 24, and it was quite memorable. Facing the Chicago Cubs at Pittsburgh's Forbes Field, Hall struck out 11 in a 12–5 Pirates win. At the time he had no idea that the team record for strikeouts in a game was 12, set by Babe Adams in 1909. "I didn't know I was anywhere near the record," Hall later remembered, "until someone told me after the game. I just kept firing away."[15]

Since he hadn't had much time to develop as a pitcher, Hall's pitch selection at the time was minimal. "I had only a fastball and control then," he said, "and all I knew was to throw hard and get the ball over."[16]

In time, he expanded his repertoire. When Hall was later playing for the Phillies, in 1967, the press reported that the tall right-hander "knows all the tricks of pitching" and "throws harder than he seems to." By then he threw three pitches, having added to his "sneaky fastball" both "a good slider and fine change." Of utmost importance, it was also noted, Hall "can hit a dime with any of his pitches." Yet he threw with a delivery that was anything but efficient. "The ball comes right out of his shirt," a sportswriter wrote, "because of the unusual, awkward-looking motion he uses."[17] The delivery made it difficult for hitters to pick up the ball as it left his hand.

Hall admitted that his delivery looked awkward. "The best description I've heard of what I look like on the mound," he said, "is a drunken giraffe on roller skates."[18] A reporter described the delivery this way: "He draws his arm back and strides stiff-legged toward the plate, then when his arm is only halfway back, he brings it forward sidearm and delivers not too fast."[19] It might not have been the classic way to pitch, but no one could argue with the results.

By the end of 1955 the Pirates had penciled Hall into their rotation for the following season. Appearing in 15 games in 1955, with 13 starts, he ended with a 6-6 record and a 3.91 ERA. But instead of a continuation of that relatively successful debut, the next several years proved disastrous. During Hall's first winter pitching in Mexico, Rickey had encouraged him to try to develop a pitch to supplement his fastball. Rickey suggested a knuckleball. Rather than mastering the knuckler, though, Hall injured his arm throwing the pitch.

Over the next two seasons, as Hall battled his injury, he pitched just 72 innings and compiled an 0-7 record. He was on the disabled list once in each season, and was unable to recover his effectiveness. Finally, Pirates manager Bobby Bragan, who admittedly "wasn't a Dick Hall man from the start,"[20] had seen enough, and on June 17, 1957, Hall was assigned outright to Columbus. There he pitched 91 innings in 14 games and finished with a record of 4-7.

Hall didn't pitch at all in 1958. Two noteworthy things happened that year, though. First, he was transferred to the Pirates' Salt Lake City affiliate. During spring training with Salt Lake City, Hall developed hepatitis and spent the entire season on the voluntarily retired list. Out of action for the year, Hall conscientiously prepared himself for a post-baseball career by studying accounting at the University of Utah's Graduate School of Business. It was a move that served him well once his baseball career was finished.

As it turned out, his career was just getting started. By 1959 Hall's arm was finally healthy, and he celebrated with a wonderful season. That year, pitching in Salt Lake City, Hall led the Pacific Coast League in wins (18), percentage (.783), ERA (1.87), and shutouts (6) and was named the PBL's Most Valuable Player. Interviewed years later, Hall remembered that he won $55 that season, too. Larry Shepard was the Salt Lake City manager. At the beginning of the season, Hall said, Shepard told the mound staff, "If you pitch an entire game, win, and walk no one, I'll give you five dollars."[21] The result was Hall's $55 windfall.

With confidence in the right-hander seemingly renewed, the Pirates recalled Hall in September 1959; he pitched in two games, made one start, didn't earn a decision, and walked only one in 8⅓ innings. But that marked the end of his Pirates career. On December 9, Hall was traded, along with infielder Ken Hamlin and a player to be named later (eventually catcher Hank Foiles), to the Kansas City Athletics, for catcher Hal Smith.

The trade was "a real shock," Hall recalled. "I'd been in the Pittsburgh organization eight years, when all of a sudden I got traded." Moreover, "I couldn't name a single player on the Kansas City team."[22] His feelings weren't assuaged any when the Pirates went on to win the World Series in 1960, while the Athletics finished last in the American League.

Yet Hall was renewed in Kansas City. Used as a starter throughout the year (29 times), he finished the season 8-13 with an ERA of 4.05. Impressively, too, he walked just 38 batters in 182⅓ innings. Then he was traded again. On April 13, 1961, Kansas City sent the thirty-year-old Hall and outfielder Dick Williams to the Baltimore Orioles for pitcher Jerry Walker and outfielder Chuck Essegian. This time, Hall recalled, "I was fine" with the trade.[23] And over the next six years he developed into a vital component of the Orioles' pitching staff, first as a starter and eventually as a reliever as his "elbow again gave me trouble."[24]

By the mid-1960s Hall had become one of the premier relievers in the game, largely by virtue of his hard work. Indeed, noted the press, "No player is more attentive to training and mechanics than the scholarly Swarthmore grad."[25] (Pitching coach Jim Frey commented: "Turkey is one of the best-conditioned players I've ever seen."[26]) The rewards for Hall's hard work were impressive ERAs (3.09, 2.28, 2.98, 1.85, and 3.07 from 1961 through '65) and a paucity of walks.

Although he developed a reputation as an intellectual—"a brilliant guy," was how Rex Barney described him[27]—Hall's approach to pitching was rather simple. With his unique delivery ("A lot of people say, oh, you were a side-arm pitcher, but I really threw 'short-arm,'" he remembered), Hall threw a rising fastball, and "I'd just throw on the outside corner, trying to get them to hit it to center field." As a result, batters "couldn't hit down the line," and "when I was throwing good, I'd throw a lot of pop-ups and fly balls."[28]

In 1963 he won five games and saved 12, but his most impressive stretch occurred between July 24 and August 17, during which Hall retired twenty-eight men in order. "That was my first perfect game," Hall said. "I never had one before and this one took 25 days."[29]

During those years, Hall also gained renown as a Yankee killer. In 1963 and '64, over a span of ten relief appearances against New York, he pitched 18⅔ innings, allowed only two runs, and posted a 3-1 record, with one save. "I know he's been good against us for a couple years," said manager Yogi Berra at the time, "but I don't know why. The ball sure looks good to hit, but we don't hit it."[30] On June 24 in Baltimore, in the top of the eighth inning, Bobby Richardson and Mickey Mantle singled with no outs, and Hall promptly retired the next three hitters on three pitches.

Between 1961 and 1966, Hall's record with the Orioles was 44-27 (.620), with 48 saves. In 599⅔ innings, he allowed 496 hits and walked only 100, 29 intentionally. By 1966, though, Hall's ERA had soared to 3.95; midway through the season he developed tendinitis near his right elbow, and the pain limited his work. He didn't pitch at all in the Orioles' World Series win that year over the Dodgers, and he wasn't surprised when Orioles general manager Harry Dalton called him at one o'clock on the morning of December 16 to tell Hall he'd been traded to the Phillies for a player to be named later. "Looking at it objectively," Hall told the Philadelphia press, "it wasn't much of a shock."[31]

In 1967 Hall was outstanding for the Phillies, posting a 2.20 ERA with 8 saves in 86 innings. On

June 15, he made his first start in four years, replacing an ailing Jim Bunning and recording a surprising 4–1 complete-game victory over the Pirates at Connie Mack Stadium. However, the following year he again developed a sore elbow, pitched just 46 innings, and posted an ERA of 4.89, and on October 29 was given his unconditional release. When no team came calling, Hall once again contacted Harry Dalton, who, as Hall remembered, invited the veteran to "come down to spring training; we'll give you a shot."[32]

With the soreness in his elbow gone after a winter's rest, Hall pitched 11 scoreless innings in spring training and made the 1969 team. "The way he has looked, Hall could pick up the phone right now and get five jobs," commented manager Earl Weaver as spring training ended.[33] During the regular season, pitching 65⅔ innings, Hall won 5 games, saved 6, and posted a 1.92 earned run average. Moreover, in the entire season he issued just 3 unintentional walks.

The thirty-nine-year-old finally made a postseason appearance. On October 4, 1969, at Memorial Stadium, in the first American League Championship Series game ever played, Hall was the winning pitcher in a 4–3 Orioles victory over the Minnesota Twins. It was his only ALCS appearance that year. In the Orioles' World Series loss to the Mets, in Game Four, at Shea Stadium, Hall was charged with the loss.

Three weeks later, Hall took an important test. For eight straight winters he had worked at the accounting firm of Main, Lafrentz; during his illness in 1958, he had also studied accounting. He knew what he would do with the rest of his life, so after the World Series he sat for the CPA exam. Several months later he was notified that he had passed, recording a score that tied him for second in the state of Maryland among several hundred who took the three-day test.

Despite being the oldest active player in the American League in 1970 (he turned forty on September 27), Hall threw 61⅓ innings and finished 10-5 with an ERA of 3.08 and three saves. He issued just six walks, only four of them unintentionally. In Game One of the 1970 ALCS, again versus Minnesota, Hall was the winner, allowing only one runner in 4⅓ innings. And in Game Two of the 1970 World Series, in Cincinnati, Hall entered the game in the bottom of the seventh inning with runners on first and second and two outs, and over the final 2⅓ innings retired Tony Perez, Johnny Bench, Lee May, Hal McRae, Tommy Helms, and pinch hitters Bernie Carbo and Jimmy Stewart to save the Orioles' 6–5 victory.

After that appearance, the Reds offered their opinions of the forty-year old veteran's offerings: "His pitches don't seem to be moving, but I guess it's deceiving. He keeps getting people out," said Tommy Helms. Tony Perez lamented, "He's got that funny motion. He throws a change-up or a palm ball. I don't know what it is. Oh, that pitch he gave to me was a good one to hit." And Johnny Bench told reporters, "I tried to go right on him, then I changed my swing and I got all screwed up."[34]

During the game, Bench had hollered at Hall from the dugout, "How can you be out there with that garbage?" and Hall had just grinned. "Even though I wasn't throwing too well," Hall said, "the Reds weren't hitting the ball squarely."[35]

In 1971 Hall, at the age of forty-one the oldest player in baseball, and pitched his final season. In 27 games, he threw only 43⅓ innings, won 6 games and saved 1, but finished with an ERA of 4.98. On October 11, in Game Two of the World Series against the Pirates at Memorial Stadium, he earned a save for Jim Palmer in what turned out to be Hall's final Major League appearance. It was only fitting that it should be against the Pirates, the team with which it had all begun.

"I guess one of the things I like about baseball," Hall said in 1970, "is that, unlike football, force isn't necessary. The pitch comes in one direction, you hit in another, and you run in still another. You might call it a cat-and-mouse game, this battle between the pitcher and hitter. I enjoy it. I like the competitive approach. Yes, I really enjoy the challenges in baseball. And if I can get paid for it, why not?"[36]

As of 2009 Hall had been married fifty-three years, and he had four children and nine grandchildren. He began working as an accountant during his career, and did it full-time until 2001 and part-time for several years after. He suffered a stroke in 2001, from which he mostly recovered. He told the *Baltimore Sun* in 2009, "I've had one knee replaced and my [right] shoulder is shot—I can't throw a ball 50 feet. But I can walk and play golf, and that's good enough."[37] Living in the greater Baltimore area, he played golf twice a week with former Orioles Billy Hunter and Ron Hansen.

For the better part of nineteen Major League seasons, Dick Hall got paid to throw his sneaky fastball over the outside edge of the plate. And for the better part of nineteen years, it's safe to say that Dick Hall provided a pretty good return on that investment.

Chapter 31. July 1970 Timeline

Malcolm Allen

All headlines below are from the next day's edition of the *Baltimore Sun*.

July 1—PALMER HURLS BIRDS TO 3–0 SHUTOUT WIN OVER CLEVELAND—The Orioles improved to 8-0 against the Tribe in 1970 behind Jim Palmer's eight-hitter. Brooks Robinson doubled three times and scored two of Baltimore's runs.

July 2—TRIBE NIPS BIRDS, ENDS LOSS SKEIN— Indians rookie Ray Fosse extended his hitting streak to twenty-three games with a three-run homer in the first off Jim Hardin, one pitch after a disputed two-strike checked swing. A furious Earl Weaver argued with plate umpire Jake O'Donnell for several minutes, earning his first ejection of the season. Four Baltimore errors led to three unearned runs, turning a lead into a deficit, and Cleveland first baseman Tony Horton homered in the ninth to become the first player to hit for the cycle at Memorial Stadium.

July 3—ORIOLES WIN ON 4-HITTER BY CUELLAR— The Orioles scored their runs on three sacrifice flies and a wild pitch to avenge a previous shutout loss to Mickey Lolich by blanking Detroit, 4–0. Mike Cuellar overcame a forty-six-minute fourth-inning rain delay to record his ninth win.

July 4—5-RUN 9TH ENABLES TIGERS TO PULL OUT 6–5 WIN OVER BIRDS—Dave McNally's 5–1 lead went up in smoke in the ninth inning as pinch hitter Norm Cash greeted Pete Richert with a long home run to tie the game. Two batters later, Mickey Stanley went deep to win it. Terry Crowley's bid

for a two-run, game-saving blast in the bottom of the ninth fell just short, but Earl Weaver managed to keep things in perspective. "(The loss) means that the day we clinch it, we could've clinched it one day earlier," the skipper observed.[1]

July 5—ORIOLES WIN ON PALMER'S 3-HITTER— The Baltimore faithful booed Detroit's Denny McLain roundly in just his second start back from a suspension for his part in a bookmaking operation. McLain was wild, yet effective, but Jim Palmer outpitched him by hurling his second straight shutout, 2–0. Boog Powell drove in both Baltimore runs to take over the AL lead in RBIS.

July 6—The Orioles blew a 3–2 ninth-inning lead in an exhibition in Norfolk, Virginia, losing to the International League All-Stars on a base hit by Angel Mangual.

July 7—BIRDS BEAT YANKS IN TENTH, 6–2— Commissioner Bowie Kuhn restored fan voting to choose the starting lineups for the All-Star Game in 1970 after twelve years, and Boog Powell learned he'd received more votes than any other American League player. Frank Robinson got the most support among AL outfielders, and Earl Weaver chose Davey Johnson to start at second base with fan choice Rod Carew out with a knee injury. That night against second-place New York at Memorial Stadium, the Yankees were down to their last out before forcing the game into extra innings. Mike Cuellar earned the victory anyway, though, pitching a scoreless tenth before Brooks Robinson settled matters with a game-winning grand slam. Number Five's blast inside the left-field foul pole on a 3-2 pitch from Yankees relief ace Lindy McDaniel was his first "granny" since 1962.

July 8—BIRDS EDGE YANKS WITH 3-RUN NINTH—Dave McNally was roughed up hours after he, Mike Cuellar, and Jim Palmer were named to the American League's All-Star pitching staff. Rookie Yankees reliever Ron Klimkowski knocked Frank Robinson down in the second inning, but coughed up a New York lead two frames later when Boog Powell and Frank took him deep back-to-back. After the Yankees regained the lead on former Oriole Curt Blefary's home run in the eighth, Frank Robinson ignited Baltimore's ninth-inning rally with his fourth hit of the night: a mammoth, 450-foot dinger to the base of the new scoreboard construction in left-center field. Still down, 8–7, the Birds quickly loaded the bases, but after Lindy McDaniel struck out Terry Crowley and Elrod Hendricks, red-hot Don Buford (25 for his last 50) stroked a two-run single past first baseman Danny Cater for a 9–8 Orioles victory. Davey Johnson raced home from second base with the winning run, touching home plate with his left hand just ahead of Thurman Munson's tag. The next day, New York coach Elston Howard—who had been in pinstripes since 1955—said, "Last night's loss was the toughest I can ever remember as a Yankee."[2]

July 9—YANKS HAND BIRDS 7-5 LOSS IN RAIN-SHORTENED CONTEST—On a rainy Thursday night in Baltimore, it looked for a moment as if the Orioles might get a rain-shortened 5–4 victory and a sweep when umpire Hank Soar called for the tarpaulin in the bottom of the fifth. The determined Yankees refused to leave the diamond, though, and seized control of the game with three unearned runs the following inning after rookie Bobby Grich's throwing error. New York earned

a 7–5 victory in a game halted after eight innings, but left town in third place anyway.

July 10—CAIN'S HIT HELPS SINK BIRDS, 4–2—In front of a big Friday night crowd (44,568) at Tiger Stadium, Jim Palmer's scoreless innings streak ended at nineteen, and the Orioles got outhit 12–4 and lost to Detroit southpaw Les Cain. Sparkling Baltimore defense kept the score closer than it probably should have been. Earlier in the day, Brooks Robinson was added to the AL All-Star squad as a reserve.

July 11—HOME RUNS LIFT BIRDS TO 6–5 WIN—Mike Cuellar struggled through seven innings but helped himself to his eleventh victory by collecting a career-high three hits, including his second homer of the season. Though Paul Blair was in the late stages of a 5-for-53 slump, his Gold Glove defense was in top form when he scaled the fence in left-center to haul in Al Kaline's 400-foot drive for the final out.

July 12—BIRDS SPLIT IN TWIN BILL WITH TIGERS—The largest Tiger Stadium crowd (53,959) in nine years saw Detroit clobber Dave McNally for three homers and a season-worst seven runs in less than three innings in the matinee of a Sunday doubleheader. The Tigers tied a record by laying down three sacrifice bunts in the second inning, one of which caused Earl Weaver to file a formal protest of Baltimore's 7–3 defeat, arguing that Detroit's Mickey Lolich interfered with Andy Etchebarren. In the nightcap, the Orioles pounded Denny McLain and four relievers, 13–3. Boog Powell homered into the distant center-field bleachers and collected four RBIs, Elrod Hendricks drove a long ball into the right-field upper deck, and Merv Rettenmund added four hits. Dick Hall retired the last fourteen Detroit hitters to earn the win with 6⅓ innings of one-hit-shutout relief. Don Buford got the big enemy crowd cheering in the eighth for his leaping, somersault catch of a drive by Don Wert. The Orioles headed into the All-Star break with a 54-33 record, and a six-game American League East lead over the second-place Tigers.

July 13—All-Star break.

July 14—At brand-new Riverfront Stadium in Cincinnati—only two weeks old—Jim Palmer started the All-Star Game for the American League and hurled three shutout innings. Frank Robinson, Boog Powell, and Davey Johnson combined to go 1-for-11 against the Senior Circuit, but Brooks Robinson came off the bench to single against Gaylord Perry and rap a two-run triple off Bob Gibson. After the National Leaguers scored three times in the bottom of the ninth to tie the game, they prevailed in the twelfth when Pete Rose steamrolled over Cleveland catcher Ray Fosse to score the winning run on Jim Hickman's two-out hit. Some observers were appalled by Rose's aggressive play, which made the NL the winner for the thirteenth time in the last fifteen All-Star Games, but Earl Weaver remarked, "That's just part of the game. Fosse was just trying to block him from the plate."[3]

July 15—All-Star break.

July 16—BIRDS TUMBLE TWINS, 5–1—Mike Cuellar went the distance for his fourth win in a row on a cool and breezy Thursday night as Baltimore beat the only American League team with a better first-half record.

July 17—TWINS DOWN BIRDS, 6–5, IN 10 INNINGS—Memorial Stadium's largest regular-season crowd in nearly two years—40,169 for T-shirt Night—saw their Orioles cough up leads in the seventh and ninth innings after leading most of the way. Minnesota prevailed on backup catcher Tom Tischinski's two-out hit for his first RBI of the sea-

son. In the seventh, Twins reliever Stan Williams drew a warning from plate umpire Nestor Chylak after one of his pitches hit Frank Robinson on the hand and two others came close to the chin of Elrod Hendricks.

July 18—TWINS BEAT BIRDS WITH 4-RUN SIXTH—Frank Robinson stroked four hits and Boog Powell flashed great reflexes to start a double play, but Harmon Killebrew and Frank Quilici rapped two-run homers off Dave McNally in the sixth to help Minnesota win the series.

July 19—BIRDS SPLIT PAIR WITH WHITE SOX—A Sunday doubleheader at Comiskey Park took nearly eight hours to complete thanks to a pair of rain delays. Jim Palmer pitched the Orioles to an 8–2 victory in the opener, with center fielder Merv Rettenmund temporarily preserving the shutout in the sixth. Rettenmund crashed through an unlocked gate in the fence to make a grab with two aboard, then toppled into the Baltimore bullpen. Chicago sent Tom Phoebus to an early shower in the first inning of the second game, and Earl Weaver joined him two innings later after getting tossed by plate umpire Lou DiMuro for disputing a checked-swing call. Recalling that DiMuro was the umpire who awarded first base to the Mets' Cleon Jones on a disputed hit-by-pitch in the 1969 World Series after a baseball with shoe polish on it was shown to him, Weaver approached DiMuro with a ball of his own, lifted his left foot to rub shoe polish on it, and dropped it at the umpire's feet. An angry DiMuro picked up the baseball and hurled it into the Orioles' dugout on a bounce, whereupon coach Billy Hunter tried to throw it back at him. Hunter missed, and by the time Chicago won the game 7–3, only about 1,000 fans remained in the ballpark.

July 20—ORIOLE BATS UNLOAD ON CHISOX—Elrod Hendricks homered for the fifth time in seven games, driving in a career-high six runs, four on a grand slam off White Sox southpaw Barry Moore. Baltimore stormed to a 14–5 win with its second highest scoring output of the season, trailing only the eighteen runs the team scored on April 29, also at Comiskey Park.

July 21—ORIOLES NIP KANSAS CITY IN 9TH, 2–1—Rookie Royals lefty Bob Johnson struck out eleven Baltimore batters, but Terry Crowley's ninth-inning double off the left-field wall drove in Brooks Robinson with the tie-breaking run.

July 22—BIRDS EDGE ROYALS IN 13TH BY 4–3—Four Baltimore relievers combined to hurl 5⅓ innings of one-hit relief after Kansas City came back to tie in the bottom of the eighth, allowing the Orioles to prevail on Chico Salmon's perfect two-out bunt single. Two pitches after swinging at a Ted Abernathy submarine ball that was over his head, Salmon expertly pushed a ball to the first-base side of the mound as Davey Johnson raced home with the decisive run.

July 23—BIRDS NIP ROYALS BY 5–4 SCORE—Starting at shortstop in place of Mark Belanger, rookie Bobby Grich made three sparkling defensive plays and tripled home the Orioles' fifth and final run as Baltimore beat Kansas City for the twentieth time in a row.

July 24—KAAT HURLS TWINS PAST BIRDS, 8–0—Mike Cuellar was bombed for six runs in less than five innings, and the Orioles' offense moved only one runner past first base. Minnesota's Harmon Killebrew homered for the fifth straight game against Baltimore, and Birds shortstop Mark Belanger uncharacteristically committed three errors.

July 25—BIRDS EDGE TWINS WITH LATE HOMER—At windy Municipal Stadium, Don Buford was almost hit in the head when he misjudged Harmon Killebrew's fourth-inning fly, turning it into an RBI double. After Dick Hall hustled for his first hit of the year in the eighth, though, Buford redeemed himself by belting a two-run homer to lead Baltimore to a 6–5 victory.

July 26—BOOG BELTS GRAND SLAM IN 11–1 WIN—Fifteen of sixteen Orioles hits were singles as they trounced fifteen-game-winner Jim Perry, but Boog Powell clobbered a grand slam to the base of the scoreboard in right-center and drove in six to lead the way. Dave McNally began a personal nine-game winning streak with his first triumph in almost four weeks after noticing while watching game films that he was overstriding.

July 27—TWINS DOWN ORIOLES, 5–2, RAP PALMER—Rookie Bert Blyleven, only nineteen years old, beat the Birds as Minnesota took the season series from Baltimore, seven games to five. No other team posted a winning record against the Orioles in 1970.

July 28—ORIOLES WIN AS CUELLAR TAKES 14TH—Back in Baltimore with temperatures in the high eighties, Mike Cuellar went the distance on a three-hitter to beat the White Sox 4–2 without allowing an earned run.

July 29—HARDIN LOSES AS CHISOX EDGE BIRDS, 2–1, ON 9TH FRAME RUN—Jim Hardin got a decision for the first time in nine starts since May 26, but it wasn't the one he wanted as Bob Spence's sacrifice fly drove in the winner in the Chicago's only win at Memorial Stadium in 1970.

July 30—No game scheduled.

July 31—BIRDS TOP ROYALS AND TIE RECORD—The Orioles beat Kansas City for a record-tying twenty-first straight time as Dave McNally became the third fourteen-game winner on the Orioles staff by limiting the Royals to five singles.

AL East Standings, July 31:

Team	W	L	GB
Baltimore	64	39	—
Detroit	57	45	6.5
New York	56	46	7.5
Boston	52	49	11.0
Cleveland	49	54	15.0
Washington	46	56	17.5

Chapter 32. **Pete Richert**

Adam Ulrey

AGE	W	L	PCT.	ERA	G	GS	GF	CG	SHO	SV	IP	H	BB	SO	HBP	WP
30	7	2	.778	1.98	50	0	25	0	0	13	54.2	36	24	66	1	4

No one in the history of Major League Baseball had a first appearance like that of hard-throwing left-handed pitcher Pete Richert. In his debut with the Los Angeles Dodgers on April 12, 1962, against the Cincinnati Reds at Dodger Stadium, Richert set a record by striking out the first six batters he faced. With the Dodgers trailing 4–0, he entered the game with two outs in the top of the second inning and struck out Vada Pinson for the final out. Richert then recorded a four-strikeout third inning in which his victims were Frank Robinson (his future Baltimore Orioles teammate), Gordy Coleman (who reached first base on a passed ball by catcher Johnny Roseboro), Wally Post, and Johnny Edwards; his record-breaking sixth strikeout was of Tommy Harper leading off the fourth.

In addition, Richert as of 2010 remained the only Major League pitcher to record a four-strikeout inning in his debut. He held the Reds hitless in his 3⅓ innings of relief, and became the winning pitcher after the Dodgers scored seven runs in the fifth inning. He threw forty pitches to the twelve batters he faced, and only seven were called balls, according to the scoresheet kept by the Dodgers' statistician, Allan Roth. (Four years later, while pitching for the Washington Senators, Richert tied another consecutive-strikeout record.)

Despite his strikeout heroics, it remains a question whether Richert is better known for his whiffs or for the bizarre play while he was on the mound in the tenth inning of the fourth game of the 1969 World Series that helped propel the New York Mets to the world championship.

Peter Gerard Richert was born on October

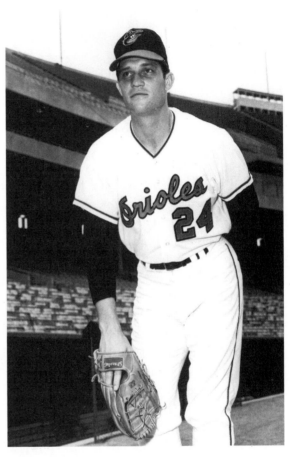

Pete Richert began his career as a starter for the Dodgers, but he led the Orioles with thirteen saves in 1970.

29, 1939, in Mineola, New York. His father, Edward, had been a catcher on the Columbia University varsity, and played semipro ball on Long Island. Edward died when the young pitcher was fifteen. There had been a close relationship between the two. "He was a Yankee fan and so was I," Pete said. "He used to take me to Yankee Stadium when I was a kid. Like millions of kids who go to Yankee Stadium through the years, I imagined myself out there pitching. You know how kids are. My father actually believed I'd make it someday to the big leagues and that I would be pitching in Yankee Stadium. Life does some funny tricks."[1]

In high school Richert was not very big, standing five feet seven and weighing 150 pounds. (By the time he reached the Major Leagues he was five feet eleven and weighed 165 pounds.) He was tough, though, and helped lead Sewanhaka High in Floral Park to the Long Island championship in his senior year. He also pitched in the Babe Ruth League and the Connie Mack division, for older teenagers, where he was scouted by Los Angeles Dodgers, the New York Yankees, and the Milwaukee Braves. In the end, the Dodgers' Al Campanis and Charlie Russo signed Richert. There were reports when he came up to the Dodgers that Richert got a $35,000 bonus from the Dodgers, but Richert later said it was actually $2,000.[2]

After graduating from high school it was onto the Minor Leagues, and the eighteen-year-old Richert's first stop was with the Reno Silver Sox of the California League. He handled himself pretty well, starting 27 games and going 10-13 with a 4.59 earned-run average with 215 strikeouts in 200 innings. He also walked 143 batters. The next season the Dodgers moved Richert up to the Green Bay Bluejays of the Class B Three-I League, where he improved his strikeout-to-walk ratio, fanning 173 in 156 innings and cutting his walks down to 99. He won 10 games and lost 8, and lowered his ERA to 3.29. At Double-A Atlanta in 1960, he had a breakout season, leading the Southern Association in victories (19), shutouts (6), complete games (18), and strikeouts (a league-record 251). He lost nine games. He added a twentieth victory in the playoffs. He was named to the Southern Association All-Star team and the National Association's Double-A All-Star team. He was selected as the Minor Leaguer showing the greatest improvement during the 1960 season.

Richert was moved up to the Triple-A Spokane Indians in 1961 but was sidelined the first six weeks of the season with arm troubles. Only a quick finish allowed him to finish 5-10 with a 4.50 ERA in 21 starts. He stuck with the Dodgers after spring training in 1962 but despite his record-breaking April 12 debut he could not crack the Dodgers' starting rotation of Sandy Koufax, Don Drysdale, Johnny Podres, and Stan Williams, and two months into the season he was demoted to Omaha, where he experienced a career-threatening crisis.

"My arm snapped," he told *The Sporting News*:

I threw a pitch and the arm felt like it was broken. I was afraid to throw after that. I babied the arm. One day, [manager Danny Ozark] handed me the ball. "Pete," he said, "this is it. If you're going to pitch big-league ball, let's find out right now. Throw as hard as you can. If the arm snaps, goodbye. If it doesn't, you're free of this fear. Now throw as hard as you can." I guess it was like a drowning man reviewing his life. I was 22 years old. All my life I wanted to be a major-league pitcher. My dad did too. It was his dream, his great ambition for me. He died before I made it to the big leagues. It was his faith that got me started in the first place. All this went through my mind. I told Danny I was ready. I fired as hard as I could. Nothing happened. I felt great. I risked my baseball life on that one pitch. I won.[3]

Eventually recalled by the Dodgers, Richert wound up getting twelve starts and won five games while losing four. The Dodgers blew a first-place lead and were tied by the San Francisco Giants. Then the Giants won the pennant in a three-game playoff.

In 1963 Richert again pitched sparingly with the Dodgers, going 5-3 with a 4.50 ERA and spending some time with Los Angeles' Spokane farm team (5-1, 2.25 ERA). The Dodgers won the pennant and swept the Yankees in the World Series. Richert did not pitch in the Series. He started the 1964 season with Los Angeles but after three games was sent down to Spokane after getting hit pretty hard (9.95 ERA). At Spokane he worked on his mechanics, wound up 7-8 with a 3.52 ERA, and earned a call-up to the Dodgers in September, when he struck out 22 in 28 innings with an ERA of 2.34. On December 15, 1964, he was traded along with Frank Howard, Ken McMullen, Phil Ortega, and Dick Nen to the Washington Senators for Claude Osteen, John Kennedy and $100,000.

Inserted into the Washington rotation, Richert won 15 games and lost 12 for the eighth-place (out of ten teams) club, with a 2.60 ERA, fifth best in the American League. He was picked to play in the 1965 All-Star Game at Minnesota's Metropolitan Stadium, and he responded with two scoreless innings, striking out Willie Mays and Willie Stargell.

The Senators finished in eighth place again in 1966 but Richert had another good year, finishing 14-14 with a 3.37 ERA. On April 24 he tied an American League record (since broken) by striking out seven Detroit Tigers in a row. He went to the All Star Game again, and was charged with the loss when former teammate Maury Wills drove in the winning run for the National League in the bottom of the ninth inning.

Richert credited his success to a change in outlook—"my mature attitude." He credited manager Gil Hodges for exiling him to the bullpen the season before, where "I got straightened out and started to pitch the way I should."[4] Given that Richert had a fastball that had a lot of motion, a slider, a changeup, and a curve, Hodges said, "Pete is cocky, but he has something to back it up. He's confident when he steps out on the mound and he thinks he can beat anybody. That's the kind of player I like. Pete is a good athlete and he is a good hitter. I'd rate him with Sam McDowell as the best left-hander in the league."[5]

Despite Hodges' high opinion of Richert, the pitcher was traded in May 1967 to the Baltimore Orioles for pitcher Frank Bertaina and first baseman Mike Epstein. Richert was 2-6 as a starter when the deal was made. The Orioles kept him in the starting rotation, and though he had a decent ERA (3.00 for Baltimore, 3.47 for the season) and a good hits-to-innings ratio, he went 7-10 for the Orioles, and his 9-16 record was the worst he would put up.

Richert's twenty-nine starts in 1967 were the last he would make in his career; in 1968 he became a reliever. He won six games out of the bullpen, four of them in the nine-day period beginning on August 5.

The Orioles won the American League pennant in 1969, 1970, and 1971, and Richert was a prominent member of their strong and flexible bullpen. In 1969 he won 7 games, lost 4, saved 12, and had a 2.20 ERA. In the World Series against the New York Mets, Richert relieved Dick Hall in the fateful tenth inning of Game 4 with runners on first and second and nobody out. When the Mets' J. C. Martin laid down a sacrifice bunt, Richert fielded the ball, and his throw to first hit Martin, the error allowing the winning run to score from second. Television replays showed that Martin had been running inside the baseline, and should have been called out for interference.

The 1970 season was Richert's best as a reliever. Throwing his fastball 90 percent of the time, he won 7 games, lost 2, saved 13, and had a 1.98 ERA. He recorded the save for Jim Palmer in Game One of the World Series and the Orioles went on to defeat Cincinnati in five games.

Richert's pitching numbers slipped in 1971: 3-5 with a 3.47 ERA and four saves. He pitched briefly in Game Seven of the World Series, won by the Pittsburgh Pirates. In 1972 he was back in Los Angeles, sent to the Dodgers with Frank Robinson in a six-player deal. In two seasons with the Dodgers he had 13 saves. Before the 1974 season the

Dodgers traded Richert to the St. Louis Cardinals for Tommy Agee. In June the Cardinals sent him along to the Philadelphia Phillies. He pitched sparingly for both teams. After the season Richert was found to have a blood clot in his pitching arm, and his career ended. He was thirty-five years old. He did get to work the World Series as a baseball analyst.

Pete started an organization called Athletes for Youth. Richert and others traveled to speak to young people about the dangers of drugs. They also visited methadone treatment centers and spoke with addicts.

Pete served as a pitching coach and assistant GM for many teams in the Pacific Coast League and the California League from 1989 to 2001. He and his wife, Adele, have raised three children and as of 2010 lived in Rancho Mirage, California.

Chapter 33. Paul Blair

Michael Huber

AGE	G	AB	R	H	2B	3B	HR	TB	RBI	BB	SO	BAV	OBP	SLG	SB	GDP	HBP
26	133	480	79	128	24	2	18	210	65	56	93	.267	.344	.438	24	9	3

Paul Blair is considered one of the premier defensive center fielders of his era. He made his Major League debut on September 9, 1964, and played in 1,947 games over a seventeen-year Major League career, with his final game coming on June 20, 1980. He batted and threw right-handed but tried switch-hitting for a brief time.

Paul L. D. Blair was born February 1, 1944, in Cushing, Oklahoma, but his family moved to Los Angeles when Paul was young. He grew up a Dodgers fan, once remarking, "I was always a Dodger fan, back when they were in Brooklyn. I was a Dodger fan, mainly because of Jackie Robinson, but [Duke] Snider and [Carl] Furillo, too."[1] Paul graduated from Manual Arts High School in Los Angeles in 1961, where he lettered in baseball, track, and basketball. His baseball team finished dead last in 1960 but jumped to first in 1961. At the age of seventeen, Blair got a tryout from the Dodgers, but he was rejected. The Dodgers' scouts thought the six-foot-one-inch ballplayer was too small to make it to the Majors. The Mets' scouts disagreed.

Paul was signed by the New York Mets on July 20, 1961, as an amateur free agent, at the position of shortstop. Floyd "Babe" Herman signed him to his first contract for $2,000. "The first day the coach told us to run out to our positions," Paul once told a reporter. "Well, seven players went to shortstop and six went to second but only one went to right. And I knew I could throw better than him and run better than him. So I ran out to right and played there. Then the center fielder got hurt and I moved to center."[2] The Mets had assigned the new outfielder to Santa Barbara of the

Paul Blair's 1970 season was marred by his May 31 beaning by California's Ken Tatum. He returned to hit eighteen home runs and play his usual marvelous center field.

California League in 1962, where he batted .228 with 147 strikeouts. He was then sent in October to the Florida Instructional League and hit extremely well. He also met and became good friends with fellow outfielder Cleon Jones. The Mets had left Blair unprotected after a season with Santa Barbara, and the Orioles drafted him in the 1962 first-year draft. When Jones and Blair would meet after that, Cleon the Met would say, "You got your break when you got drafted," and Paul the Oriole would reply, "You got your break when I was drafted."[3] The Orioles sent Blair to Stockton, California, in 1963, and then to Elmira, New York, in 1964. Paul appeared as a pinch runner in his Major League debut on September 9, a 4–3 loss to the Washington Senators, but he did not bat or play in the field. In 1964 he appeared in a total of eight games, but he only batted in the final game.

It was in Elmira, where he was playing in the Eastern League, that Paul Blair met Evelyn Cohen and they became engaged. Paul and Evelyn waited until the 1965 American League season started to exchange their wedding vows. The happy couple was wed on the baseball diamond in Elmira on April 15. They would have two children: Terry was born on September 23, 1965, and Paula was born on May 29, 1968.

Before the 1965 season, Blair completed a six-month tour of duty with the U.S. Army Reserve at Fort Jackson, South Carolina, as a communications specialist. He opened the 1965 season in center field for the Orioles, despite not being mentioned as a starting player during spring training. Manager Hank Bauer said that Blair would hold that position "until he plays himself out of it."[4] His intuition and speed allowed him to play shallow and run balls down. Earl Weaver, Blair's second manager in Baltimore, believed that saving a run is just as good as scoring a run. And Paul Blair saved many runs by patrolling the center of the Orioles' outfield. His amazing quickness allowed him to track down balls that should have dropped in for hits. Paul would often say, "In the outfield I felt there was no ball I couldn't get to. I played the shallowest center field of anyone."[5]

In an interview in 1997 in USA *Today Baseball Weekly*, Blair explained his defensive approach to the game: "I was taught to play defense. Back in our day it was pitching and defense. Our philos-

ophy was don't make the little mistakes that cost you ballgames. That is the way we won over such a long period of time."[6]

In Game Three of the 1966 World Series, Blair hit a solo home run against Claude Osteen and the Dodgers, giving Wally Bunker all the run support he needed for a 1–0 victory. In Game Four, his acrobatic leaping catch off the bat of Jim Lefebvre saved a home run and preserved a 1–0 win for Dave McNally, as part of the Orioles' stunning four-game sweep of Los Angeles. After the 1966 season, to continue to improve his hitting skills, Blair played winter ball with the Santurce club in the Puerto Rican League.

On May 17, 1967, the Baltimore Orioles became only the eighth team in the history of the American League to hit four home runs in the same inning (Andy Etchebarren, Sam Bowens, Boog Powell, and Dave Johnson connected in a nine-run seventh inning). Paul Blair, Frank Robinson, and Brooks Robinson also homered in that game, marking the only time in history that seven different teammates each hit a round-tripper in the same game. Blair's twelve triples in 1967 led the American League and remain the Orioles' season record. He was also a great bunter and fundamentals player. He recorded at least ten sacrifice hits four times in his career, including having 13 in 1969 (which led the league) and 17 during the 1975 season.

In 1967 Blair hit .293 with an on-base percentage of .353, and a slugging percentage of .446. That batting average was fifth best in the league. He also clubbed 11 homers, with 64 RBIs and 27 doubles to go with a league-leading 12 triples. As fast as he was, however, Blair concedes that he was never much of a base-stealer, with a career high of 27 in 1974 and 20 or more only three times. At the end of the 1967 season, the speedy center fielder was rewarded for his seasonal stats, as Blair picked up several prizes, including a portable stereo from the radio station WFBR as the Most

Valuable Oriole, an engraved silver tray from the Maryland General Assembly, a color TV set from the National Brewing Company after twice hitting home runs in Home Run Derby innings, and a black-and-white TV set.

In the winter of 1967, Blair again played in the Puerto Rican League, as the Orioles wanted him to continue to improve his hitting. However, in December of that year, Paul broke his right ankle, causing him to miss most of the 1968 spring training.

According to a June 2, 1968, article in *The Sun Magazine*, Blair's nickname "Motormouth" was the inspiration of Harry Dunlop, who was Blair's 1963 manager at Stockton, the Orioles' farm team in the California League. "We were coming out of the dugout," Blair said, "and Curt Motton and I were arguing. We were hitting about .320 apiece, but I had outhit him the day before—4-for-4, I think it was—and I was reminding Curt about it. Dunlop heard us and said, 'Motton, Blair's getting to be as bad as a motor, isn't he?'"[7] Frank Robinson and Curt Blefary revived the nickname in the big leagues, and it stuck. Everyone on the Orioles knew that Blair was a big league hitter and a big league talker.

Blair's most productive year was probably 1969, when he hit .285, had an on-base percentage of .327 and a slugging percentage of .477. Showing more power, he smacked 32 doubles and 26 homers, stole 20 bases, scored 102 runs and had 178 hits in 150 games. He also had 76 runs batted in. Defensively, the loquacious Oriole won one of his eight Gold Gloves for the excellence he showed while roaming center field.

Paul ended the 1969 season as the only center fielder to have more than 400 put-outs. The next best outfielder was Del Unser with 339. Fans would wrack their brains to remember the last time they saw a ball land between Blair and the center field fence. During the 1969 campaign, the center fielder hit an inside-the-park home run at Memori-al Stadium. The date was August 8, 1969, and it was the first inside-the-park homer at that stadium since Billy O'Dell had hit one in 1959. That year, 1969, would mark the first time the fans voted the Orioles center fielder to the All Star Game. He would also be honored as a *Sporting News* All-Star at the conclusion of the season.

In 1970 Blair had two significant events in baseball. The first could well be the best single offensive display of his career. He hit three home runs and knocked in six runs in a game on April 29, 1970, as the Orioles beat the Chicago White Sox, 18–2. The second event was career-altering. Unfortunately, in addition to his remarkable defensive prowess, Paul Blair is remembered for receiving a severe beaning by California Angels pitcher Ken Tatum on May 31, 1970. He was carried off the field with a broken nose and serious eye and facial injuries; Blair claims he never saw the pitch. He missed the next three weeks of the season but came back to play a total of 133 games that season and insists it did not affect him. Nevertheless, Blair never equaled the offensive output from his successful 1969 season. In 1971 he attempted switch-hitting, but went 11-for-57 and gave up the experiment.

The Orioles played the Cincinnati Reds in the 1970 World Series. Paul Blair set a record by garnering nine base hits in the five-game series. The center fielder clubbed .474 in that Series, outhitting all players on both sides, but everyone remembers instead what his Hall of Fame teammate at third base, Brooks Robinson, did defensively against Lee May, Johnny Bench, and the Big Red Machine.

In general, Blair was known around the league as a fastball hitter who liked the ball inside. He often crowded the plate, even after his accident in 1970. He himself admitted he was too stubborn to hit the outside pitch to right field, preferring instead to pull the ball. Part of his success at the plate came from batting ahead of Hall of Famer Frank

Robinson. Blair once said, "With him behind me, I knew at two and oh or three and one counts what they'd throw me. They're not going to walk Paul Blair to get to Frank Robinson, so they're going to throw me a fastball. After Frank [left the Orioles], they were throwing breaking balls. And the slider was a pitch I had trouble with. I wasn't disciplined enough to take those pitches and walk."[8]

In 1972 Blair's batting average dipped to .233, and his on-base percentage was only .267. Something had to be done. On June 15, 1973, Blair started seeing a Baltimore psychiatrist. After a suggestion from Chan Keith, a baseball writer for the *Baltimore News American*, Paul visited Dr. Jacob H. Conn and received hypnosis therapy, restoring confidence in his ability to avoid inside pitches. According to the doctor, in one session, he was able to unlearn three years of ducking out of the way every time a ball came inside. Over the next two weeks, he was hitting .522. In a dozen games, he collected 24 hits in 46 at-bats, including six doubles, a triple, and three home runs. He drove in eleven runs and scored ten. On May 29, he had been batting just .218, but a month later, he was fourth in the league at .321. He ended the season at .280.

Paul Blair accomplished a rare feat in 1973 when he hit an inside-the-park grand slam homer against the Kansas City Royals. The game was August 26 and featured Jim Palmer matched up against Paul Splittorff. Blair drove a ball into the gap. Royals outfielders Amos Otis and Steve Hovley collided in midair, and Blair rounded the bases. On September 3, 1973, Blair hit a three-run inside-the-park home run against Boston's John Curtis. At the end of the 1973 season, Blair earned another Gold Glove selection.

In 1974 Paul Blair again led all American League outfielders with 447 put-outs in centerfield (in 1969 he had 407). In fact, nine times in his career, he had more than 300 put-outs in the out-field. His defense kept him in the lineup, despite his batting .218 in 1975 and only .197 in 1976.

On January 20, 1977, the Orioles traded the contract of the thirty-two-year-old Blair to the New York Yankees for Elliott Maddox, twenty-seven, and Rick Bladt, thirty. At the time, Blair was the Orioles' all-time leading base stealer with 167. He also ranked third in the Orioles' record books (behind Brooks Robinson and Boog Powell) in games, at-bats, runs, hits, total bases, and runs batted in. His career average with Baltimore was .254. He had played in all five American League Championship Series and all four World Series in which the Birds were involved. His eight Gold Gloves contributed mightily to the Orioles' success.

Blair left Charm City to become a reserve for the Yankees for two seasons (both World Series championship seasons for the Bronx Bombers), and then was released just into the 1979 season. After a month off, in May 1979, the Cincinnati Reds signed Blair to a one-year contract. His acquisition gave the Reds thirty-one Gold Gloves on the team: Bench (10), Blair (8), Morgan (5), Concepcion (4), and Geronimo (4). Unfortunately, Blair, new to the National League, did nothing for the Reds, batting .152 in 77 games and just 145 at bats, then went back to New York for 1980. He played in 12 games as a defensive replacement (just two at bats), and retired at the age of thirty-six.

After his playing days were over, Paul Blair became an outfield instructor for the New York Yankees in 1981. He was named the head baseball coach at Fordham University in August 1982 and coached the 1983 season, compiling a record of 14-19. That position lasted only one year, but Blair kept in touch with Major League teams, offering his services again as an instructor. He last did it at the Major League level for the Houston Astros in 1985. In 1989, at the age of forty-five, he played 17 games for the Gold Coast Suns of the Senior Professional Baseball Association. The club split its home games between Miami and Pompano Beach, Florida, and hired future Hall of Famer Earl Weaver as its manager. Despite fine performances from Bert Campaneris (.291 with 16 stolen bases) and Joaquin Andujar (5-0 with a 1.31 ERA), the team did not make the playoffs. After its first season, the Gold Coast Suns ceased operations.

In 1995 the former Major Leaguer accepted a coaching job for the Yonkers Hoot Owls, one of six teams in the new independent professional Northeast League (the Hoot Owls became the Bangor Blue Ox in 1996). Between the time he stopped playing and began coaching, Paul devoted his time to high school coaching, operating a baseball camp, and working as a sports coordinator for a clothing firm. He was also the head baseball coach at Coppin State College from 1998 to 2002. Granted, he inherited a desperately inexperienced team, but under his leadership, the team posted a disappointing 30-185 record. Although Paul Blair the player had been associated with very successful Major League teams, Paul Blair the coach could not attain the same success. He retired to Owings Mills, Maryland.

Paul Blair had two great postseason series for the Orioles in his career. In the 1969 American League Championship Series against Minnesota, he hit .400 and slugged .733 with a homer and six RBIs, and in the 1970 World Series against the Reds, he hit .474 and slugged .526, also scoring five runs. Blair's five hits in the final game of the 1969 American League Championship Series against Minnesota is still a record. Indeed, the former Orioles center fielder is the only player ever to get five hits in a single ALCS game. Twice he was named to the American League All-Star squad (1969, 1973). He played in a total of fifty-two postseason games during his seventeen-year baseball career, and his team won nine of thirteen postseason series. He played in six World Series and won four World Series rings, two with the Orioles (1966 and 1970) and two with the Yankees (1977 and 1978). The player once known as Motormouth received votes for the American League's Most Valuable Player in four different seasons. At the time Paul Blair retired, his eight Gold Gloves were a record for an outfielder, since broken by Ken Griffey Jr. Blair's career fielding percentage was .987, as he only had 57 errors in 4462 chances. He batted .250 for his career during a time when the league batting average was just .254.

Chapter 34. **Terry Crowley**

Malcolm Allen

AGE	G	AB	R	H	2B	3B	HR	TB	RBI	BB	SO	BAV	OBP	SLG	SB	GDP	HBP
23	83	152	25	39	5	0	5	59	20	35	26	.257	.394	.388	2	5	0

They say I'm a good pinch-hitter, but maybe if I ever came to the plate 500 times, they might learn I'm a good hitter, period."

—*Terry Crowley, quoted by Jim Henneman in* The Sporting News

Terrence Michael Crowley was born on February 16, 1947, in Staten Island, New York, and grew up rooting for the Yankees. Despite his admiration for pinch-hitting expert Johnny Blanchard, Crowley was a left-handed pitcher in high school, and he drew the attention of professional scouts. Starring at Curtis High in Staten Island, the school that sent Bobby Thomson of "Shot Heard 'Round the World" fame to the Major Leagues, Crowley got to pitch for the city championship as a junior. But he hurt his arm and couldn't even throw—much less pitch—when he returned for his senior year. Not surprisingly, the demand for Crowley's services in pro ball dipped accordingly. "Some teams had made offers and said they would wait until my arm got better," he said. "But I couldn't realistically go away to play pro ball when I couldn't move my left shoulder."[1]

Instead, Crowley enrolled at the Brooklyn campus of Long Island University, the institution that Hall of Famer Larry Doby once attended on a basketball scholarship. He never went back to the mound, but Crowley got his baseball career back on track with a first-team All-American performance as a sophomore. Now married to the former Janet Boyle, with whom he had a baby daughter, Carlene, Crowley was drafted by the Baltimore Orioles in the eleventh round of the 1966 June am-

Terry Crowley was another victim of the Orioles' crowded outfield, but he was a valuable reserve in his 1970 rookie season.

ateur draft, but was in no particular hurry to sign unless the price was right.

The Orioles inked one draftee after another, but Crowley kept refusing to sign. Scout Walter Shannon came to watch him play, and after following Crowley around "for a good two months,"[2] finally offered a bonus of $27,500 with only a few weeks remaining in the Minor League season. Crowley signed, reported to Miami, and batted .255 in 19 Florida State League games with only one extra-base hit in his first taste of professional baseball.

He returned to Miami in 1967 and batted .262 with a league-leading 24 doubles in 135 games. Surprisingly, Crowley, a six-foot, 180-pounder never known for his speed, added 10 triples and 21 steals. However, he managed only 3 homers and 49 RBIs. "The wind blew in from right field so hard, it was impossible for a lefty to hit a home run," Crowley remembered. "The whole league was like that."[3]

After the season the Orioles put Crowley on their forty-man roster, and after he did a stint in the Florida Instructional League, they promoted Crowley to the Double-A Elmira Pioneers in 1968. "Crow" hit .271 without a home run in 55 Eastern League games playing for Cal Ripken Sr., but he earned a promotion to Triple-A Rochester after a red-hot June. There, he began to hit with power for the first time as a professional, launching 8t home runs to go with a .268 average in 75 games. The Orioles sent him back to the Florida Instructional League after the season, and Minor League director Jim McLaughlin speculated that "Crowley may just come up in September for a look after a season in Triple-A."[4]

That's exactly what happened, but not before Crowley overcame a slow start at Rochester to become a unanimous in-season All-Star selection by International League managers. He batted .282 with 28 home runs and 83 runs batted in, walked 69 times, and led the league with 246 total bases. On September 4, 1969, he fouled out as a pinch hitter in his Major League debut at Tiger Stadium but notched three hits in his first start (against the Indians) when the Orioles returned home. He got into seven games that September, hitting .333 (6-for-18), and at just twenty-two years of age, his future appeared very bright.

Nevertheless, Crowley was a long shot to make the Orioles in 1970. The team's 109 victories had given it the American League pennant in 1969, and no starting jobs were open in the outfield or at first base. Even two reserve outfielders had spots

secured, but Crowley forced his way into the mix by hitting .380 in Grapefruit League play. Utility infielder Bobby Floyd became the odd man out, and Crowley was wearing a Baltimore uniform on Opening Day in Cleveland. He didn't get into the game, instead winding up in the hospital for an overnight stay when a foul liner one-hopped its way into the Orioles' dugout and struck him above the ear. He was fine, though, and started the series finale in right field.

Though Crowley began the season as the Orioles' twenty-fifth man, his contribution to the team's 108-54 record and second consecutive American League East title was substantial. His first Major League home run was a three-run blast off the Minnesota Twins' Dave Boswell at Memorial Stadium on May 1 that gave Baltimore a lead it wouldn't lose. He added game-winning home runs in Detroit and Cleveland before the season was through. He batted .257 in 83 games (34 starts). His totals of 5 homers and 20 RBIs in 157 at bats were pretty good, and his .394 on-base percentage was exceptional. Perhaps most telling was Crowley's .290 average as a pinch hitter, a difficult role for any player, but particularly for a twenty-three-year-old rookie. "It's a job usually handled by a veteran," remarked Crowley. "It's a big adjustment to go from playing every day to pinch-hitting."[5]

He made only one plate appearance in the postseason but earned a World Series ring as the Orioles romped through the Minnesota Twins and Cincinnati Reds by winning seven times in eight tries. "It was like, hey, this is the way it's supposed to be," said Crowley. "We pretty much had an All-Star at every position. We had a fantastic pitching staff. It was a great time."[6]

The Orioles hoped Crowley would head to Puerto Rico to sharpen his skills in the Winter League, but with daughter Carlene about to turn seven and sons Terry Jr. and Jimmy still in diapers, Crowley elected to stay home and be daddy. When spring training rolled around for 1971, he pulled a hamstring in a running drill, didn't hit when he was able to play, and wound up getting sent back to Rochester. "It was an emotional adjustment, no doubt, going from the world champions back to the Minors," he said. "I had to fight not only the opposing pitchers, but my situation as well."[7]

Crowley was recalled to Baltimore a few times that season but managed only a .174 average in 23 at bats over 18 games. At Rochester, he hit clean-up, played first base, and helped the team to a Junior World Series title by smashing five homers in the playoffs. Still, the season was a disappointing setback, and he did go to the Puerto Rican League that winter trying to turn things around.

Fellow Orioles Don Baylor, Rich Coggins, Dave Leonhard, and Fred Beene were also on the Santurce squad, but Crowley gained his most valuable experience of the winter away from the baseball field. Though physically fine, he'd been placed on the disabled list after a disagreement with manager Ruben Gomez, and found himself sitting around the pool one day when heavyweight boxing contender Joe Roman happened by and the two became friends.

"I had boxed informally as a kid," Crowley recalled. "We always had the gloves, and my dad and uncles always taught me how to fight because they were into the fight game a little bit. When I actually started to fool around with Joe Roman, it was fun and I could handle myself a little bit. I could move around, and I found that doing it every day for the first time, I got to improve."[8]

In addition to sparring, Crowley spent about three weeks following the training regimen of Roman, who in 1973 became the first Puerto Rican to fight for the heavyweight championship. (George Foreman knocked him out in one round.) "Boxers are fantastically dedicated guys," marveled Crowley the following spring. "They get up at 4 o'clock in the morning and go out and run for an hour or so. Every morning. They never miss. I've nev-er seen anyone work so hard in athletics and, boy, does it pay off. I feel in great shape."[9]

Crowley wasn't sure where he fit in the Orioles' plans heading into 1972, but one major obstacle had been removed when Baltimore traded Frank Robinson to the Los Angeles Dodgers. Crowley wound up more or less platooning in right field with his good friend and roommate Merv Rettenmund. "Merv Rettenmund was one of funniest, wittiest, sarcastic type guys that you could ever be around," said Crowley. "He was a great teammate. Guys loved him, and he was a really funny guy."[10]

Crowley got into a career-high 97 games in '72 and hammered 11 home runs in 247 at bats. In June, he shared the cover of *The Sporting News* with teammates Don Baylor and Bobby Grich, and received praise from Baltimore coach Billy Hunter in the accompanying story. "I am more surprised at what Crowley has accomplished than the other two," Hunter said. "We always knew that Terry was a natural hitter, but he has impressed me even more by working very hard at other phases of the game."[11] But, a .193 second-half batting average dropped Crowley's season mark to .231, and the Orioles missed the playoffs for the first time in four years after a September swoon.

Crowley lifted weights with Rettenmund nearly every day that offseason at a Baltimore YMCA, seemingly in preparation for a great opportunity. The American League adopted the designated hitter rule for the 1973 season and Crowley made his first-ever Opening Day start as the first DH in Orioles history. Veteran Tommy Davis, a two-time batting champion, seized the job in May, though, and Crowley wound up hitting just .206 with 3 home runs in 54 games. Fed up, he let it be known that he'd welcome a trade. The Orioles sold him to the Texas Rangers in December for a reported $100,000.

After another winter in Puerto Rico to get some at bats, Crowley expressed optimism about joining

MALCOLM ALLEN

a new team. "If I could get about 350 or 400 at-bats, I think I could hit between 15 and 20 home runs and help this club a great deal," he said. "I'll DH, play first or the outfield, platoon, anything. All I'd like is the opportunity to play in some predictable fashion."[12]

Crowley didn't even make it through spring training with the Rangers, however. Texas placed him on waivers and he ended up with the Cincinnati Reds. There, he was reunited with Rettenmund, whom the Orioles had also traded away because he wasn't satisfied playing part time. The pair of ex-Orioles earned one more World Series ring when the Reds went all the way in 1975, but mostly endured two miserable years of dwindling playing time and disappointing production with Cincinnati. Crowley hit .240 with one homer in 1974, then .268, again with a single homer the following year, and saw his at bats drop from 125 in 1974 to 71 in 1975.

Just before the 1976 season opener, Cincinnati sent Crowley and Rettenmund packing in separate deals. The two friends were so glad to be leaving the Reds that, *The Sporting News* wrote, they went joyriding back and forth over one of the Reds' spring training fields in Tampa. More than three decades later, Crowley still wasn't talking. "No comment," he replied with a laugh. "Let [Rettenmund] tell you that story."[13]

Traded to the Atlanta Braves, Crowley was soon reminded that the grass is not always greener. After he went hitless in seven pinch-hit appearances, the Braves tried to option him to Triple-A. He refused, became a free agent, and wound up back at Rochester a few weeks later after re-signing with the Orioles. Baltimore brought him back to the big leagues in late June, and he hit .246, primarily as a pinch hitter the rest of the way.

Just before the 1977 season got underway, the Orioles, in a surprise move, decided to keep rookie first baseman Eddie Murray, and Crowley was sent back to Rochester again. "Very mad" is how he de-scribed his reaction.[14] With four children (daughter Karen arrived in August 1976) between seven months and thirteen years of age, being back at Rochester nine years after his first tour there was not a welcome career move. "I think I'm the best hitter in this league, but I have to prove it," Crowley said.[15]

"He doesn't belong in this league," observed Tidewater Tides skipper Frank Verdi.[16] "He was right," replied Crowley when the quote was relayed to him years later.[17]

Playing every day for the first time since 1969, Crowley set out to bat .300 with 30 home runs, and accomplished his goal by the first week of August. The Orioles brought him back to the Majors a week later, and he remained a big leaguer for the next six years. "Terry has what you call a classic swing," observed Hall of Famer Frank Robinson. "It's one you don't tamper with."[18]

From 1977 through 1981, Crowley delivered a .314 average as a pinch hitter for the Orioles. "People say you can't carry Crowley for what he does," said Earl Weaver midway through Baltimore's pennant-winning 1979 season. "But he's already got us three games."[19]

"I've been doing it for so long that people just naturally think I'm older," Crowley said in 1978. "I've been around for a while, and I've been in a couple of World Series. A year ago, people thought I was washed up, though I was only 30 years old."[20]

American League managers voted Crowley the circuit's best pinch hitter in 1979, and he made them look good in Game Three of that season's American League Championship Series with a hit that would have driven in the pennant-clinching run had the Orioles been able to hold the lead in the bottom of the ninth inning. Baltimore did advance to the fall classic the next day, however, setting the stage for one of the most memorable hits of Crowley's career.

The Orioles were trailing the Pittsburgh Pirates 6–3 in Game Four of the World Series entering the eighth inning, but pulled within a run when John Lowenstein smacked a two-run double to the right-field corner. After Pirates ace reliever Kent Tekulve issued an intentional walk to set up the double play, Crowley stroked a pinch-hit double to the same location as Lowenstein's hit to knock in the tying and go-ahead runs. Baltimore took control, three games to one, and Crowley's hit would be remembered even more fondly if the Orioles hadn't dropped the final three games of the series.

"Once you get to the World Series, everything is gravy," Crowley said. "I had some pressure-filled pinch hits that got us to different pennant-winning teams. Not only that year, but other years that were pressure-filled. If you get a hit, we win the game. If you don't, we drop into second place. But the one thing about the hit off Tekulve, people started to notice, 'Hey, this guy's done that before.' That was the one that probably got me the most notoriety."[21]

The Orioles won 100 games in 1980 and, though they missed the playoffs (the Yankees won 103), it was an especially gratifying year for Crowley. He got 233 at bats, the second highest total of his career, blasted 12 home runs, and drove in 50 runs while batting .288. He was rewarded with a two-year contract extension to keep him employed through 1983.

Crowley was frustrated, however, when he found himself back in his familiar pinch-hitting role, struggling for at bats again in 1981. "I'm coming off one of the most productive years on the club," he said. "What's wrong with letting me prove I can do it again?"[22]

"Terry's got an awful lot of value as a pinch-hitter," manager Earl Weaver said. "You can't be too good at your job, and that's his job. I think the object of everyone to help the club is to do what he does best, and one of the things Crowley does as well as anyone is pinch-hit. It isn't that I'm disappointed with what he can do as a DH, but he's excellent as a pinch-hitter."[23]

Though Crowley came off the bench to hit two home runs in 1982, including a walk-off grand slam against the Royals, his average as a pinch hitter dipped to .194 that season. Nevertheless, when the Orioles had to choose between Crowley and his friend Jim Dwyer for the final roster spot coming out of spring training in 1983, a story in a Baltimore newspaper was headlined "DWYER SET TO GO." Crowley hit .357 that spring, so it was a surprise when the Orioles decided to release him instead. Baltimore general manager Hank Peters called it "one of the toughest things I've ever had to do in this job."[24]

Crowley was about to accept an offer to become the Orioles' Minor League hitting instructor when the Montreal Expos called in late May. But he got only 44 at bats all year, batted .182, and decided to call it a career. "I had some phone calls to go play, but my back was hurting pretty good at that time, and I thought it best and wisest to get into my coaching career, to try to become a hitting coach."[25]

Crowley spent 1984 as the Orioles' Minor League hitting instructor, then served on Baltimore's Major League staff as the hitting coach from 1985 through 1988. In 1986 the Orioles drafted his son Terry Jr., a shortstop, in the eighth round. (Crowley's younger son, Jimmy, was the Red Sox's eleventh-round pick in 1991.) When the Orioles lost 107 games in 1988, all the coaches lost their jobs except the popular Elrod Hendricks. Crowley spent 1989 and 1990 working with Boston Red Sox Minor Leaguers.

He returned to the Majors in 1991, becoming the hitting coach for a Minnesota Twins club that surprised nearly everybody by going from "worst to first" to win the World Series. He remained there through 1998, and explained part of his approach to instructing hitters this way: "If they're good enough to get here to this level, then they must be doing something right. Unless there's something I see that absolutely prevents them from having success at this level, I'll basically leave them alone and try to help them improve their own style, to improve on their own."[26]

"You know, it's like a signature," he continued. "If you can read it, it's not too bad, but when it gets to the point that I can't read it, I've got to straighten their swing out a little bit."[27]

"If there's a hitter who's capable of hitting home runs, hitting with power and driving in runs, that's what I'll strive for. I'd hate to see a player just being a singles hitter if he could hit with some power."[28]

The way Crowley fought to get at bats during his playing career helps him communicate to his pupils the importance of making the most of every plate appearance. "Sometimes I go into detail with them to try to make them understand you can develop good habits just as well as you can fall into bad habits. Once you get in the groove and start hitting the ball good, you have to work as hard as you can to stay there, because in the blink of an eye you can fall into a slump or start to struggle."[29]

Crowley left Minnesota after eight seasons and returned to Baltimore in 1999 for a second stint as the Orioles' hitting coach that lasted a dozen years. He outlasted six managers and was invited back for a twenty-fifth season on a Major League staff in 2011 but opted for the reduced travel of a newly created hitting evaluator position instead. Crowley was to evaluate Oriole Major and Minor Leaguers, possible trade and free agent targets, and potential draftees.

"I think I was lucky. I had a pretty good swing, and I had some ability and I made the best of it. I would like to have played more. That's the only regret I have. I wish I could've played more, but I turned out to be a pretty good pinch hitter, so I guess everything worked out."[30]

Chapter 35. **Bobby Grich**

John McMurray

AGE	G	AB	R	H	2B	3B	HR	TB	RBI	BB	SO	BAV	OBP	SLG	SB	GDP	HBP
21	30	95	11	20	1	3	0	27	8	9	21	.211	.279	.284	1	2	0

Bobby Grich was one of the best second basemen in baseball over a seventeen-year Major League career that began in 1970. During his first season, Grich played with the Orioles primarily as a utility infielder. Known for his sharp fielding and consistent hitting, Grich became a regular in 1972 and played in his first All-Star Game that season. In 1974 writer Larry Eldridge made this observation about the twenty-five-year-old Grich: "Grich is one of those rare ballplayers who excel in every aspect of the game—a strong hitter, a slick fielder, and a steady performer whose day-to-day contributions can carry a team almost single-handedly. He's the driving force for the Baltimore Orioles now in their down-to-the-wire race with the New York Yankees, and he may well be the most valuable player in the American League, even though somebody else with more glamorous statistics will undoubtedly get the award."[1]

Robert Anthony Grich was born on January 15, 1949, in Muskegon, Michigan. Grich spent most of his childhood in California, where his father was a clerk in the shipping industry in Long Beach for thirty-five years. Grich's mother was a waitress for a few years at a fine-dining restaurant in Long Beach before staying at home. Shortly after moving to California following World War II, Grich's father had been an amateur boxer who compiled a career record of 40-2-2, and Grich recalled, "Everyone I ever met who saw him fight said he was a terrific fighter with fast hands."[2]

Grich's father had objected to his "skinny" son playing baseball. Still, his mother coaxed Grich to play, even against older children. Grich played both baseball and football at Woodrow Wilson

Bobby Grich was hitting .383 for the Rochester Red Wings at the midseason of 1970 when he was finally summoned to Baltimore. He would not get a starting position until 1972, but he was soon one of the league's best players.

High School, and he had to decide which sport to pursue in college and professionally. Football coach Tommy Prothro of the University of California at Los Angeles was recruiting Grich to play there, and one newspaper account later said that Prothro "practically guaranteed [Grich] a clean shot at the Heisman Trophy his senior year."[3]

Even though Grich signed a letter of intent to play at UCLA, the Orioles drafted him in the first round of the 1967 amateur draft, and Grich accepted their offer. At six feet two and 190 pounds, Grich said, "I figured I was too small to make a career out of pro football. I would have liked to have given pro football a shot, but I figured I could play pro baseball during the summer and work on my degree during the offseason."[4] Grich went on to study at Fresno State College.[5]

The right-handed-hitting Grich broke in as a shortstop and initially struggled in the Minor Leagues, hitting .254 with Bluefield in 1967, then .228 with 8 home runs for Stockton in 1968. Moving up to Dallas–Fort Worth in 1969, the twenty-year-old made some adjustments, began to hit more to right field, and raised his average to .310. His improved hitting, coupled with his great glove at shortstop, made him a top prospect. In changing his style from a singles hitter to one who drove the ball with power, Grich credited Baltimore hitting instructor Jim Frey: "[Frey] made me into a hitter by teaching me to punch the ball into right field during the 1968 season," said Grich. "[In 1970], I concentrated less on hitting to the opposite field and more on going for the long ball."[6]

Grich excelled for the rest of his time in the Orioles' Minor League system. He was leading the International League in hitting with a .383 average and nine home runs at Rochester when he was called up to the Major Leagues on June 29, 1970. After batting only .211 in 30 games for the Orioles, however, Grich did not play in the 1970 World Series.

In spite of his offensive struggles with Baltimore, Grich remained confident. Pitcher Dave McNally even remarked about how sorry he felt for Harry Dalton, the team's general manager: "When the time comes for Harry to tell Bobby he's going to Rochester, I'd advise him to have someone else in the room. Grich is liable to start throwing punches." Writer Phil Jackman recounted that Frank Robinson came by when Grich was talking about hitting and remarked, "What does a rookie like you know about hitting?" Grich replied to Robinson: "Tell you something, pal. I'll be hitting for ten years around here after you're gone."[7]

Grich indeed was sent back down to Rochester to start the 1971 season, and remarked at the time that it may have been a fortuitous move: "I don't like to sit and watch other people play ball," said Grich. "The Orioles sent me to Rochester to play a season at shortstop and improve my stroke at the plate."[8]

At Rochester in 1971 Grich won the International League Most Valuable Player Award with a .336 batting average and 32 home runs. Had he not batted in the second position in the lineup, he might have challenged for the RBI title as well. (Grich, who knocked in 83 runs, was behind league-leader Richie Zisk, who batted in 109.) Grich also showed signs of being a superb fielder. "People are always comparing me with [Orioles shortstop Mark] Belanger, and I think my own fielding is underrated," he said. "I have a lot of pride in my fielding, and I work hard at it."[9]

Pitcher Dave Leonhard concurred: "Belanger may have a shade more range, but the difference is hardly noticeable. They can both throw well, too. The big difference is in their bats. Bobby has so much more power."[10] In the International League managers' poll, Grich was chosen as the best player, best defensive infielder, and best thrower in the league, and he shared the Silver Glove award with Charlotte's Charles "Buck" Guth, since they both had .974 fielding averages.

As one writer noted in August 1971, "In Bobby Grich, the Orioles have one of the most coveted youngsters in the whole Minor League galaxy, a sort of Brooks and Frank Robinson rolled into one."[11] After he retired, Grich said in a 1987 interview, "I played out of my head [in 1971]. It was a storybook season. It couldn't have been any better."[12] Grich played in seven games for the Orioles at the end of the 1971 season, hitting the first of his 224 career Major League home runs.

Grich played frequently for the Orioles in 1972, appearing primarily at shortstop and second base. The twenty-two-year-old Grich batted .278 with 12 home runs and 50 RBIs in his first full season. Even the MVP voters took notice, as he finished in fourteenth place in the American League's voting.

The Orioles finished in third place in the American League East in 1972, and Grich stated that he felt the team had underperformed. He was also critical of his own play in the field: "I am disappointed with my defense this year," said Grich, who made 18 errors in 127 games. "There was a July and August stretch when I seemed to do okay at short. The rest of the year, I haven't been too good, though. Considering what [manager] Earl [Weaver] was trying to accomplish, he had no other choice. I haven't done my job as well as I should have."[13]

As Grich began to become an offensive force, he earned Weaver's praise. Late in Grich's first season, his manager said, "Grich has Hall of Fame potential as a hitter and fielder." Yet Grich never forgot his first encounters with Weaver as a rookie: "I'd just flown in. I was 21 years old and nervous as can be. I felt I've got to tell Weaver I'm here. The door was open to his office. I knocked on the side of the doorway. He looked up from his desk. He said, 'What do you want?' Just like that. I was kind of taken aback. I said: 'I just wanted you to know I'm here.' He said: 'Is that all?' That was my greeting to the big leagues."[14]

When he became a regular, Grich earned Weaver's respect. "I admired Weaver as a manager, I learned a lot from him: that most of the game is fundamentals, fundamentals are what consistently win ballgames, that defense is a bigger part of the game than offense." Even so, Grich said, "Weaver and I never talked. He just wasn't a guy who'd talk to you. If he wanted you to adjust, he'd send one of his coaches over. You could never be sure where you stood with him. . . . After I started playing for Weaver, doing a good job, he started joking

with me a little more. Unless you're playing good ball for him, he really doesn't give a can of beans for you. It was like: 'You're a good player, oh yeah, Bob, how's the wife and kids?' But I didn't forget how he treated you when you were a peon."[15]

By 1973 Grich had established himself as a regular with Baltimore and as a budding star. The team had traded incumbent second baseman Davey Johnson to make room for the younger Grich, who was able to settle in full time at one position for the first time. Grich welcomed the change: "Now that I can settle in at second base . . . maybe I can perfect four or five [different kinds of pivots]—crossing the bag with either foot, straddling the base, the jump throw, and moving back. Also, coming across the base on the move."[16]

Grich won his first of four consecutive Gold Glove Awards at second base in 1973. Since shortstop Mark Belanger also won a Gold Glove Award in every year from 1973 through 1976 as well, the Orioles had the strongest middle-of-the-infield defensive combination in baseball during that time. In 1973 Grich also played in all 162 games and duplicated his 12 home runs and 50 RBIs from the year before. That season ended in disappointment, however, as the Orioles lost the American League Championship Series to the Oakland Athletics in five games, with Grich getting only two hits in 20 at bats and driving in only a single run on a solo home run.

Still, Grich continued to improve his play. In 1974 he tied his career high set the year before with 17 stolen bases, while hitting 19 home runs and driving in 82 runs. Near the end of that season, in which Grich finished ninth in the league in the MVP voting, writer Larry Eldridge made this analogy: "Leo Durocher once said of Eddie Stanky: 'He can't hit, he can't run, and he can't throw, but I wouldn't trade him for any second baseman in the league.' Imagine what he would have given for Bobby Grich, who provides the same kind of leadership qualities that made Stanky valuable and can do all those other things too." Eldridge even noted that Weaver commented that "Grich has more range than any other second baseman in the league."[17] Although Grich improved his batting average to .250 in the 1974 ALCS, the Orioles lost to the Oakland Athletics for the second season in a row.

Off the field, Grich expressed a desire to skydive—though he never did it—and he was taking flying lessons in the hope of flying solo around the world. "Maybe [I'll] take a long voyage and explore remote areas," said Grich in August 1974. "I'll need an estate of about $2,000,000," he said. "If I get that, with some wise investments, I should never have to work. If I can get a 10 percent return, that would give me $200,000 a year, enough to do almost anything I want. . . . To get $200,000, I need home runs, RBIs, and a good average. I've got to be a good offensive player. A defensive player won't make a lot of money. I learned that during arbitration last winter."[18] (Grich was able to fulfill his desire to travel, having visited all fifty states and Europe five times, as well as Australia, New Zealand, Scotland, and Ireland.[19])

During the next two seasons with Baltimore, Grich was near his best. He finished in the top ten in the American League in on-base percentage in both 1975 and 1976, and he continued to show a good eye at the plate, finishing third in the league in walks during each year as well. He did, however, get caught looking on a third strike on June 1, 1975, to become the final out in Nolan Ryan's fourth no-hitter.

The Orioles finished in second place in the American League in both 1975 and 1976, and on November 1, 1976, Grich was granted free agency. After having acquired Reggie Jackson and Ken Holtzman, the Orioles were expected to overhaul the team completely, and there had been rumors during the 1976 season that Baltimore was trying to trade Grich.[20]

Since he was a California Angels fan growing up, Grich fulfilled a longtime dream by signing with the team. While the New York Yankees had pursued Grich hard in free agency, Grich commented after signing a $1.58 million contract with the Angels: "I had better offers, but you can't put dollar signs on what Southern California has to offer."[21]

Things had been going well for Grich: as writer Dick Miller recounted, "He was living the good life. At 29, he was single and with the rugged good looks of the Marlboro man."[22] Yet Grich's transition to the Angels was interrupted by injury. During the offseason before the 1977 season, Grich injured his back lifting an air conditioner. "I spent three weeks of spring training in traction, but the season was getting close so I came back. I guess I forced the pain out of my mind, but I never felt right. My body ached every day." After hitting a game-winning home run on June 8, Grich knew that he could not continue playing with the injury. "When I touched second base, I began to feel the pain," he said. "I knew if I could feel the pain after hitting a game-winning home run, I was hurting."[23] Grich had surgery on his ailing back less than a month later, on July 3, to remove a herniated disk. He was limited to fifty-two games that season, the fewest of his Major League career after he became a regular.

Even when Grich came back in 1978 he was not the same player. He drove in only three runs in July and three in August. For the season, Grich hit only 6 home runs in 144 games and stole merely 4 bases. "I knew it would take [Grich] a full season to come back from the operation, but people wanted results faster. I didn't want to ruin Grich's mental approach," said his manager, Jim Fregosi. As Grich struggled, Fregosi tried holding him out of the lineup. Grich tried adjusting his batting stance before settling on a new approach: "I raised my hands around my head and took the loop out of my swing. Before, I was coming underneath every pitch. Finally, my swing was level."[24]

In the offseason, Grich became an even more devoted weight-lifter. "But instead of lifting two or three times a week, I was lifting five or six. I felt like I might be slipping a bit, on my way down, but I was going to work hard. Besides, [my strong performance in] September [1978] showed me I still had some ability."[25]

Grich's recovery led him to have perhaps his best overall season in 1979. That year, he hit a career-best 30 home runs, batted in 101 runs, and batted .294 for the American League West–winning Angels. Remarkably, Grich achieved these impressive statistics while often batting eighth in the lineup. That 1979 team included several familiar faces, as Grich was reunited with former Baltimore teammates Don Baylor, Larry Harlow, and Merv Rettenmund. Grich received his fourth career All-Star selection in 1979, and he was voted by both United Press International and the Associated Press as the top second baseman in the American League.

"I read *The Power of Positive Thinking* once and one thing I remember is that you have to have a mental picture of yourself being a success before you can get there," said Grich. "I pictured myself having a year like '79. To have the people in the American League recognize me as the best second baseman in the league, it was one of the goals I set for myself."[26] From May 31 through June 19, Grich hit safely in twenty consecutive games, the second-longest hitting streak in California Angels history. On July 15, with the Angels trailing by a run, he hit a game-winning two-run home run to right field to give California an improbable 5–4 comeback victory over the New York Yankees.

Unlike the stability Baltimore had provided at shortstop with Mark Belanger, the Angels did not have an established shortstop after Grich arrived. Among others, he played with Dickie Thon, Rance Mulliniks, Bert Campaneris, Jim Anderson, and Fred Patek. "If I just watch them a few times, I know how the shortstop is going to come to me,"

said Grich. "It's no big deal playing with a number of shortstops. Really, it's not that difficult."[27]

Grich remained a top performer for the Angels and was a key member of their division-winning teams in 1979, 1981, and 1986. In 1979 the Angels lost the ALCS to the Orioles in four games. During the strike-shortened 1981 season, Grich hit 22 home runs, tying for the American League home-run title with Tony Armas, Dwight Evans, and Eddie Murray. In so doing, Grich become the first American League second baseman to win or share the title since Napoleon Lajoie in 1901 and the first Major League second baseman since Rogers Hornsby in 1929. Still, Grich's performance in the postseason was never up to the level he displayed in the regular season; he batted .154, .200, and .182, respectively, in the Angels' three ALCS losses.

Grich's contract with the Angels was due to expire after the 1981 season, and his future was a source of constant debate in the press. His hot bat also made him very marketable as a potential free agent. After the 1981 season resumed following the strike, Grich in one week got twelve hits in twenty-four at bats, with five home runs and eight runs batted in. "If I'm not the player of the week," he said, "I'd like to shake the hand of the man who is."[28] Ultimately, Grich signed a new four-year contract with the team. "I want very much to finish my career with the Angels, and hopefully, I will contribute to a pennant or two," he said after signing the new contract.[29]

After the 1982 season, Grich was unable to play as consistently because of injury and was often replaced by Rob Wilfong. Grich also played more of a utility role, as he had done earlier in his career, appearing periodically at first base and third base. On November 26, 1985, he re-signed with the Angels for another season.

In 1986, while Grich split time at second base with Wilfong, the Angels won the American League West title. The team was on the verge of advancing to the World Series, leading the Boston

Red Sox in the best-of-seven ALCS three games to one. In the sixth inning of Game Five, Grich hit a home run to put the Angels ahead 3–2. The Angels lost that game, however, and ultimately lost the ALCS to the Red Sox in seven games. It was the fifth time that one of Grich's teams had failed to advance to the World Series.

After that playoff loss in 1986, Grich announced his retirement in the Angels' locker room. "That series was an emotional roller coaster for everyone involved," he said. "I thought we had it. I had been thinking about retiring for a while, but when we lost, I'd had enough. It was time to try something else."[30] Grich's retirement was accelerated by an injury he sustained early in the season: "[I] blew out my thumb the first game at home that season and was out six weeks. That's when I figured that [1986] would be my last year."[31] Grich finished his seventeen-year Major League career with 1,833 hits, 320 doubles, 864 RBIS, and a .266 batting average.

Grich married his second wife, Zetta, in 1992. His stepson, Brandon Lodge, played for the UCLA baseball team, and Grich also raised a daughter, Brianna. In retirement, Grich helped to produce an instructional video working with several former Major Leaguers, including Gary Carter, J. T. Snow, Mike Schmidt, Rod Carew, and Rollie Fingers. As of 2010 he was working on an instructional device called Thro-Trac, which he described as "help[ing] young boys baseball players and young girls softball players throw properly over the top with their arms up."[32]

Grich also worked for six years with Fidelity National Title Insurance Company, where he sold commercial real estate title insurance. An avid golfer with a 2.5 handicap, Grich said that he had played eighty-nine of the top hundred golf courses in the United States (according to a 1989 list published in *Golf Digest*). He also was assistant general manager of the Mission Viejo Vigilantes of the Western Baseball League. Grich in 1988 became the first inductee into the California Angels Hall of Fame.

Grich has also worked in the marketing and sales department for the Anaheim Angels, where, he said, "I had sold five suites and numerous ads over the past eight years."[33] He also worked with the team's speakers bureau, appeared at many of the team's fantasy camps, and devoted time to many charities, including the Cystic Fibrosis Foundation.

Chapter 36. **Moe Drabowsky**

R. J. Lesch

AGE	W	L	PCT.	ERA	G	GS	GF	CG	SHO	SV	IP	H	BB	SO	HBP	WP
34	4	2	.667	3.78	21	0	10	0	0	1	33.1	30	15	21	1	0

He terrorized teammates with snakes. He tossed firecrackers under benches and into bullpens. He was a master of the fine art of the hotfoot. Often forgotten is that Moe Drabowsky could pitch a little, too. In a seventeen-year Major League career with eight teams, it was his two stints with the Orioles that brought him lasting fame, including a star performance in the 1966 World Series and a return trip to Baltimore in 1970.

He was born Miroslav Drabowski in Ozanna, Poland, on July 21, 1935. His mother, Frances Galus, was an American citizen who met her future husband while visiting relatives in Ozanna. "We lived on a farm," Moe recalled in a 1966 interview. "I remember a stream I fished in. I remember a barn, and some of the animals."[1]

In 1938, when Hitler began to invade and annex Eastern Europe, the Drabowski family left Poland. Moe arrived in the United States with his mother in 1938. She was 8½ months pregnant with his sister, Marian, at the time. Their father, Michael, joined the family later, before Germany invaded Poland, and the family settled in Connecticut.

"Language was a barrier when I started school," recalled Moe, "because we didn't speak English at home."[2] Miroslav picked up English from the radio and from school over time, to the point where he all but forgot Polish. With his new home and tongue came a new anglicized name, Myron Walter. From boyhood on, however, nobody ever called him anything but Moe. Eventually, in high school or college, his last name was misspelled "Drabowsky," and Moe went with that spelling for the rest of his life.

Drabowsky's pitching career began in earnest

Reacquired by the Orioles in June 1970, Moe Drabowsky brought versatility, and practical jokes, to the bullpen.

at Loomis Prep School in Windsor, Connecticut. There he was 8-0 in his senior year, including a no-hitter. He then attended Trinity College in Hartford, Connecticut. "I went on a scholastic scholarship," he said, "but lost it when I joined a fraternity and started partying."[3] He didn't lose his fastball, which helped him to a 17-5 record, including another no-hitter, with 111 strikeouts in 70 innings. He also developed his interest in business and finance, and studied economics with, if not academic zeal, at least enough diligence to prepare him for a career as a stockbroker.

During the summer, Moe pitched for the Truro Bearcats in the Nova Scotia Amateur League in Canada. In 1955 he posted a 9-9 record, striking out 135 batters in 120 innings, and in 1956 he went 6-2 with 69 strikeouts in 60 innings. There he caught the eye of scout Lennie Merullo, who signed him for the Chicago Cubs. Sources disagree on the size of the bonus Drabowsky received; it is given as anywhere from $40,000 to $80,000. In any case, under the rules of the day, it was large enough to obligate the Cubs to keep Moe on the Major League roster for two years. As a result, he went right from Nova Scotia to the National League.

He was calm in his first official Major League game, a one-inning scoreless relief appearance in Milwaukee on August 7, 1956. "But the next night in Cincinnati," Drabowsky told the *Chicago American* at the time, "I really had the jitters. The first man I faced was Ted Kluszewski. I was so worried I threw him four straight balls."[4] Drabowsky walked two more batters but struck out three to get through another scoreless inning.

On August 18, pitching coach Dutch Leonard asked, "How would you like to do some throwing tonight?" "I'd like it," Drabowsky replied. "Then you're starting against the Cardinals tonight," Leonard told him.[5] Drabowsky won his third appearance, his first start, going seven innings in an 8–1 win over St. Louis in Busch Stadium.

"Being a bonus player," Moe said, "naturally I take a lot of good-natured kidding. In the pepper games during batting practice anyone who makes an error has to buy the other guy a Coke. When Don Kaiser, Jerry Kindall, and I play, the veterans yell, 'Hey, here come the bonus boys. Forget the Cokes—this one's for Cadillacs!'"[6] No doubt Moe's infectious good nature eased some of the transition pains he might otherwise have felt. It didn't hurt that he seemed to take to big-league mounds right away. Through September 8 Moe had posted a 1.56 ERA over 40 innings. "I was a lit-tle disappointed with my control," he said, though he had added a changeup to his fastball and curve by the end of his Chicago stint.[7] His contract allowed him to return to Trinity College at that point, though the Cubs did call on Moe for two more appearances, one in Brooklyn on the 14th and one in New York on the 19th after he'd been back in school for five days. The Dodgers touched him for four runs, three earned, in a complete-game loss, and the Giants got four runs off him in three innings in relief. The two appearances raised his ERA to 2.47 for the season, which did nothing to diminish Cubs hopes for their bonus phenom.

Moe was supposed to join the Major League club after the school year ended in 1957, and return to school in the fall as he had in 1956. However, he spent the entire season with the Cubs, going 13-15 in 239⅔ innings and striking out 170. He continued to struggle with his control, but his 3.53 ERA was better than the National League average.

After a stint with the U.S. Army Reserve and a throat ailment, he reported late and underweight to the Cubs in 1958. He arrived in time to surrender Stan Musial's 3,000th hit on May 13, 1958. Pinch-hitting for Sam Jones in the sixth inning, with the Cardinals down 3–1 in Chicago, Musial took two balls and fouled off two more before slapping a Drabowsky curve ball into left field for a double. The hit sparked a four-run game-winning rally for the Cards.

On June 27, 1958, Drabowsky married Elizabeth Johns, a former airline stewardess, in St. Paul's Cathedral in Pittsburgh. They met on a flight when Moe traveled from Chicago to New York to visit his parents. Johns, a Pittsburgh native, was a baseball fan who confessed to a reporter that she had harbored a crush for Gil Hodges since she was ten years old. (She might have had mixed feelings about Hodges's .394 batting average against Drabowsky, or his 4 home runs in 33 at-bats.) The couple had two daughters, Myra and Laura.

On July 11, 1958, however, the newly married Drabowsky's career changed dramatically. "I had two strikes on Bob Skinner," he later recalled. "I reached way back for the strikeout pitch, and heard something snap in my elbow."[8] The strikeout ended the fourth inning, but the Pirates tagged Moe for five runs on two singles, three walks, and a homer the next inning. Moe skipped a turn, then tried to pitch on July 19 against Milwaukee and lasted only a third of an inning. "The arm responded to treatment at first," said Drabowsky, "then I had trouble again. I strained my shoulder favoring the elbow. One thing led to another."[9] Drabowsky made four starts in late August, going 1-2. He was 8-7 with a 3.80 ERA at the time of the injury, but finished 9-11, 4.51.

Drabowsky's arm never felt quite right during the next four years. By July 1960, with an ERA hovering around 10.00, he went to the Minors for the first time in his career. He won all five of his starts for Houston, with an ERA of 0.90, and pitched more effectively upon his return to the Cubs in August. But Drabowsky no longer figured in the Cubs' plans. They traded him to the Milwaukee Braves before the 1961 season. He struggled for the first half of the season before being sent to Louisville. The Cincinnati Reds picked up Drabowsky in the 1961 Rule 5 Draft, and used him in the bullpen in 1962 until August, when his contract was sold to the Kansas City Athletics.

There his career was resurrected under the tutelage of the Athletics' pitching coach, former Yankees great Ed Lopat. During this period Moe also began to study films of his pitching, taken by his wife, Elizabeth, in an attempt to improve his mechanics. His fastball was no longer as overpowering, and he learned to rely on location and placement. "I really learned a lot about pitching from Eddie Lopat at Kansas City," said Drabowsky years later. As his pitching coach in 1962, Lopat "provided me with a brand-new outlook and rekindled the confidence." Hired as Kansas City's

manager for 1963, Lopat "gave me a chance to pitch and my arm never felt stronger or better. My confidence was restored and suddenly I realized I was far from washed up."[10]

Drabowsky began 1963 in Portland, starting two games and relieving in 17, and going 5-1 with a 2.13 ERA. Returning to Kansas City, he started in 22 of his 26 appearances. Moe went 7-13 for the Athletics, but posted a 3.05 ERA in the process (in a league where starters averaged 3.65).

Drabowsky began to feel comfortable enough to indulge the sense of humor for which he would become notorious. There are few accounts of his pranks before 1963. The most common observation about him before this time was that he came to the Majors with "a copy of *The Sporting News* in one hand and a copy of the *Wall Street Journal* in the other."[11] Although Drabowsky continued to ply his trade as a stockbroker during the off-season, the serious, studious portrait gave way to that of the madcap bullpen prankster and eventually crowded out almost every other image of the man. On August 18, 1963, for example, in a game when Lopat was ejected, umpire Ed Hurley had to order Drabowsky to stop throwing in the Kansas City bullpen when two of his pitches just happened to sail into right field. It was a sign of antics to come.

In 1964 Drabowsky got into a salary dispute with Athletics owner Charles O. Finley. Drabowsky, who did a pretty good Finley impersonation, amused himself during this period by calling the other holdouts using his Finley voice. "But Mr. Finley," his teammates would say, "$16,000 isn't enough money." According to Drabowsky, "I found out what all the other holdouts were making."[12] The knowledge apparently didn't help Moe much, as he reported late and unhappy, and got off to a terrible start. In July 1964, after Mel McGaha replaced Lopat as manager, Drabowsky was moved back to the bullpen, where he was marginally more effective. He spent most of 1965 in Vancouver (Pacific Coast League), mostly starting, and

R. J. LESCH

still showing he could be effective (at least at the Triple-A level) as a starter. On August 21, 1965, Drabowsky fanned twenty-one batters in a seven-inning game. He allowed three hits, and stranded all three runners. However, he came back to the Kansas City bullpen in August and essentially remained in the bullpen for the rest of his career.

During the off-season, once again available in the Rule 5 Draft, Drabowsky waited to see where he would end up. The Cardinals expressed interest in him, but didn't have the chance to select him. When Cleveland took Baltimore's first choice, pitcher Bob Heffner, Orioles general manager Harry Dalton heard from Charlie Lau, a former Drabowsky roommate. "If you can, get Drabowsky from Kansas City," said Lau, "and we'll win the pennant."[13] Dalton made the pick, then offered Moe $10,000; Drabowsky held out for $15,000, but signed for $12,500.

Up until 1966, Drabowsky is a footnote in baseball history despite occasional flashes of brilliance. In addition to the Musial milestone, as he put it, "I'm in the records for some real beauties."[14] On June 2, 1957, he hit four batters with pitches in 3⅔ innings, tying a Major League record. He plunked future teammate Frank Robinson twice in that outing. He was the losing pitcher on July 13, 1963, when Early Wynn finally captured his 300th win. He narrowly missed another chance at trivia-quiz immortality on April 30, 1961, when Willie Mays hit four home runs against the Braves. During the game, Mays also flied out to center against Drabowsky in the fifth inning. Drabowsky recalled years later that Mays hit the ball to the warning track. "Right now I'm sorry that I didn't give up that home run because it would have been a great feat," Moe said.[15]

In 1966 Drabowsky joined a relief corps that already included Stu Miller, Dick Hall, and Eddie Fisher. Not pitching well in the first two months of 1966, he asked pitching coach Harry Brecheen if he could throw every other night in the bullpen.

The routine helped Drabowsky, as did the talent around him. "Maybe Moe got back his confidence when he joined us," said Sherm Lollar, the bullpen coach for the Orioles. "We were a contender and could support his pitching."[16] Drabowsky became part of a lights-out relief corps.

As the weather warmed up, so did Drabowsky's sense of humor. He wore a four-foot gopher snake around his neck one day as he strolled into work in Anaheim, scaring Paul Blair out of the clubhouse. A small garter snake placed in Camilo Carreon's pocket sent Cam through the roof. Drabowsky liked snakes so much that he cultivated relationships with pet-shop owners, who would let him borrow the snakes. Luis Aparicio was a frequent target, but was forgiving enough to team up with Moe on other pranks. On one occasion Drabowsky and Aparicio swiped a huge papier-mâché Buddha from a Chinese art show in their hotel and placed it outside Charlie Lau's door.

During this season, Moe pulled off one of his best-known pranks. On May 27, in the second inning of a game against his former teammates in Kansas City, Drabowsky called the Athletics bullpen, imitated KC manager Alvin Dark, and ordered that Lew Krausse begin warming up. A few minutes later, Drabowsky called again and ordered Krausse to sit down again. Finally, on the third call, Drabowsky's voice was recognized.

The story has grown in the years since, placing the prank at a critical point in an important game. Several versions of the story name the starting pitcher as Jim Nash, insisting that Nash was pitching a shutout in the sixth inning, and that Drabowsky's prank so unnerved Nash that the Orioles were able to mount a rally and win the game. This version resembles a September 21 game, which Nash left for a pinch hitter after six innings with a 6–1 lead, only to see his bullpen cough up nine runs to lose the game to the Orioles. This is well after the original story was in the paper. The original story needs no such dramatic flourish, now or at the time. As a boy in South Dakota put it in a letter to Drabowsky written sometime after the June reports of the incident, "Baseball needs more nuts like you."[17]

The Orioles entered the 1966 World Series as underdogs against the Los Angeles Dodgers. During Game One, Dave McNally had trouble pitching from Dodger Stadium's high mound: "I couldn't find my rhythm," said McNally. "Ordinarily I like steep mounds, but I couldn't adjust to this." In the third inning, McNally walked the bases loaded with one out. "They quit swinging on me. They didn't have to swing," he said.[18] Frank and Brooks Robinson had given Baltimore a 3–0 lead with first-inning back-to-back homers, but with the lead now in jeopardy, manager Hank Bauer summoned Drabowsky. "He had just so-so stuff when he was warming up," said Charlie Lau, who wasn't on the World Series roster but worked in the bullpen.[19] Moe struck out Wes Parker, walked Jim Gilliam to force in a run, and got Johnny Roseboro on a foul pop to end the inning.

From then on Drabowsky was unhittable. He fanned the next six batters he faced, to tie a World Series record for consecutive strikeouts. In the seventh inning he gave up a walk and a single, but neither runner scored. He closed out the game with perfect eighth and ninth innings as the Orioles won, 5–2. In all, Drabowsky struck out eleven Dodgers in 6⅔ innings, and gave up two walks and just one hit. He hit the corners unerringly and, as Shirley Povich noted, got all eleven strikeout victims swinging.

"Just what is a guy like me doing in fast company like this?" marveled Drabowsky after the game, his arms around Frank and Brooks Robinson. "I couldn't wish for a situation to arise that would call for me to be a hero. I did hope, though, that I'd be able to see a little action in the Series."[20] Asked about his six straight strikeouts, he chuckled, "It's about time I got in the books for something except the wrong end of the record." Wes Parker's two-strike single had broken the string. "If I had known about the record," said Drabowsky, "I might have pitched to him differently. I gave him a slow curve because I was ahead of him, but I might have given him my best pitch, a fastball."[21]

The Orioles did not fare as well in 1967. "When we slipped to fifth place, Hank Bauer stopped us from charcoaling sausages in the bullpen," Drabowsky noted. "That shows what you can get away with when you're winning."[22] The Orioles rebounded in 1968, and Drabowsky continued to pitch effectively throughout his stay in Baltimore.

Drafted by the expansion Kansas City Royals after the 1968 season, Drabowsky added another trivia question answer to his résumé: he was credited with the win in the first Royals regular-season game, on April 8, 1969. Drabowsky was a bullpen fixture for the Royals the next season and a half. Moe kept his Orioles teammates in his sights, however. During the first game of the 1969 World Series, Moe hired a plane to fly over Memorial Stadium in Baltimore before the game, trailing a banner reading "Beware of Moe." (One source has it "Good Luck Birds. Beware of Moe.") The next day, a package delivered to the Baltimore clubhouse contained, according to *The Sporting News*, "one large and thoroughly irritated blacksnake."[23]

By 1970, Drabowsky was enough of a bullpen maestro to offer up his five C's to relief pitching: comfortable grip, confidence, challenging the hitter, control, and concentration. He shared his insights on his role with a reporter that spring: "If it looks like I might get in, I try to visualize a particular hitter, his strike zone and the areas to avoid. I'll do this with several key hitters that I don't want to beat me. But you can't keep going over this through the entire game or pretty soon you'll psych yourself and start giving the hitter too much credit. Then it will be even harder to get him out. I just like to try to get it planted in my mind and then forget about it."[24]

And: "It is difficult for the hitter to protect both

the inside and the outside part of the plate. He has to give somewhere. You try to find out where. If I show him I can nip the outside corner twice, then he has to adjust to protect the outside corner. When he does that, the pitch in on him will be effective. One pitch complements another. If I can't hit that outside corner, then the pitch inside is not effective."[25]

And, on Eddie Lopat: "Until he came along I could never see throwing a ball on purpose. To show you what I mean, let's say I'm coming in to pitch the ninth and I don't know what the hitter will be looking for. If I've had luck getting him out with a slow curve, he may be looking for it. In that case, the best thing for me to do is bust a fast ball low and away, but not for a strike. Then I've got to watch the hitter's reaction. If the ball is by him before he's ready then I know he was looking for the curve."[26]

Moe was hospitalized in early June "after developing a reaction to the medication he was taking."[27] He bounced back, and won in his second appearance. "I was watching the scoreboard in Kansas City one night in 1970 [June 15] and noticed that the Orioles were ahead 6–2 in the fifth inning or so. Next time I looked up they were losing 8–6 in the eighth, so I got a premonition that they might be in the market for some relief pitching."[28] (In fact, Baltimore went up 4–2 after the first inning that night, was up 6–3 after the sixth, then gave up six runs to the Brewers in the eighth.) Sure enough, Moe was dealt back to Baltimore.

The Orioles' 1970 bullpen, already excellent, featured Dick Hall, Pete Richert, and Eddie Watt. Drabowsky contributed a save and four relief wins to the Orioles' stretch drive. Drabowsky did not pitch in the 1970 League Championship Series against Atlanta. In the World Series he yielded one run in 2⅓ innings of work in Game Two, the run coming on a Johnny Bench solo home run, and pitched a scoreless inning to finish Baltimore's only loss of the Series in Game Four.

Asked whether he had cooked up any pranks for his Cincinnati opponents, Moe professed caution, noting that such things could backfire during a World Series. He couldn't resist taking aim at another target, however: Commissioner Bowie Kuhn, who was reportedly the victim of one of Drabowsky's most elaborate hotfoot attempts. Drabowsky ran a trail of lighter fluid all the way from the trainer's room to a match slipped into the sole of Kuhn's shoe as he sat in the clubhouse before one of the games. "You never saw a shoe come off so fast in your life," Drabowsky said.[29]

Moe spent 1971 with the St. Louis Cardinals, for whom he finished 6-1 with 8 saves in 51 games. Off the mound, his return to the National League gave him a new set of victims. He threw cherry bombs in Chief Noc-A-Homa's teepee in Atlanta, and twice gave sportswriter Hal Bock a hotfoot on a road trip to New York (the last act drawing a censure from National League president Chub Feeney). After starting the next year with the Cardinals, he ended up back in the American League with the Chicago White Sox. He was pitching to Tommy Harper one day in August. "I threw a fastball," he told a reporter, "and I watched that ball go to the plate, and I said, 'When in the world is that ball going to get to the plate?' I said, 'Hey, my career is over.'"[30]

Drabowsky joined Garden City Envelope Company in Chicago, where he worked through 1982. He moved on to a Canadian-owned communications firm, then returned to baseball in 1986 as a coach with the Chicago White Sox. There had been no money in coaching when he left baseball in 1972, but now he found he could afford to return to the game he loved. Attitudes had also changed, though. "Players seem to be more serious now," he said in a 1987 interview. "I would tend to believe they don't have as much fun. You don't find the same kind of characters in the game today. Egos are a big factor. And the guys are making so much money."[31]

Drabowsky was no less dedicated where the craft of pitching was concerned, and he coached in the Minors with Vancouver, and with the Chicago Cubs in 1994, before settling into a position with the Orioles at their spring training and rehabilitation camp in Sarasota. He continued to make use of film study, as he had with his own pitching motion in the 1960s, before it became ubiquitous. His infectious enthusiasm and passion for the craft of pitching rubbed off on the pitchers he worked with. "The kids adored him," said his wife, Rita, who married Drabowsky in 1990.[32]

Rita warned him that she was off-limits where snakes and other pranks were concerned, but Moe kept in form against other targets. At Oriole Fantasy Camp, where Moe was a fixture, firecrackers slid under the stall doors in the restroom. After games, players who performed well received the White Rope Award, a white rope draped over the shoulders, or a Brown Rope Award for an error or misplay. Naturally, with Moe around, sometimes the brown ropes would have a wriggle of their own. He could take as well as he gave, though, as he proved when friends on the local police force once arrested him, right off the ballfield, for cruelty to animals. When the police car reached the station and his friends began to process Moe for the "crime," Moe began to wonder whether he had indeed gone too far! His friends waited for him to crack before admitting to the gag.

Diagnosed in 2000 with multiple myeloma, a type of bone-marrow cancer, Drabowsky was given six months to live. He stretched that into six years through grit, determination, and medical therapies that included stem-cell transplants. Drabowsky also found coaching therapeutic, and continued working with Oriole pitchers up until a few months before his death.

The end came for Moe Drabowsky on June 10, 2006, at the University of Arkansas for Medical Sciences (UAMS) Medical Center in Little Rock, Arkansas. Drabowsky could look back on a Hall of Fame career, not the Hall in Cooperstown, but the National Polish-American Sports Hall of Fame, which inducted him in 1999. The most fitting tribute to Drabowsky, however, came at a Fantasy Camp banquet after his passing. Seated at the head table, Rita Drabowsky snuck a dollop of shaving cream onto the button of a guest speaker's Orioles cap. The shaving cream remained on top of the cap all through the dinner, unbeknownst to the speaker, and through the start of his speech, to the delight of the crowd. Moe would have loved it.

Chapter 37. August 1970 Timeline

Malcolm Allen

All headlines below are from the next day's edition of the *Baltimore Sun*.

August 1—BIRDS SNAP MARK WITH 9-TO-1 WIN—On a hot Saturday night at Memorial Stadium, Merv Rettenmund went 4-for-5 and Jim Palmer pitched a complete game six-hitter as the Orioles broke the record for consecutive wins against an opponent by beating the Royals for the twenty-second time in a row.

August 2—BIRDS HOLD OFF ROYAL RALLY, 10–8—The Orioles kayoed KC starter Jim Rooker with a five-run first, then held on to complete a 12-0 season series against the Royals. Curt Motton homered and tripled in a career-best five-RBI performance, and Paul Blair went 4-for-5 in the early stages of a ten-game hitting streak in which he'd bat .512.

August 3—No game scheduled.

August 4—ORIOLES HALT RED SOX BEHIND MC-NALLY, 5–2—In front of the second-largest home crowd of the season (39,011), the Birds romped, 13–1, in an entertaining pregame exhibition against their wives, then won the game that really mattered behind two homers off the bat of Paul Blair.

August 5—PALMER WINS 16TH, SHACKLES BOSTON ON 4-HITTER—Jim Palmer's fourth shutout tied him for the Major League lead in that category, as he matched his career high in wins and led the Orioles to their twelfth win in fifteen games.

August 6—BIRDS WIN, 7–1, BEHIND HARDIN FOLLOWING 4–0 LOSS TO TRIBE—A season's-longest fifteen-game road trip began in Cleveland with the Orioles making fourteen ground-ball outs in a 4–0 shutout loss to former Baltimore farmhand Dean Chance. Baltimore earned a split when Jim Hardin celebrated his twenty-seventh birthday with his first win since May 26 (also against the Indians), helping himself by matching his career high with three RBIs.

August 7—TRIBE TOPS ORIOLES ON 7-RUN 7TH—Tom Phoebus had a 4–0 lead and a perfect-game bid going with one out in the bottom of the sixth inning, but Cleveland's offense erupted an inning later against three Baltimore pitchers and the Indians triumphed 10–4.

August 8—BIRDS BEAT YANKEES ON HOMERS, 4–2—Boog Powell and Merv Rettenmund homered off herky-jerky southpaw Mike Kekich on consecutive third-inning pitches to spoil Old Timers Day at Yankee Stadium in front of 47,194.

August 9—BIRDS GAIN SPLIT WITH WIN IN 11TH—After blowing a four-run seventh-inning lead, the Orioles lost the first game of a doubleheader, 6–4, on Roy White's walk-off homer in the bottom of the eleventh. After coughing up a six-run lead in the nightcap, built in part by Terry Crowley's and Elrod Hendricks's back-to-back homers, the Birds fought back to prevail 12–9 in extra frames despite issuing a season-high thirteen walks. Frank Robinson started the decisive rally with a pinch-hit double after missing six games with a jammed shoulder, getting safely to second with a head-first dive and hustling home with the winning run on Don Buford's fourth hit of the game.

August 10—No game scheduled, as the Orioles traveled to the West Coast in a 342-seat 747. Meanwhile, the Twins lost their third straight to the A's, 7–3, making Baltimore's 71-42 record the best in the American League. Minnesota's losing skid went on to reach nine in a row, so the Birds held the top spot the rest of the way.

August 11—3 BIRD HOMERS TOP ANGELS FOR CUELLAR—Paul Blair and both Robinsons went deep in support of Mike Cuellar's shutout pitching in a 7–0 Orioles win. Cincinnati Reds advance scout Rex Bowen began tailing the Orioles, telling *The Sun*, "They're the best team in baseball. Well, maybe you should say the best team in the American League."[1]

August 12—ETCHEBARREN LEADS ORIOLES TO 5–4 VICTORY OVER ANGELS—The Orioles pushed their AL East lead to 10½ games thanks largely to Andy Etchebarren, who was playing about fifteen minutes from his birthplace, Whittier, California. Etchebarren drove in three runs with a homer and two singles, and stole two bases for the only time in his career. Not only that, when pinch runner Jay Johnstone attempted to score the tying run in the bottom of the eighth by knocking Etchebarren head over heels, the Orioles backstop held onto the baseball for the final out of the inning.

August 13—ANGELS EDGE BIRDS ON REPOZ' HOMER—Jim Palmer threw seven innings of two-run ball on the first anniversary of his no-hitter, but the Angels beat Baltimore 3–2 on Roger Repoz' leadoff homer off Moe Drabowsky in the eighth.

August 14—A'S BLANK ORIOLES AS DOBSON WINS, 4–0—After telling reporters a few weeks back that

he'd consider leaving Baltimore after the season if the right three-year offer came along, Earl Weaver met with club vice president Harry Dalton in Oakland and agreed in principle to remain with the Birds. Unfortunately, Earl's fortieth birthday party was spoiled as the Orioles were held scoreless by Chuck Dobson and Mudcat Grant.

August 15—BIRDS CRUSH A'S, CUELLAR POSTS NO. 17—After the media learned that Earl Weaver had agreed to return in 1971, the Orioles snapped a two-game slide with a crisp all-around performance and won 7–1.

August 16—BIRDS NIP A'S, 2–1, ON SALMON HR—Chico Salmon homered off the left-field foul pole for the second Sunday in a row. Salmon's fifth-inning dinger off Catfish Hunter proved to be the game-winning blow as Dave McNally became the first Major Leaguer with eighteen victories.

August 17—BIRDS WIN ON POWELL'S HOMER, 3–2—Jim Palmer retired sixteen straight Brewers before a seventh-inning interference call against Andy Etchebarren ignited a game-tying Milwaukee rally. Boog Powell untied it in the eighth with his twenty-ninth homer—on his twenty-ninth birthday.

August 18—MILWAUKEE STIFLED BY HARDIN, 3–0—Baltimore managed only three hits against right-hander Marty Pattin but won anyway, thanks to Jim Hardin's second shutout of the season.

August 19—18TH WIN RECORDED BY CUELLAR—Merv Rettenmund rammed a two-out, eighth-inning single up the middle to drive in Brooks Robinson and break a 2–2 tie. Earl Weaver used a different starting lineup in every game of Baltimore's longest road trip of the season, and the Orioles went home after winning ten of fifteen.

August 20—No game scheduled.

August 21—ORIOLES GIVE MCNALLY HIS 19TH VICTORY—The Orioles tuned up with a father-son game, then rode Dave McNally's first shutout of the season to a 5–0 victory over the Angels.

August 22—ANGELS NIP BIRDS, 3–2, IN TENTH—California scored single runs in the ninth and tenth innings to eke out a victory. Jim Fregosi's game-winning shot through the box on a full-count pitch nearly took Eddie Watt's leg off.

August 23—BIRDS TALLY IN 9TH TOPS ANGELS, 6–5—Mark Belanger and Bobby Grich, who entered the contest batting .194 and .193 respectively, each singled in the bottom of the ninth to set up Paul Blair's two-out, game-winning hit.

August 24—No game scheduled.

August 25—MCNALLY CAPTURES 20TH IN 5–1 VICTORY—On the night the new scoreboard debuted at Memorial Stadium, Dave McNally beat the A's to match the Orioles' record for career victories with 110. The southpaw also became the first American League pitcher with three consecutive twenty-win seasons since Bob Lemon from 1952 to 1954. You had to go back to Hal Newhouser in 1944-46 to find another AL lefty who had done it.

August 26—JIM PALMER TAKES 18TH IN 5–1 WIN—Athletic Felipe Alou's solo homer accounted for the only run against Palmer's ledger as the blossoming right-hander decreased his ERA to 2.55, the lowest mark among qualifiers in the Major Leagues.

August 27—F. ROBINSON BELTS PAIR IN 6–4 WIN—Mike Cuellar got fourteen ground-ball outs to become a twenty-game winner for the second season in a row, and Frank Robinson rapped two of Baltimore's three home runs off Oakland's

Chuck Dobson with a pair of bombs to left-center. The Orioles' AL East lead grew to twelve games, and a loss by the Cincinnati Reds in Philadelphia made the Birds' 83-45 record the best in the Major Leagues.

August 28—DON BUFORD SLAMS FOR BIRD SPLIT—Jim Hardin suffered a hard luck 2–1 defeat in the opener of a doubleheader, but Don Buford's grand slam off Dave Baldwin propelled the Orioles to a split in the nightcap. Elrod Hendricks added Baltimore's only pinch-hit homer of the season an inning later, and Pete Richert earned the win in relief with a lights-out performance in which he struck out six Brewers in three perfect innings.

August 29—BIRDS WIN, 6 TO 1, OVER MILWAUKEE—Dave McNally beat the Brewers with a seven-hitter and passed Milt Pappas's club mark with his 111th Orioles victory. The southpaw also matched his career best with three hits, including a three-run double off knockdown artist Bobby Bolin that helped send the Milwaukee hurler to an early shower in the second inning.

August 30—BIRDS DROP 5–2 GAME TO BREWERS—Milwaukee starter Skip Lockwood entered the contest with a 1-10 record but outdueled Jim Palmer into the eighth to snap the winning streak of Baltimore's Big Three of McNally, Cuellar, and Palmer at thirteen. Paul Blair recorded ten putouts in center field in defeat.

August 31—BIRDS WHIP YANKEES IN 10–2 ROMP—Don Buford bounced the first pitch of the ballgame into the seats for a ground-rule double, and sloppy New York defense led to a four-run top of the first for the Orioles at Yankee Stadium. A comedy of errors gave Baltimore five unearned runs overall, and the Birds entered September with a twelve-game division lead.

AL East Standings, August 31:

Team	W	L	GB
Baltimore	86	47	—
New York	74	59	12.0
Detroit	69	63	16.5
Boston	68	63	17.0
Cleveland	64	69	22.0
Washington	63	69	22.5

Chapter 38. **Andy Etchebarren**

Ben Klein

AGE	G	AB	R	H	2B	3B	HR	TB	RBI	BB	SO	BAV	OBP	SLG	SB	GDP	HBP
27	78	230	19	56	10	1	4	80	28	21	41	.243	.313	.348	4	10	3

Five years after being signed to a Minor League contract by the Baltimore Orioles, Andy Etchebarren found himself starting behind home plate for the Orioles on Opening Day, April 12, 1966, against the Boston Red Sox at Fenway Park. The twenty-two-year-old rookie not only settled into the lineup, but thrived as Baltimore's number one catcher. Etchebarren caught in sixty-three of the Orioles' first sixty-eight games and by the end of June led all American League catchers in RBIs and was turning heads with his defensive prowess, toughness, and ability to handle Baltimore's star-studded rotation. By early July Etchebarren had secured a place on the American League All-Star team and thrust himself solidly into the Rookie of the Year discussion. Then he suffered a fractured bone in July that hobbled him for several weeks.

Nonetheless, Etchebarren played an integral role in Baltimore's run to the 1966 pennant and subsequent sweep of the Los Angeles Dodgers in the World Series. He placed seventeenth in the American League Most Valuable Player voting. Teammate Frank Robinson walked away with the MVP award, but his success was bizarrely linked to Etchebarren. At a party in August, Robinson slipped and fell into a pool. Not knowing how to swim, Robinson began sinking before Etchebarren dived into the pool and rescued him.

Apart from his lifeguard skills, Etchebarren's quickness behind the plate and ability to handle pitchers so impressed Baltimore manager Hank Bauer that Bauer entrusted him to catch every inning in the World Series. Etchebarren went 1-for-12 in the Series and earned the distinction of being the last Major Leaguer to face Sandy Koufax,

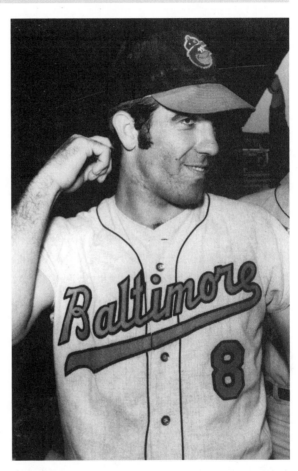

An All-Star in his first two seasons, Andy Etchebarren split the catching duties for the Orioles in 1970.

grounding into a double play to end the top of the sixth inning of Game Two. Etchebarren's impressive rookie campaign was probably his finest and, instead of foreshadowing even greater seasons, stands as a microcosm of his entire big-league career—a career that was slowed by nagging injuries but highlighted by Baltimore's pennant runs.

Andrew Auguste Etchebarren was born on June 20, 1943, the son of a French mother and a Basque American father. He first caught the eye of Harry Dalton in 1961 when Dalton, eventually the Orioles' general manager, was earning his stripes as the farm director and Etchebarren was a star at La Puente High School in La Puente, California, an eastern suburb of Los Angeles. A two-sport athlete, Etchebarren turned down several football offers, including one to the United States Naval Academy. After Dalton secured Etchebarren's commitment to the Orioles in 1961 with an $85,000 signing bonus, Etchebarren began to earn a reputation in the Minors for his defense, ability to manage pitchers, clutch hitting, and toughness. He also began to draw comparisons to Yogi Berra —less for his ability than for his facial features. Etchebarren was even cruelly dubbed "Lurch" by fans of the *Addams Family* TV show and was later derided by broadcaster Joe Garagiola, who suggested that Etchebarren could profit from crashing into the screen behind home plate at Yankee Stadium because the collision "might rearrange some of those parts."[1]

After Minor League stops in Class C Aberdeen in 1961 and Single-A Elmira in 1962, Etchebarren made his Major League debut on September 26, 1962. Completing the Orioles battery on that day was Dave McNally, who was also making his debut and hurled a two-hit shutout against the Kansas City Athletics. The achievement was not lost on Etchebarren, who later called McNally the best pitcher he ever caught. In the second inning, Etchebarren singled and drove in the second Orioles run of the 3–0 victory.

After the 1962 season, Etchebarren spent a few more years in the Minors, first back with Aberdeen, now a Single-A club, and ultimately landing with the Rochester Red Wings of the International League in 1965. It was at Rochester that Etchebarren cemented his reputation for toughness by play-ing through injuries and even remaining in a game after being knocked unconscious when he hit his head while diving after a foul ball. By 1965, it was obvious that Etchebarren was ready for the Majors defensively, but his bat remained a question mark despite his three-run homer off Yankees pitcher Bill Stafford in one of his five late-season games. In his five seasons in the Minors, Etchebarren compiled a batting average of .242, and never finished a season over .255.

Etchebarren's chance finally came in the 1966 season, after Baltimore's top catcher, Dick Brown, suffered the misfortune of being diagnosed with a brain tumor and his backup, Charlie Lau, was hampered by an elbow injury. Suddenly faced with vacancies at the position, the Orioles thrust Etchebarren into Major League action and acquired Vic Roznovsky from the Chicago Cubs. After receiving his shot, Etchebarren had a memorable rookie year, hitting just .221 but with 11 homers and 50 runs batted in, while starting 118 of the club's 162 games. Etchebarren remained the Orioles' catcher in 1967, playing in 112 games and finding himself on the American League squad for the All-Star Game for a second consecutive season. (He played in neither game.) His defense and game-calling were highly prized, though he hit just .215 in 1967.

Despite his defensive prowess, 1967 was the last year in which Etchebarren was the Orioles' primary catcher. It was also the last season in which he was 100 percent healthy; his appearances in 1968 dwindled to 74, the result of both injuries and the emergence of left-handed-hitting catcher Elrod Hendricks. The two began sharing duties as the Baltimore backstops. A midseason change of managers in 1968, with Earl Weaver replacing Hank Bauer, may have dealt a blow to Etchebarren's chances at resuming his lead role, because Bauer had been a strong advocate of Etchebarren, once calling him the quickest catcher he had ever seen, and Weaver loved Hendricks's superior bat. Weaver typically used Etchebarren against left-handed pitchers.

Etchebarren and Hendricks resumed sharing catching duties in 1969, with Hendricks playing in 105 games and Etchebarren in 73. Although he would have preferred to have earned the main job, Etchebarren conceded that Weaver's decision to platoon him and Hendricks was a good one for the club because the catching duo had a strong combined season in 1969. They helped lead the Orioles to 109 victories and their second pennant in four years. Etchebarren started Games Two and Five of the World Series, but failed to get a hit in six at bats during the Series, a five-game defeat to the Mets.

Etchebarren continued to share catching duties with Hendricks in the 1970 season, making 78 appearances and finishing the season with a .243 batting average. In the 1970 World Series triumph over the Reds, Etchebarren started Game Three and Game Five, catching victories pitched by Dave McNally and Mike Cuellar. As in the 1969 World Series, Etchebarren struggled at the plate, striking out three times and netting only one hit in seven at bats. In 1971 he appeared in 70 games and raised his batting average to .270, his career high. Etchebarren also swatted nine home runs, his highest total since his rookie season. In 1971 the Orioles won their third consecutive pennant. The Orioles took the World Series to Game Seven, but they lost to the Pittsburgh Pirates. Etchebarren appeared only in Game Four, going 0-for-2, including grounding into a double play and getting hit by a pitch.

In 1972 Etchebarren squandered the opportunity to regain the starting job when Elrod Hendricks became disabled by a calcium deposit in his neck early in the summer. Instead of seizing the opportunity, Etchebarren saw his batting average plummet to a career-low .202 and he lost the lead job to Johnny Oates. By 1973 Etchebarren's shot at the starting catcher role appeared bleaker than ever. Elrod Hendricks remained in the lineup to hit against right-handed pitching, and the Orioles obtained power-hitting Earl Williams from Atlanta in the offseason. Despite their depth at catcher, manager Weaver turned to Etchebarren during the stretch run. The insertion of Etchebarren into the starting lineup during the run to the postseason was motivated largely by his ability to handle pitchers, but Etchebarren's greatest postseason performance at the plate came in the 1973 American League Championship Series against the Oakland Athletics. Etchebarren appeared in four games, hitting .357 and driving in four runs. Before the series, Oakland manager Dick Williams teased Etchebarren by sarcastically saying that he feared Etchebarren for the strength that he must have built up from not playing all season. In response, Etchebarren clubbed a three-run home run off Vida Blue to help the Orioles win Game Four of the ALCS before the club was eliminated by Oakland in Game Five.

At the start of the 1974 season, Etchebarren was fed up with backing up Earl Williams at catcher and was growing tired of being away from his wife and children, who remained at home in Hacienda Heights, California. Harry Dalton had left the Orioles in 1971 for the California Angels. Confronted with a young and inexperienced team, Dalton began a quest to bring Etchebarren to Anaheim. Etchebarren saw in the Angels not only an opportunity to have a strong shot at a top catching position but also a chance to be closer to his wife and two daughters. Etchebarren demanded either a three-year contract or a trade to the Angels and threatened retirement if neither of the two alternatives materialized. When Baltimore refused to acquiesce to Etchebarren's demands, spring training began with Etchebarren back in California tending the family liquor store. Not surprisingly, Etchebarren missed baseball too much and within two weeks after the start of spring training came to terms with new Baltimore general manager Frank Cashen, without securing either a three-year contract or a trade to the Angels.

At the start of the 1975 season, Etchebarren was named the Orioles' everyday catcher. But in the first week of the season, he suffered two injuries, a strained Achilles tendon and a fractured elbow. When the Orioles failed to reactivate Etchebarren after he was given a clean bill of health, Etchebarren filed a grievance through the Major League Baseball Players Association. Although he was reinstated, Etchebarren's days with the Orioles seemed numbered as he had only one plate appearance after his reactivation. Etchebarren informed the Baltimore front office that he would retire if they refused to trade him and he even refused to sit for the Orioles' 1975 team photo.

When the June 15 trading deadline arrived, Etchebarren and the Orioles went separate ways, with the Orioles leaving for a series in Cleveland and Etchebarren traveling on his own for California, thinking his playing days were behind him. While Etchebarren was en route west, he was sold to the Angels. The news didn't reach Andy until fifty of his closest friends greeted him at his house in Hacienda Heights and surprised him with the news. The move was a happy one for Etchebarren, who had enthusiastically entertained the idea of a move to Anaheim ever since Harry Dalton became the Angels' general manager. Dalton held Etchebarren's baseball knowledge in very high regard and believed that he would be very helpful to the young and inexperienced Angels team. Etchebarren's motivations were both professional and personal—with the Angels he would have a shot at an everyday position at Anaheim Stadium, a mere twenty-minute drive from his home.

Etchebarren immediately replaced Ellie Rodriguez as the Angels' everyday catcher. But within two weeks of his first start for the Angels, Etchebarren's health woes returned as he suffered a broken right thumb and he finished the season

appearing in only thirty-one games for the Angels. In 1976 new Angels manager Norm Sherry named Etchebarren the Angels' primary catcher, and he appeared in 103 games and finished the season with a .227 batting average. By 1977, Etchebarren was thirty-three years old and the elder statesman of the young Angels team. Although it was clear that he was in the twilight of his playing career, his future in baseball as a coach appeared secure when he re-signed with the Angels in 1977 as a player-coach. Etchebarren finished the 1977 season appearing in 80 games and hitting .254.

In 1978 Etchebarren joined his third big-league team. His contract was sold to the Milwaukee Brewers, where Harry Dalton was now the general manager. But Etchebarren was plagued by injury, and 1978 was his last as a player in the Major Leagues. He had elbow surgery in June, and he finished the season appearing in only four games with six plate appearances. He retired as a player after the season. Etchebarren finished his career with a .235 average, 49 home runs, and 309 RBIs. While his offensive numbers are largely unimpressive, he will be remembered for the role he played on four pennant-winning teams, his defense, toughness, and baseball acumen.

After retiring, Etchebarren decided to take a break from baseball and he bought a racquetball club in Hacienda Heights. After three years of running the club, Etchebarren itched to get back into baseball, and once again Harry Dalton came back into the picture. Etchebarren accepted Dalton's offer of a job as the Brewers' Minor League catching instructor. Then he worked his way back up to the big leagues, managing in Stockton in 1984 and becoming the Brewers' first-base coach in 1985 and bench coach under manager Tom Trebelhorn in 1987. By 1993, Etchebarren found himself back in the Orioles organization and became the manager of the Bluefield Orioles in 1993. After a stint as the Baltimore bench coach in 1996 and 1997, Etchebarren managed at Bluefield again in 1998, at Frederick in 1999, at Bowie in 2000, and in Rochester in 2001 and 2002. He was a roving Minor League instructor from 2003 to 2006, and managed short-season Aberdeen from 2005 through 2007, leaving the Orioles organization after the latter season. He later served as the bench coach for the Southern Maryland Blue Crabs of the independent Atlantic League, before becoming in 2009 the manager of the York Revolution of the same league. He held that post in 2010 as well. Etchebarren is a true baseball lifer.

Chapter 39. **Bobby Floyd**

Chip Greene

AGE	G	AB	R	H	2B	3B	HR	TB	RBI	BB	SO	BAV	OBP	SLG	SB	GDP	HBP
26	3	2	0	0	0	0	0	0	0	0	2	.000	.000	.000	0	0	0

When Baltimore Orioles shortstop Bobby Floyd fielded the final out to preserve Jim Palmer's no-hitter on August 13, 1969, it was undoubtedly one of the highlights of the little-used Floyd's career. His was not a household name. The quintessential good-field, no-hit utility infielder who usually played only when a starter was hurt or needed a rest, Floyd took part in only 214 Major League games for two teams in seven seasons, but he was always ready to fill in when needed at any infield position. He saw time at second base, third base, and shortstop, and was a Major League-caliber fielder. But Floyd never managed to hit well enough to solidify a starting position.

Despite his brief playing career, Floyd did not leave the game. Once his playing days ended, he remained in the sport full-time. "Baseball's a great game," Floyd said in 2010. "I love it. And I've been fortunate enough to make a living at it."[1] From Minor League manager to Major League bench coach to player personnel evaluator, Floyd carved out a long and varied career with several organizations. But traveling to such far-off places as the Dominican Republic to assess the baseball talents of aspiring seventeen- and eighteen-year-olds must have seemed light years from football games on the beaches of El Segundo, California.

Born in Hawthorne, California, in Los Angeles County, on October 20, 1943, Floyd grew up in nearby El Segundo. He was the youngest of three children. His childhood was filled with athletics. Whether in structured Little Leagues, Babe Ruth League, American Legion, or simply sandlot pick-up games, Bobby and his friends played not only baseball, but football and basketball as well. In

Bobby Floyd was little used by the Orioles before his June trade to the Royals, but he carved out a few more years with Kansas City as a utility infielder.

fact, "we would often play all three sports in the same day," he remembered. "We'd go down to the beach and play football in the mornings, then go back to town and play basketball and baseball 'til the evening."[2]

By the time he arrived at El Segundo High School, Floyd was well prepared for intramural athletics. (He wasn't the only professional baseball player to graduate from El Segundo High: Ken and George Brett and Scott McGregor all attended the school.) As a senior, Floyd was the starting quarterback on the football team, having apprenticed the previous season to Pete Beathard. (Beathard's older brother, Bobby, went on to a storied career as a general manager in the National Football League.) As a hard-hitting shortstop, in his senior year Floyd led El Segundo to a Southern California championship. He was rewarded for his outstanding play by being chosen to participate in Los Angeles's CIF-City All Star Game.

Floyd owed the foundations of his success to his parents. For many years his mother was a librarian at the high school. His father, who coached Bobby in Little League and was meticulous about such things as caring for the baseball diamond, worked for Standard Oil. Floyd remembered his father as a hard worker who had no hobbies other than his family, but who impressed upon the young Bobby a strong work ethic and positive values, teaching him that "nothing comes without hard work."[3] Bobby absorbed his father's lessons and carried that work ethic to the baseball diamond.

Although he had an opportunity to sign with Ed Burke, a scout for the Philadelphia Phillies, Floyd accepted a baseball scholarship to UCLA, where he gained experience and maturity. After two years of collegiate competition, in August 1963 he felt he was ready for the challenge of the next level and signed with Burke, who was then working for the Baltimore Orioles.

An important part of Floyd's development was the two summers he spent in the Basin League in South Dakota, considered a showcase for collegians. The six teams each played a fifty-game schedule in sixty days, with the top four teams meeting for the playoff championship. Floyd played for the Winner Pheasants in 1962, when he led the league in batting (.344), and 1963. "That was quite a team," he recalled. "We had little jobs at South Dakota. I don't remember what they were, but that's what the NCAA required."[4] The players lived with host families.

The 1963 Winner club, managed by part-time Orioles scout Harry Wise, won the championship. One of its stars was seventeen-year-old pitcher Jim Palmer, who was hailed by some observers as the hardest thrower they'd ever seen. Many years later, Floyd recounted his first impressions of the future Hall of Famer as "a tremendous athlete, a natural,"[5] and said it was easy to see Palmer was going to be a star. The 1963 Winner team also included future Major Leaguers Jim Lonborg, Merv Rettenmund, and Carl Morton. As for Floyd, he hit safely in fourteen of the team's first fifteen games, played forty-six games at shortstop, and hit .307. His performance convinced Burke to sign him.

First, Floyd had to fulfill a military obligation. As a member of the U.S. Marine Corps Reserve, he attended boot camp and served a six-month hitch that conveniently ended a week before the start of spring training in 1964. Starting in April 1964 Floyd spent several years making his way through the Orioles' Minor League system. He claimed not to have received a lot of guidance along the way. "You improved or you didn't go higher," he said. "They just let you play. If you had the talent you were going to move up."[6]

Floyd began his career with Elmira, New York, in the Double-A Eastern League, playing for Earl Weaver. When he hit just .088 after 34 at bats, the Orioles reassigned him to Single-A Stockton in the California League, which proved much more to his liking (.269 in 123 games). The next season Floyd hit his stride playing for Tri-Cities, Washington, in the Northwest League, finishing with a .275 average while stroking seven home runs and driving in seventy runs. The home run and RBI figures were the highest Floyd produced at any level, but were only part of his accomplishments that season. Floyd also led Northwest League shortstops in put-outs (260) and chances (661), and when the season ended he was named to the league All Star team.

In 1966 he returned to Elmira, two years after struggling there. Although Floyd hit just .248, he was again stellar defensively, leading Eastern League shortstops in fielding (.965), put-outs (230), assists (382), and double plays (74). For the next two seasons, Floyd was the starting shortstop for the Triple-A Rochester Red Wings. He had by now made most of the stops in Baltimore's Minor League system, and played at one time or another with most of the players who later propelled the Orioles to an extended period of excellence: Mark Belanger, Dave Johnson, Boog Powell, and Jim Palmer among others. Forty years later he recalled how much he enjoyed the camaraderie of his teammates.

"There were no egos" among the young Orioles prospects, he said. "Everyone was treated the same, whether you were a superstar or just one of the team." All in all, they were "just a great group of guys," and it was fun to have been a part of it. "Of course," he added, "it helped that during many of those years the Orioles and their farm teams did an awful lot of winning."[7]

That's what Rochester did for Earl Weaver in 1967. The team came up just short, losing the International League pennant to Richmond in a playoff after the two teams ended the regular season tied for first place. Floyd hit .243 in 105 games and played his customary steady defense. The next year Floyd broke out to hit .287 with 6 home runs and 52 RBIs. Sportswriter Doug Brown wrote in *The Sporting News* that in the spring of '67 Floyd discovered the book *Psycho-Cybernetics*, described as "a new technique for using your subconscious power." Floyd himself called it "the use of the mind as a machine." Simply put, Floyd thought only about positive outcomes. "If you keep thinking about repeated failures," he told the sportswriter, "that's the way you'll react in a tense situation." Conversely, "Think positively and chances are that's the way you'll react."[8] (It's worth noting that Floyd later returned to school, at the University of Missouri at Kansas City, as a psychology major.)

Whether or not his improvement was attributable to his new mental approach, Floyd had one of his best seasons in 1968. Rochester returned to the semifinal playoffs, although the Red Wings lost to Columbus, three games to two. On July 22 in Louisville, Floyd represented the International League in a game against the Cincinnati Reds, won by the Minor Leaguers, 3–1. After the season, he was named shortstop for the Triple-A East All Stars. None of those accolades could compare, however, to the excitement Floyd felt on September 15, the day after the playoffs ended, when the Orioles called him up for the final three weeks of the season. After five years in the Minor Leagues, he had finally made it to the Majors, working again with Earl Weaver, who had become the Orioles' manager. Although Floyd played sparingly (only five games) during those three weeks, he collected his first Major League hit, a double off Cleveland's Sam McDowell, and run batted in, and fielded cleanly every ball that was hit to him at shortstop. The season ended, he went home to prepare for spring training, hopeful for the coming season.

Fresh from a second-place finish in the American League, the Orioles had few needs on their roster in 1969. They were well stocked at virtually every position. The team acquired veteran infielder Chico Salmon on the eve of the season, and he and Floyd both made the club and shared reserve duties. Floyd's greatest baseball thrill, he later said, was being a member of the 1969 American League champion Baltimore Orioles. Although he rarely played that season, he spent the entire year in the Major Leagues and was on the Orioles roster in the World Series against the New York Mets. "I knew I wasn't going to play [against the Mets] unless Earl Weaver needed a pinch runner,"[9] Floyd said, and indeed he did not play in the Series. Still, he played thirty-nine regular-season games at second base, third base, and shortstop, and earned a full World Series share of $14,904.21.

In the Majors Floyd was unable to duplicate the batting progress he'd made the previous year at Rochester. In 84 at bats, he batted just .202, slugged an anemic .250, struck out 17 times, and grounded into 4 double plays. His one RBI proved an important one: on July 16 against Cleveland, Floyd's sacrifice fly tied the game and the Orioles went on to win, 6–5. It was a rare offensive highlight in a largely ineffective offensive performance.

During the off-season, Floyd worked hard to stay in shape. The Orioles formed a basketball team that played high-school faculties. Floyd participated on the team, along with Paul Blair, Brooks Robinson, Eddie Watt, Pete Richert, Dick Hall, Jim Palmer, and Dave McNally. In January he participated in twice-a-week workouts led by Orioles coach Billy Hunter at the Baltimore YMCA. Despite the preparation, the 1969 season proved to be Floyd's only full year with the Orioles.

When the Orioles acquired Chico Salmon in 1969, they expected to use him as a frequent pinch hitter for Mark Belanger, a notoriously weak hitter. Weaver said in the spring that "if there are two spots open in the infield, one will be a glove and the other a bat"[10]; Floyd would be the glove, and Salmon, a lifetime .252 hitter, the bat. As it turned out, Belanger hit .287 in 1969, and the Orioles felt comfortable keeping just one backup infielder in 1970. Unfortunately for Floyd, Salmon won the position, and on the last day of spring training, Floyd was sent to Rochester.

Naturally disappointed, Floyd dutifully reported to the Red Wings, joining a team managed by Cal Ripken Sr. and featuring future stars Bobby Grich and Don Baylor. The team got off to a great start, opening the International League season with a 9-1 record after reeling off eight wins in a row. In one of those victories, on April 27 over Louisville, the Red Wings' Roger Freed was on third base in the sixth inning when Floyd executed a perfect suicide squeeze bunt down the third base line, scoring Freed and igniting a five-run rally, in an eventual 9–2 Rochester win. Two days later, again versus Louisville, Floyd hit his first home run of the season, although Rochester lost, 8–6. After 35 games Floyd was batting .290 and enjoying a fine season. On May 31 Orioles center fielder Paul Blair was hit in the face by a pitch and was placed on the injured list. Floyd was recalled to take his spot on the roster.

This opportunity proved very brief, just three games, with three plate appearances resulting in two strikeouts and a sacrifice bunt. On June 15, at the trading deadline, the Orioles traded Floyd to the Kansas City Royals for pitcher Moe Drabowsky. After nearly seven years in the Baltimore organization, the twenty-six-year-old Floyd was going to a second-year expansion club. "I felt like it was a good break,'" he recalled. "I was finally going to get an opportunity to play. I knew I was never going to be a starter in Baltimore."[11]

Royals general manager Cedric Tallis believed the infielder would be a good addition to the club. "Floyd has a chance to help out our club substantially at short or second base," he said. "We felt the opportunity to obtain an infielder who could help us for a long time was something we couldn't afford to pass up."[12] Manager Bob Lemon immediately installed Floyd at shortstop. "We want to find out what Floyd can do," Lemon said. "It would be kind of stupid to make a trade for him and then sit him on the bench."[13] But after four starts and ten hitless at bats, Floyd was sent to Triple-A Omaha. Among the starts was one against Bert Blyleven of the Minnesota Twins, Many years later Floyd recalled that Blyleven was the toughest pitcher he faced in the Major Leagues. "People always talk about his curveball," Floyd said, "but, man, he threw hard."[14] So too, he said, did Andy Messersmith, whose pitches Floyd characterized as simply "nasty."

Floyd joined Omaha on July 2 and, *The Sporting News* reported, immediately "solved a defensive problem at a position (shortstop) where three players had been given extended trials."[15] He also contributed with the bat, posting a .292 average in 62 games as Omaha captured its second straight American Association championship. Floyd returned to the Royals in September and hit well, finishing the 1970 season with a .311 average in 17 games for the Orioles and Royals.

At the winter meetings in December 1970, the Royals obtained Fred Patek from Pittsburgh to be their everyday shortstop. After a poor spring, Floyd began the 1971 season in Omaha and also changed positions, moving to second base. He adapted well to the change, particularly the throw to his right, about which he told sportswriters, "I'm working on it every day."[16] He put together an eight-game early-season hitting streak. On June 28, the Royals recalled Floyd to replace Patek, who had been injured. This time Floyd struggled at bat, hitting just .152 in 31 games.

Things didn't improve much in 1972. Despite a poor spring, Patek's spring illness made Floyd the club's starting shortstop on Opening Day. Remaining with the club for only a month, he again failed to hit much and was back in Omaha in May. Floyd hit well there, .300 in 55 games, and was soon back in Kansas City, recalled in July to replace injured third baseman Paul Schaal. But again he failed to hit (just .179 for the season).

Floyd enjoyed his best extended Major League stay in 1973. A member of the Royals the entire season, he hit .333 in 78 at bats as a backup infielder. In 1974 the promising twenty-year-old infielder Frank White made the team, effectively ending Floyd's chances. While he made the team in the spring, he managed just one single in nine at bats before his demotion to Omaha. He hit .270 for the club that season, then returned to hit .234 as a player-coach in 1975. After the season, he retired as a player.

From 1977 to 1985 Floyd managed in the Seattle Mariners system. In 1986 he went to work as a Minor League manager for the New York Mets. (His 1988 Kingsport Mets won the Appalachian League championship.) Starting in 1989 he was the Mets' Minor League field coordinator, a job he held for twelve years. He was a Mets coach in 2001 and 2004. In 2002 and 2003 he managed the Mets' Norfolk team in the International League. As of 2010 he was still working in baseball and had no plans to end his long career in the game. After all, he's got a lifetime of baseball experience to impart to young players.

Chapter 40. **Roger Freed**

Joe Wancho

AGE	G	AB	R	H	2B	3B	HR	TB	RBI	BB	SO	BAV	OBP	SLG	SB	GDP	HBP
24	4	13	0	2	0	0	0	2	1	3	4	.154	.294	.154	0	0	0

On the night of May 1, 1979, the St. Louis Cardinals were playing the Houston Astros at Busch Stadium in St. Louis. Roger Freed, the Cardinals' much-traveled first baseman-outfielder, had been restless, relegated to pinch-hitting duty in the first month of the season. Like many pinch hitters, he was unable to find his stroke but was expected to come through when the team needed a key hit. He had failed in five previous at bats, except for a walk. Freed had also been reading that he might be demoted if the Cardinals decided they needed another pitcher. "I talked to Roger before the game and told him we weren't going to move him," said manager Ken Boyer. "I told him to relax and keep swinging. Roger realizes his role as a pinch hitter. It's not an easy job coming off the bench and getting just one chance, but I believe he has the ideal mental attitude to do the job for us."[1] (Unfortunately for Freed, Boyer changed his mind later in the season.)

As the night wore on, the Astros and Cards found themselves in a 3–3 tie as the game reached the eleventh inning. The Astros went ahead in the top of the frame, scoring three runs—one of them courtesy of a double off the bat of Houston relief pitcher Joe Sambito. Sambito, one of the best relievers in the game, collected 22 saves to go with an earned run average of 1.77 in 63 relief appearances that season, but on this night, he let the Cardinals load the bases in the bottom of the eleventh as he surrendered two walks and a single by center fielder Tony Scott. True to his word, Boyer called on Freed to pinch-hit for left fielder Jerry Mumphrey. After working the count full, Freed blasted a grand slam, the ball clearing the wall in

Another highly touted Baltimore outfield prospect, Roger Freed drove in 130 runs for Rochester in 1970 before his late-season call-up to Baltimore.

left-center field, delivering a 7–6 win for St. Louis. The few fans remaining from the sparse attendance of 6,349 cheered wildly. "This is the biggest, most pleasing experience anyone could have in a lifetime," said Freed. "Something like this really makes me feel like a part of the ballclub—like I'm an asset to the team. You get to feeling like dead weight when you're not contributing in some way."[2]

Freed's feat was a high for him in a season and career mostly of lows at the Major League level.

And not long after hitting his dramatic blast, he was out of the Major Leagues.

Roger Vernon Freed was born on June 2, 1946, in Los Angeles, California, to William and Margie Freed. Roger was the oldest of four children, having three younger sisters. William Freed worked as a pitchman, demonstrating and selling products at carnivals, circuses, and county fairs. Because of William's work, the Freed family was on the move for much of Roger's childhood; he changed schools often as they moved from town to town.

Freed attended Baldwin Park High School, near Los Angeles, and was a four-sport letterman (baseball, basketball, football, and track). After graduation, he enrolled at Mount San Antonio Junior College in Walnut, California. He helped lead their baseball team to the California Junior College baseball championship in 1965, and was named to the All-Eastern Conference team.

Baltimore scout Ed Burke signed Freed, and he was assigned to Aberdeen, South Dakota, of the short-season Northern League for 1966. Freed hit .266 but led the league in home runs (13) and runs batted in (58). He returned to Aberdeen in 1967 and finished among the league leaders in many offensive categories: tied for first in home runs (13), third in batting average (.303), and first in walks (61).

Freed also spent time in 1967 with Class A Stockton in the California League, where his offensive figures suffered (.180 in 122 at bats). He was back at Stockton in '68 and showed good power, smacking 31 home runs and 14 doubles, with 131 RBIs. Freed was named to both the league and Class A West All-Star teams. He continued to blaze a trail through the Orioles organization in 1969, hitting 22 home runs and driving in 90 runs for the Dallas–Fort Worth Spurs. He emerged in the field as well, leading all outfielders in the Texas League in fielding (.984) and in assists (17). "Freed will play in the big leagues," said his Stockton Ports manager, Joe Altobelli. "He has two strong

things going for him—his bat and his arm. He can hit a ball as far as anyone. In fact, I predict he'll hit more homers in the majors than in the minors."[3]

Bolstered by a lineup that included Bobby Grich and Don Baylor, the 1970 Rochester Red Wings flexed their offensive muscle, hitting 113 home runs and scoring 757 runs. The centerpiece of the 1970 team was Roger Freed. From his first at bat at the Triple-A level, when he smashed a 430-foot home run in Columbus, Ohio, he did not stop hitting all season long. Freed was named the International League Player of the Year by Topps and Minor League Player of the Year by *The Sporting News* after hitting .334 with 24 home runs, 30 doubles, 168 hits, and 130 RBIs. He was the third player in the Orioles organization in five years to be so honored (following Mike Epstein in 1966 and Merv Rettenmund in 1968).

Freed was further rewarded for his fine season when Baltimore promoted him to the big-league roster as a late season call-up. He made his Major League debut on September 18, 1970, at Baltimore's Memorial Stadium. Starting in right field and batting fourth, Freed went hitless in four trips to the plate. The next day he stroked his first hit in the big leagues with a single to center field off the Cleveland Indians' Phil Hennigan.

As the Orioles captured the World Series title over the Reds, the future looked bright for Freed. He had succeeded at every level of Minor League baseball, leaving nothing more to prove to the Orioles, or so he hoped. He was ready to compete at the big-league level. However, the baseball adage that "you can never have enough pitching" prevented Freed from taking that final step in an Orioles uniform. After the season Baltimore dealt its prized prospect to the Philadelphia Phillies for left-handed pitcher Grant Jackson (who had finished 5-15 for the Phillies with a 5.29 ERA) and two reserve outfielders, Sam Parilla and Jim Hutto. It seemed a curious trade for the Orioles in that they received little in return and Freed had two options left. Parilla never played again in the Majors and Hutto did not make it to Baltimore's big-league roster until 1975, playing in only four games. But the Orioles had a loaded outfield with starters Frank Robinson, Paul Blair, and Don Buford. With up-and-coming reserve Merv Rettenmund hitting .322 in 1970, there was nowhere for Freed to play. (Jackson wound up having several fine years in the Orioles bullpen.)

Freed was immediately tabbed the starter in right field for the Phillies by manager Frank Lucchesi. "You always hate to say a job is filled, but let's be honest about this," said Lucchesi. "Roger Freed is going to be the right fielder. We didn't make a trade involving the players we gave up to get a utilityman. If he falls on his face in July, we'll have to do something else, but for now, he's the right fielder."[4]

The Phillies moved into a new ballpark in 1971. Veterans Stadium was one of the "cookie cutter" stadiums that sprang up around the country in this era, with a turf field considered the future for all parks. In the second home game of the year, Freed connected for a grand slam off Montreal's Howie Reed to break open a 3–1 Phillies lead in the fifth inning. One member of the Phillies' staff later told the writer Allan Lewis, "That grand-slam might have been the worst thing that could have happened to him."[5] From April 19 to June 18, Freed hit .208 with 1 home run and 8 RBIs in 49 games. He finished the year hitting .221 with 6 home runs and 37 RBIs for last-place Philadelphia. He started 93 games in right field, the most he would ever start in a Major League season.

Freed showed little improvement in 1972. Though he played in 73 games, he started in only 27 games in right field, sharing the job with Oscar Gamble, Tom Hutton, and Mike Anderson. His home-run total was again 6, but he drove in only 18 runs while hitting .225. When the Phillies again finished in the basement (59-97) of the Na-

tional League East, Paul Owens replaced Lucchesi as manager.

In December the Phillies sent Freed and Gamble to Cleveland for outfielder Del Unser and third baseman Terry Wedgewood. Freed was assigned to Oklahoma City, Cleveland's affiliate in the American Association. Indians general manager Gabe Paul assured Freed that he would be given a shot to make the team in spring training, but it was Gamble who gained a roster spot and Freed spent the 1973 season in the Minors, leading the 89ers with 30 home runs. The Indians finished in last place in the American League East, and their right fielder, Rusty Torres, hit .205, but Freed was never recalled to the Majors.

In December 1973 the Indians traded Freed to Cincinnati for pitcher Steve Blasteric. Again, there was no room on the Major League roster, and the Reds sent him to Indianapolis (American Association). Freed still had no problem hitting in the Minors, finishing 1974 with 19 home runs and 71 RBIs. One positive element from the season was the relationship that grew between Freed and Indianapolis manager Vern Rapp. Later in his career Freed described Rapp as "the best manager I ever played for. We're very close friends."[6] Rapp was a Minor Leaguer from 1946 through 1960 who never made it to the Major Leagues. Perhaps he and Freed commiserated with each other about life in the bush leagues. Freed earned a call-up to the Reds in September and hit a three-run pinch-hit home run against San Diego on September 18.

After Freed spent all of spring training with the Reds in 1975, Cincinnati sold his contract to Monterrey of the Mexican League. He hit .285 with 19 home runs and 130 RBIs while playing in 103 games. The Montreal Expos purchased his contract and sent him to Denver, their top farm team in the American Association, in 1976. Rapp had been recently hired as the Bears' manager and urged the team to pick up Freed. "When I came over here [to Denver], I felt I needed somebody who had played for me previously," said Rapp.[7] Rapp's judgment looked sound. Freed once again captured *The Sporting News* Minor League Player of the Year award, the only person ever to earn the honor twice. He swatted a career-high 42 home runs, drove in 102 runs, and batted .309. He finished 3-for-15 for the Expos in a brief September call-up.

By this point Freed had been typecast as a good Minor League hitter, and he was left unprotected by the Expos in the Rule 5 draft. Montreal general manager Charlie Fox said he felt that Freed had "too many holes to be a big-league hitter."[8] St. Louis claimed Freed, and once again he was reunited with Rapp, who had been hired to replace Red Schoendienst as manager. This time Freed stayed in the Major Leagues.

Freed was used primarily as a pinch hitter off the bench and at times spelled Keith Hernandez at first base. As a pinch hitter he was 9-for-23 with two walks, good for a .391 batting average. He had a fan club that frequently folded stadium seats to spell out a giant "Freed" in the upper deck of Busch Stadium. One of his highlights for the 1977 season came on August 22 in St. Louis. The Cardinals scored seven runs in the ninth inning to overcome a 6–1 deficit to the Dodgers. Freed provided the decisive blow when he pinch-hit for pitcher Al Hrabosky, and hit a three-run home run off Charlie Hough to secure the come-from-behind victory. "That's the biggest hit, yes sir," said Freed. "I kept fouling some good pitches. His knuckleball was hopping all over. I knew I hit it hard, but I didn't know where it was going to go. I didn't know whether it was going to be a line drive to the shortstop or what. When I looked up and saw it was going out, I couldn't believe it."[9] For the season, Freed batted .398 (33-for-83) with 5 home runs. He made the final out of the season on a force play against New York, thus ending his bid for a .400 season.

Freed enjoyed more success in 1978 as he hit .379 (11-for-29) in a pinch-hitting role (.239 overall in 92 at bats). As in the previous year he also saw some time at first base to give Hernandez a breather. Although he did not provide any theatrics with game-winning homers, he did collect twelve RBIs in his substitute role. On May 5 Cardinals starter Bob Forsch was throwing a no-hitter against the Phillies and clinging to a 1–0 lead through six innings. In the bottom of the sixth Freed pinch-hit for Tony Scott with the bases loaded, and delivered a bases-clearing double. The lead gave Forsch some breathing room and he went on to pitch a 5–0 no-hitter. Rapp was replaced at the helm when Cardinals great Ken Boyer took over early in the season. The change of managers did not help the final outcome as St. Louis finished in fifth place, twenty-one games off the pace.

Freed started the 1979 season in St. Louis. He had a moment of glory with his walk-off grand slam against Houston on May 1, but was demoted to Springfield of the American Association at midseason. "He hadn't many at bats with us and he didn't have many in spring training," said Boyer. "And the way (Hernandez) is playing, there is no need to rest him. And if I did rest him, I'd play (Dane) Iorg at first base. This way, Roger can get 35 to 40 at bats (at Springfield) and get his stroke back."[10] If Freed refused to go, he would surrender his 1979 salary. "It's a numbers game," the unhappy Freed said. "But they won't find a job for me someplace else. I've been up and down before. I don't feel this is the end of my career, but I could see it coming. What I don't understand is why can't somebody else use me? Why not give me a chance in the American League. I haven't given anybody any trouble. I come out and do my work."[11] He did return to the Cardinals and finished the season at .258 with 2 home runs in 31 at bats. Besides the walk-off grand slam against Houston, his other home run also came in a pinch-hitting role, on June 12 off Burt Hooton of the Los Angeles Dodgers in a 9–3 loss.

The Cardinals released Freed at the end of spring training in 1980. He signed with Philadelphia and was assigned to Oklahoma City of the American Association. After playing in fifty-seven games, he was released and finished the season at Syracuse, the Toronto Blue Jays' Triple-A affiliate in the International League. After that he ended his playing career. Freed seemed to be classified as a "4A Player"—too good for Triple A but not quite good enough to stick in the Major Leagues. He ended his career with 143 home runs in Triple-A baseball.

After retiring as a player, Freed worked as a Minor League batting instructor in the Dodgers organization, and in 1981 as manager of the Erie (New York) Cardinals, the Cardinals' short-season affiliate. In 1985 he managed Saltillo in the Mexican League.

Freed died on January 9, 1996, at the age of forty-nine. He had been hospitalized with a ruptured appendix the month before, but the cause of his death was related to a heart condition. He was survived by his wife, Linda, and three daughters, Melinda, Merrie, and Michalle. He was buried in Oakdale Memorial Park in Glendale, California.

Chapter 41. **Dave McNally**

Mark Armour

AGE	W	L	PCT.	ERA	G	GS	GF	CG	SHO	SV	IP	H	BB	SO	HBP	WP
27	24	9	.727	3.22	40	40	0	16	1	0	296	277	78	185	7	8

A longtime left-handed pitching ace for one of baseball history's best staffs, Dave McNally was also a legend and hero in his native Billings, Montana, where he lived his entire life outside of baseball. Though a World Series pitching (and hitting) star, he might be best known in some circles for the role he played in ending the "reserve clause" in baseball contracts.

David Arthur McNally was born on October 31, 1942, in Billings, the youngest of four children, three boys and one girl. His father, James, was an oil salesman who died in the Allies' fight to conquer Okinawa in July 1945. Beth McNally, now a widow, worked in a welfare office and raised her four children. All the kids helped out, working as much as they could, though Dave's year-round sports playing kept him too busy to hold down a job for long.

McNally played Little League baseball and then attended Billings Central Catholic High School. The school did not field a baseball team, due to both Montana's short spring and the long travel that would have been required (McNally's basketball team regularly traveled 200 miles to play conference games). Instead, he played and starred for the powerhouse Billings Royals Post 4 American Legion club, which was in the midst of winning fourteen state titles in succession. Legion ball was huge in Montana, with eighty-game seasons and travel all over the Northwest. "School would let out," McNally recalled, "and immediately we would go on a five-, six-state tour in our air-conditioned bus. Not only did we have our local Legion post behind us, but everybody else in town too. A

A star pitcher for several years with the Orioles, Dave McNally won twenty-four games in 1970 and hit a memorable grand slam in the World Series.

good team would come into town and we'd draw 4,000 to 5,000 people."[1]

McNally played on the 1958 club that went to the national Legion World Series, the 1959 club that lost in the regional, and the 1960 club that reached the national finals. In 1960 McNally finished 18-1 and once struck out twenty-seven batters in a single game, including five in an inning. His only loss came in the final game, when he was beaten by a New Orleans club that included Rusty

Staub. "He was just a great athlete," recalled teammate Pete Cochrane. "He was a solid guy, a good leader, just outstanding."[2]

In September 1960, still not quite eighteen years old, McNally signed with Baltimore Orioles scout Jim Wilson for $80,000. "It came down to the Orioles and Dodgers," McNally recalled. "If I'd known about the Kiddie Corps [several young pitchers in the Orioles system] I probably would have signed with the Dodgers."[3] With all the Minor League seasons over, McNally was sent to an instructional league in the fall, before he reported the next spring to the Orioles' Double-A Texas League club in Victoria, Texas. The Texas League proved too tough for the eighteen-year-old (0-3, 6.16 earned run average in four starts), so he was transferred to Appleton, Wisconsin, to play for the Class B Fox Cities Foxes of the Three-I League. Playing for Earl Weaver for the first time, McNally pitched in 25 games, finishing 8-10 with a 4.18 ERA.

In 1962 McNally again played for Weaver, this time for the Class A Elmira Pioneers of the Eastern League. The team featured future Major League teammates Andy Etchebarren, Mark Belanger, and Darold Knowles, as well as legendary Minor League fireballer Steve Dalkowski, but the nineteen-year-old McNally was the biggest star. Pitching in 34 games, including 28 starts, he finished 15-11 with a 3.08 ERA. His fine effort led to a recall to the big club in September, and he was even given a start on September 26. McNally faced off against the Kansas City Athletics in Baltimore's Memorial Stadium, and the left-hander tossed a two-hit shutout, retiring the final seventeen men to face him. "I was scared to death," recalled McNally of his debut.[4]

Even with his fine effort to end the season, McNally was still a long shot to stick with Baltimore in 1963. The Orioles were a fine club, having won eighty-six games in 1962, and featured several young starters, including Steve Barber, Chuck Estrada, and Milt Pappas. Dalkowski was expected to make the team as a left-handed reliever, but he suffered a pinched nerve in his elbow in spring training. McNally made the club in his place, at least until May 15, when teams had to reduce their rosters to twenty-five players. He pitched a single inning in New York on April 14 (retiring all three batters), then got an emergency start in April 20 when Estrada had a sore elbow. McNally responded with a complete-game seven-hitter over the Cleveland Indians, 7-1. Although he had his share of rocky outings, he ended up pitching in 29 games, 20 of them starts, in his rookie campaign, finishing 7-8 with a 4.58 ERA. The following year the twenty-one-year-old had a similar role, starting 23 times among his 30 games, with a 9-11 record and an improved ERA of 3.67. He ended the season well, with a one-hit shutout over the Washington Senators, allowing only a double (to Don Lock) in the seventh inning.

In 1965 McNally kept his role as the team's fifth starter and occasional reliever. After a mediocre start (he had an ERA of 4.19 at the end of May), he pitched very well the last four months, finishing the season 11-6 with a 2.85 ERA in 29 starts and 198 innings. In midsummer he quit smoking and gained weight (from 188 to 202 pounds on his five-foot-eleven frame), and later credited his improved pitching to his excess pounds. For the second straight season he finished with a flourish, this time a two-hit, ten-strikeout victory against Cleveland. After the season he started smoking again, and battled the Orioles over his weight for the next few years.

Heading into the 1966 season, the twenty-three-year-old McNally was seen as a key member of a young and talented rotation that included Steve Barber (28), Wally Bunker (21), and Jim Palmer (20). The club had lost Milt Pappas, its most consistent hurler over the past several seasons, and the key man in a trade to the Cincinnati Reds that landed Frank Robinson. With Robinson immediately the best player in his new league, the Orioles ran away with the American League pennant. McNally was the team's most consistent starter, finishing 13-6 with a 3.17 ERA in 33 starts. He also had a hot stretch as a hitter, getting his average over .250 in midsummer. When asked how he was doing it, he replied, "I don't have to explain my hitting. I mean, did Ted Williams have to explain?"[5]

With plenty of time to prepare for the World Series, manager Hank Bauer chose McNally to pitch the first game against the Dodgers' Don Drysdale in Los Angeles. Unfortunately, McNally was uncharacteristically wild, allowing two hits and five walks in just 2⅓ innings before being removed. The Orioles were leading 4–1 at the time, and reliever Moe Drabowsky pitched brilliantly in 6⅔ innings of relief to close out the 5–2 victory. Baltimore won the next two games as well, behind shutouts from Palmer and Bunker. To pitch the fourth game, Bauer again gave the ball to McNally. This time the lefty did not disappoint, throwing a four-hit shutout to close out the Series, the Orioles' first-ever championship. "I had a lot of things going for me that day," he recalled. "The movement on my fastball was sufficient, and I had a pretty good curveball and changeup."[6] A photograph of McNally and third baseman Brooks Robinson rushing into each other's arms is one of the more indelible images in Orioles history.

McNally was a devoted family man, having married Jean Marie Hoffer, his high-school sweetheart, in 1961, when both were teenagers. The couple eventually raised five children: Jeff, Pamela, Susan, Annie, and Michael. During the 1966 season the McNallys bought a house in Lutherville, Maryland, and spent most of the next several years there. In the offseason, Dave worked at the brewery of Orioles owner Jerry Hoffberger.

Heading into 1967 as the certifiable staff ace, McNally suffered a sore elbow in the spring and had a lost year, finishing just 7-7 with a 4.54 ERA. With injuries suffered by fellow pitchers Barber,

Bunker, and Palmer, the Orioles fell to sixth place in the American League. Early in the year McNally felt fine only because he was not throwing as hard as he normally did, and he was getting hit. When he decided to let loose, he had intense pain in his elbow. He made only twenty-two starts, eleven fewer than in the previous season. In December he could barely comb his own hair with his left arm. He was just twenty-five, but his career seemed to be in danger.

After several weeks of light throwing, by March, McNally's elbow had recovered, and he soon became reacquainted with an old friend—his slider, a pitch he had used in the Minors but had not gotten to work for several years. He had relied solely on his curve and fastball for five years, until one day, in a spring bullpen session, he casually tossed a "short curve" to catcher Andy Etchebarren. "Great slider," the catcher hollered.[7] The surprised McNally threw a few more, and—just like that—he had a third pitch. The slider became a key part of his arsenal for the rest of his career. With three excellent pitches, McNally dominated AL batters in 1968, finishing 22-10 with a 1.95 ERA (third best in the league), 5 shutouts, and 19 complete games. He finished fifth in the league's Most Valuable Player voting, was named Baltimore's MVP, won the league Comeback Player of the Year award, and was named as the left-handed starter on *The Sporting News* American League All-Star team.

One batter who hit McNally well, in 1968 and throughout his career, was Senators slugger Frank Howard. In a September 1968 game in Washington, McNally allowed a home run to Howard in the fourth inning, but the score remained 1–1 in the seventh. With one man on and Howard up again, manager Earl Weaver sent pitching coach George Bamberger out to tell McNally to throw curveballs. The pitcher refused, insisting on his slider. Howard hit the next pitch well out of the park in deep right-center field, after which Weaver

MARK ARMOUR

told McNally he would go out to the mound himself the next time. For his career, Howard hit .336 with 13 home runs in 110 at bats against McNally. Other than Howard, only Willie Horton, with ten, hit more than six home runs off McNally.

Another key to McNally's success might have been the ascension of Earl Weaver to club manager in midseason of 1968. Weaver asked his starters to work fast, and also to pitch deep into games. McNally won Weaver's first game, a two-hit shutout, in two hours and twelve minutes on July 11, before winning eleven more in a row. "McNally worked quick," first baseman Boog Powell remembered. "It was 'Let's go boys; let's get it over with and get out of here; we've got better things to do.' He didn't have overpowering anything, but he was a magician with the stuff he had."[8]

After closing 1968 with fourteen wins in his final sixteen decisions, McNally started the 1969 season 15-0, finally losing when he allowed a seventh-inning grand slam to Minnesota's Rich Reese on August 3. McNally tied Johnny Allen's league records of fifteen wins to start a season, and seventeen consecutive wins over two seasons. His best performance might have come on May 5 in Minnesota, when his no-hit bid was broken up by a Cesar Tovar single with one out in the ninth. McNally quickly enticed Rod Carew to ground into a double play, and settled for a one-hitter.

The Orioles easily dominated the new American League East in 1969, winning 109 games and finishing 19 games ahead of the Detroit Tigers. McNally slumped in August but recovered to finish 20-7 with a 3.22 ERA. The Orioles faced the Minnesota Twins in the first-ever American League Championship Series, and won it in three straight games. In the second game, McNally pitched a masterful eleven-inning three-hit shutout, winning 1-0. In the World Series, the Orioles faced the New York Mets and lost in five games. McNally lost the second game 2–1, allowing the winning run on three two-out singles in the top of the ninth

inning. He also pitched the fifth game, but left after seven innings in a game tied at 3–3. McNally had hit a two-run home run in the fourth to keep the Orioles in the game. The Mets scored two in the eighth off Eddie Watt to win the World Series. McNally put up a 2.61 ERA in 16 innings, but lost his only decision in the Series.

The next year was more of the same for the Orioles and McNally. This time Baltimore won 108 games and led its division by 15 games. McNally finished 24-9 with a 3.22 ERA, and teamed up with Mike Cuellar (24-8) and Jim Palmer (20-10) to form most of the best rotation in the game. McNally again got the Game Two assignment in the playoff rematch against the Twins, and came through with the win (11–3) to help the club to another three-game sweep. In the World Series, McNally started the third game and beat the Cincinnati Reds, 9–3. Most memorably, he helped his own cause in the sixth inning by crushing a Wayne Granger pitch to deep left for a grand slam. McNally remains the only pitcher to hit a grand slam in the World Series, and one of only two pitchers (along with Bob Gibson) to hit two home runs in World Series play. (McNally's two home runs were his only hits in sixteen lifetime Series at bats.) This victory put the Orioles up three games to none, and they soon wrapped up the series in five games for their second championship in five years.

The 1971 Orioles won "only" 101 games but still claimed the division title by twelve games over the Tigers. The team is most famous for having four twenty-game winners, the first team to accomplish this feat since the 1920 Chicago White Sox. McNally missed six weeks in July and August with a sore arm, but still became the first Oriole to win number twenty when he shut out the Yankees on September 21. Cuellar got his twentieth on September 24, Pat Dobson on the 25th, and Palmer on the 26th. McNally ended up leading his team in wins, finishing 21-5 in just 30 starts, with a 2.89 ERA. He then beat the Oakland Athletics in the first game of the playoffs, and watched his team complete a three-game sweep, its third in the first three years of the League Championship Series.

In the first World Series game against the Pittsburgh Pirates, McNally allowed three unearned second-inning runs but held the line, finishing with a three-hitter and a 5–3 victory. He was less effective in Game Five, losing 5–0 to Nelson Briles as the Orioles fell behind 3–2 in the Series. McNally pitched in relief in the final two games, earning a victory in Game Six when he got one out and the team rallied in the bottom of the tenth. He got one out the next day as well, but the Orioles fell 2–1 to Steve Blass to lose the Series four games to three.

After his fourth straight twenty-win season (a record of 87-31 over the four seasons), McNally signed a contract calling for $105,000 for 1972, the six-figure salary a coveted number in those pre-free-agent days. In fact, he was the first AL pitcher ever in the $100,000 circle. "He's worth every cent," said Orioles pitching coach George Bamberger. "Nobody in baseball has worked as hard as he has. He never pouts or moans no matter how he's hurting. If he has a run of bad luck, he just shrugs it off. There are pitchers who are faster and maybe have better curveballs, but the difference is McNally knows exactly how to use what he has."[9]

Although he began the 1972 season with two straight shutouts, and four in his first five starts, it would prove to be a frustrating season for McNally and the Orioles. After featuring the league's best offense the previous three years, the 1972 team dropped from 4.7 to 3.3 runs per game, and the team fell to third place despite its stellar pitching. All four of the twenty-game winners from 1971 had fine seasons, but only Palmer returned to the twenty-win circle. McNally posted an excellent 2.95 ERA over 36 starts and 241 innings, but could manage only a 13-17 record. He threw a career-high six shutouts, meaning that in games in which he surrendered at least one run, he went only 7-17.

In 1973 McNally had to settle for a 17-17 rec-ord, despite a fine 3.21 ERA and 17 complete games in 38 starts. The Orioles returned to the postseason in 1973, holding off the Boston Red Sox by eight games in the East before falling in five games to the Athletics. McNally pitched and lost the second game, his first ALCS loss after three wins. In 1974 his record improved to 16-10 despite a rise in his ERA to 3.58. Once again he lost his lone playoff start, as the Orioles fell to the A's in the playoffs for the second straight year.

After the 1974 season, the thirty-two-year-old McNally was the winningest all-time Baltimore pitcher with a 181-113 record, plus a 7-4 postseason log. Nonetheless, he startled the Orioles in November by asking to be traded. "I need a change of scenery to see if it'll straighten me out and give me a little extra life," he told a writer in November. "I haven't been pitching the way I'm capable, and maybe a trade would wake me up."[10] Although the writer speculated that McNally might have had difficulties with manager Earl Weaver, or that he was upset over several difficult contract negotiations in recent years, McNally would not comment. Frank Cashen, the club's general manager, later remembered the battles with his pitcher. "McNally was a tough son of a bitch," Cashen said. "*Intractable* is a good word for him."[11] This was an era when having an agent, which McNally did, was considered an affront. On December 4, he was dealt with outfielder Rich Coggins and a Minor Leaguer to the Montreal Expos for pitcher Mike Torrez and outfielder Ken Singleton. Although McNally was the big name in the deal, it turned out to be a great trade for Baltimore. Torrez won twenty games for the Orioles in 1975, and Singleton had several fine seasons.

McNally's stay in Montreal was brief yet historic. He believed that the Expos reneged on agreements they had made at the time of the trade (he had to give his permission to finalize the deal). Failing to come to terms on a contract, he played on without one (the club renewed his 1974 contract, with a small raise, pending an agreement). After four starts he was 3-0 with a 3.19 ERA, for a club whose record was just 4-7. Nine outings later, McNally's record had fallen to 3-6, 5.24. On June 9, 1975, he announced his retirement from baseball. "It got to the point," he said, "where I was stealing money."[12] He thought he was letting his team and his teammates down, and could no longer do it. "I was trying to tell myself that it would come around. If I had arm trouble or any kind of arm injury, then I could say that I had an excuse. There is absolutely nothing wrong with my arm."[13] He apologized to the fans of Montreal. He did not sign his official retirement papers, a move that proved to be significant.

Wrapping up his affairs in Montreal did not take long. McNally had rented a room downtown, and his family had not yet left their suburban Baltimore home. Once the children were out of school in late June, the McNallys sold their house and moved back to Billings. In a likely unrelated development, on June 17 McNally began hiccupping, a condition that lasted for twelve days and required hospitalization at Baltimore's Sinai Hospital.

His days in the baseball news were not quite over. For the past several years the players union had considered a legal challenge to baseball's reserve clause (which annually bound all contracted players to their clubs for the next season). The way to combat the clause, union leader Marvin Miller felt, was for a player to play an entire season without a contract and then file a grievance claiming free agency. In 1974 San Diego outfielder Bobby Tolan had done this very thing, but the Padres signed him just before his arbitration hearing. In 1975 Dodger pitcher Andy Messersmith was playing without a deal, but many figured that the Dodgers would also get a contract done before a hearing could be reached. With McNally retired and no longer interested in signing a contract, Miller asked him to join the case. McNally, a former union rep with the Orioles who understood

what was at stake, agreed, and soon Expos General Manager John McHale was in Billings offering him a big raise and a two-year deal to come back.

In any event, neither McNally nor Messersmith signed their contracts, the grievances were filed, and the hearing was held in late November of 1975. On December 23 arbitrator Peter Seitz ruled in favor of the pitchers, making both men free agents, effectively ending the reserve clause and changing baseball forever. Though he was now free to sign with any team, McNally had no interest in pitching—he had filed his grievance to help other players. He did not attend the hearing or even leave Montana. He never played baseball again.

Meanwhile, he and his brother Jim had bought a car dealership in 1973 that Jim had been running. Soon after Dave returned home, they bought a second dealership, which Dave took over. Later they bought a third. He once told the writer Maury Allen, "I follow baseball casually, but I follow the automobile business more carefully."[14] Though he worked long hours at his job, he played enough golf to have an eight handicap for many years.

His son Jeff was drafted by the Milwaukee Brewers in 1980, but instead went to Stanford and never played professionally. Jeff's friend Jeff Ballard also attended Stanford, and went on to pitch seven years in the Major Leagues, becoming Billings's second-best baseball product. By 1997 Dave and Jean had seven grandchildren.

McNally received many honors in his retirement years. He was named to the Baltimore Orioles Hall of Fame in 1978, only the third inductee—following Brooks Robinson and Frank Robinson. In 1999 he was named Montana's athlete of the century by *Sports Illustrated*. The same year he was one of eight pitchers named to the Orioles' All-Century team—only Jim Palmer and Mike Mussina received more votes among pitchers.

A lifetime chain smoker, McNally battled prostate cancer and lung cancer beginning in late 1997. He held on for five years, but finally succumbed on

December 1, 2002, in Billings. He is buried in Yellowstone Valley Memorial Park. Many teammates and friends praised McNally on hearing the news. "Dave was an unbelievable competitor," remembered Earl Weaver. "He did it with cunning and intelligence. He loved to set you up with a change, fool you with that tremendous curve and then throw the fastball by you. Plus he was 100 percent gentleman. He was the kind of guy you wanted your son to be."[15]

"I think the proudest thing I have left from those days is the respect of my teammates," McNally recalled late in his life. "They knew when I went out there, they got everything. I didn't leave anything on the bench."[16]

Chapter 42. **Johnny Oates**

Jacob Pomrenke

AGE	G	AB	R	H	2B	3B	HR	TB	RBI	BB	SO	BAV	OBP	SLG	SB	GDP	HBP
24	5	18	2	5	0	1	0	7	2	2	0	.278	.333	.389	0	0	0

In the first years of Tommy Lasorda's Hall of Fame career as manager of the Los Angeles Dodgers, he kept several large photographs on the walls of his office at the team's spring training complex in Vero Beach, Florida. There was one of himself and Walter Alston, his legendary predecessor, and another with Hall of Fame sluggers from the Dodgers' "Boys of Summer" days in the 1950s. Finally, there was a photograph of his third-string catcher swinging a bat. Johnny Oates rarely struck that pose while playing for Lasorda—he made only 126 appearances for the Dodgers skipper in three seasons.

When asked why the journeyman catcher's picture was up on the wall with all of those Hall of Famers, Lasorda replied, "He's just a terrific guy, one of my favorites." It was a sign of the high esteem in which the baseball world always held Johnny Oates.[1]

For many respected men who die before their time, reputations are often enhanced after their lives are over. Johnny Oates's legacy was forged long before his death at the age of fifty-eight in 2004 from an aggressive form of brain cancer.

As a player for eleven seasons, Oates was a favorite of managers—Earl Weaver in Baltimore, Lasorda in Los Angeles, Dick Howser in New York—and as a manager, who guided the Texas Rangers to their first playoff appearance in franchise history, Oates was favored by his players. He managed four MVPs in his eleven seasons at the helm, and finished with a 797-746 career record. As of 2010, Oates and Hall of Famer Frank Robinson were the only two men to play for, coach, and manage the Baltimore Orioles.

The five games Johnny Oates played in 1970 were the start of a long career in the Major Leagues as a player, coach, and manager.

But it was Oates's honesty and integrity that earned him respect from those who crossed his path. Baseball executive Doug Melvin, who hired him for two managerial positions, said, "He touched a lot of people, and that's what makes people special in this world. He always had a relationship with his players that goes beyond just a working relationship. That's rare. Not everybody is like that, especially in a highly competitive field as this one."[2]

Johnny Lane Oates was born on January 21, 1946, in Sylva, North Carolina, a town nestled in the Great Smoky Mountains in the western part of the state. He was the fourth of Clint and Madie (née Franks) Oates's five children. Clint eked out a living cutting cabbage, with Madie's help. The family had no indoor plumbing or electricity, and an army cot served as a couch in their living room. With the encouragement of his father, who had played for sandlot and mill teams, Johnny learned to play baseball on the hillside with his brothers, avoiding the snakes when an errant throw went into the brush.[3]

Clint learned to cut sheet metal and took a job at Fort Bragg in Fayetteville, North Carolina, where Johnny began playing organized ball on a Royal Ambassador team. (The Royal Ambassadors are a Southern Baptist–sponsored program for young boys.) He was a catcher from the beginning—in his first game, the coach asked Oates if he could play the position. "No, I can't," he said. "Yes, you can," his father said from the stands. And so he did.[4]

When Johnny was in the eighth grade, the family moved to Petersburg, Virginia. Clint took his son to his first Major League game, at Washington's Griffith Stadium, in 1961. He recalled seeing Mickey Mantle hit a home run that weekend, and one of his prized possessions later in life was a baseball autographed by the Yankees slugger.[5]

Oates starred in baseball, basketball, and football at Prince George (Virginia) High School, hitting .523 as a senior to earn all-conference honors. He entered Virginia Polytechnic Institute in 1965. He played two years of varsity baseball for the Hokies and became the first player from that school to be drafted when he was selected by the Chicago White Sox in the second round in 1966. Oates decided to return to school for his junior season, but was selected again by the Baltimore Orioles with the tenth overall pick of the secondary draft in January 1967. He signed with the Orioles on the provision that he would stay in school until June to finish his spring classes, and he lat-

er graduated with a degree in health and physical education. Oates's No. 15 became the first baseball jersey retired at Virginia Tech in 2002, and a memorial award was established in 2006 to honor the player who exemplified Oates's faith, character, and perseverance.[6]

On August 12, 1967, Oates married his high-school sweetheart, Gloria Jackson. They had continued dating for five years even though Gloria had gone to East Carolina University in Greenville, North Carolina, and Johnny was at Virginia Tech. It was a relationship that would last more than four decades, producing three children. Gloria understood and accepted her new role as a baseball wife. "Even if he's 3,000 miles away, he always calls and says, 'I'm with you,'" she said years later.[7]

After a week in the rookie-level Appalachian League, Oates joined the Orioles' Class A affiliate in the Florida State League. In Miami, his manager was Cal Ripken Sr., who had been a catcher a decade earlier in the Orioles organization. Ripken was charged with teaching his twenty-one-year-old prospect about the position. He would stand at the mound and hit hard fungoes at Oates, saying, "If you can block these, you can block any pitch." The pair talked baseball for hours. Oates said later, "I don't think there was anyone who knew more about the game."[8]

Oates reported to the Orioles' spring training camp in 1968, catching batting practice and warming up the pitchers. "I was excited," he said, "maybe a little bit in awe. They had Frank Robinson, Brooks, Boog, a championship-type ball club. . . . It was my first association with all those people I'd seen on TV." But Oates still needed a lot of seasoning in the Minor Leagues, and was sent back to Miami that season. He played well enough to earn a call-up in 1969 to the Double-A Texas League, where he hit .288 and made just 4 errors in 66 games for Dallas–Fort Worth.[9]

In 1970 Oates got his first taste of the big

leagues, when he made five appearances for the eventual World Series champion Orioles in the final month of the regular season. He made his Major League debut on September 17, 1970, when he pinch-hit for shortstop Mark Belanger to lead off the ninth inning in a game at Washington's Robert F. Kennedy Stadium, just two hours north of where he had grown up in Virginia. Facing sixteen-game winner Dick Bosman, Oates singled to left field in his first at bat but was stranded there as the Orioles lost 2–0. Oates got his first start the next day at home against Cleveland. He went 1-for-4 and threw out a pair of would-be base stealers at second.

But Oates's time in Baltimore was frustrating. Stuck behind veterans Andy Etchebarren and Ellie Hendricks, the twenty-five-year-old spent the entire 1971 season at Triple-A Rochester, where he hit .277 in 114 games and made just six errors. The Red Wings finished first in the International League, but Oates was itching for a chance to return to the big leagues.

In 1972 he took advantage as injuries limited Etchebarren and Hendricks, and Oates made the majority of the starts for Hall of Fame manager Earl Weaver. But Baltimore's run of three consecutive American League pennants ended, and when the Orioles had a chance that off-season to acquire Atlanta's slugging catcher, Earl Williams, Oates was deemed expendable and included in a trade to the Braves with second baseman Davey Johnson and pitcher Pat Dobson.

Oates was a pleasant surprise for the Braves, batting as high as .310 near the end of April 1973, and seemed a lock to keep his place in the lineup even after his average fell off. However, in mid-July—an Atlanta paper said he was "just coming into his own" then[10]—Oates sustained the first of a series of injuries that hampered the rest of his playing career. He strained a ligament in his knee running out a ground ball against the New York Mets and did not return to the team until early September.

Nagging injuries continued to limit Oates in 1974; although he played a career-high 100 games (including a pinch-hitting appearance on April 8, the day that Henry Aaron hit his record-breaking 715th home run), he made just ten starts after Clyde King replaced Eddie Mathews as the Braves' manager in July. Oates made his displeasure known to Braves general manager Eddie Robinson, who sent him to Philadelphia with Dick Allen after the latter had refused to report to the Braves to start the 1975 season. "This will give Oates a chance to play more regularly," Robinson said at the time.[11]

Oates thrived in Philadelphia, and so did the Phillies. After making five pinch-hit appearances, Oates began a career-high eleven-game hitting streak on June 10 at San Diego. He hit .313 during the streak, raising his average thirty-eight points; he also reached base in eighteen consecutive games. The Phillies surged to second place in the NL East behind Pittsburgh, finishing above .500 for the first time in a decade.

But Oates was still hurting, and he had surgery to repair ligaments in his left knee at Philadelphia's Methodist Hospital in November, returning in time to open the 1976 season as the Phillies' starting catcher. His good health lasted almost nine innings. On Opening Day Pittsburgh's Dave Parker crashed into Oates and knocked the ball from his grasp to score the game-tying run in the ninth. A broken left shoulder kept Oates out until June 3, by which time he had lost his job to Bob Boone. "One play turned my entire year around," Oates said.[12]

The Phillies won their first National League East Division title that year, and Oates made a token appearance in the final game of the League Championship Series against the Cincinnati Reds. But in the off-season, a month before his thirty-first birthday, he was traded again—this time to

Los Angeles, where he was expected to back up catcher Steve Yeager. New manager Tommy Lasorda took a liking to Oates immediately. A later *Los Angeles Times* profile explained why: "Oates understands his job and does it well. Maybe that's why he is such a favorite. He doesn't make a manager nervous. . . . No waves, no rocking boats."[13]

Oates did not see much playing time in a Dodgers uniform, but he did earn two National League championship rings—and reached base twice in the late innings of Game Five of the 1978 World Series, singling off the Yankees' Jim Beattie for his only postseason hit. (He had also played two innings in Game Five of the previous year's World Series against New York.)

By 1980, the Dodgers had little room for a weak-hitting, injury-prone, thirty-four-year-old backup catcher. Oates was released at the end of spring training and offered a job in the organization. He preferred to keep playing, however, and on a recommendation from former Dodgers teammate Tommy John, the Yankees signed him as a free agent a week later.

He saw the writing on the wall. "The only time I caught," Oates said, "was when we were 10 runs behind or 10 runs ahead. But Dick Howser made me feel so good about myself." The following year, the Yankees offered him a Minor League contract but later guaranteed his Major League salary after John and fellow pitcher Tommy Underwood stood up for him with management.[14]

In May, the Yankees were taking batting practice before a game in Cleveland when manager Gene Michael approached the catcher. Oates recalled, "I knew what was coming. They just told me to come into the office and talk, and I told them whatever they had to tell me I could take standing up in the dugout."[15] He was sent to Triple-A Columbus as a player-coach, but he didn't take the field ever again. Oates ended his career with a .250 average in 593 games, but he took more pride in his defense, having caught eight pitchers with at least 200 victories (Steve Carlton, Tommy John, Jim Kaat, Phil Niekro, Jim Palmer, Gaylord Perry, Don Sutton, and Luis Tiant.) "I was a very lucky ballplayer because I was always with the right team at the right time," he said.[16]

Like many ballplayers, Oates didn't hang 'em up without a few regrets. "The one thing that disappoints me most about my career is that I didn't enjoy it," he said. "I was always worried about being released, being traded. I was a fringe player and all I thought about was surviving from one day to the next."[17]

In 1982 Oates took the reins of the Yankees' Double-A affiliate in Nashville, Tennessee. His immediate task, aside from adjusting to life as a young manager, was to help develop the most promising catcher in the organization, Scott Bradley, who went on to play nine seasons in the Majors.[18] In the meantime, Oates led the Nashville Sounds to a 77-67 finish in the Southern League and earned a promotion to Columbus in 1983, when he led the Triple-A Clippers to an 83-57 record and a berth in the Little World Series.

Oates was offered a chance to return to the Major Leagues in 1984 as a bullpen coach with the Chicago Cubs, who needed an experienced catcher to help Jody Davis shore up his defense. Under Oates's guidance, Davis became an All-Star for the first time, and Chicago won the National League East title. Oates stayed on as bullpen coach for two more seasons, then replaced Ruben Amaro as bench coach under manager Gene Michael. After Michael resigned in 1987, Oates was considered one of the leading contenders to get the Cubs' head job, but he lost out to Don Zimmer.

For the first time, Oates began to consider life after baseball. Several years before, he had become involved with the Virginia franchise of an advertising specialty company as a sales associate. Soon the Orioles came calling, asking their former player to manage again in Triple-A in 1988. Saying "baseball was in my blood," Oates accepted the job with Rochester and proceeded to win the International League's manager of the year award. (The Red Wings also had the league's MVP, Craig Worthington, and rookie of the year, Steve Finley.)[19] After being passed over for the Toronto Blue Jays' managerial job that off-season, Oates returned to Baltimore for the first time in nearly two decades to serve as Frank Robinson's first base coach in 1989.

He also enjoyed reuniting with Cal Ripken Sr., his old manager. Oates and his wife, Gloria, often spent time at the Ripkens' house in Aberdeen, swimming and throwing horseshoes. According to Cal Ripken Jr., Oates "lived for the day when Dad would bring the first box of his Better Boys in the clubhouse" so he could make his favorite sandwiches, tomato and mayonnaise, a staple of his youth in the mountains of North Carolina.[20]

It didn't take long before Oates's name was mentioned as Robinson's possible successor. He managed the Orioles to a 2-1 record during the latter's suspension in June 1990. When the Orioles lost 24 of their first 37 games in 1991, Oates's time had come. On May 23, he became the ninth manager in franchise history. General Manager Roland Hemond said at the time, "I had my eye on him. I had concerns at some point that he'd be managing another club. . . . We're fortunate to have him around."[21]

The strain that Oates had felt as a fringe player in the Major Leagues increased exponentially when he became a manager. As his Orioles lost their first four games, Oates lost nine pounds, and his diet was reduced to a bowl of soup and half a sandwich per day. He lost weight so quickly, reported the *Washington Post*, that Hemond was prompted to deliver a huge ice cream sundae to Oates's office after his first victory.[22] He remained a nervous wreck that whole season. He kept the walls of his office at Memorial Stadium bare until the Orioles players' "kangaroo court" fined him for waiting five days to begin managing—and then

instructing him to use the money to start decorating. By then, it was nearly time to move into Camden Yards.[23]

Oates had a lot to look forward to in 1992. Besides the sparkling new stadium, and the league's reigning MVP in Cal Ripken Jr., Oates had also signed a multiyear contract—for only the second time in his life—and could now concentrate on building a winner in Baltimore. He lured an old teammate, Rick Sutcliffe, to be the Orioles' ace, and the veteran right-hander responded with sixteen victories. The Orioles won 89 games in Oates's first full season, their most since winning the World Series in 1983, but the end of the year was marred when Oates was forced to fire his old friend Cal Ripken Sr. from the coaching staff.[24]

Oates's tenure in Baltimore came under further strain after Peter Angelos took over as owner in 1993. Although the Orioles won 85 games that year (with Oates earning Manager of the Year honors from *The Sporting News*) and finished the strike-shortened 1994 season with a .563 winning percentage—the highest of Oates's career to that point—he still faced constant questions about his job security. Angelos seemed "bent on firing him," and before baseball finally came back from the work stoppage, he did.[25]

Oates wasn't out of a job for long. In Texas, general manager Doug Melvin—who had hired him in Rochester back in 1988—brought him in to manage the Rangers, a franchise with four eighty-win seasons in the last six but that couldn't quite get over the hump and into the postseason. It was Johnny Oates who finally led them there.

Rangers outfielder Rusty Greer said, "I don't think it's any coincidence that Juan [Gonzalez] won two Most Valuable Player awards under Johnny or that Pudge [Ivan Rodriguez] won his MVP under Johnny. Johnny got the most out of each player and knew what buttons to push. He allowed each player to be themselves."[26]

What Oates hadn't been doing was allowing

his family to be themselves. By his own admission, "the job had me so wrapped up that it . . . ruled my life." He had missed all three of his kids' baptisms and graduations. But that all changed before his first game with the Rangers. His wife, Gloria, woke up one morning during spring training with a major panic attack and was rushed to the hospital. "My wife is dying and my focus is still on *baseball*?" Johnny asked himself. As Gloria recovered, Oates took a two-week leave of absence from the team—missing Opening Day—and went home to Virginia to begin counseling with his wife, and to renew his faith. He vowed not to let his intensity cause him to lose perspective about his job. Soon, he noticed that his team had better focus, too.[27]

In 1996, with MVP Gonzalez leading the way and Oates a changed man in the dugout, the Rangers powered to 90 wins, their first American League West title and the first playoff appearance in franchise history. For his efforts, Oates shared the American League's Manager of the Year Award with the Yankees' Joe Torre. Torre, however, got the best of him in the division series, winning three out of four games as New York went on to claim its first championship in nearly two decades.

The Yankees became Oates's nemesis in the playoffs for the rest of the decade—the Rangers also won the AL West in 1998 and '99 but were swept by New York in the first round each year. But getting past the Bronx Bombers would soon be the least of his concerns. New owner Tom Hicks assembled an unbalanced team, heavy on hitting but low on pitching, that sank into last place; Oates decided to step down from the Rangers in May 2001. He handed over the team to his friend and third base coach, Jerry Narron. He spent the rest of the year with his family, taking daily walks with his wife, spoiling his grandchildren, watching ballgames on TV. It was his first summer without baseball since he was eleven years old.

Two days after the 2001 World Series ended,

Oates, then fifty-five, learned he had cancer. Not just any cancer, but glioblastoma multiforme, one of the most aggressive forms of brain tumors and the same ailment that had killed former Royals pitcher Dan Quisenberry and his former manager Dick Howser. Oates's diagnosis was grim: he was given fourteen to eighteen months to live, even after doctors had removed the tumor through surgery. He promised his daughter Jenny that he would live to see her wedding the following August, and he did. "This is not a script I've written for myself," he said. "I'd rather be managing a ballclub somewhere. But this is what I've been dealt. And I'm at peace with it."[28]

The outpouring of support for Oates from his baseball friends was immense. On Opening Day 2002, he returned to Camden Yards to throw out the first pitch for the Orioles and was given a standing ovation. He had already been inducted into the Virginia Tech Sports Hall of Fame (1983); Virginia High School Sports Hall of Fame (1992); Salem-Roanoke Baseball Hall of Fame (1994); Texas Baseball Hall of Fame (1997); Rochester Red Wings Hall of Fame (2000); and Jackson County (North Carolina) Sports Hall of Fame (2001)—now, he added the Virginia Sports and Texas Rangers halls of fame to that list. In 2003 the Rangers honored Oates along with Nolan Ryan, Jim Sundberg, and Charlie Hough in an on-field ceremony in Arlington. Oates received the loudest applause from a sellout crowd. That night, the humble former manager said, "The difference between these guys and myself is they're here because of what they did. I'm here because of what others did for me."[29]

Oates's cancer returned in April 2003. This time, neither surgery nor chemotherapy could keep the tumor away. With his wife and brother at his side, Oates died on December 24, 2004, at Virginia Commonwealth Medical Center in Richmond. He was fifty-eight.

Posthumously, Oates was honored by the Virginia General Assembly and his No. 26 was retired by the Rangers in 2005. Buck Showalter, his former player and coach and one of his best friends, renamed the Rangers' manager's office for Oates. "There is not a day that goes by that I do not use some of the advice that he gave me over the years," Showalter said. "Nobody epitomized more than Johnny what we want to do and how we should handle ourselves as professionals in this game."[30]

Chapter 43. **September 1970 Timeline**

Malcolm Allen

All headlines below are from the next day's edition of the *Baltimore Sun*.

September 1—PETERSON, YANKS DROP BIRDS, 4–2—The Orioles got 5⅓ hitless innings of relief work from Marcelino Lopez and Pete Richert but couldn't overcome the early hole a pair of Jim Hardin gopher balls put them in. Baltimore hitters grounded into double plays in four of the last five innings.

September 2—YANKEES RALLY IN 7TH, NIP BIRDS 3–2—Merv Rettenmund went into the left-field seats to rob a Roy White of a home run in the first, and Mark Belanger and Paul Blair also made outstanding defensive plays to help Baltimore carry a two-run lead into the seventh inning stretch. The Yankees struck for three runs after two were out in the bottom of the frame, however, slicing the Orioles' AL East lead to ten games. "Ten games?" said Earl Weaver as he munched on a postgame sandwich. "Come on, October 1."[1]

September 3—BIRDS BLAST YANKS, 8–4, WITH 6 IN 6TH—The Orioles took advantage of three errors by New York second baseman Horace Clarke, as Jim Palmer beat the Yankees for the ninth time in eleven career decisions. *The Sun* mentioned Baltimore's magic number for the first time, noting that the win had reduced it to sixteen.

September 4—B. ROBINSON 5-FOR-5 IN ORIOLE WIN—Don Buford homered on Boston righty Mike Nagy's second pitch of the game, and Brooks Robinson delivered his first five-hit performance since 1960. Not all of the news was good, however. Mike Cuellar surrendered a grand slam to Tony Conigliaro and didn't record an out, with Earl Weaver also failing to last the first inning because umpire John Rice ejected him. Two innings later Merv Rettenmund pulled his hamstring when he tripped over first base, but Brooks Robinson's second home run of the night—a three-run blast in the seventh—gave the Birds an 8–6 victory.

September 5—HOME RUN BY JOHNSON TOPS BOSOX—Baltimore beat Boston's Ray Culp for the fourth time in five tries. Davey Johnson singled off the Green Monster to drive in the tying run in the seventh, and blasted a home run over it with two outs in the ninth to lead the Orioles to a 3–2 win.

September 6—BIRDS BOW TO BOSTON IN 11TH, 9–8—The Orioles got five unearned runs in the fourth inning to build a 6–0 lead, but gave it all back and lost on Pete Richert's wild pitch in extra innings. Tony Conigliaro, who scored the winning run for the Red Sox, reached base when Richert hit him with a pitch. Baltimore stranded fourteen runners.

September 7—TIGERS BALK PALMER BID FOR 20, 5–2—Detroit's Jim Northrup knocked in four runs to derail Jim Palmer's attempt to become a first-time twenty-game winner. Boog Powell provided the only Baltimore offense, reaching 100 RBIs with his thirtieth home run of the season, his first since August 17.

September 8—BIRDS STOP TIGERS, 6–3, ON 2 HOMERS—Mike Cuellar flew to Houston to be with his ill daughter, and emergency starter Marcelino Lopez responded with 5⅔ innings to earn his first win of the season despite a career-high seven walks. Boog Powell blasted a Mickey Lolich pitch into the right-field upper deck in the first, and Frank Robinson went deep in the third. With Triple-A affiliate Rochester eliminated from the playoffs, the Orioles recalled Don Baylor, Fred Beene, Roger Freed, and Johnny Oates.

September 9—BIRDS TAKE 1 TO 0 DUEL FROM YANKS—Brooks Robinson, Paul Blair, Mark Belanger, and Davey Johnson received their 1969 Gold Glove awards in a pregame ceremony before helping Mike Cuellar tie for the Major League lead with twenty-two victories. New York rookie Steve Kline pitched well, but two-out hits by Frank and Brooks Robinson in the bottom of the sixth produced the game's only run. The bad news for Baltimore was that Elrod Hendricks had to leave the game after a high pitch from Cuellar broke the middle finger on the catcher's throwing hand.

September 10—MCNALLY 6-HITS YANKS FOR 20 AS ORIOLES TAKE FINALE, 2–1—Months earlier, former Oriole Curt Blefary told his Yankee teammates they could still overtake the Orioles because Baltimore's uniforms didn't feature a big red S on the chest. Recalling the statement, Frank Robinson approached Blefary during batting practice and popped open his Orioles jersey to reveal a Superman logo. When the game started, the Birds got a home run from Andy Etchebarren, who was playing because of Elrod Hendricks's injury the night before. An eighth-inning Yankees threat ended when John Ellis's smash with two aboard was turned into an inning-ending double play by Davey Johnson. Ellis symbolized New York's frustration afterward; *The Sun* reported that "for a mo-

ment it appeared [he] might heave his helmet onto 33rd Street."[2]

September 11—BELANGER TOPS BOSOX WITH SINGLE—Things continued to go right for the Orioles. After Don Buford snapped a 1-for-28 slide with a leadoff double in the bottom of the thirteenth, Red Sox manager Eddie Kasko was ejected for fruitlessly arguing that Buford missed first base. When play resumed, Mark Belanger stroked a game-winning single to center.

September 12—BIRDS DOWN BOSOX, 5–1, ON 3 HOMERS—Baltimore's AL East lead grew to thirteen games as Tom Phoebus pitched a five-hitter to win for the first time since May 9. Mark Belanger unloaded his only home run of the season, and Frank Robinson and Boog Powell added back-to-back blasts to beat Boston southpaw Gary Peters.

September 13—ORIOLES HAND BOSOX 13–2 LOSS—Baltimore's largest scoring night of 1970 at Memorial Stadium completed a sweep of the Red Sox, and Paul Blair added insult to injury by robbing Tony Conigliaro of a ninth-inning home run.

September 14—No game scheduled. With the magic number down to three and the second-place Yankees preparing to meet Boston in a doubleheader, the Orioles could clinch the AL East as soon as the next day.

September 15—ORIOLES WIN, 6–2, TO GAIN 7TH IN ROW—With the RFK Stadium field in terrible shape after a Washington Redskins exhibition game, the Senators' normally surehanded shortstop Eddie Brinkman committed an error that led to four unearned runs. Though the Yankees swept a doubleheader from the Red Sox to remain alive mathematically speaking, Dave McNally shaved the Orioles' magic number to two with his eighteenth career victory against the Senators in twenty-two decisions.

September 16—NATS ROOKIE BALKS FLAG CLINCHING BY BIRDS WITH 2–0 WIN—Freak triples off Jim Palmer in consecutive innings derailed the right-hander's bid for a twentieth victory. Aurelio Rodriguez got to third after Don Buford's attempt to snare his sinking drive with a shoestring grab missed, while Ed Stroud's three-bagger came on a single that took a very bad hop. Both Senators scored, and that was all freshman right-hander Bill Gogolewski needed to get his second Major League victory. Palmer surrendered yet another triple, to Frank Howard, the Washington Monument's only one of the season.

September 17—ORIOLES GAIN TITLE DESPITE ANOTHER 2–0 LOSS TO NATS—The Orioles were on a bus to RFK Stadium when they learned the Yankees had lost an extra-inning afternoon affair to Boston, thus clinching the AL East for Baltimore. The Birds then lost their shortest game of the season, getting shut out by Dick Bosman in just one hour and forty-eight minutes before kicking off their champagne and cigars celebration by tossing a uniformed Earl Weaver into the shower.

September 18—BIRDS TRIP INDIANS IN 11TH, 4 TO 3—Playoff tickets went on sale in Baltimore, and the Orioles snapped their scoreless-innings streak at twenty when Don Baylor drove a two-run single over Vada Pinson's head in his first Major League at bat. The game went into extra innings, and Baylor won it by driving home Paul Blair with hit number two.

September 19—INDIAN ROOKIE HALTS BIRDS, 4–2—Without any Robinsons in the starting lineup for the second straight game, the Orioles lost to right-hander Jim Rittwage, who was making his first Major League start.

September 20—BIRDS WIN AS PALMER GETS NO. 20—Jim Palmer fired a four-hitter to beat Cleveland 7–0, tying for the Major League lead with his fifth shutout and finally notching his twentieth win on his fourth try. The Orioles became the first American League team with a trio of twenty-game winners since the 1956 Indians. "I hate to ruin all the press about three 20-game winners," Palmer said. "But the season is nothing if we don't win the playoffs and get to the World Series."[3] A few days after ex-Oriole Jackie Brandt suggested he back off the plate a little, Mark Belanger went 4-for-4 with three RBIs and got his batting average over .200 for the first time since May 27. It was a good day for Baltimore sports fans. A few hours after the Orioles' victory, the NFL Colts won their season opener in San Diego, 16–14, on Jim O'Brien's last-minute field goal.

September 21—BIRDS TRIP TIGERS BY 4–3 IN 12TH—Marcelino Lopez threw thirteen consecutive balls at one point in the second inning, but still had a chance for a victory until Detroit tied the game against the Baltimore bullpen with two outs in the ninth. After rookie Johnny Oates led off the bottom of the twelfth with one of two triples he would hit in eleven Major League seasons, red-hot Mark Belanger stroked the game-winning hit for the Birds. Boog Powell's first-inning homer was Baltimore's first in six games, ending their longest home-run drought of the season.

September 22—BIRDS WHIP TIGERS FOR 100TH WIN—On Fan Appreciation Night with temperatures in the high eighties, Andy Etchebarren knocked in six runs with a single, a double, and a homer to lead Baltimore to a 10–2 triumph. Later in the evening, the Twins clinched the AL West in Oakland, setting up a rematch of last year's ALCS.

September 23—With an ongoing electrical power crisis throughout the Mid-Atlantic region, the Orioles postponed their scheduled night game against the Tigers until the following afternoon. In addition to letting them do their part as responsible citizens, the move allowed the Orioles to pencil in Mike Cuellar to pitch the ALCS opener on four days' rest instead of five, which they feared might be too long a layoff.

September 24—BIRDS SCORE WIN BEHIND CUELLAR, 7–4—The smallest home crowd of the season (3,069) showed up on short notice in ninety-degree weather to see Mike Cuellar break his own club record for victories with his twenty-fourth win. The Cuban southpaw went the distance for the twenty-first time in 1970 despite allowing a season-high dozen hits. Paul Blair went 4-for-5 with two home runs and a stolen base to lead the offense. Baltimore outhomered opponents 16 to 4 over the last sixteen games.

September 25—BIRDS DOWN INDIANS, 9–7, IN 13 FRAMES—The Orioles blew a five-run lead in the bottom of the ninth and left sixteen runners on base, but won anyway on Terry Crowley's two-run homer off rookie Rich Hand in extra innings.

September 26—BIRDS DROP INDIANS, 7–4, IN 11TH—Jim Palmer retired the first nineteen Cleveland hitters before Ted Uhlaender doubled in the seventh to break up his bid for a perfect game. A ninth-inning Indians rally forced extra innings for the second straight contest, but Baltimore regained the lead when Cleveland pitcher Fred Lasher made a throwing error after fielding a sacrifice bunt. Frank Robinson homered with a man aboard to add insurance; the Birds' 176th home run of the season, it established a new club record. Mark Belanger tied a team mark by scoring a career-best four runs.

September 27—ORIOLES WIN 7TH IN ROW, NIPPING TRIBE—Dick Hall, the oldest player in the

American League, hurled three perfect innings on his fortieth birthday to earn the win as Baltimore beat twenty-game-winner Sam McDowell, 4–3, on Curt Motton's seventh-inning single.

September 28—No game was scheduled, though a court allowed the NFL Colts to play their Monday night home opener at Memorial Stadium less than twenty-four hours before the Orioles commenced their final regular-season series. Normally, the Colts were expected to make every effort to allow at least thirty-six hours for field repairs, and Earl Weaver was not happy. "There is nothing that equalizes two teams more than a lousy field," remarked the Birds' skipper.[4] The Colts were chopped up, 44–24, by the Kansas City Chiefs.

September 29—BIRDS DUMP NATS TWICE IN 3–2 GAMES—Brooks Robinson recorded the 1,000th RBI of his career in the opener of a twin bill, and the Orioles won the game on Mark Belanger's sacrifice fly in the bottom of the tenth. Baltimore forced the nightcap into extra frames with a pair of unearned runs in the bottom of the ninth, then extended its winning streak to a season-high nine games when Frank Robinson doubled home Curt Motton two innings later.

September 30—MCNALLY GAINS 24TH WIN—The Orioles won their tenth straight game when Merv Rettenmund stroked a two-out, two-run single in the bottom of the seventh. Brooks Robinson followed with a two-run triple to make it 6–2, and Dave McNally shook off concerns about his recent sore arm with a complete game four-hitter to match Mike Cuellar for the club lead in wins.

October 1—BIRDS TOP NATS, SET CLUB MARK—The Orioles finished the regular season with their eleventh straight win—a club record—by sending the Senators to their fourteenth consecutive loss. Davey Johnson's single off Horacio Pina in the bottom of the ninth knocked in Merv Rettenmund with the game-winner, and Baltimore ended the season 108-54, winning the American League East by a full fifteen games.

Final AL East Standings, 1970:

Team	W	L	GB
Baltimore	108	54	—
New York	93	69	15.0
Boston	87	75	21.0
Detroit	79	83	29.0
Cleveland	76	86	32.0
Washington	70	92	38.0

Chapter 44. **Fred Beene**

Todd Newville and Mark Armour

AGE	W	L	PCT.	ERA	G	GS	GF	CG	SHO	SV	IP	H	BB	SO	HBP	WP
27	0	0	.000	6.00	4	0	1	0	0	0	6	8	5	4	0	0

Fred Beene proved that big things can come in small packages. Affectionately known as "Beeney" throughout much of his professional baseball career, the five-foot-nine, 160-pound Beene defied skeptics who thought he was too small to succeed on a Major League mound. At times, the criticism of his physical attributes proved frustrating for the slick-fielding right-hander who possessed a crafty assortment of pitches. Because he wanted to play in the big leagues so badly, Beene paid no attention to what some thought of his stature. He knew he could pitch in the Majors, and so did his father.

"I was small and I had to battle all those perceptions about my size," said Beene. "I always heard that I was too little to pitch in the big leagues. I did have talent, but because of my size, I couldn't be lacking in other areas. Having perseverance and not giving up helped me get to the big leagues. What my dad taught me and having pride in what I did helped me to become a Major League pitcher."[1]

Freddy Ray Beene was born on November 24, 1942, in Angleton, Texas, about fifty miles south of Houston near the Gulf of Mexico, to William Andrew Beene and the former Inez Fay Steadman. Fred had one sister, Lena, who was three years his junior. "My dad was my biggest influence," Beene said in an interview in 2005. "He never pitched an inning anywhere except in a cow pasture. He was a farmboy who just loved baseball. He taught me about pitching inside and changing speeds and location. That's what pitching is all about and he preached that to me. I threw a perfect game when I was ten years old. I didn't walk a guy and I struck out all eighteen hitters."[2]

After high school Beene played collegiate base-

Fred Beene had the misfortune of emerging from the great Orioles system at a time when starting pitching jobs were scarce. He did manage a 12-7 big league record with three teams.

ball for Sam Houston State, where he helped propel his team to victory in the 1963 NAIA title game. Burleigh Grimes and Dee Phillips were responsible for signing Beene to his first pro contract with the Baltimore Orioles. "Burleigh was in the room when I signed at a Holiday Inn in Joplin, Missouri, after the national tournament," Beene recalled. "Burleigh said if I were bigger, I could get more money. That talk was already starting. But Dee knew me and he scouted me. He knew what kind of athlete and competitor I was. He wanted me pretty bad. And Burleigh told me a lot of good things that day."[3]

Beene began his professional career in 1964 with Fox Cities in Appleton (Wisconsin) of the Single-A Midwest League. There, the diminutive righty forged an impressive 11-5 record in his pro debut along with a sparkling 2.22 earned run average and 102 strikeouts in just 77 innings of work. In 1965 Beene continued to excel, at the Double-A level. He fashioned a 7-7 record for Elmira (New York) of the Eastern League along with a 2.25 ERA and 99 whiffs in 132 innings. He worked a league-leading 62 games for manager Earl Weaver that campaign—none more grueling and demanding than on May 8 against Springfield in front of just 386 fans. Beene entered the scoreless game in the top of the sixteenth, and pitched twelve innings to pick up the 2-1 victory. He allowed a run in the twenty-sixth, but Elmira tied it up in the bottom of the inning and won it in the following inning. At the time, this was the longest game in professional baseball history.

In 1966 Beene returned to Elmira and finished 10-12 with a 2.16 ERA and 129 strikeouts in 150 innings. Late that season he advanced to Triple-A Rochester, where he went 2-1 in four contests with a 2.57 ERA. In 1967 Beene finished 2-1 in 12 games for Elmira, with a minuscule 1.67 ERA before again advancing to Rochester, where he was 5-1 with a 2.95 ERA in 22 outings. The Orioles system was filled with young pitching prospects, and Beene was having difficulty standing out despite his success.

In 1968 he returned to Rochester and put up an 8-7 record with a 2.68 ERA in 48 games. On September 18 the twenty-five-year-old finally made his Major League debut in the Orioles' 4–0 loss to the Boston Red Sox. Beene surrendered two hits, one walk, and one earned run while striking out one. It was his only inning of big-league action that sea-

son. Joe Foy was Beene's first Major League strikeout victim.

In 1969 Beene joined Rochester for the fourth time, fashioning an impressive 15-7 record with a 2.98 ERA and 132 strikeouts in a league-leading 193 innings. He walked just 47 hitters. At the end of the Minor League campaign, Beene was again called up to Baltimore. In two contests, against Boston and Cleveland, Beene didn't allow an earned run. As a late call-up, Beene was not on the Baltimore roster for the World Series, which the Orioles lost to the New York Mets in five games. After an off-season in Puerto Rico in which he threw a no-hitter for Santurce, Beene went back to Rochester in 1970 and finished 9-3 with a 3.20 ERA in 13 games. He got more late-season action with the Orioles, getting into four games. Beene was certainly one of Baltimore's best pitching prospects.

Beene was in a professional bind. Though he had dominated Minor League hitters for several years, he was pitching in an organization with a historically strong pitching staff. The Orioles won three straight pennants beginning in 1969 and had three twenty-game winners in 1970 while using a four-man rotation. The Orioles had little use for Beene's talents. "I was with the Baltimore organization for eight years," Beene said. "I was one of their top guys to be called up, but there weren't many chances for me. Earl Weaver liked the older, veteran players. The Orioles were a good team and they dominated during that time. There just wasn't room for me."[4]

"[General manager] Harry Dalton was a good guy. He called me into his office after the [1970] season and said he would trade me if they could get a good deal for me. He realized I had a tough fight and probably deserved to be in the big leagues. It just wasn't happening for me in Baltimore. He said if they could trade me to another club, they were going to do it."[5] True to Dalton's word, in December Baltimore sent Beene, fellow pitchers Tom

Phoebus and Al Severinsen, and shortstop Enzo Hernandez to the San Diego Padres for pitchers Pat Dobson and Tom Dukes.

Just before the trade, Beene had gone back to Puerto Rico to play winter ball. "On Opening Night, I blew out my elbow," he said. "I threw a slider to Ken Singleton and I thought I had [broken] my arm. Something snapped and the doctor in Puerto Rico said I might not pitch again. But I went to Baltimore and got an American doctor to look at me. The day I went to Baltimore to have my arm examined, they made the trade."[6] When Beene's arm did not improve after a short stint with San Diego's Pacific Coast League farm team in Honolulu, the Padres sent him back to Baltimore on May 16, 1971. He returned to pitch for Dallas–Fort Worth in the Texas League and went 2-2 with a 2.06 ERA in five games. He later returned to Rochester, where he was 7-1 with a 4.44 ERA. Beene showed he still had command of the strike zone, walking just 35 batters in 108 innings for the two teams while surrendering 107 hits.

"I went to Rochester to heal up," Beene said, "and I finally got some good news." On January 19, 1972, the Orioles traded Beene for the second time, to the New York Yankees for Minor Leaguer Dale Spier. "Pete Ward was a coach at Rochester at the time," Beene said. "He recommended to the Yankees that they trade for me—on the sly, of course, since he was still working for the Orioles. I was very happy they traded me because I thought that I might be through at that point."[7]

That spring Beene was intent on making the Major League roster, and he wowed the Yankee organization. "When I got to spring training," he recalled, "they had about five sore-armed pitchers. I had been pitching in Puerto Rico over the winter and I was in pretty good shape. I got into the first exhibition game that spring and I was mowing them down pretty good for about six outings with the Yankees. [Manager] Ralph Houk called me into his office and said I had made the club. . . . I

was finally one of the main twenty-five guys out of spring [training]. I wasn't just waiting to be called up later in September. What a feeling it was!"[8]

Beene had a fine rookie season, finishing 1-3 with a 2.34 ERA and 3 saves in 29 games. In 1973 he did even better—he fashioned a perfect 6-0 record along with a microscopic 1.68 ERA in 19 games. He walked just 27 and yielded only 67 hits in 91 innings while striking out 49. Opposing batters hit just .209 against Beene, who helped anchor a solid bullpen that also featured Lindy McDaniel (12-6, 2.86 ERA) and closer Sparky Lyle (27 saves, 2.51 ERA). "I thought the DH would ruin me in 1973 since you don't need as many pitchers on a team," said Beene, referring to the introduction of the designated hitter in the American League that season. "But it actually worked to my benefit because I became one of the first long relievers in the game. It was a new niche for a lot of pitchers."[9]

Just when Beene thought he had finally established himself, he received a professional setback. On April 26, 1974, the Yankees dealt four pitchers—Beene, Tom Buskey, Steve Kline, and Fritz Peterson—to the Cleveland Indians for first baseman Chris Chambliss and pitchers Dick Tidrow and Cecil Upshaw. "To say the least, the clubhouse was in an uproar," Beene said. "They traded four good ol' boys from the club and broke up the party. Guys were upset and didn't leave the clubhouse until well after midnight."[10]

"You don't trade four pitchers," veteran pitcher Mel Stottlemyre said at the time. "You just don't." Catcher Thurman Munson said, "You've got to be kidding." The trade shocked and angered players and fans alike. Former catcher and Yankee coach Elston Howard was especially vociferous in his criticism of the deal.[11]

For Beene, the trade was particularly traumatic. "I was leaving a place where my role had been established," he said. "I had a spot and I felt secure with the Yankees. It had taken me a long and trying time to finally make it to the big leagues. I felt like I was a very important part of that Yankee pitching staff. One of the keys to being successful in the Major Leagues is to function in the role that you are best suited for. I had established that with the Yankees."[12]

Before the trade, Beene had appeared in 6 games for New York with 1 save and a 2.70 ERA. After going to Cleveland, he was 4-4 with 2 saves and a 4.93 ERA in 32 games. In 1975 Beene's pitching arm bothered him again, leading to sixty-two days on the disabled list and just a 1-0 record with a 6.94 ERA in 19 games.

As it turned out, 1975 was the last time he pitched in the Majors. He spent a year and a half with Cleveland's Triple-A affiliate in Toledo, finishing 7-9 and 5-10 as a starting pitcher. In July 1977 he was sold to Philadelphia, and he spent the rest of that year and all of the next two seasons with the Phillies' Oklahoma City club, finishing 2-2, 12-5, and 10-5. The 1979 club won the American Association pennant, after which Beene chose to retire.

"That last game in Oklahoma City against Evansville was my last game as a pitcher," Beene said. "I remember that pretty well. I went about four innings and didn't pitch too good. I knew those last three or four years in the Minors that I was possibly a game away from being done for good. I had so many physical problems. I really wanted to pitch well, but I struggled and I was defensive out there on the mound. So I hung it up."[13]

After retiring as a player, Beene became the pitching coach for the Tidewater Tides in the International League, the top Minor League franchise of the New York Mets. After that he scouted for the Milwaukee Brewers before finally retiring from baseball in 2001. "After scouting for twenty years," Beene said, "I determined the biggest factors in a prospect are his ability to adapt and his perseverance. It's not always the talent."[14]

In 1982 Beene signed a six-foot-three, 215-pound pitcher from Brownwood, Texas, who played for Ranger Junior College. By the age of twenty-five, that prospect had hurt his arm and was out of pro ball, opting instead to settle down, raise a family, and coach high-school baseball near his home in Big Lake, Texas. Ten years later, on September 18, 1999, Jim Morris made his Major League debut with the Tampa Bay Devil Rays, a story Morris later turned into a book and a movie.

Though Beene spent sixteen years playing professional baseball, he remembers most fondly the two years and one month he pitched for the Yankees—years that resulted in a 7-3 record and 1.99 ERA in 158 innings. He often sees Fritz Peterson, Sparky Lyle, Mel Stottlemyre, and others at autograph shows or reunions. His days in the Minors also evoke positive memories for Beene. "Rochester is king of Minor League cities," he said. "They put me in their Hall of Fame. That's one of the biggest honors I ever received. They thought of me as the little guy and their battle hero. I really liked it there in Rochester and I appreciate that recognition because I did give my heart and soul to that city while trying to make it to Baltimore."[15] Beene won forty-six games for Rochester over parts of six seasons.

Beene and his wife, Carolyn, raised two children, Darrell and Monica, and retired to a two-acre place about fifteen miles east of Huntsville, Texas. "My wife is the church secretary," Beene said, "and we travel a great deal with them. We've been on about ten cruises the last couple of years. We've been to Europe, Australia, and everywhere just about."[16] Beene also enjoys deep-sea fishing in the nearby Gulf of Mexico. He and his son, Darrell, operate several retail warehouses that sell fireworks.

Fred Beene had two obstacles to overcome to make it as a professional pitcher: his height and the wealth of fellow pitchers in the Baltimore organization. He overcame both to pitch 112 games in the Major Leagues and pick up a lifetime's worth of memories.

Chapter 45. Chuck Thompson

Matt Bohn

For nearly half a century, one man's voice defined baseball in Baltimore. Chuck Thompson, referred to as "the voice of God in Baltimore" by fellow sportscaster Ted Patterson,[1] was the play-by-play broadcaster of Baltimore baseball for nearly every season from 1949 through 2000. Cal Ripken Jr. grew up listening to Thompson on the radio and recalled late in his career, "When the Orioles were doing some great things on the field, the excitement and familiarity of his voice just made it that much better," he said. "When I hear his voice now, I'm just flooded with memories."[2] Orioles broadcaster Fred Manfra said simply, "Chuck Thompson was sports in Baltimore as I was growing up."[3]

Born Charles Lloyd Thompson on June 10, 1921, in Palmer, Massachusetts, to Lloyd and Maggie (Moon) Thompson, Chuck lived with his family in Springfield, Massachusetts, for a time before moving to Reading, Pennsylvania, in 1927. Among Thompson's fond memories of his early childhood were being introduced to radio by a babysitter at the age of three or four. "The sitter would put earphones on my head and I would listen to KDKA in Pittsburgh. For me, that was fascinating," Thompson remembered years later.[4]

After moving to Reading, the Thompson family maintained close ties to Massachusetts. Chuck spent his childhood summers staying with an aunt in Palmer. It was in Palmer that he developed a great love of baseball. During these summers, Thompson would play baseball with children in his aunt's neighborhood, as well as listening to Boston Red Sox games on the radio with his grandmother. "A man has to have some background that dedicates him to a career in sports and I suppose

Chuck Thompson was the beloved voice of the Baltimore Orioles for fifty years.

my grandmother helped to set the stage for that when many, many years ago, she had this boarding house in Brookfield [Massachusetts] and Connie Mack used to stay there, back in the days when he was a semipro," Thompson said years later. "There were many stories about baseball and this helped to bring about a love for the game that has endured."[5] Thompson remembered trips to Fenway Park as the highlights of his childhood summers spent in Massachusetts.

By the time he was in junior high school in Reading, Chuck played basketball and soccer.

He was also active in sandlot baseball and played football at Reading High School. In the summer of 1938, just after his junior year of high school, Thompson began singing with the Joe Lombardo band. Thompson's stint singing with the band led indirectly to his radio debut.

One night in 1939, while he was singing with the band, a neighborhood girl dared Thompson to get into radio. Thompson initially was against the idea. In 1966 he recalled, "She kept daring me to go to the program director of the local radio station for a singing audition and finally I did. But when I did, mainly because I had played ball in high school, the audition developed into a sports broadcast. I'm sure it turned out the right way because this gave me my start."[6] Soon after being hired at Reading station WRAW, Thompson got his first "big break": broadcasting a college game between Albright and Carnegie Tech that was being fed back to Pittsburgh. Thompson recalled, "In those days, the N. W. Ayer Advertising Agency out of Philadelphia controlled high-school and college broadcasts on the Eastern Seaboard, from New England into the South."[7] He credited agency executive Les Quailey with teaching him much about how to do play-by-play on radio. It was while working at WRAW (as well as its sister station WEEU) that Thompson married his high-school sweetheart, Rose Heffner. The two were married on November 15, 1941. Their marriage lasted until Rose's death nearly forty-four years later. They had three children.

After a dispute over pay, Thompson left WRAW in early 1942. After spending a few weeks working at Youngstown, Ohio, radio station WKBN, he got an offer to work at WIBG in Philadelphia. "For the most part, I was a staff announcer to WIBG and did sports programs twice a day," Thompson said.[8] He also provided play-by-play for Temple University football and occasionally covered Harvard, Princeton, or Dartmouth games.

By the time Thompson arrived at WIBG, the United States was involved in World War II. He wrote a half-century later in his memoir, "Hovering over my budding career was the war and my impending induction. So I decided to take matters into my own hands and take an exam to enter the Marines."[9] Rejected by the Marines because of his inability to distinguish between green and gray on an eye exam, Thompson was inducted into the U.S. Army in October 1943. He served with the 30th Division in Europe. Returning from the war in 1945, Thompson got his job back at WIBG.

Late in the 1946 baseball season, a faulty elevator at Shibe Park led to Thompson's Major League broadcasting debut. Thompson was at the microphone between games of a doubleheader to describe a ceremony taking place on the field honoring Philadelphia Phillies radio announcers Byrum Saam and Claude Haring. Thompson recalled, "In those days, the ballpark elevator was hand-operated and required a key to be put into motion. But when Saam and Haring were ready to come back upstairs, the operator was nowhere to be found."[10] The second game began with Thompson alone at the microphone. "With Saam and Haring still absent, I tried to describe the game—without a scorecard, lineup, or anything," Thompson remembered.[11] By the time Saam and Haring arrived in the booth, it was the bottom of the first inning. Quailey of N. W. Ayer was present in the booth and persuaded them to let Thompson continue. Thompson said, "This impromptu audition led to me being added to the broadcast team in 1947 for the Phillies' and A's home games. I've wondered many times over the years what would have happened had the elevator man been on hand to bring Saam and Haring back on time. Would I have wound up in play-by-play? Would I have wound up in baseball?"[12] Thompson spent the 1947 and 1948 seasons providing two innings of radio play-by-play for each Phillies and A's home game.

In 1948 Thompson was assigned to provide color commentary for the Navy-Missouri football game over the Mutual Radio network. When play-by-play broadcaster Connie Desmond became ill just before the broadcast, Thompson had his trial by fire; he had to step into Desmond's place, providing play-by-play on a national football broadcast with little preparation. "Frankly, I was almost totally lost, without lineups, numerical charts or spotters' boards—and talking to listeners on more than 200 stations across the country," he said.[13] With the help of Les Quailey (who had once been a spotter for network sportscaster Ted Husing), Thompson got through the broadcast. He didn't realize it at the time, but the football broadcast led to his broadcasting in Baltimore. "My appearance had been set up by the Gunther Brewing Co. and the Ruthrauff and Ryan advertising agency as an on-air audition while they sought to replace Baltimore legend Bill Dyer as the broadcaster of International League Orioles games,"[14] Thompson wrote. Because announcer Byrum Saam was already firmly established in Philadelphia, Thompson had been advised that his chances of advancing in that city were small. Owing in large part to his performance on the Navy-Missouri football broadcast, Thompson was hired as voice of the International League Orioles in 1949.

One of Thompson's earliest memories of broadcasting the Orioles had nothing to do with the game he was broadcasting. "It was my second or third game here," he said, "and I saw one of the Orioles climb up the screen behind home plate, jump into the seats, and beat up a spectator. Apparently the spectator had been very abusive and they didn't have the kind of help they have today, ushers or security guards, to take care of things. So one of the umpires asked this player to handle the situation."[15] Broadcasting all home games and doing telegraphic recreations for road games, Thompson covered Baltimore's International League games for five seasons. Beginning in 1949, he also worked broadcasts of Navy football and the All-America Conference Baltimore Colts.

When Major League Baseball returned to Baltimore in 1954, Thompson was not included on the broadcast crew. "The National Brewing Co. was to be the major Orioles sponsor and I was disqualified because of my previous connections with the Gunther Brewing Co.," Thompson remembered.[16] "It was made more frustrating because the ballclub and the fans wanted me to do the games and so did Bailey Goss, who was the color man."[17] By late 1954, however, Thompson was invited to meet with Jerry Hoffberger, president of the National Brewing Company (and later the owner of the Orioles). Hoffberger told Thompson that they wanted him to be part of the Orioles' on-air crew the following season.

Hoffberger was also responsible for one of Thompson's notable trademarks: his fedoras. "He saw me standing hatless during a network telecast from Baltimore's Memorial Stadium as I conducted an interview during a National Football League game," Thompson said. "Jerry, who had seen the telecast in California, called his office the next day and said, 'Tell that son-of-a-gun to put a hat on.' He was paying the bills, so from then on I wore a lid on my bald head when I was on camera."[18]

Another Thompson trademark developed during his early years in Baltimore was the expression "Go to war, Miss Agnes!" This was picked up from a golfing partner who refused to swear. "He was a great guy and, like any golfer, he had real frustrations," Thompson explained. "But instead of cussing, he'd come up with the phrase 'Go to war, Miss Agnes!' It sounded so funny. I picked it up and used it to emphasize something big and exciting on the ballfield and it just caught on."[19] Eventually, Thompson dropped it. "I phased that expression out of my lexicon as the Vietnam War dragged on. It was something I could no longer justify, because of the mounting American casualties."[20]

Another famous phrase of Thompson's was borrowed from Bob Robertson, a spotter who worked with him on Colts football games. When things were going well for the Orioles, Thompson would exclaim, "Ain't the beer cold!" Thompson eventually retired this trademark expression as well. "Eventually I received lots of mail from people in the Carolinas, the area sometimes referred to as the Bible Belt."[21] Respecting the opinions of listeners who objected to the reference to beer, Thompson stopped using the expression in the 1970s.

When National Brewery lost the rights to the Orioles broadcasts after the 1956 season, Thompson became a member of the Washington Senators' broadcast crew. Working with Bob Wolff, Thompson described the games for the Senators from 1957 through 1960. Returning to the Orioles' broadcasting crew in 1962, Thompson remained on the air describing Baltimore baseball through the end of the twentieth century.

Thompson worked on the NBC-TV Game of the Week in 1959 and 1960. He was also at the mike on the NBC radio network during Game Seven of the 1960 World Series. "I called Mazeroski's homer on radio and, for some unknown reason, gave the final score as 10–0 instead of 10–9," Thompson recalled later. "Not only that, I told the listening audience that the homer had been hit off Art Ditmar instead of Ralph Terry." It was one of the most exciting moments he had described over the air, but for Thompson, "easily the most embarrassing moment of my career behind the microphone." But he didn't try to undo it. "When the Pirates' broadcaster Bob Prince called me during the off-season and asked if I'd like to redo the ending for a souvenir record the Pirates were going to produce, I declined. I figured it had gone on the air that way, so it would not be honest to change it."[22]

Baseball and football were not the only sports Thompson covered during these years. In 1963-64, he handled telecasts for the Baltimore Clippers of the American Hockey League. Outside of his baseball work he was probably best known for providing radio and network television play-by-play

for the NFL Baltimore Colts for several decades. Thompson's most noted football moment came on December 28, 1958, when he and Chris Schenkel were at the mike for the NBC television network to describe the championship game between the Colts and the New York Giants. Flipping a coin before the game to decide how play-by-play duties would be divided, Schenkel won the coin toss and opted to broadcast the second half. When the game went into overtime, Thompson returned to play-by-play and got to describe the action as the Colts won the game. He later recalled the significance of the telecast, noting, "The sudden-death game, witnessed by some 50 million people on television, probably did more to establish the NFL as a TV property than any other game played previously or since."[23]

In 1966 Thompson saw the Orioles make it to the World Series for the first time, sweeping the Dodgers in four games. It was the first of many championship Orioles teams he would describe, but he always claimed his fondest memories were of the 1966 team. "The Orioles also played in the World Series in 1969, 1970, 1971, 1979, and 1983, but like the first kiss, I'll always be fondest of the first one," he said.[24] Thompson was part of the NBC television broadcast crew for the World Series in 1966, 1970, and 1971.

The year 1966 was also important to Thompson's career for another reason: it was that year in which he began working on with Bill O'Donnell. The two came to form a memorable team on Orioles radio and television broadcasts through the 1982 season. Not only did they have a close working relationship, but they formed a good friendship as well. O'Donnell noted in 1980, "I would guess that of the last 100 dinners we've had on the road, 95 we've had together."[25] Thompson described their partnership as a "wonderful association."[26] When O'Donnell was stricken with cancer and died after the 1982 season, Thompson was devastated. Broadcast colleague Tom Marr said a few years later, "It was a tough year. Bill was dying of cancer, everybody was hoping and pulling for him. It was devastating, really tough on Chuck. Chuck experienced a total personality change. He was very depressed the whole season."[27] After that 1982 season Thompson confined his Orioles broadcast duties to television only.

Thompson retired from broadcasting after the 1987 season. His retirement period was brief, however, as he was lured back by the Orioles to cover eighty-one games on WBAL radio in 1991, providing three innings of play-by-play on games when Orioles announcer Jon Miller had television commitments. Continuing to work a partial schedule on Orioles broadcasts every season throughout the 1990s, Thompson provided a sense of continuity on Baltimore airwaves as the Orioles moved from Memorial Park to Oriole Park at Camden Yards.

In 1993 Thompson received the Ford C. Frick Award from the Baseball Hall of Fame. His selection for the award, the highest honor that can be given to a baseball broadcaster, overwhelmed him. "I don't know if I'll ever get over the enormity and the prestige of this," Thompson said on learning of his selection. "I never felt this would happen—I didn't think I was good enough."[28] Thompson's former Colts broadcast colleague Vince Bagli summed up how many of his peers and fans felt about Thompson's selection for the award: "It was well-deserved. It was overdue."[29]

By the 2000 season Thompson was losing his eyesight because of macular degeneration. That season he appeared on some Orioles radio broadcasts but was no longer able to do play-by-play, instead providing commentary and anecdotes from his years as an Orioles broadcaster. "If something happens that may remind me of something, or a certain pattern becomes obvious to me, we might talk about that," Thompson said. "I'm just kind of sitting in, I guess, to have the voice heard again on WBAL."[30] Though Thompson's eyesight was not expected to improve, he wanted to do the play-by-play one last time. "If my eyes were ever recovered

enough to read, you can bet your boots I'd come out to the booth to see if I could do it. I would do one inning and just shut the book and go away and forget about it."[31]

Thompson's wife, Rose, died in 1985. On September 24, 1988, he remarried, to widow Betty Kaplan. In his autobiography, Thompson wrote, "Among the wonderful things she has done for me was to take me back to the church. Thanks to Betty, I joined church again, attend as regularly as I can, and do whatever I can to help the congregation."[32] In later years, Chuck and Betty were members of St. Leo Catholic parish, where he sometimes lent his booming voice to calling bingo games. Chuck's daughter, Sandy Kuckler, died of breast cancer in 2001.

On March 6, 2005, Chuck Thompson died after suffering a stroke. He was eighty-three. His memorial Mass was held at Baltimore's Cathedral of Mary Our Queen and was attended by Maryland Governor Robert L. Ehrlich Jr., Orioles owner Peter Angelos, and former Orioles broadcaster Jon Miller. Former Baltimore Orioles outfielder Ken Singleton assessed Chuck's approach to broadcasting, stating, "To him, the game came first. Chuck was just the messenger—and a damn good one."[33] Cal Ripken Jr. summed up Thompson's place in Baltimore Orioles history, saying, "He'll forever be associated in my mind with what was right with the Orioles."[34]

Chapter 46. **Bill O'Donnell**

Matt Bohn

For seventeen seasons Bill O'Donnell covered Baltimore Orioles baseball in a calm, objective style. O'Donnell, who was said to be as unflappable off the air as he was on, once commented, "If you're always getting excited, you will lose your credibility when it is time to be excited."[1] A highly respected sportscaster, O'Donnell also covered network baseball, football, and basketball before his untimely death at the age of fifty-six.

Bill O'Donnell was born on June 4, 1926, in the Bronx, New York, the son of William and Eleanor O'Donnell. Growing up in the Bronx, he attended Fordham Prep. At the age of fourteen, he was working as a copyboy for the *New York Times*, and he later worked for the *New York World-Telegram*. O'Donnell served in the Pacific as a combat correspondent with the U.S. Marine Corps during World War II.

Discharged from the marines in 1946, O'Donnell attended Fordham University and later Mohawk College (now Mohawk Valley Community College) in Utica, New York, where he completed his degree. He worked as a sportswriter and copy editor for the *Utica Daily Press* from 1946 until January 1948, when Elliott Stuart, manager of Utica radio station WIBX, offered him a position as sports director at the station. In addition, O'Donnell hosted a daily sports radio show.

While working at WIBX O'Donnell got his first opportunity to provide sports play-by-play. By the fall of 1948, he was covering Hamilton College football over the airwaves. Yearning for the opportunity to do the same for baseball, O'Donnell spent many nights in the summer of 1949 seated

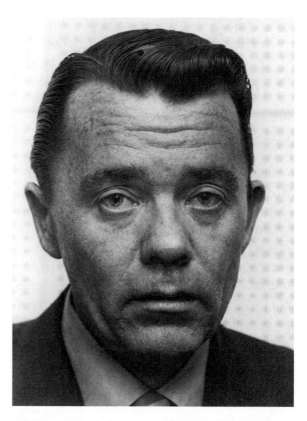

Bill O'Donnell had a long network broadcast career but is perhaps best known for his work calling Orioles games during their greatest years.

in the stands at McConnell Field, describing the games of the Eastern League Utica Blue Sox into a tape recorder. After the games he would listen to the tapes, critiquing his performance and taking note of ways to improve. In the summer of 1950 Blue Sox General Manager John Wise allowed O'Donnell to broadcast all Sunday Blue Sox home games as well as re-creations of road games. In 1982 O'Donnell recalled, "The seed for my baseball broadcasting career was planted before I came to Utica, but it blossomed in Utica."[2]

Utica was important to O'Donnell personally as well as professionally. He married Patricia Martin on September 10, 1949, at Our Lady of Lourdes Catholic Church. The marriage was a lasting one, and they had five children. O'Donnell said in 1978, "In this business, there is no gray, it's all black and white. Your success and lack of success depends a lot on the person you marry. You marry the right person and it is heaven, you marry the wrong person, it could be hell."[3] O'Donnell credited his wife with being the major factor in his personal and professional success.

O'Donnell continued to work on improving his play-by-play skills in Utica. "I remember always listening to tapes of those games, plus our Clinton hockey games, Hamilton College football, and occasionally basketball broadcasts, attempting to improve both style and presentation," he said.[4]

O'Donnell's chance to continue working on Blue Sox radio broadcasts ended when the Eastern League team left Utica after the 1950 season. "But it turned out to be a break," he remembered years later. "It enabled me to accept a position in Pocatello, Idaho, to broadcast games in the Pioneer League, plus Idaho State football and basketball games."[5] The opportunity to broadcast in Idaho came about when baseball clown Billy Mills (a close friend of O'Donnell's) was entertaining fans before a game in Pocatello and learned that the club was unhappy with its announcer and was looking for a replacement. Mills recommended O'Donnell and he was hired. He joined radio station KWIK, which broadcast the Pocatello Cardinals' games. "The play-by-play schedule there was fruitful and it gave me the 'live' broadcast experience that was necessary," O'Donnell recalled years later.[6]

By 1953 O'Donnell had moved to Syracuse, New York, becoming the sports director of WSYR radio and television. He provided some local base-ball coverage, working telecasts of the International League Syracuse Chiefs in 1954, and describing weekend games of the New York–Penn League Auburn Yankees in 1961. But O'Donnell's stint at WSYR was most notable for the thirteen years he spent as the voice of Syracuse University football. It was an exciting time for the team. Years later, he remembered, "My association with Syracuse football came during the developmental years of Ben Schwartzwalder's program, leading to his national championship of 1959. I was not only able to be a part of the football growth and success, but also to describe the outstanding achievements of Jim Brown, the late Ernie Davis, and Floyd Little, among others."[7] O'Donnell recalled, "Syracuse Coach Ben Schwartzwalder and his staff were so good to me. They would let me sit in on coaches' meetings and watch films. I even had access to scouting reports. As a result of that experience, I think I gained a greater insight into the game."[8]

While still working at Syracuse, O'Donnell began to gain national recognition through network television assignments. In 1958 he was selected by NBC-TV to cover the NBA Western Division playoff series. In 1965 O'Donnell became one of the network's play-by-play announcers for AFL football. "It was a season of hectic, but valuable weekends; describing Syracuse football games on Saturday and then speeding from college stadiums to airports for flights to AFL telecasts around the country on Sundays," he recalled.[9]

In 1965 O'Donnell got his first opportunity to broadcast play-by-play for Major League Baseball, covering a doubleheader between the Orioles and Angels over Baltimore radio. Early in 1966, when broadcaster Curt Gowdy left the Boston Red Sox booth to focus on network assignments for NBC, O'Donnell applied for the opening with the Boston broadcast team. Notified that he was one of three finalists for the job, O'Donnell was told he would need a "major-league push" to get the job.[10]

O'Donnell remembered, "I decided to call the Orioles for a recommendation for the Red Sox job because I had worked that doubleheader for them. I didn't know it at the time, but the same morning that I called Baltimore, the Orioles held a meeting in which they decided to add an announcer to their staff. I called them for a recommendation that morning and before I even asked the question they told me to wait by the phone that day because I was going to be getting a call from the Orioles."[11] He was offered the job as an Orioles radio and television broadcaster the same day. "I felt like my prayers had been answered," he said. "It was truly the broadcaster's dream come true—and little did I realize some greater thrills were to follow like clinching the pennant later that summer in Kansas City and the four-game series sweep over the Dodgers."[12]

As well as broadcasting the Orioles' games, O'Donnell continued to cover many network assignments. In 1970 he told Utica columnist Phil Spartano, "Last fall in the eighth inning of the third and final playoff game with Minnesota, Chet Simmons of NBC-TV sports walked into our booth and asked me to call him the next morning. I was sure it meant an assignment to work the World Series. That's what it turned out to be. Right after breaking into radio with WIBX I had always hoped to someday broadcast a World Series. It took a long time but the wait was worthwhile, even though the Mets won it in five games."[13] O'Donnell also broadcast the 1971 World Series and the 1975 American League Championship Series for the television network, as well as serving as a play-by-play voice of NBC's backup Game of the Week from 1969 to 1976.

O'Donnell also continued to work other sports. After spending 1966 to 1968 on radio broadcasts of Baltimore Colts football, he broadcast NFL football on NBC-TV from 1970 to 1975, as well as NCAA football on ABC-TV in 1969. Throughout his career, he kept a busy schedule. By 1982 he report-edly worked a schedule of 180 baseball games (including exhibition games), thirty-two basketball games, and ten football games a year.

In 1981 O'Donnell was diagnosed with cancer. Broadcast partner and close friend Chuck Thompson recalled, "Bill underwent cancer surgery in 1981, and made enough progress to return to work. But a year later, he had another operation and never fully recovered. Sometime after the second operation, he wanted to come back to the booth and do his share." Thompson remembered, "The night he returned, we went in to an extended rain delay. As long as I live, I'll remember Bill stretched across three metal chairs in the back of the booth during the delay, trying to conserve as much energy as possible for the resumption of the game. I begged him to go home. But professionals don't quit—and Bill completed the game."[14] Bill O'Donnell died in his sleep at Johns Hopkins Hospital on October 29, 1982, at the age of fifty-six.

Twenty-five years after his passing, O'Donnell was recognized for his contributions to the Orioles. In 2007 the team honored him with the Herbert E. Armstrong Award, presented to non-uniformed personnel who have made significant contributions to the club and to baseball. Fans and colleagues of O'Donnell have maintained that one other honor should be bestowed on the long-time Orioles voice. Chuck Thompson summed it up, saying, "I hope that sometime, somehow, that those who have the say in Cooperstown will remember that Bill O'Donnell belongs there."[15]

Chapter 47. **John Gordon**

Stew Thornley

John Gordon established his "Touch 'Em All" call for home runs in New York and had it resonate with fans in his first year at Minnesota, when the Twins won the World Series in 1987. He had also broadcast for a world championship team in Baltimore, in 1970, joining Chuck Thompson and Bill O'Donnell in the midst of a run of pennants by the powerhouse Orioles.

John Gordon Gutowsky was born in Detroit on July 7, 1940. His father, Otto, was a manufacturer's representative, selling wire, and his mother, Evelyn, a homemaker. He grew up with two older brothers, Otto Jr. and Larry. Gordon spent a lot of time watching the Tigers at Briggs Stadium, as a guest of his grandfather when he was younger and later as a soda vendor in the bleachers. At Redford High School Gordon pitched on the baseball team in addition to playing football and basketball. He accepted a scholarship offer to Indiana University from baseball coach Ernie Andres and pitched on the freshman team under Gene Ring.

Gordon was originally a health, physical education, and recreation major before taking a year off from school. When he came back, no longer a member of the baseball team, he switched his major to broadcast journalism. WFIU, the university's radio station, provided football and basketball (which was still led by coaching legend Branch McCracken) broadcasts to a statewide network. Dick Enberg, then in graduate school, was the main announcer, and Gordon succeeded him in broadcasting for the teams. His broadcast partner was Pat Williams, then a graduate student at Indiana while also playing baseball in the Philadelphia Phillies organization during the summer. "John was an

John Gordon has worked in the broadcasting business for more than forty years, and he called his first big league action with the great 1970 Orioles.

undergrad and we were thrown together," recalled Williams. "We had so much in common—sports background, loved the whole scene, similar personalities: upbeat, enthusiastic. We clicked."[1]

During the summers Gordon worked at a pair of radio stations in Saginaw, Michigan. When he arrived and introduced himself to WSAM program director Bruce Malle as John Gutowsky, Malle asked him what his radio name was. At that point, John Gutowsky became John Gordon in professional life (and remained John Gutowsky away from work). In Saginaw Gordon filled in where needed, on the control board as a disc jockey, writing copy, or monitoring Tigers broadcasts. After leaving Indiana he went to WCEN Radio in Mount Pleasant, Michigan, where he broadcast football and basketball for Central Michigan University as well as two area high schools.

In February 1965 Pat Williams, now done playing, became general manager of the Philadelphia Phillies' Class A team in the Western Carolinas League in Spartanburg, South Carolina. "I arrive full of vim and vigor ready to start my front-office career," he said. "We've got a radio station to do the games but no broadcaster. I said, 'I've got a broadcaster in the pipeline.' I tracked John down in Mount Pleasant and said, 'You ready to move south?'"[2] Gordon and Williams worked and lived together for the next four years before Williams went to the Philadelphia 76ers to begin a prominent front-office career in the National Basketball Association, one that includes cofounding the Orlando Magic.

A promotional whiz who drew praise from Bill Veeck, Williams helped the Spartanburg Phillies lead all Class A teams in attendance in 1965 despite finishing seventh in an eight-team league. "We were promoting up a storm," said Williams. "Every night was Mardi Gras. And John was our key voice. We're promoting all that through the broadcasts, trying to capture the excitement."[3]

Gordon expressed fond memories of the Phillies' home, Duncan Park, a small ballpark built into the side of a hill and lined with trees. He said the park did not have a press box when he arrived, but he helped the son-in-law of the team owner build a modest structure with booths for the public-address announcer, broadcasters, and print media. More importantly, while in Spartanburg Gordon met Nancy Rasor, whom he married in 1968.

The 1966 and 1967 Spartanburg Phillies won the league pennant while featuring future Major Leaguers Denny Doyle, Larry Bowa, Barry Lersch,

Ken Reynolds, and John Vukovich. In 1968 Gordon was honored as the South Carolina sportscaster of the year by the Sportscasters and Sportswriters Association.

After five seasons in Spartanburg, Gordon went to Baltimore and joined the WBAL broadcast team of Chuck Thompson and Bill O'Donnell in announcing Orioles baseball. He estimated that he worked about thirty-five of the fifty televised games and ninety games overall each season on radio and television, as well as broadcasting football and basketball games of the U.S. Naval Academy. The Orioles won the World Series in Gordon's first year in Baltimore, the middle year of three straight pennants for the club. However, Gordon was the third announcer of the crew and got "weeded out" after the 1972 season when the National Brewing Company lost the broadcast rights to Orioles baseball.[4]

He went to work for the University of Virginia in Charlottesville, broadcasting football and basketball for the Cavaliers for the next three years before returning to baseball for the Columbus (Ohio) Clippers, a New York Yankees affiliate. He also announced football and basketball for Ohio State University. In 1979 the Clippers, managed by Gene Michael, won the International League pennant and playoffs with a pitching staff that included Ron Davis and Dave Righetti. With Joe Altobelli managing the team in 1980, Columbus won the pennant and playoffs again, but it was Gordon's last year with the team.

At about this time he almost got a job broadcasting the Pittsburgh Pirates; when he did not, he planned to get out of baseball. He did sports on WTVN-TV in Columbus and broadcast the Liberty Bowl between Ohio State and Navy in late 1981. While in Memphis at the Liberty Bowl, Gordon got a call from Gene Michael, who had managed at Columbus while he was with the club in 1979. Michael, by this time with the parent team and a confidant of owner George Steinbrenner, asked Gordon if he wanted to come to New York to broadcast Yankees games. Gordon started there in 1982 and worked through 1986.

"New York was a great experience," said Gordon, but the broadcast booth got crowded.[5] In 1986 Billy Martin was part of the broadcast team, and Gordon was relegated to pregame and postgame broadcasts. He looked for other opportunities, and one came up in Minnesota. In December of 1986, he flew to Minneapolis on the same plane with Tom Kelly (whom he had known when Kelly had played for Toledo in the International League in 1978). Kelly had finished the season as the Minnesota Twins' interim manager and was going to interview for the position on a more permanent basis. Both Gordon and Kelly were successful in their job quests.

Dave Mona, then with WCCO Radio as well as an owner of Mona Meyer McGrath & Gavin, a public relations firm working with the Twins on a number of assignments, recalled the interview. "After the 1986 season the Twins, along with WCCO Radio and Channel 9, wanted to bring in some fresh broadcast talent," wrote Mona in e-mail correspondence with the author:

> They put out the word through sports and broadcast channels and were flooded with audition tapes. There must have been 50–60 that made the first cut. A group of us listened to all of them and got it down to about 5 or 6. We were looking for someone who didn't sound like everyone else and who had a good, strong call. I think we got it down to about five or six finalists and we brought in about four people. One of them was John Rooney, who ranked high on everyone's list.
>
> John Gordon's tape set him apart from almost everyone else. It was amazing how casual most people were. They sent in maybe an inning or two from several different games. John's presentation was maybe the most professional of the group. He actually included some production and narration.

For instance, he would say, "A lot of my work with the Yankees is on putting together pre- and postgame shows. We want our fans to get to know the players. Here's an example of a pre-game interview with . . ." Now that may sound pretty common today, but 25 years ago, he got style points far beyond most of the competition.[6]

Gordon and Rooney were both hired (the latter leaving after one season to broadcast for the Chicago White Sox), and Gordon worked on both television and radio for two years before switching exclusively to radio.

Regarding Gordon's hiring, which came around the same time that the Twins interviewed, but did not sign, pitcher Jack Morris, *The Sporting News* correspondent Moss Klein wrote, "The Twins may have blundered on Morris, but they did make a fine off-the-field move by adding John Gordon, formerly with the Yankees, to their TV-radio team. Within weeks, the hardworking Gordon will know more about the Twins and their inner workings and farm system than announcers who have been with the club for years."[7]

Just as he had in Baltimore, Gordon showed up just in time in Minnesota to ride a championship wave. The Twins, after having finished sixth in the seven-team American League West Division in 1986, finished first in the West and then won the league playoffs and World Series in 1987.

Listeners were serenaded by Gordon's home-run call of "Touch 'Em All," which he had ample opportunity to use as the Twins, led by Kent Hrbek, Tom Brunansky, Gary Gaetti, and Kirby Puckett, hit 196 home runs that season. Gordon told *Minneapolis Star and Tribune* reporter Jon Roe that he got the expression from Dick Enberg, his colleague at Indiana University. "I realized that Dick wasn't doing baseball, and I started using it with the Yankees. But if there had been a lot of bad reaction from Twins listeners, I wouldn't have used it anymore."[8]

Gordon has had many broadcast partners in Minnesota, with his longest run coming alongside Herb Carneal, a recipient of the Ford Frick Award from the Baseball Hall of Fame in 1996. Also a former Orioles announcer, Carneal called Twins games from 1962 until his death just before the 2007 season. As of 2010, Gordon had also worked with former Twins Dan Gladden and Jack Morris (who, after not signing with the Twins in 1987, joined the team in 1991, another championship season).

Gordon and his wife became active in the Fellowship of Christian Athletes and in the 1990s started an annual "Touch 'Em All" golf tournament, which benefits the Fellowship, the Twins Community Fund, and Twins Chapel. Gordon appeared in the movie *Little Big League*, playing an announcer named Wally Holland.

Upon arriving in Minnesota, John and Nancy lived in the Twin Cities year-round. In 2008 they moved to Florida and started to rent a home in the Twin Cities during the baseball season.

They have two children. John Jr. (who goes by Gordy and worked in the front office of the Cleveland Indians) was born in Spartanburg. He moved to the Twin Cities with his wife and two children. Jean was born in Baltimore and went to Indiana University, where she met her future husband. They have two children and live in Fortville, Indiana. Gordon is a past member of the Society for American Baseball Research (SABR) and loved Bob Davids's *Baseball Briefs* column in the SABR Bulletin.

"He was a grinder," recalled Pat Williams of Gordon. "If anybody built a foundation of good solid experience, it was John. He paid his dues at every level. He did not jump-start anywhere. With that kind of foundation, long-term success is much more likely."[9]

Chapter 48. **Brooks Robinson**

Maxwell Kates

AGE	G	AB	R	H	2B	3B	HR	TB	RBI	BB	SO	BAV	OBP	SLG	SB	GDP	HBP
33	158	608	84	168	31	4	18	261	94	53	53	.276	.335	.429	1	18	4

The stage was the fifth game of the World Series, on October 15, 1970. The Baltimore Orioles had taken a lead of three games to one over the Cincinnati Reds. Brooks Robinson had already delivered a game-winning home run in the opener, robbed Tony Perez and Johnny Bench of base hits with a pair of diving catches in Game Three, and cracked a two-out RBI single in Game Four. Robinson had not been an offensive factor in the Orioles' 9–3 lead in Game Five. In fact, he was called out on strikes in the eighth inning. As he returned to the dugout with his head hung, the fans "gave him a standing ovation for his dream series."[1] And why not? Robinson was batting .429 for the Series with seventeen total bases and nine hits, including two doubles and two RBIs in Game Three. Meanwhile, the bulk of his twenty-four fielding chances occurred during key moments of the games. The Reds had one final chance in the top of the ninth, and leading off the inning was Johnny Bench, soon to be named his league's Most Valuable Player. Bench lined a foul ball that appeared to be out of Robinson's reach. Yet it was plays such as these for which Lee May nicknamed him "Hoover the Vacuum Cleaner." Robinson dived headlong into dirt in foul territory and miraculously snared the baseball, a startling and fitting finale to an extraordinary World Series performance. Compared with this catch, throwing out Pat Corrales on a soft bouncer to end the game and win the World Series appeared almost anticlimactic.

The lasting memory of Brooks Robinson for many remains his wizardry in the 1970 World Series. But countless others will remember the man behind the statistics, records, and awards. "When

Brooks Robinson's amazing deeds in the 1970 World Series are perhaps the high point of his long and glorious career in Baltimore.

fans ask Brooks Robinson for his autograph," remembered the late Orioles broadcaster Chuck Thompson, "he complied while finding out how many kids you have, what your dad does, where you live, how old you are, and if you have a dog. . . . His only failing is that when the game ended, if Brooks belonged to its story—usually he did—you better leave the booth at the end of the eighth inning. . . . By the time the press got [to the clubhouse] Brooks was in the parking lot signing autographs on his way home."[2]

Success did not compromise the integrity or upstanding character of Brooks Calbert Robinson. Even into his eighth decade, he remained as honest and genuine as the day he graduated from high school in Little Rock, Arkansas. He conducted himself with class throughout his twenty-three seasons in a Major League uniform, and fulfilled extraneous obligations with joy and enthusiasm. As of 2010 Robinson had lived most of his married life in Baltimore, where he helped raise four children, endorsed local businesses, and was active in his family's church. Brooks Robinson continued to greet total strangers as if they were childhood neighbors.

Robinson was born in Little Rock on May 18, 1937, of mixed German-English extraction. His father was instrumental in the development of his baseball skills. "I was hardly big enough to hold a glove up when he taught me to catch a rubber baseball," remembered Brooks. "And one of my earliest memories is the day he cut off an old broom so the handle was about the right size for me to swing. . . . Mom and the neighbors could always tell where I was by the ping of the rocks against those old broomsticks." When he was older, Robinson developed his fielding skills with a paper route of 150 customers, including Bill Dickey, the New York Yankees Hall of Fame catcher of an earlier era. Given an English composition assignment about his career ambition in the eighth grade, Robinson entitled his paper "Why I Want to Play Professional Baseball." More specifically, he wanted to play third base for the St. Louis Cardinals.[3]

Although he also played football and basketball in high school, baseball was the sport he most excelled at. One of many the scouts to observe the wunderkind and his glovework at American Legion games was Lindsay Deal, a former Minor League teammate of Baltimore manager and general manager Paul Richards. "He's no speed demon," wrote Deal to Richards, "but neither is he a truck horse. Brooks has a lot of power, base-ball savvy, and is always cool when the chips are down."[4] After Robinson graduated from Central High School in 1955, he and his parents considered several baseball offers before he signed with Baltimore Orioles scout Arthur Ehlers for $4,000. The Orioles were a lowly organization at the time, just a season removed from their transfer from St. Louis. Ehlers used the organization's position to convince Robinson that "with us, you have the chance to move up faster than with probably any other club."[5]

Robinson began his professional career in York, Pennsylvania, with a reputation as a weak hitter. Even the public address announcer for the Piedmont League club did not take the new prospect seriously, announcing him as "Bob Robinson" in his first plate appearance. Years later Robinson credited Paul Richards for seeing his "raw ability and for [refusing] to listen to the people that didn't think I'd ever hit in the big leagues."[6] Robinson batted .091 (2-for-22) in a brief September call-up.

"I thought Paul was kidding when he had me watch the kid work out one day," recalled teammate Gene Woodling. "He couldn't hit, he couldn't run, and his arm wasn't that strong." Robinson spent the next four years splitting time between the Major and Minor Leagues. He was playing for San Antonio in May 1956 when he learned that the Orioles had acquired veteran third baseman George Kell from the Chicago White Sox. San Antonio manager Joe Schultz reassured Robinson that Kell was "a stopgap measure" until the nineteen-year-old was ready for the Major Leagues.[7]

It took Robinson a few tries to finally stick in the Major Leagues. He hit .272 in 154 games for San Antonio in 1956 before another September recall (.227 in 15 games). He hit his first Major League home run on September 29 in Griffith Stadium off Senators pitcher Evilio Hernandez. Robinson was the Orioles' starting third baseman at the start of the 1957 season but returned to San Antonio after struggling—he wound up hitting

.266 in the Minors and .239 in the Majors for the season.

His first full Major League season was 1958, when he played 145 games but hit just .238 with three home runs. He had hit just .232 in his first 216 Major League games. He was returned to the Minor Leagues again early in the 1959 season, this time to Vancouver, British Columbia, of the Pacific Coast League. He hit well (.331 in 42 games) and he got back to Baltimore (for good, it turned out) in July. After one final difficult month (.183 in July), he hit over .340 the final two months and claimed the job he would hold for another sixteen years.

Robinson's Vancouver manager, Charlie Metro, later recalled a freak accident that nearly ended his career. "Our dugout in Vancouver had a screen hanging over some hooks," said Metro. "A guy took half the screen down but forgot the hooks. Robinson came over for a foul, slipped, and threw his arm up. A hook caught his arm at the right elbow. I grabbed his arm—he had a 24-inch cut. If he had fallen, he would have been done."[8]

Robinson's finest hour in 1959 came off the field. On August 26 he and his Orioles teammates boarded a flight in Kansas City bound for Boston. After taking his seat, he became mesmerized by one of the stewardesses, and wisely asked for a glass of iced tea. After his third iced tea, possibly his fourth, Robinson followed the air hostess to the galley, offering that "all the rest [of the players] are married. So remember, if any of them try to talk to you, I'm the only single, eligible bachelor on the plane."[9] Robinson eventually collected enough confidence to ask the young lady's name, and she introduced herself as Connie Butcher from Detroit. After she accepted Robinson's dinner invitation once the flight landed in Boston, the third baseman knew that Connie was the woman he wanted to marry.

After six noncompetitive seasons in the American League, the Orioles surprised most everyone by challenging the New York Yankees for the pennant in 1960. Baltimore was tied for first as late as September 15, but the Yankees won their final fifteen games to leave the Orioles behind. Despite his tender age of twenty-three, Robinson emerged as a leader on the very young club. He had a fine individual season, hitting .294 with 14 home runs and 88 RBIs, and hitting for the cycle on July 15 in Chicago. His fine season earned him a trip to his first two All-Star Games, his first Gold Glove, and his selection as the Orioles' MVP. He finished third in the voting for league MVP, behind only Roger Maris and Mickey Mantle. Although he did not get to play in the World Series, he did marry Connie Butcher on October 8 at her family's summer home in Windsor, Ontario.

The new bridegroom picked up right where he left off in 1961, batting .287 mainly in the lead-off position as the Orioles finished well behind the Yankees. The next year, under new manager Billy Hitchcock, Robinson set career highs with 23 home runs and 86 RBIs while batting .306. New teammate Robin Roberts reflected that Robinson was "quicker than [former teammate Willie] Jones and had the fastest reflexes I've ever seen."[10] Robinson fell off quite a bit in 1963, hitting just .251 with 11 home runs, and the team's poor play cost Hitchcock his job. Hank Bauer took over for the 1964 season.

Robinson had perhaps his best season in 1964, and the Orioles were part of a summer-long scramble for the pennant, a race again won by the Yankees. Missing only two innings of the Orioles' 163 games played, Robinson had 194 hits, 28 home runs, and a league-best 118 RBIs. He hit a torrid .464 in September to lift his average from .294 to .317. After the season Robinson was named the American League's Most Valuable Player, and also won his fifth consecutive Gold Glove (he eventually won sixteen straight). The Yankees finally dropped back in 1965, and the Orioles won 94 games, but the Minnesota Twins, not the Orioles, took advantage of the opening and won the pennant easily. Robinson suffered a broken thumb when hit by a Hank Aguirre fastball and played 144 games (after missing just one game the previous four seasons), batting .297 with 18 home runs.

In the following off-season the Orioles underwent some changes. Jerold Hoffberger, chairman of National Brewing Company, bought a majority stake in the team, and he hired Harry Dalton to be the general manager. As Brooks Robinson was the club's only right-handed power threat, Dalton made a big deal with the Reds to acquire outfielder Frank Robinson. For the next six years the two Robinsons defined the franchise and led the team to its greatest run of success.

Many would have understood if Brooks Robinson felt threatened by the arrival of Frank Robinson, a great player and renowned leader. Frank was the first African American star in Baltimore, and one of the first in the American League. Brooks, on the other hand, grew up in Little Rock, a city that had integrated its schools nine years earlier only with the help of the National Guard. Brooks was elated by the trade, declaring the new Oriole to be "exactly what we need."[11] If anything, Frank eased the burden on Brooks as a clubhouse motivator. As Hank Bauer recalled, Frank "was definitely the missing cog," who "took away the pressure on Brooks and Boog [Powell]. He helped the young players just by talking to them."[12]

More importantly, Frank's presence greatly strengthened the Orioles' offensive attack. On Opening Day in Boston, Frank was hit by a pitch. Brooks followed by belting a two-run homer, which proved to be just sufficient in a thirteen-inning 5–4 victory. Although Frank won the Triple Crown, Brooks also provided valuable contributions to the team's runaway pennant—the club's lead was more than eight games every day after mid-July, and they eventually won by nine over the Twins. Robinson played the entire All-Star Game in St. Louis, and though the American League

lost 2–1, his triple and two singles earned him the game's MVP award.

The Orioles' opponents in their first World Series were the heavily favored Los Angeles Dodgers, champions from 1963 and 1965. The upstart Orioles did not pay attention to the doubters, and they swept the Dodgers in four straight games. In Game One, both Brooks and Frank Robinson homered in the first inning to start the Orioles to their 5–2 victory. The Orioles finished the job with three straight complete-game shutouts from their pitchers. For Brooks Robinson, runner-up to Frank in the league's MVP vote, the Series was a highly satisfying event. "You dream about signing a big league contract," he later wrote. "You dream about getting to the majors. And you dream about getting to the World Series. I remember thinking, 'Now if you never win anything else again, at least you've done this.'"[13]

The Orioles fell back to sixth place in 1967, beset by injuries to pitchers Jim Palmer and Dave McNally and off years from several hitters. Robinson hit .269 with 22 home runs, fine production for the mid-1960s. Although the American League lost the All-Star Game once again, Robinson was responsible for the junior circuit's only run, a round-tripper off Ferguson Jenkins. The Orioles moved up to second place the next year, although a midsummer slump cost manager Bauer his job in favor of Earl Weaver. Brooks received a favorable first impression of his new manager, describing him as "intense and just insecure enough to have us playing all out all the time."[14]

While 1969 marked an off year for Robinson (.234 with 23 homers and 84 RBIs), the Orioles crushed American League opponents all season en route to a 109-53 record and a sweep of the Twins in the playoffs. Despite losing the World Series to the upstart New York Mets, the Orioles came back the next year and did it all again, this time sporting a record of 108-54 and another sweep of Minnesota. Three of Robinson's eighteen home runs that year were particularly noteworthy. He broke a 2–2 deadlock on May 9, hitting the 200th round-tripper of his career off Chicago's Tommy John. On June 20, he delivered a three-run blast to eclipse a 2–2 tie against Washington's Joe Coleman for his 2,000th hit. A walk-off home run off Boston's Sparky Lyle, though not a career milestone, was exemplary of Robinson's grit and tenacity. Earlier in the game he had sustained minor head injuries as starter Mike Nagy beaned him. That year, Robinson brought his average back up to .276 and drove in 94 runs in the Orioles' cause.

Robinson's dominance of the 1970 World Series made him more famous than he ever had been before. Along with all the formidable defensive plays, he also hit .429 with two home runs (after having hit .576 in the Twins series). However, few remember that the memorable Game Five almost did not take place that day. As Phil Jackman of the *Baltimore Evening Sun* reported: "It was about 30 minutes before the fifth game . . . but it didn't look as if the show would go on. It was pouring. Brooks Robinson walked into the dugout and Andy Etchebarren, sitting there, kiddingly said, 'Brooksie, make it stop raining.' Number 5, raising his eyes, said, 'Stop raining.' It did. 'I'm getting out of here,' Etchebarren said, scurrying towards the clubhouse." Perhaps there was some validity to the remark of umpire Ed Hurley that Robinson "came down from a higher league."[15]

Teammates and adversaries alike offered their admiration of Brooks Robinson after the Series. Boog Powell provided the ultimate compliment, saying that in the late innings of a tight ballgame, "I'd rather have him up there instead of me." It was of little surprise to anyone that Robinson was named the 1970 World Series Most Valuable Player, receiving a new Dodge Charger. To this, Pete Rose of the vanquished Reds suggested, "If we knew he wanted a car so [badly], we'd have bought one for him ourselves."[16]

How could the thirty-four-year-old improve on his magnificent 1970? He could not, but the next year his 20 home runs, 92 RBIs, and .272 batting average were enough to earn him his fourth and final Most Valuable Oriole award. Baltimore ran away with the American League East again, racking up 101 wins and sweeping Oakland in the playoff series. Two of Robinson's more memorable regular-season contests were against the Athletics. On July 18 in Oakland, his grand slam proved to be the difference in a 7–3 victory. On July 27 he beat Rollie Fingers with a two-run homer in the bottom of the ninth. The following night Robinson reminded everyone that he was mortal after all, committing three errors in one inning and hitting into two double plays.

Baltimore took a 2–0 lead over Pittsburgh in the World Series, as Robinson reached base five times in an 11–3 victory in Game Two. Fans at Memorial Stadium, if they opened to page 44 of their World Series Program, could view a beautiful Norman Rockwell art print of Robinson used as an advertising piece for a sporting goods company. Entitled *Gee Thanks, Brooks*, it displayed the third baseman signing an autograph for a boy sitting in the first row of seats. Having autographed hundreds of copies of the portrait, Robinson became familiar with every detail in the painting, even identifying which of the spectators was Rockwell himself. Despite winning the first two games, the Orioles lost the 1971 World Series to the Pirates, whose star Roberto Clemente had a World Series as memorable as Robinson's had been the year before.

Shortly after returning from an eighteen-game barnstorming tour of Japan, the Orioles announced a trade that sent Frank Robinson to the Los Angeles Dodgers. Without their catalyst and fearless leader in the lineup, the Orioles reverted to the middle of the division in 1972 thanks to a collapsing offense. A lifetime .274 hitter to that point, Robinson batted only .250. The Orioles returned to their divisional apex in 1973 and 1974 but could not defeat Oakland in the Championship Series either year. Robinson retained his attitude as a team player, as was evident when the Orioles overcame a 4–0 deficit in Game Four of the 1973 Championship Series to win 5–4 on a pair of home runs by Bobby Grich and Andy Etchebarren: "I remember being out in the field thinking in the sixth inning that I'll probably be home raking leaves the next day. Instead we were playing the next day with a trip to the World Series on the line."[17]

In 1975 the thirty-eight-year-old Robinson won his sixteenth consecutive Gold Glove Award, a fitting accomplishment for a player who committed only 263 errors in 9,165 chances. But he also hit .201, and just .211 in 71 games the following year. By the end of the 1976 season, Doug DeCinces had supplanted Robinson as the regular third baseman, and the end appeared imminent. When Billy Hunter left Baltimore to become the manager of the Texas Rangers, Robinson replaced him on the coaching staff. Before he hung up his spikes, he saved one final moment in the sun—in the rain, actually—for Baltimore's fans. On April 19, 1977, the Orioles trailed the Indians by three runs in the bottom of the tenth inning. After Lee May singled in one run, there remained two Orioles on base as Robinson emerged to pinch-hit for Larry Harlow. Dressed in the garish orange uniform of the era, he took the count to 3-2 against Dave LaRoche and fouled several pitches before producing a game-ending home run for a 6–5 victory. It was Robinson's 268th and final home run.

The Orioles paid tribute to their retired star on September 18, 1977, as they celebrated Thanks Brooks Day. Before the game, Robinson was driven around the perimeter of the field in a 1955 Cadillac convertible as the crowd of 51,798 offered a standing ovation. Doug DeCinces ran on the field, removed third base from the dirt, and presented it to Robinson. The bitterness of losing Reggie Jackson to free agency remained a vivid memory when Gordon Beard wrote in his Associated Press column that "Brooks never asked anyone to name a candy bar after him. In Baltimore, they name their children after him."[18] Following the season, Brooks was selected, along with Frank Robinson, as charter members of the Baltimore Orioles Hall of Fame.

In 1978 Robinson became an Orioles broadcaster. He also became a popular advertising representative, lending his name to products like Rawlings Sporting Goods, Mike Meagher's All-Star Dodge, Crown Petroleum, and Esskay Hot Dogs. These were products used by families in the Baltimore area—much like his own family, which would grow to include sons Brooks David, Chris, and Michael, daughter Diana, and several grandchildren. As the autograph industry expanded in the 1980s, Robinson became a regular on the baseball card show circuit. Over the decades, Robinson has scrawled his signature on thousands of items, including some that collectors would not expect. In an interview with the *Baltimore Sun*, he admitted that on various occasions, he has been asked to sign a pet rock, an Easter egg, a photo of Frank Robinson, and even a plane ticket.[19]

In 1983 Robinson was inducted into the Baseball Hall of Fame. Standing before a sea of black and orange from the podium in Cooperstown, Robinson paid homage to his teachers, Paul Richards and George Kell. Of his predecessor at the hot corner, he once offered that "George Kell taught me everything he knew about playing third. He also taught me how to conduct myself as a big leaguer, to be a role model, and someone kids and all fans could look up to." Fittingly, fellow Arkansas native Kell was also enshrined in the Hall that very day. In his own speech, Kell remarked to Robinson that he found it "almost unbelievable that we have traveled the same path for so long with the same goals in mind. And we wind up here in Cooperstown on the same day."[20]

Robinson remained an Orioles broadcaster until 1993 when he and Connie retired to Southern

California. In 1991 he was central to the closing ceremony at Memorial Stadium. He and Baltimore Colts Hall of Famer Johnny Unitas were invited to throw out the first pitches before the final game on October 6 against the Detroit Tigers—Unitas threw a football.

The Robinsons later returned to Maryland, and as of 2010 Brooks remained active in baseball as the part-owner of four Minor League teams, including the York Revolution in the independent Atlantic League. Early in the 2008 season Robinson was honored by the Revolution as a life-size bronze statue of his likeness was unveiled. A few years ago Robinson received a surprise Christmas gift from his son—the original Norman Rockwell portrait bearing his likeness. It was hung in the family recreation room in Timonium. Robinson received a health scare in early 2009 when he was diagnosed with prostate cancer but early treatment was successful.[21]

Brooks Robinson once defined professional sports as "a good life that allows you to do what you love to do all the time, and at the same time provide support for yourself and your family. But it is important to understand what goes on in a professional athlete's mind during his brief playing career. To us, making money is secondary—we just want to play."[22] He played for parts of twenty-three seasons, and for most of that time established a standard for his position.

Chapter 49. **The 1970 Orioles Postseason**

Mark Armour

The Orioles made a shambles of the American League East race in 1970, winning 108 games and finishing fifteen games ahead of the Yankees. Unlike the 1969 team, which lost five of its final six regular season games en route to the playoffs, the 1970 squad won its final eleven and finished 21-7 in September. If the players believed they had coasted, or been overconfident, in 1969, they had not let the same thing happen again.

In the playoffs the Orioles again faced the Minnesota Twins, whom they had swept in three straight games in 1969. The Twins were the underdog but had plenty of reasons to believe that this year could be different. The club had won ninety-eight games, the third highest total in baseball, and had beaten the Orioles seven times in their twelve meetings, the only team to win the season series against Baltimore. The 1969 series was closer than the final result would indicate—the Orioles won the first game in eleven innings and the second in twelve. The rematch would start with two games in Minnesota's Metropolitan Stadium, which the Twins believed would help them start the series well.

The Twins were led by a group of hitting stars: slugging third baseman Harmon Killebrew (41 home runs, 113 RBI), right fielder Tony Oliva (23 home runs, 107 RBI, .325 average), and center fielder Cesar Tovar (.300 average, 120 runs). Star second baseman Rod Carew hit .366 in just 51 games—but he broke his leg in June and would be available only to pinch-hit in the series. The club also had twenty-four-game winner Jim Perry, who would win the Cy Young Award that season, and veteran left-hander Jim Kaat to anchor a solid pitching staff. The Twins had a lot of talent.

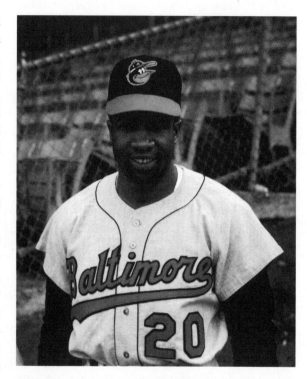

The Orioles' determination to complete the mission that had fallen short in 1969 culminated in a waltz through the 1970 postseason. Frank Robinson was their team leader.

Alas, it would not be enough. On Saturday, October 3, the Twins scored first and the game was tied, 2–2, after three innings, but the Orioles broke through for seven runs in the fourth, highlighted by a grand slam from twenty-four-game winner Mike Cuellar. Though Cuellar could not get through the fifth himself, the Orioles held on for a 10–6 victory, with Don Buford and Boog Powell adding home runs to the cause and Dick Hall pitching 4⅔ scoreless innings for the victory.

For Game Two, the Orioles sent Dave McNally, another twenty-four-game winner, to the mound.

The game was a tight one, 4–3, through eight innings, but the Orioles had another seven-run inning in the ninth to seal it away, 11–3. McNally went the route, backed by home runs from Frank Robinson and Davey Johnson.

The series moved to Baltimore on Monday afternoon, with the Orioles handing the ball to twenty-game-winner Jim Palmer, ten days shy of his twenty-fifth birthday but already one of the game's best pitchers. Palmer responded with a complete-game seven-hitter and twelve strikeouts in the easy 6–1 victory. The only Minnesota run was scored in the fifth when Frank Robinson lost Cesar Tovar's fly ball in the sun, leading to a two-out triple. Leo Cardenas singled in the run, making the score 5–1, but Palmer was too much for the Twins on this day. The Orioles had their sweep, and would return to the World Series for the second straight year, and the third time in the last five seasons.

The Orioles' opponent would be the Cincinnati Reds, in their first postseason since earning their enduring nickname "the Big Red Machine." The Reds won 102 games and cruised to the National League West title by 14½ games, before dispatching the Pittsburgh Pirates in three straight playoff games. The Reds earned their nickname with their wonderful offense, led by a collection of stars: twenty-two-year-old catcher Johnny Bench (45 home runs, 148 RBI), third baseman Tony Perez (40 home runs, 129 RBI, .317 average), first baseman Lee May (34 home runs, 94 RBI), right fielder Pete Rose (.316 average, 205 hits, 120 runs), and center fielder Bobby Tolan (.316 average, 57 stolen bases). It was truly a machine.

Not that there weren't causes for concern for rookie manager Sparky Anderson. Unlike the Orioles, the Reds were not able to keep cruising over the latter part of the season. Sitting at 70-30 on July 26, with a 12½-game lead, Cincinnati finished 32-30 over the final sixty-two games. The primary problem was a series of injuries to the pitching staff. Longtime ace Jim Maloney went down with an arm injury in April and did not return. Rookie sensation Wayne Simpson began the season 13-1 before hurting his shoulder and made only two short appearances after July. Anderson managed to hang on behind Jim Merritt (20-12), Gary Nolan (18-7), Jim McGlothlin (14-10), Tony Cloninger (9-7), and a fine bullpen. In the Pittsburgh series, the Reds' pitchers allowed just three runs.

The Orioles were the favorites, but they had been in 1969 as well, and the Reds looked a lot stronger than the Mets did. The Series began on October 10, a Saturday afternoon affair in Cincinnati. It was the first World Series game played on an artificial surface, as the Reds had moved from Crosley Field to the new Riverfront Stadium on June 30. The Reds touched Palmer for a run in the first and two in the third, but the Orioles battled back behind home runs by Powell, Ellie Hendricks, and Brooks Robinson to take the game, 4–3. Robinson set the tone not only with his game-winning home run, but with a great defensive play to rob May of an extra-base hit in the sixth.

Later in the same sixth inning the Orioles benefited from a controversial play at home plate. With Bernie Carbo on third base, Reds pinch hitter Ty Cline hit a chopper in front of home that catcher Hendricks fielded. Carbo surprised everyone by trying to score, and in sliding home he took out plate umpire Ken Burkhardt, who had his back to the play making the fair/foul call on the batted ball. Replays showed that Carbo did not touch the plate, and that Hendricks did not have the ball in his glove when he tagged the runner. Nonetheless, Burkhardt called Carbo out, and the Reds were denied a run they could have used.

On Sunday the Reds started well again, taking a 4–0 lead into the fourth only to see the Orioles chase McGlothlin with six hits and five runs in the fifth inning. Although Cuellar could not get through the third, a flock of relief pitchers held on for the 6–5 victory.

The series moved to Baltimore's Memorial Stadium on Tuesday afternoon, and the Reds knew that no team had ever lost the first two games of a World Series at home and come back to win. The Orioles changed the script somewhat in Game Three, scoring two runs in the first on Brooks Robinson's two-run double, then adding solo home runs by Frank Robinson and Don Buford to give McNally a 4–1 lead after five. In case that wasn't enough, McNally himself crushed an opposite-field grand slam into the left-field bleachers in the sixth, extending the lead to 8–1. He coasted to a complete-game 9–3 victory, highlighted by two more outstanding plays by Brooks Robinson at third base.

Going for the sweep on Wednesday, the Orioles turned to Game One winner Jim Palmer, who was just good enough to take a 5–3 lead, backed by another Brooks Robinson home run, into the eighth inning. After Palmer walked Perez and allowed a single to Bench, Weaver removed Palmer in favor of Eddie Watt, who had not pitched in two weeks. Watt threw one pitch to Lee May, who hit it into the left-field bleachers. The Reds suddenly led 6–5, and that would prove to be the final score.

The Reds were still alive, a point they reiterated with four hits and three runs off Mike Cuellar in the first inning of Game Five. Cuellar had not pitched well in either of his two postseason outings, and it looked like another rough performance from the Cuban star. A dugout conference after the first with Weaver, catcher Andy Etchebarren, and pitching coach George Bamberger led to the decision to stop throwing the screwball, Cuellar's best pitch, which had deserted him in recent weeks. Cuellar righted the ship, allowing just two hits the rest of the way.

Frank Robinson hit a two-run home run in the bottom of the first, and the Orioles added a pair of runs in both the second and third innings to win rather easily, 9–3. Brooks Robinson had one final fielding gem in the ninth inning, diving toward the line to catch Johnny Bench's screaming line drive, winding up in foul territory but holding the ball up for the umpire to see. Robinson, voted the Series' Most Valuable Player, ended with a .429 batting average and a national reputation as an extraordinary defensive star.

More importantly, the Orioles had finished the job. They had spent a year answering questions about their loss to the Mets, and they responded the only way they could—with a convincing dominance of their division, of the Twins, and finally, of a great Cincinnati Reds team. Several of the Oriole players had been on the team that won the 1966 Series, but that victory over the Dodgers was a surprise. The pressure on the 1970 Orioles was to keep winning, because anything short of a world championship would have been a supreme disappointment. Keep winning they did, in one of the more impressive championship runs in baseball history.

Epilogue

Mark Armour

The Baltimore Orioles had entered the 1970 season on a mission, determined to make up for their shocking loss in the 1969 World Series. The 1969 and 1970 teams were virtually the same, and it is only their performance in the Series that puts the 1970 team in front.

The 1970 Orioles are often mentioned when historians rank the greatest teams in baseball history. In *Baseball Dynasties*, published in 2000, Rob Neyer and Eddie Epstein each listed their choices for baseball's fifteen greatest teams.[1] Epstein ranked the Orioles as the third best club ever, and Neyer placed them second. Most serious analysts agree that they are comfortably within the top ten.

Along with their second World Championship, the 1970 Orioles received many individual honors. Brooks Robinson was named the World Series MVP for his amazing performance at bat and in the field. Boog Powell won the American League Most Valuable Player award, while three Orioles—Dave Johnson, Brooks Robinson, and Paul Blair—garnered Gold Glove Awards for their great defensive play. Harry Dalton was named baseball's Executive of the Year by *The Sporting News*.

Though the Orioles had several outstanding teams in the coming years, they would not win another World Series until 1983. After losing a great seven-game series to the Pirates in 1971, the Orioles traded Frank Robinson, and the core of the great 1969–71 clubs slowly drifted away. A largely different group returned to the postseason in 1973 and 1974, and lost another World Series in 1979. They would have the best record in the American League in the 1970s, as they had in the 1960s.

Among the great 1970 Orioles, Jim Palmer, Frank Robinson, Brooks Robinson, and manager Earl Weaver have been inducted into the Baseball Hall of Fame. In a tribute to the Oriole Way, many of the team's coaches and players went on to manage other teams, and six of them (George Bamberger, Don Baylor, Jim Frey, Dave Johnson, Johnny Oates, and Frank Robinson) later won Manager of the Year honors of their own, keeping alive the influence of this great organization.

The 1970 Baltimore Orioles are a team with a story worth remembering.

Notes and References

This section first lists a number of key sources that were consulted repeatedly while researching this book, followed with chapter-by-chapter notes and bibliographies.

General References

Baltimore Orioles Yearbook, 1966–1980.

Berney, Louis. *Tales from the Orioles Dugout*. Champaign IL: Sports Publishing LLC, 2004.

Eisenberg, John. *From 33rd Street to Camden Yards*. New York: Contemporary Books, 2001.

Gesker, Mike. *The Orioles Encyclopedia*. Baltimore: Johns Hopkins University Press, 2009.

Johnson, Lloyd, and Miles Wolff, eds. *The Encyclopedia of Minor League Baseball*. Baseball America, 1997.

Palmer, Jim, and Jim Dale. *Together We Were Eleven Foot Nine: The Twenty-Year Friendship of Hall of Fame Pitcher Jim Palmer and Orioles Manager Earl Weaver*. Kansas City MO: Andrews McMeel, 1996.

Patterson, Ted. *The Baltimore Orioles: Four Decades of Magic from 33rd Street to Camden Yards*. Rev. ed. Dallas: Taylor Publishing Company, 2000.

Pluto, Terry. *The Earl of Baltimore*. New Century, 1982.

Robinson, Brooks, and Fred Bauer. *Putting It All Together*. Portland: Hawthorn Books, 1971.

Robinson, Brooks, and Jack Tobin. *Third Base Is My Home*. Waco TX: Word Books, 1974.

Robinson, Frank, and Berry Stainback. *Extra Innings*. New York: McGraw-Hill, 1988.

Seidel, Jeff. *Baltimore Orioles: Where Have You Gone?* Champaign IL: Sports Publishing LLC, 2006.

Spatz, Lyle, ed. *The SABR Baseball List and Record Book*. New York: Scribner, 2007.

Weaver, Earl, with Berry Stainback. *It's What You Learn after You Know It All That Counts*. New York: Doubleday, 1982.

Baseball-reference.com

Retrosheet.org

SABR Encyclopedia of Baseball. http://sabrpedia.org/wiki/Main_Page

SABR Minor League Database

The player files in the A. Bartlett Giamatti Research Center, the National Baseball Hall of Fame and Museum, Cooperstown NY.

1. The Oriole Way

1. *Chicago Tribune*, September 15, 1954, C1.

2. Kevin Kerrane, *Dollar Sign on the Muscle: The World of Baseball Scouting* (Fireside/Simon & Schuster, 1984), 145.

3. Earl Weaver with Berry Stainback, *It's What You Learn after You Know It All That Counts* (Doubleday, 1982), 235. An extensive description of the Thomasville camp is in John Eisenberg, *From 33rd Street to Camden Yards* (Contemporary Books, 2001), 71–76.

4. From an untitled, undated manuscript by Paul Richards, in the author's files.

5. Donald Honig, *The Man in the Dugout* (Follett, 1977), 201.

6. Jim Russo with Bob Hammel, *SuperScout* (Bonus Books, 1992), 41.

7. Eisenberg, *From 33rd Street to Camden Yards*, 70.

8. Lou Gorman, *High and Inside: My Life in the Front Offices of Baseball* (McFarland, 2008), 42.

9. Eisenberg, *From 33rd Street to Camden Yards*, 212.

10. Terry Pluto, *The Earl of Baltimore* (New Century Publishers, 1982), 96.

11. Pluto, *Earl of Baltimore*, 97.

12. Eisenberg, *From 33rd Street to Camden Yards*, 233.

13. *Boston Globe*, April 4, 2010, 10.

14. Frank Deford, "The Best Damn Team in Baseball," *Sports Illustrated*, April 12, 1971, online archive, http://sportsillustrated.cnn.com.

2. Earl Weaver

1. *Baltimore Sun*, July 12, 1968, C1.

2. "Baltimore's Soft-Shelled Crab," *Time*, July 23, 1979, Time Archive, http://www.time.com/time/arcguve.

3. Earl Weaver and Berry Stainback, *It's What You Learn after You Know It All That Counts* (Doubleday, 1982), 133.

4. John Eisenberg, *From 33rd Street to Camden Yards* (New York: Contemporary Books, 2001), 185.

5. Terry Pluto, *The Earl of Baltimore* (New Century, 1982), 70.

6. Mike Klingaman, "Orioles to Hail '70 Champs at Today's Game," *Baltimore Sun*, June 26, 2010, http://articles.baltimoresun.com/2010-06-26/sports/bs-sp-orioles-1970-reunion-20100623_1_orioles-earl-weaver-champs.

7. *Baltimore Sun*, October 16, 1970, C1.

8. Earl Weaver and John Sammis, eds., *Winning!* (William Morrow, 1972), 153.

9. Frank Deford, "The Best Damn Team in Baseball," *Sports Illustrated*, April 12, 1971, SI Vault, http://sportsillustrated.cnn.com/vault/.

10. *Baltimore Sun*, September 23, 1979, 25.

11. Earl Weaver with Terry Pluto, *Weaver on Strategy* (Brasseys, 2002), 39.

12. Pluto, *Earl of Baltimore*, 81.

13. Pluto, *Earl of Baltimore*, 173.

14. Pluto, *Earl of Baltimore*, 168.

15. "Baltimore's Soft-Shelled Crab."

16. Weaver and Stainback, *It's What You Learn*, 223.

17. *Baltimore Sun*, October 3, 1979, B3.

18. Weaver and Stainback, *It's What You Learn*, 10.

19. Weaver and Stainback, *It's What You Learn*, 51.

20. Weaver and Stainback, *It's What You Learn*, 54, 76.

21. Eisenberg, *From 33rd Street to Camden Yards*, 332.

22. Weaver with Pluto, *Weaver on Strategy*.

3. George Bamberger

1. Lowell Reidenbaugh, "Shaky at Start, Cuellar Finishes Like a Champ," *The Sporting News*, October 31, 1970, 39–40.

2. Ron Fimrite, "Prosit! He's the Toast of the Town," *Sports Illustrated*, April 30, 1979.

3. Roch Kubatko, "Shepherd with a Staff, Bamberger Was O's Ace," *Baltimore Sun*, April 7, 2004.

4. Richard Goldstein, "George Bamberger, 80, Pitching Coach, Dies," *New York Times*, April 7, 2004.

5. Ross Newhan, "He Was a Workhouse Warhorse, Very Few Are Left," *Los Angeles Times*, July 11, 1993.

6. Denny Boyd, "Let's Talk about Baseball's Bamberger," *Vancouver Sun*, April 21, 1980.

7. Boyd, "Let's Talk about Baseball's Bamberger."

8. Doug Brown, "Oriole Hurlers Please Note: Bauer Is Sick of Sore Arms," *The Sporting News*, March 2, 1968.

9. Dave Anderson, "George Bamberger, The Brewers' Ph.D. in Pitching," *New York Times*, March 8, 1979.

10. Vic Ziegel, "Bambi Meets the Mets," *New York*, March 8, 1982, 55–56.

11. "Inside Pitch," *Sports Illustrated*, June 13, 1983.

12. "Arms and the Man," *Sports Illustrated*, April 19, 2004.

Chick, Bob. "Bamberger's Pitching Theory Was Simple But Quite Effective." *The Tampa Tribune*, March 4, 2000.

Hawthorn, Tom. "Recalling the Mounties' Major Minor Legend." *The Tyee*, April 26, 2004.

Loranger, Clancy. "Mountie Bamberger Steps out as ERA Leader—2.36." *The Sporting News*, September 3, 1958.

4. Jim Frey

1. *Chicago Tribune*, March 11, 1984.

2. *Kansas City Star*, 1979, day and month unknown, clipping from Jim Frey's player file at the National Baseball Hall of Fame Library, Cooperstown NY).

3. *Kansas City Star*, November 10, 1979, clipping from Frey's player file at the National Baseball Hall of Fame Library.

4. *Kansas City Star*, 1979.

5. *Kansas City Star*, 1979.

Akron Beacon Journal
Chicago Tribune
Cincinnati Enquirer
Kansas City Star
Kansas City Union
New York Post
New York Times
The Sporting News

5. Billy Hunter

1. Billy Hunter, interview by John Grega, April 28, 2003, SABR Oral History Project.

2. *St. Louis Browns Fan Club Spring Newsletter 2006*, clipping in Billy Hunter's player file at the National Baseball Hall of Fame Library, Cooperstown NY.

3. Ronnie Joyner, "Billy Hunter" [clipping], date unknown, in Hunter's file at the National Baseball Hall of Fame Library.

4. *Sports Collectors Digest*, April 18, 1997.

5. Hunter, interview, April 28, 2003.

6. John Eisenberg, *From 33rd Street to Camden Yards* (New York: Contemporary Books, 2001), 166.

7. Billy Hunter, interview by Paul Brown, February 17, 1992, SABR Oral History Project.

8. *The Sporting News*, July 27, 1968.

9. *New York Daily News*, June 15, 1974.

10. *The Miami Herald*, March 8, 1975.

11. Eisenberg, *From 33rd Street to Camden Yards*, 166.

12. Untitled source, October 15, 1977, clipping in Hunter's file at the National Baseball Hall of Fame Library.

13. *The Sporting News*, August 27, 1977.

14. Hunter, interview, April 28, 2003.

Two interviews with Hunter from the SABR Oral History Project were provided by Eileen Canepari of the SABR office. I accessed the February 17, 1992, interview conducted by Paul Brown, and the April 28, 2003, interview conducted by John Grega.

Various articles, Towson University media guides and 1978 Texas Rangers media guide provided by Dan O'Connell, associate director of athletic media relations, Towson University. Received December 2008. Mr. O'Connell's assistance is greatly appreciated.

Various undated articles and newspaper clippings in Gordon W. Hunter's player file at the National Baseball Hall of Fame Library, Cooperstown NY. Special thanks to Gabriel Schechter for his assistance.

6. George Staller

1. John Steadman, "Hitchcock Rings Bell with Choice of Orioles Tutors," *The Sporting News*, November 8, 1961.

2. William C. Kashatus, *Diamonds in the Coalfields: 21 Remarkable Baseball Players, Managers, and Umpires from Northeast Pennsylvania* (Jefferson NC: MacFarland, 2001), 40.

3. William C. Kashatus, *One-Armed Wonder: Pete Gray, Wartime Baseball, and the American Dream* (Jefferson NC: MacFarland, 2001), 30.

4. Tommy Holmes, "Early Call Placed for Rising Dodgers," *The Sporting News*, February 15, 1940.

5. *The Sporting News*, June 14, 1945.

6. "Orioles Fire Coaches Ermer/Staller," *The Sporting News*, October 13, 1962.

7. Earl Weaver with Terry Pluto, *Weaver on Strategy* (Dulles VA: Brassey's, 2002), 119.

8. Doug Brown, "They're Still Birds of Paradise at Home," *The Sporting News*, November 1, 1969.

9. Phil Jackman, "Grapevine Gives Birds True Line of Maddox," *The Sporting News*, May 2, 1970.

7. Looking Ahead to the Season

1. John Eisenberg, *From 33rd Street to Camden Yards* (New York: Contemporary Books, 2001), 219.

2. William Leggett, "Baseball 1970," *Sports Illustrated*, April 13, 1970, 65.

3. Joe Trimble, "American League," *Street and Smith's Official Baseball Yearbook*, 1970, 39.

4. C. C. Johnson Spink, "Flag Winners? Spink Picks Braves and Orioles," *The Sporting News*, April 11, 1970, 9.

8. Don Buford

1. Jerome Holtzman, "Rookie Buford Earns Old Pro Keystoner Tag," *The Sporting News*, April 4, 1964.

2. Paul Wilkes, "Don Buford and the Dignity of a Dirty Uniform," *Sport*, December, 1968.

3. Jean Marbella, "Like Father, Like Son: Damon

Buford Follows in Dad Don Buford's Major-League Footsteps," *Baltimore Sun*, June 20, 1993.

4. Tony White, "Freedom of Choice Is Buford Household Tradition," *Baltimore Afro-American*, August 2, 1997.

5. White, "Freedom of Choice Is Buford Household Tradition."

9. Dave Leonhard

1. Dave Leonhard, telephone interview with author, January 26, 2010.

2. Jim Palmer and Jim Dale, *Together We Were Eleven Foot Nine: The Twenty-Year Friendship of Hall of Fame Pitcher Jim Palmer and Orioles Manager Earl Weaver* (Kansas City MO: Andrews and McMeel, 1996), 36.

3. Phil Berger, "Hopkins' Accidental Big Leaguer," *The Johns Hopkins Magazine* 19, no. 2 (Summer 1968): 16.

4. Berger, "Hopkins' Accidental Big Leaguer," 16.

5. Lou Hatter, "Leonhard Chants New Lyrics to Old Oriole Song of Spring," *The Sporting News*, March 17, 1963.

6. Berger, "Hopkins' Accidental Big Leaguer," 16.

7. Berger, "Hopkins' Accidental Big Leaguer," 18.

8. Berger, "Hopkins' Accidental Big Leaguer," 18.

9. Both quotes are from Berger, "Hopkins' Accidental Big Leaguer," 18.

10. Doug Brown, "Orioles in '68 or I Quit,' Says Perpetual Prospect Leonhard," *The Sporting News*, November 25, 1967; Leonhard, interview.

11. Berger, "Hopkins' Accidental Big Leaguer," 20.

12. Doug Brown, "Mother-in-Law Punctures Leonhard's Balloon," *The Sporting News*, May 18, 1968, 20.

13. Berger, "Hopkins' Accidental Big Leaguer," 20.

14. Both quotes are from Berger, "Hopkins' Accidental Big Leaguer," 18.

15. Berger, "Hopkins' Accidental Big Leaguer," 21.

16. Undated clipping in Dave Leonhard's player file at the National Baseball Hall of Fame Library, Cooperstown NY.

17. Berger, "Hopkins' Accidental Big Leaguer," 21.

18. "Orioles 'Fringe' Pitcher Plugs Gap for Champs," United Press International, May 24, 1971; Leonhard, interview.

19. Phil Jackman, "Ticket Back to the Bushes Irks Dave Leonhard—He Balks," *The Sporting News*, April 24, 1971.

20. Thomas E. Van Hyning, *The Santurce Crabbers: Sixty Seasons of Puerto Rican Winter League Baseball* (Jefferson NC: McFarland, 1999), 119.

21. Leonhard, interview.

22. Palmer and Dale, *Together We Were Eleven Foot Nine*, 37.

23. Van Hyning, *The Santurce Crabbers*, 119.

24. Leonhard, interview.

25. Leonhard, interview.

26. Van Hyning, *The Santurce Crabbers*, 119.

27. Van Hyning, Thomas E., and Eduardo Valero, *Puerto Rico's Winter League: A History of Major League Baseball's Launching Pad* (Jefferson NC: McFarland, 2004), 253.

28. Leonhard, interview.

29. Palmer and Dale, *Together We Were Eleven Foot Nine*, 36.

30. Palmer and Dale, *Together We Were Eleven Foot Nine*, 166.

10. Curt Motton

Thanks to Curt Motton, his widow, Marti Franklin-Motton, and the Motton family for their e-mail correspondence.

Epigraph: Ralph Ray, "Who Needs Speed? Not with Orioles Arsenal," *The Sporting News*, October 16, 1971, 15.

1. Doug Brown, "Orioles Chirping Over May and Motton," *The Sporting News*, May 25, 1968, 8.

2. Brown, "Orioles Chirping."

3. Al C. Weber, "May, Motton Spell Muscle for Wings," *The Sporting News*, June 3, 1967, 35.

4. Larry Whiteside, "Can Motton Crash Brewer Lineup?" *The Sporting News*, January 8, 1972, 36.

5. Tom Keegan, "Elrod Gives the Nod to Worst, Best and Rest," *Baltimore Sun*, May 25, 1994.

6. Doug Brown, "Motton Sees Some Things Right in Winter Troubles," *The Sporting News*, February 7, 1970, 32.

7. Doug Brown, "Motton's Timely Touch in Clutch Hitting Turns on Orioles," *The Sporting News*, September 13, 1969, 4.

8. Brown, "Motton's Timely Touch."

9. Brown, "Motton's Timely Touch."

10. Jeff Seidel, *Baltimore Orioles: Where Have You Gone?* (Champaign IL: Sports Publishing LLC, 2006), 82.

11. Brown, "Motton's Timely Touch."

12. Seidel, *Where Have You Gone*, 82.

13. Roy Firestone, post at Orioles Dugout website, January 23, 2010, http://www.orioleshangout.com.

14. "Curt Motton," *Baltimore Sun*, January 22, 2010.

15. Seidel, *Where Have You Gone*, 82.

11. Jim Palmer

1. *The Sporting News*, July 27, 1963, 35.

2. Joel Cohen, *Jim Palmer—Great Comeback Competitor* (Putnam, 1978).

3. John Eisenberg, *From 33rd Street to Camden Yards* (Contemporary Books, 2001), 198.

4. Eisenberg, *From 33rd Street to Camden Yards*, 199.

5. Jack Zanger, "The Arm That Came Back," *Sport*, August 1969.

6. Eisenberg, *From 33rd Street to Camden Yards*, 273.

7. Eisenberg, *From 33rd Street to Camden Yards*, 275.

8. Eisenberg, *From 33rd Street to Camden Yards*, 273–74.

Palmer, Jim, and Jim Dale. *Together We Were Eleven Foot Nine: The Twenty-Year Friendship of Hall of Fame Pitcher Jim Palmer and Orioles Manager Earl Weaver.* Andrews McMeel, 1991.

12. Dave May

Thanks to Dave May for providing background and details on his career. David May Jr. also helped with background information and arranging contact between the author and his father.

1. Wayne Minshaw, "No Brave Future for Wynn and May," The *Sporting News*, October 16, 1976, 18.

2. Ed Rumill, "Opportunity Knocks at May's Door," *Christian Science Monitor*, June 12, 1972, 8.

3. Rumill, "Opportunity Knocks," 8.

4. Steve Pate, "Evaluating the Trade," *Dallas Morning News*, August 11, 1977, B3.

5. Doug Gelbert, *The Great Delaware Sports Book* (Montchanin DE: Cruden Bay Books, 1995), 106.

6. Scott Ostler, "In the Cage," *Los Angeles Times*, March 18, 1981, E3.

7. Dave May, telephone interview with author, January 15, 2009.

8. Charlie Van Sickel, "The Dutch Rub: Dutch Smorgasbord," *Tri-City Herald*, December 9, 1965, 21.

9. Larry Whiteside, "Fast-Dealing Brewers Corral 3 Pinch-Hitters," *The Sporting News*, June 27, 1970, 6.

10. May, interview, January 15, 2009.

11. May, interview, January 15, 2009.

12. Larry Whiteside, "May Solving Brewers' Center Field Headache," *The Sporting News*, October 3, 1970, 17.

13. Larry Whiteside, "Brewers Peg Attack on May Comeback," *The Sporting News*, November 11, 1972, 45.

14. Lou Chapman, "No Flag, but Brewers Gained Respect in 1973," *The Sporting News*, September 15, 1973, 14.

15. Lou Chapman, "Transplant in April Brings Protest Shower from May," *The Sporting News*, April 27, 1974, 20.

16. "Dave May to Erase 'Trivia' Tag," *Chicago Defender*, March 12, 1975, 24.

17. Minshaw, "No Brave Future," 18.

18. Steve Pate, "Marshall Picks up 6–0 Victory," *Dallas Morning News*, June 16, 1977, B1.

19. May, interview, January 15, 2009.

20. May, interview, January 15, 2009.

21. Dave May, telephone interview with author, March 15, 2009.

22. May, interview, March 15, 2009.

23. May, interview, January 15, 2009.

24. May, interview, March 15, 2009.

25. May, interview, January 15, 2009.

26. May, interview, March 15, 2009.

Appleton (WI) Post Crescent, 1963–64

Atlanta Constitution, 1975–76

Dallas Morning News, 1977

Fresno Bee, 1963

Kingsport (TN) Times-News, 1962

The Sporting News, 1962–80
Syracuse Post-Standard, 1966
Tri-City Herald (Kennewick, Washington), 1965

13. April 1970 Timeline

1. *Baltimore Sun*, April 21, 1970.
2. *Baltimore Sun*, April 24, 1970.

14. Tom Phoebus

1. Phil Jackman, "Pat Dobson Acquired to Fill No. 4 Spot on Oriole Staff," *The Sporting News*, December 19, 1970, 38.
2. Walter L. Johns, "Orioles' Tom Phoebus," *Cumberland News*, March 24, 1967, 34.
3. "St. Joes Wins on No-Hitter," *Baltimore Sun*, April 22, 1959, 23.
4. Mike Klingman, "Catching Up with Former Oriole Tom Phoebus," *Baltimore Sun*, April 28, 2009.
5. Doug Brown, "Phoebus First Rate Oriole Hill Frosh—May Be Starter," *The Sporting News*, March 4, 1967.
6. Bill Vanderschmidt, *Rochester Democrat and Chronicle*, September 14, 1964, September 22, 1964, 2D.
7. Doug Brown, "Red Wing-to-Oriole Trip Short Haul for Phoebus as Bird Flies," *The Sporting News*, January 1, 1966.
8. Klingman, "Catching Up."
9. Bill Vanderschmidt, "No-Hitter for Phoebus," *Rochester Democrat and Chronicle*, August 16, 1966, 1A, 1D, 2D.
10. Mike Gesker, *The Orioles Encyclopedia* (Baltimore: Johns Hopkins University Press, 2009), 406.
11. Gesker, *Orioles Encyclopedia*, 406.
12. Lou Hatter, "Phoebus Hurls 4-Hit Shutout in Debut to Halt Bird Loss," September 19, 1966, C1; "Music Calmed Tom Phoebus," *Baltimore Sun*, September 19, 1966, C6.
13. Lou Hatter, "F. Robinson Hits No. 47 For Orioles," *Baltimore Sun*, September 21, 1966, C1, C3.
14. Lou Hatter, "Rookie Sees Scoreless String Go," *Baltimore Sun*, September 26, 1966, C1, C2.
15. *Baltimore Orioles Media Guide*, 1970.
16. Lou Hatter, "Salary Hike for Phoebus," *Baltimore Sun*, April 29, 1968, C5.

17. Jackman, "Pat Dobson Acquired," 38.
18. Irv Grossman, Press Release, San Diego Padres Baseball Club, April 17, 1971.
19. Klingman, "Catching Up."

15. Dave Johnson

1. Edward Kiersch, "Davey's Destiny," *Cigar Aficionado*, September 1999.
2. Kiersch, "Davey's Destiny."
3. John Eisenberg, *From 33rd Street to Camden Yards* (New York: Contemporary Books, 2001), 134.
4. Furman Bisher, "An Oriole's Aim," *Sport*, April 1967.
5. Kiersch, "Davey's Destiny."
6. Mark Kram, "Mr. Hornsby, Meet, Uh, Mr. Johnson," *Sports Illustrated*, September 17, 1973.
7. Phil Jackman, "Orioles' Johnson Unhappy, Blasts Club Brass," *The Sporting News*, May 30, 1970.
8. Wayne Minshew, "Braves Sure They Landed Quality in 6-Player Swap," *The Sporting News*, December 16, 1972, 52.
9. Wayne Minshew, "Johnson Credits HR Binge to Aaron," *The Sporting News*, November 10, 1973, 30.
10. Robert Whiting, *You Gotta Have Wa* (New York: Macmillan, 1989), 163.
11. Tom Verducci, "Out in the Cold Again," *Sports Illustrated*, February 23, 1998.
12. Harvey Araton, "Former Mets Manager Johnson at Ease in Florida," *New York Times*, July 30, 2010.

16. Jim Hardin

1. "Man in a Hurry," *Oriole News*, June–July 1969.
2. Doug Brown, "Hardin Giving Hitters a Hard Time," *The Sporting News*, June 22, 1968, 3.
3. Brown, "Hardin Giving."
4. Doug Brown, "Hardin Scores as Strong Man of Orioles' Hill," *The Sporting News*, September 23, 1967, 12.
5. Brown, "Hardin Giving."
6. Brown, "Hardin Giving."
7. Brown, "Hardin Giving."
8. Jim Palmer and Jim Dale, *Together We Were Eleven Foot Nine: The Twenty-Year Friendship of Hall of Fame Pitcher Jim Palmer and Orioles Manager Earl Weaver* (Kansas City MO: Andrews McMeel, 1996), 24.

9. Brown, "Hardin Giving," 3.

10. Palmer and Dale, *Together We Were Eleven Foot Nine*, 24.

11. Palmer and Dale, *Together We Were Eleven Foot Nine*, 24.

12. Jim Palmer, interview with author, May 17, 2008, Oriole Park, Camden Yards.

13. Palmer, interview.

14. Oscar Kahan, "Pitchers Moan, Batters Skeptical of Low Hill," *The Sporting News*, March 29, 1969, 15.

15. Doug Brown, "Back Pains Plague Hardin, So Do Tough AL Sockers," *The Sporting News*, June 14, 1969, 10.

16. "Gophers Hurt Hardin," *The Sporting News*, August 2, 1969, 24.

17. Wayne Minshew, "Braves Salvage Jewel off Junk Heap: Jim Hardin," *The Sporting News*, July 29, 1972, 3.

18. "The Death of Ex-Oriole Jim Hardin," Misc Baseball (website), http://miscbaseball.wordpress.com /2009/05/21/the-death-of-ex-oriole-jim-hardin/.

19. Both quotes in this paragraph are from "Death of Ex-Oriole Jim Hardin."

17. Elrod Hendricks

Grateful acknowledgment to Ellie Hendricks for providing his memories (in personal interviews with the author, July 1999 and May 2001, in the clubhouse at Yankee Stadium, home of his childhood favorites) and to Jim Palmer (personal interview with the author, May 2001, Yankee Stadium, May 2001). Unless otherwise noted, quotes from Hendricks and Palmer are from these interviews.

1. Bob Cairns, *Pen Men* (New York: St. Martin's Press, 1993), 300.

2. "Hank Aaron Comes to Terms with Milwaukee for $40,000," *Los Angeles Times*, February 2, 1959.

3. Pat Jordan, *A False Spring* (New York: Dodd, Mead, 1975).

4. Thomas E. Van Hyning, *Puerto Rico's Winter League* (Jefferson NC: McFarland, 1995), 129.

5. Van Hyning, *Puerto Rico's Winter League*.

6. Ron Luciano and David Fisher, *The Umpire Strikes Back* (New York: Bantam, 1982).

7. Jim Henneman, "Elrod's Endless Appeal," *Baltimore Sun*, November 7, 1994, C1.

8. Lou Hatter, "Hendricks Shelved by Mystery Ailment," *The Sporting News*, May 27, 1972.

9. Lou Hatter, "Hendricks Ready if Williams Runs into Traffic," *The Sporting News*, June 2, 1973.

10. Frank Robinson and Berry Stainback, *Extra Innings* (New York: McGraw-Hill, 1988), 2–3; Thomas E. Van Hyning, *The Santurce Crabbers* (Jefferson NC: McFarland, 1999), 119.

11. Henneman, "Elrod's Endless Appeal," C1.

12. Norman L. Macht, "The Night Elrod Pitched," *The National Pastime*, no. 16 (Cleveland: SABR, 1996).

18. Chico Salmon

1. *Baltimore Sun*, October 12, 1970, n.p.

2. *New York Times*, July 26, 1970, 5.

3. *The Sporting News*, July 15, 1967, 30.

4. *The Sporting News*, June 11, 1966, 9.

5. *The Sporting News*, April 17, 1971.

6. *Baseball Digest*, February 1969, 63.

7. *The Sporting News*, April 10, 1969, 19.

8. *Baseball Digest*, June 1968, 6–7.

9. *The Sporting News*, May 20, 1967, 18.

10. *The Sporting News*, June 18, 1966, 8.

11. *The Sporting News*, May 22, 1966, 6.

12. *The Sporting News*, July 23, 1966, 19.

13. *The Sporting News*, July 16, 1966, 45.

14. *Cleveland Plain Dealer*, March 9, 1967, 66.

15. *Cleveland Plain Dealer*, June 14, 1968, 56.

16. *St. Petersburg Times*, October 16, 1968, C-1.

17. *The Sporting News*, April 12, 1969, n.p.

18. *Baltimore Sun*, August 18, 1969, C1.

19. *The Sporting News*, April 17, 1971.

20. *The Sporting News*, March 25, 1972.

21. *Baltimore Sun*, August 23, 1972, C5.

22. *Cleveland Plain Dealer*, April 7, 1973.

23. *Baltimore Sun*, May 24, 1994.

19. May 1970 Timeline

1. *Baltimore Sun*, May 22, 1970.

20. Boog Powell

1. *Baseball Digest*, February 1987, 88.

2. *Miami News*, March 7, 1962, 2C.

3. *Baseball Digest*, February 1987, 86.

4. *The Sporting News*, February 28, 1962, 14.

5. *The Sporting News*, February 28, 1962, 5.

6. *The Sporting News*, March 14, 1962, 31.

7. *The Sporting News*, April 20, 1963, 17.

8. *The Sporting News*, August 24, 1963, 16.

9. *The Sporting News*, September 12, 1970, 6.

10. *The Sporting News*, November 28, 1970, 39.

11. *The Sporting News*, June 24, 1972, 4.

12. *The Sporting News*, October 7, 1972, 13.

13. *The Sporting News*, October 5, 1974, 3.

14. *The Sporting News*, March 15, 1975, 42.

15. *The Sporting News*, April 26, 1975, 5.

16. *Utica Observer-Dispatch*, August 24, 1975, 61.

17. *Baltimore Sun*, July 15, 1986, 6D.

18. *Baltimore Sun*, April 10, 2010.

21. Clay Dalrymple

Grateful acknowledgment to Clay Dalrymple for his phone interviews with the author (May 11 and May 23, 2008). Thanks also to SABR member Alfonso Tusa for Dalrymple's Venezuelan stats.

1. Bob Fowler, "Twins Sing the Praises of Unsung Borgmann," *The Sporting News*, July 28, 1979, 17.

2. Unless otherwise noted, quotes and information from Dalrymple are from the phone interviews the author conducted with him on May 11 and May 23, 2008.

3. Debra Moon, *Chico: Life and Times of a City of Fortune* (Charleston SC: Arcadia Publishing, 2003), 134.

4. Eddie Mullens, "Mullen It Over," *Amarillo Globe-Times*, July 30, 1957, 12.

5. *The Sporting News*, August 27, 1958, 42.

6. Allen Lewis, "Phillies Banking on Malkmus for 3rd Time Charm," *The Sporting News*, December 9, 1959, 16.

7. William C. Kashatus, *September Swoon: Richie Allen, the '64 Phillies, and Racial Integration* (State College: Pennsylvania State University Press, 2005), 54.

8. Allan Lewis, "Phils Size Up Dalrymple as Top Backstop," *The Sporting News*, November 8, 1961, 22.

9. Sam Carchidi, "Gene Mauch: A Strategist—An Innovator—A Great Manager," *Baseball Digest*, December 1, 2005.

10. Robert Gordon, *Legends of the Philadelphia Phillies* (Champaign IL: Sports Publishing LLC, 2005), 44.

11. Doug Brown, "Clay Ticketed for Backup Catching Job with Orioles," *The Sporting News*, February 8, 1969, 41; Phil Jackman, "Stronger Bench Causing Orioles to Raise Sights," *The Sporting News*, April 12, 1969, 27.

12. Doug Brown, "Bench-Rider Role Can Tire You Out, Dalrymple Claims," *The Sporting News*, December 13, 1969, 39.

13. Stan Hochman, "The Survivors of '64: Part Three—Clay Dalrymple," *Philadelphia Daily News*, July 18, 1989, 68.

14. Brown, "Bench-Rider Role."

15. "Clay Dalrymple Hangs 'Em Up," *Delaware County Daily Times*, Upper Darby, Pennsylvania, December 15, 1971, 27.

16. Chuck Rosciam, *The Encyclopedia of Baseball Catchers*, http://members.tripod.com/bb_catchers/catchers/.

Gutiérrez, Daniel, Efraim Álvarez, and Daniel Gutiérrez Jr. *La Enciclopedia del Béisbol en Venezuela*. Caracas, Venezuela: Editorial Norma, 2007.

www.goldenbaseball.com/Chico

Old-Time Data, Inc. The Professional Baseball Player Database, v6.0. 1995-2007. http://www.baseball-almanac.com/minor-league/

22. Mike Cuellar

1. John Eisenberg, *From 33rd Street to Camden Yards* (New York: Contemporary Books, 2001), 202.

2. *The Sporting News*, June 19, 1957.

3. *The Sporting News*, October 7, 1959; October 14, 1959.

4. *The Sporting News*, October 7, 1959; October 14, 1959.

5. *St. Louis Post Dispatch*, August 27, 1964.

6. Eisenberg, *From 33rd Street to Camden Yards*, 201.

7. Eisenberg, *From 33rd Street to Camden Yards*, 204.

8. Earl Weaver and Berry Stainback, *It's What You Learn after You Know It All That Counts* (New York: Doubleday, 1982), 239.

9. Richard Goldstein, "Mike Cuellar, Star Pitcher for Orioles, Dies at 72," *New York Times*, April 5, 2010.

E-mail correspondence with Colon Delgado, Jorge, and Alberto "Tito" Rondon of SABR's Latino Baseball Committee

Thornley, Stew. "Minneapolis Millers vs. Havana Sugar Kings." *The National Pastime,* no. 12. Cleveland OH: SABR, 1992.

23. Eddie Watt

1. Eddie Watt, telephone interview with author, December 7, 2008.

2. Watt, interview.

3. Watt, interview.

4. Watt, interview.

5. Watt, interview.

6. Watt, interview.

7. Watt, interview.

8. Watt, interview.

9. Watt, interview.

10. Watt, interview.

11. Doug Brown, "Watt's One-for-the-Road Drink Full of Bird Bitters," *The Sporting News*, December 29, 1973, 34.

12. Russ Corbitt, "Watt Hopes Wichita Pen Leads to Major Dividend," *The Sporting News*, May 24, 1975, 38.

13. Watt, interview.

14. Watt, interview.

24. Merv Rettenmund

1. Brian Hiro, "Hitters Warming up to Rettenmund's Advice," *North County Times*, June 24, 2006.

2. United States Census, Ancestry.com, and Roots Web.com, accessed December 16, 2008.

3. Merv Rettenmund, telephone interview with author, January 12, 2009.

4. Robert Markus, "Rettenmund So Wrong, He's Right," *Chicago Tribune*, October 10, 1971.

5. Rettenmund, interview.

6. Dan Nilsen, "1961 Buick Colts Baseball Team," *The Flint Journal*, http://blog.mlive.com/flintjournal/sports/2007/11/1961_buick_colts_baseball_team.html, accessed December 23, 2008.

7. Rettenmund, interview; John Ginter, "Baseball at Ball State," Ball State University Alumni Association, http://bsu.edu/alumni/march2003/sportsfeature/, accessed December 9, 2008.

8. Ed Rumill, "Rookie Balks at No. 4 Idea," *Christian Science Monitor*, March 31, 1969; Doug Brown, "Orioles Find a Place for Rookie Merv's Mighty Bat," *The Sporting News*, September 28, 1968, 11.

9. Brown, "Orioles Find a Place for Rookie Merv's Mighty Bat."

10. Rettenmund, interview; Shaun O'Neill, "Padres inside Pitch," *North County Times*, April 27, 1997.

11. "Bunker, Rookie Help Orioles Sweep A's," *Chicago Tribune*, August 28, 1968; "Orioles Beat A's 5–3 in First Game," *Hartford Courant*, August 28, 1968.

12. Rettenmund, interview.

13. Rettenmund, interview.

14. Rettenmund, interview.

15. Ron Fimrite, "Well, He's That Kind of Guy," *Sports Illustrated*, October 4, 1971.

16. Doug Brown, "Birds' Slump-Ridden Merv Making Mark as Prankster," *The Sporting News*, August 18, 1973.

17. Mark Heisler, "Homecoming for the Anaheim Chapter of the Oriole Alumni," *Los Angeles Times*, September 28, 1979; Lynn Henning, "Rettenmund Works on Batting, Psyche"; Rettenmund, interview.

18. Rettenmund, interview.

19. Phil Collier, "Rettenmund Chants a Hymn of Thanks for Padre Trade," *The Sporting News*, June 5, 1976, 11; Rettenmund, interview.

20. Rettenmund, interview; David Porter and Joe Naiman, *The San Diego Padres Encyclopedia* (Champaign IL: Sports Publishing LLC, 2002), 49.

21. Rettenmund, interview.

22. Rettenmund, interview.

23. Ross Newhan, "Angels Get 'Tough' with Blue Jays," *Los Angeles Times*, June 9, 1982.

24. Rettenmund, interview.

25. Rettenmund, interview.

26. Chris Jenkins, "An Eye on the Ball," *Baseball Digest*, September 2002.

27. Rettenmund, interview.

28. Shaun O'Neill, "Rettenmund Decides to Head South," *North County Times*, November 9, 1999; Rettenmund, interview.

29. Rettenmund, interview.

30. Rettenmund, interview.

31. Rettenmund, interview.

25. June 1970 Timeline

1. *Baltimore Sun*, June 7, 1970.

2. *Baltimore Sun*, June 26, 1970.

26. Frank Robinson

1. Ken Nigro, ed., *A 30 Year History: 1984 Orioles Yearbook* (Baltimore: Stadia, 1984), 43; Ted Patterson, *The Baltimore Orioles: Four Decades of Magic from 33rd Street to Camden Yards* (Dallas: Taylor Publishing Company, 2000), 89, 121.

2. Russell J. Schneider, *Frank Robinson: The Making of a Manager* (New York: Coward, McCann & Geoghegan, 1976), 22.

3. Brad Snyder, *A Well-Paid Slave: Curt Flood's Fight for Free Agency in Professional Sports* (New York: Viking Press, 2006), 38.

4. Frank Robinson and Berry Stainback, *Extra Innings: The Grand Slam Response to Al Campanis' Controversial Remarks about Blacks in Baseball* (New York: McGraw-Hill, 1988), 23.

5. Robinson and Stainback, *Extra Innings*, 25.

6. Robinson and Stainback, *Extra Innings*, 26.

7. Earl Weaver and Berry Stainback, *It's What You Learn after You Know It All That Counts* (Garden City NY: Doubleday, 1982), 164.

8. Robinson and Stainback, *Extra Innings*, 33.

9. Eddie Mathews and Bob Buege, *Eddie Mathews and the National Pastime* (Milwaukee: Douglas American Sports Publications, 1994), 198.

10. Tom Adelman, *Black and Blue: Sandy Koufax, the Robinson Boys, and the World Series That Stunned America* (New York: Little, Brown, 2006), 2.

11. Robinson and Stainback, *Extra Innings*, 50–51.

12. Lonnie Wheeler and John Baskin, *The Cincinnati Game* (Wilmington OH: Orange Frazer Press, 1988), 157.

13. Patterson, *Baltimore Orioles*, 121.

14. Adelman, *Black and Blue*, 13; Patterson, *Baltimore Orioles,* 83; John Eisenberg, *From 33rd Street to Camden Yards: An Oral History of the Baltimore Orioles* (New York: Contemporary Books, 2001), 172.

15. Robinson and Stainback, *Extra Innings,* 59–60; Adelman, *Black and Blue,* 5, 19.

16. Doug Brown, "Baltimore Bugle Call Rag Leaves Injuns in Tatters," *The Sporting News*, May 21, 1966, 8; Frank Robinson and Al Silverman, *My Life Is Baseball*, 2nd ed. (Garden City NY: Doubleday, 1975), 183.

17. Eisenberg, *From 33rd Street to Camden Yards*, 164; Patterson, *Baltimore Orioles*, 85.

18. Adelman, *Black and Blue*, 126.

19. Patterson, *Baltimore Orioles*, 88; Bob Brown and Fran Moulden, eds., *Baltimore Orioles 1971 World Series Souvenir Program* (Baltimore: The Baltimore Orioles, 1971), 75.

20. Patterson, *Baltimore Orioles*, 113; "O's Earmark 'Kangaroo' Fines to Corrales Kids," *Baltimore Afro-American*, August 23, 1969, 7.

21. Patterson, *Baltimore Orioles*, 96.

22. Robert Goldman, *Once They Were Angels: A History of the Team* (Champaign IL: Sports Publishing LLC, 2006), 112.

23. Schneider, *Frank Robinson*, 38, 102; Larry Burke and Peter Thomas Fornatale, *Change Up: An Oral History of 8 Key Events that Shaped Modern Baseball* (New York: Rodale, 2008), 191.

24. Schneider, *Frank Robinson*.

27. Don Baylor

1. Jack Friedman, "For Don Baylor, Baseball Is a Hit or Be Hit Proposition," *People*, August 24, 1987.

2. Don Baylor, *Nothing but the Truth: A Baseball Life* (New York: St. Martin's Press, 1990), 47.

3. Baylor, *Nothing but the Truth*, 32.

4. Baylor, *Nothing but the Truth*, 38–39.

5. Baylor, *Nothing but the Truth*, 44–45.

6. Baylor, *Nothing but the Truth*, 52.

7. Baylor, *Nothing but the Truth*, 60.

8. Baylor, *Nothing but the Truth*, 68.

9. Baylor, *Nothing but the Truth*, 92.

10. Baylor, *Nothing but the Truth*, 125.

11. Friedman, "For Don Baylor."

12. Howard Blatt, "Ultimate Player's Manager Baylor Is Tough but Fair with Rockies," *New York Daily News*, July 15, 1995.

Gutiérrez, Daniel, Efraim Álvarez, and Daniel Gutiérrez, Jr. *La Enciclopedia del Béisbol en Venezuela.* Caracas, Venezuela: Editorial Norma, 2007.

Neff, Craig. "His Honor, Don Baylor." *Sports Illustrated*, June 16, 1986.

28. Marcelino Lopez

1. Roy Firestone, post at Orioles Dugout website, August 4, 2008, http://forum.orioleshangout.com/forums/showthread.php?t=68124.

2. "Philadelphia Phillies," *Sports Illustrated*, April 9, 1962.

3. Allen Lewis, "Teen-age Hill Flash Tabbed Phils' Starter," *The Sporting News*, April 13, 1963, 38.

4. "Trav Hurler Fined $27.50, Tossed Ball over Stands," *The Sporting News*, August 3, 1963, 33.

5. Ross Newhan, "Rig and Grissom Hand Starting Job to Ex-Phil Lopez," *The Sporting News*, April 10, 1965, 15.

6. Newhan, "Rig and Grissom."

7. Newhan, "Rig and Grissom."

8. Ross Newhan, "Chance, Newman, May, Lopez—Angels Flashy Big Four," *The Sporting News*, May 15, 1965, 22.

9. Newhan, "Chance, Newman, May, Lopez."

10. Eduardo Moncada, "Lefty Lopez Earns Raves as Mr. Shutout of Latin Loop," *The Sporting News*, January 22, 1966, 25.

11. Ross Newhan, "Tired Lopez to Pass up Winter Ball," *The Sporting News*, October 8, 1966, 39.

12. Newhan, "Tired Lopez."

13. Doug Brown, "Orioles Testing Question Mark Men on Mound," *The Sporting News*, October 7, 1967, 29.

14. Doug Brown, "Tearful Exit Scene . . . Then Sweet Success for Lopez," *The Sporting News*, July 12, 1969, 11.

15. Brown, "Tearful Exit."

16. Firestone, post at Orioles Dugout website.

17. Marcelino Lopez, interview with Chuck Thompson following final game of 1970 World Series, October 15, 1970, video available at mlb.com.

18. Firestone, post at Orioles Dugout website.

19. Larry Whiteside, "Brewer Patience Pays off in Lopez," *The Sporting News*, April 24, 1971, 22.

20. Firestone, post at Orioles Dugout website.

29. Mark Belanger

1. Pat Jordan, "Years ahead of His Time," *Sports Illustrated*, July 29, 1974, 44.

2. Doug Brown, "Belanger Army Call Could Help Birds," *The Sporting News*, March 16, 1963, 69.

3. *Baseball Digest*, September 1980, 84.

4. *Baltimore Sun*, August 8, 1965, A2.

5. *The Sporting News*, March 25, 1967, 9.

6. *Baltimore Sun*, August 8, 1965, A2.

7. *Baseball Digest*, March 1967, 17.

8. Both quotes in the paragraph are from *The Sporting News*, February 25, 1967, 10.

9. *Baltimore Sun*, March 1, 1967, C4.

10. *The Sporting News*, September 21, 1968, 11.

11. *Baltimore Sun*, September 20, 1978, C7.

12. *Baseball Weekly*, June 30, 1993, 71.

13. *Chicago Tribune*, October 16, 1969; *Baseball Digest*, August 1988, 20.

14. *Baseball Digest*, December 1971, 71.

15. *The Sporting News*, August 22, 1970, 10.

16. *Wall Street Journal*, July 2, 1976, 1.

17. *Sports Illustrated*, September 26, 1977, 62.

18. *Baltimore Sun*, October 2, 1977, C12.

19. *The Sporting News*, September 30, 1978, 9.

20. *Baltimore Sun*, September 20, 1981.

21. *Baltimore Sun*, October 1, 1981.

22. *Baltimore Sun*, October 5, 1981, C1.

23. *Los Angeles Times*, May 9, 1982.

24. *Sports Illustrated*, March 8, 1993.

Belanger, Ed (brother of Mark Belanger). Telephone interview conducted by author.

Henneman, Jim (TSN Baltimore correspondent, 1976–78). Interview conducted by author.

Nigro, Ken (*Baltimore Sun* beat writer, 1969–78, and TSN correspondent 1977–79). Telephone interview conducted by author.

30. Dick Hall

1. Ed Rumill, "The Pitching Machine: Hall Has 'Built-In File on Every Hitter,'" *Christian Science Monitor*, June 25, 1970.

2. Dick Hall, interview, November 22, 1999, SABR Oral History database.

3. Rex Barney, with Norman L. Macht, *Rex Barney's Orioles Memories, 1969–1994* (Woodbury CT: Goodwood Press, 1994), 137.

4. Barney and Macht, *Rex Barney's Orioles Memories*, 212.

5. Hall, interview.

6. There are numerous speculative accounts of the size of Hall's bonus, ranging from $25,000 to $45,000. In his 1999 interview in SABR's Oral History database, however, Hall remembered the amount as $25,000.

7. Unattributed clipping in Dick Hall's player file at the National Baseball Hall of Fame Library, Cooperstown NY.

8. Ray Kelly, "Swarthmore's Dick Hall Is Finally 'Put in His Place'; Pitching Well for Bucs," *Philadelphia Sunday Bulletin*, August 14, 1955.

9. Kelly, "Swarthmore's Dick Hall."

10. Unattributed clipping in Hall's file at the National Baseball Hall of Fame Library.

11. Unattributed clipping in Hall's file at the National Baseball Hall of Fame Library.

12. Unattributed clipping in Hall's file at the National Baseball Hall of Fame Library.

13. Brooks Robinson, with Fred Bauer, *Putting It All Together* (Hawthorn Books, 1971), 58.

14. Phil Jackman, "Hall Credits Ex-Manager," *The Sporting News*, October 13, 1970.

15. "Comeback Kid," July 25, 1955, unattributed clipping in Hall's file at the National Baseball Hall of Fame Library.

16. Untitled clipping, June 16, 1967, in Hall's file at the National Baseball Hall of Fame Library.

17. Untitled clipping, July 1, 1967, in Hall's file at the National Baseball Hall of Fame Library.

18. "Cincinnati Joins Mexico in Hall's Legend," *Newsday*, October 12, 1970.

19. "Cincinnati Joins Mexico."

20. Untitled clipping, July 17, 1967, in Hall's file at the National Baseball Hall of Fame Library.

21. Hall, interview.

22. Hall, interview.

23. Hall, interview.

24. Hall, interview.

25. Untitled clipping, July 10, 1965, in Hall's file at the National Baseball Hall of Fame Library.

26. Lowell Reidenbaugh, "Hall Stands Tall; Orioles Go Two Up," *The Sporting News*, October 24, 1970.

27. Barney and Macht, *Rex Barney's Orioles Memories*.

28. Hall, interview.

29. Doug Brown, "'Perfect Game' by Reliever Hall: Retired 28 in Row over 25 Days," *The Sporting News*, August 31, 1963, 10.

30. Doug Brown, "Hitters Flunk in Facing Scholar Hall: Oriole Bull-Pen Ace Looks Awkward, Has Jerky Style," *The Sporting News*, July 25, 1964.

31. Doug Brown, "Hall Newest Victim of Player Rep Jinx," *The Sporting News*, December 31, 1966, 28.

32. Hall, interview.

33. Doug Brown, "Dick Hall Tireless and Oriole Re-tread," *The Sporting News*, April 19, 1969, 4.

34. All quotes appeared in the *Baltimore Sun*, October 12, 1970.

35. Both quotes are from "Cincinnati Joins Mexico in Hall's Legend."

36. Rumill, "The pitching machine."

37. Mike Klingaman, "Catching Up with Ex-Oriole Dick Hall," *Baltimore Sun*, May 26, 2009.

31. July 1970 Timeline

1. *Baltimore Sun*, July 5, 1970.

2. *Baltimore Sun*, July 9, 1970.

3. *Baltimore Sun*, July 15, 1970.

32. Pete Richert

1. *The Sporting News*, September 25, 1965.

2. *The Sporting News*, September 25, 1965.

3. *The Sporting News*, September 25, 1965.

4. *The Sporting News*, July 16, 1966.

5. *The Sporting News*, July 16, 1966.

33. Paul Blair

1. Robert Lipsyte, "Sports of the Times," *New York Times*, October 11, 1964.

2. USA *Today Baseball Weekly*, July 10–15, 1997.

3. Lipsyte, "Sports of the Times."

4. *The Sporting News*, May 8, 1965.

5. USA *Today Baseball Weekly*, July 10–15, 1997.

6. USA *Today Baseball Weekly*, July 10–15, 1997.

7. *The Sun Magazine*, a publication of *The Baltimore Sun*, June 2, 1968.

8. Benjamin M. Branham, "Paul Blair," Gale Contemporary Black Biography, Answers.com, http://www.answers.com/topic/paul-blair-baseball, accessed May 14, 2007.

Baltimore Orioles Media Guide, 1970.

Personal conversations with SABR members Gabriel Schechter, Malcolm Allen, and Jan Finkel.

34. Terry Crowley

Epigraph: Jim Henneman, "Crowley Fattens Up as Orioles Cinch in Pinch," *The Sporting News*, August 5, 1978, 13.

1. Terry Crowley, telephone interview with the author, May 17, 2008.

2. Crowley, interview.

3. Crowley, interview.

4. Doug Brown, "Orioles Chirp-Chirp over Fledgling Flyhawk Baylor," *The Sporting News*, November 30, 1968.

5. Crowley, interview.

6. Louis Berney, *Tales from the Orioles Dugout* (Champaign IL: Sports Publishing LLC, 2004), 102.

7. Crowley, interview.

8. Crowley, interview.

9. Phil Jackman, "Crowley in Boxing Form for O's Job," *The Sporting News*, March 11, 1972, 30.

10. Berney, *Tales from the Orioles Dugout*, 104.

11. Lou Hatter, "Baylor, Grich, Crowley: Orioles Jewels," *The Sporting News*, June 24, 1972, 3.

12. "Crowley's Confident," *The Sporting News*, March 30, 1974, 55.

13. Crowley, interview.

14. "Crowley Doesn't Belong in International League," *The Sporting News*, August 13, 1977, 33.

15. "Crowley Doesn't Belong," 33.

16. "Crowley Doesn't Belong," 33.

17. Crowley, interview.

18. Ken Nigro, "Crowley Gives O's Punch in a Pinch," *The Sporting News*, June 21, 1980, 35.

19. Ken Nigro, "'Deep Depth' Cited for Oriole Sky Course," *The Sporting News*, July 21, 1979, 12.

20. Jim Henneman, "Crowley Fattens Up," 13.

21. Crowley, interview.

22. Ken Nigro, "Pinch-Hitter Deluxe Crowley Is a Victim of His Own Talent," *The Sporting News*, April 4, 1981, 50.

23. Nigro, "Pinch-Hitter Deluxe Crowley."

24. Jim Henneman, "Crowley Shocked by Orioles Release," *The Sporting News*, April 18, 1983, 24.

25. Crowley, interview.

26. Crowley, interview.

27. Crowley, interview.

28. "Crowley Takes Over As Batting Coach," *The Sporting News*, November 26, 1990, 41.

29. Crowley, interview.

30. Crowley, interview.

35. Bobby Grich

1. Larry Eldridge, "Grich—He Can Beat You in So Many Ways," *Christian Science Monitor*, September 27, 1974, 13.

2. Bobby Grich, e-mail correspondence with author, August 20, 2009.

3. Arthur Daley, "Man with a Vowel Shortage," *New York Times*, August 6, 1972.

4. Curt Gowdy, title, date, and publication illegible, clipping from Bobby Grich's player file at the National Baseball Hall of Fame Library, Cooperstown, NY.

5. Robert Matthews, "Grich Was Best in Minors; Will He Get Shot with O's?" December 4, 1971, name of publication unknown, clipping from Grich's file at the National Baseball Hall of Fame Library.

6. "Bobby Grich," author, date, and name of publication unknown, clipping from Grich's file at the National Baseball Hall of Fame Library.

7. Phil Jackman, "O's Have Real Hardnose in Infielder Bobby Grich," *The Sporting News*, February 5, 1972.

8. Matthews, "Grich Was Best in Minors."

9. Matthews, "Grich Was Best in Minors."

10. Matthews, "Grich Was Best in Minors."

11. "Dynasty Started with Frank Robby," author, date, and name of publication unknown, clipping from Grich's file at the National Baseball Hall of Fame Library.

12. Bob Matthews, "Old Times High Times for Grich," *Albany Times Union*, July 1987.

13. Lou Hatter, "Grich Shrugs off Tributes—Points to Flaws in His Play," *The Sporting News*, October 14, 1972.

14. Mark Heisler, "Old Orioles: Four Angels with 'Scars' from Baltimore," *Dallas Times Herald*, October 2, 1979, 4-D.

15. Heisler, "Old Orioles."

16. Lou Hatter, "Grich Ready for 'Super Job' as Second Baseman," *The Sporting News*, February 24, 1973.

17. Eldridge, "Grich—He Can Beat You," 13.

18. Doug Brown, "Grich, with Itch to Travel, Turns on His Power Switch," *The Sporting News*, August 24, 1974.

19. Grich, e-mail.

20. Jim Henneman, "O's May Peddle Unsigned Grich," *The Sporting News*, May 29, 1976.

21. Dick Miller, "Star-Kissed Angels Rejoice with Grich," date and name of publication unknown, clipping from Grich's file at the National Baseball Hall of Fame Library.

22. Dick Miller, "'Never Be as Good as I Was'—Grich," March 31, 1979, name of publication unknown, clipping from Grich's file at the National Baseball Hall of Fame Library.

23. Tracy Ringolsby, "Bobby Grich from Pits to Peaks," *The Sporting News*, October 12, 1979, 21–22.

24. Ringolsby, "Bobby Grich."

25. Ringolsby, "Bobby Grich."

26. "Bobby Grich—Best Year Ever," *California Angels Spring Training Scorebook,* 1980.

27. Grich Is Going for Gold," *California Angels Yearbook*, 1980.

28. "Angels: Grich Streaking," author, date, name of publication unknown, clipping from Grich's file at the National Baseball Hall of Fame Library.

29. "Bobby Grich Is Happy with Angels Contract," *New York Times*, November 8, 1981.

30. Paul Gutierrez, "Bobby Grich, California Angels Infielder, October 20, 1986," *Sports Illustrated*, May 18, 1998, 10.

31. Grich, e-mail.

32. Grich, e-mail.

33. Grich, e-mail.

36. Moe Drabowsky

Many thanks to Steve Freeman of the Baltimore Orioles and Rita Drabowsky for sharing their memories of Moe Drabowsky. Thanks also to the Hall of Fame Library and Retrosheet.

1. David Condon, "In the Wake of the News," *Chicago Tribune*, October 6, 1966.

2. Condon, "In the Wake of the News."

3. Condon, "In the Wake of the News."

4. *Chicago American*, September 2, 1956.

5. Unattributed clipping, August 29, 1956, from Moe Drabowsky's player file at the National Baseball Hall of Fame Library, Cooperstown NY.

6. *Chicago American*, September 2, 1956.

7. Unattributed clipping, September 17, 1956, from Drabowsky's file at the National Baseball Hall of Fame Library.

8. Condon, "In the Wake of the News."

9. Condon, "In the Wake of the News."

10. James Enright, "Lopat Saved My Career: Drabowsky," *Chicago American*, October 6, 1966.

11. *The Sporting News*, February 26, 1966.

12. Unattributed clipping, 1965, from Drabowsky's file at the National Baseball Hall of Fame Library.

13. Doug Brown, March 12, 1966, unattributed clipping from Drabowsky's file at the National Baseball Hall of Fame Library.

14. Condon, "In the Wake of the News."

15. Unattributed clipping, 1972, from Drabowsky's file at the National Baseball Hall of Fame Library.

16. Condon, "In the Wake of the News."

17. *The Sporting News*, July 2, 1966.

18. Condon, "In the Wake of the News."

19. Doug Brown, *The Sporting News*, October 22, 1966.

20. Condon, "In the Wake of the News."

21. Stan Innes, October 6, 1966, unattributed clipping from Drabowsky's file at the National Baseball Hall of Fame Library.

22. Larry Merchant, July 29, 1971, unattributed clipping from Drabowsky's file at the National Baseball Hall of Fame Library.

23. Joe McGuff, "Five Cs Put Moe in Big Money as Royal Reliever," *The Sporting News*, April 18, 1970.

24. McGuff, "Five Cs."

25. McGuff, "Five Cs."

26. McGuff, "Five Cs."

27. Unattributed clipping, 1970, from Drabowsky's file at the National Baseball Hall of Fame Library.

28. *Willimantic* (CT) *Chronicle*, August 22, 1983.

29. Bill Ordine, "O's Series Hero Was Prankster, Too." *Baltimore Sun*, June 11, 2006, http://www.baltimoresun.com/sports/bal-sp.drabowsky11jun11,0,6656011.story.

30. Unattributed clipping, 1972, from Drabowsky's file at the National Baseball Hall of Fame Library.

31. Associated Press, "Prankster Pitcher Moe Drabowsky Dies at Age 70," June 12, 2006, http://sports.espn.go.com/mlb/news/story?id=2480037.

32. Rita Drabowsky, telephone interview with author, March 2010.

37. August 1970 Timeline

1. *Baltimore Sun*, August 12, 1970.

38. Andy Etchebarren

1. Doug Brown, "Handy Andy Pressure-Proof Bird Prize," *The Sporting News*, October 8, 1966, 9.

39. Bobby Floyd

1. Bobby Floyd, telephone interview with author, October 28, 2008.

2. Floyd, interview.

3. Floyd, interview.

4. Floyd, interview.

5. Floyd, interview.

6. Floyd, interview.

7. Floyd, interview.

8. Doug Brown, "Mind over Matter—Floyd's Story," *The Sporting News*, October 4, 1969.

9. Floyd, interview.

10. Doug Brown, "Orioles Have Two Vacancies . . . Starting Hurler, Spare Infielder," *The Sporting News*, March 1, 1969.

11. Floyd, interview.

12. Joe McGuff, "Deadline Trades for Floyd, Rojas Bolster Royal Infield," *The Sporting News*, July 4, 1970.

13. McGuff, "Deadline Trades."

14. Floyd, interview.

15. Bob Williams, "Champ Royals Hoist Toast to Sandy," *The Sporting News*, September 26, 1970.

16. Unattributed clipping from Bobby Floyd's player file at the National Baseball Hall of Fame Library, Cooperstown NY.

40. Roger Freed

1. *St. Louis Dispatch*, May 2, 1979, 2.

2. *The Sporting News*, May 5, 1968, 43.

3. *The Sporting News*, February 20, 1971, 36.

4. *The Sporting News*, February 20, 1971.

5. *The Sporting News*, July 17, 1971, 38.

6. *Syracuse Herald*, July 20, 1977.

7. *The Sporting News*, August 28, 1976, 34.

8. *The Sporting News*, August 28, 1976.

9. The Associated Press, August 23, 1977, unattributed clipping in Roger Freed's player file at the National Baseball Hall of Fame Library, Cooperstown NY.

10. Unattributed clipping in Freed's player file at the National Baseball Hall of Fame Library.

11. Unattributed clipping in Freed's file at the National Baseball Hall of Fame Library.

41. Dave McNally

1. Phil Jackman, "McNally Named Legion Grad of Year," *The Sporting News*, June 26, 1971.

2. Ed West, "Montana's Greatest Athlete Falls to Cancer at Age 60," *Billings Gazette*, December 3, 2002.

3. John Eisenberg, *From 33rd Street to Camden Yards* (New York: Contemporary Books, 2001), 33–34.

4. Eisenberg, *From 33rd Street to Camden Yards*, 144.

5. Doug Brown, "McNally Blossoms as Birds' Blaster," *The Sporting News*, August 13, 1966.

6. Eisenberg, *From 33rd Street to Camden Yards*, 179.

7. Doug Brown, "McNally Finds Long-Lost Slider and Takes Off," *The Sporting News*, August 17, 1968.

8. Eisenberg, *From 33rd Street to Camden Yards*, 189.

9. Barry Abramson, "Sports Mini-Profile: Dave McNally," July 8, 1972, unattributed clipping in Dave McNally's player file at the National Baseball Hall of Fame Library, Cooperstown NY.

10. Doug Brown, "Orioles Puzzle over McNally," *The Sporting News*, November 23, 1974.

11. Eisenberg, *From 33rd Street to Camden Yards*, 252–53.

12. Ian McDonald, "McNally Saw the End Coming," *The Gazette* (Montreal), June 10, 1975.

13. McDonald, "McNally Saw the End."

14. Maury Allen, "Dave McNally: Pioneer for Free Agency," *New York Post*, November 3, 1983.

15. "All-Star Pitcher McNally Dead at Age 60," CNN Sports Illustrated (cnnsi.com), December 2, 2002.

16. West, "Montana's Greatest Athlete."

42. Johnny Oates

1. John Hall, "An Old Face, Warm Smile," *Los Angeles Times*, March 4, 1980.

2. Peter Schmuck and Bill Free, "A Man of Faith, Life of Integrity," *Baltimore Sun*, December 25, 2004.

3. Johnny Oates, "Living with Full Count," interview by Toby Druin, *The Baptist Standard*, accessed at http://www.baptiststandard.com/2001/9_3/print/oates.html, October 28, 2008.

4. Tom Callahan, "Oates May Need His Old Padding," *Washington Post*, May 26, 1991.

5. Johnny Oates, "Living with Full Count."

6. Johnny Oates, "Living with Full Count;" "Johnny Oates," Hokiesports.com, accessed at http://www.hokiesports.com/baseball/jerseys/oates.html, October 28, 2008; "Hamilton, Oates, Stillwell to Join Athletic Hall of Fame," *Sylva* (North Carolina) *Herald*, April 11, 2002, accessed at http://www.thesylvaherald.com/SP-HallofFame041102.htm on November 17, 2008.

7. Johnny Oates with Dennis Tuttle, "All I Can Do Is Be Excited about Today," *The Sporting News*, April 22, 2002; Steve Berkowitz, "Now, Detail-Man Oates Must Answer Questions," *Washington Post*, May 24, 1991.

8. Richard Justice, "Oates Recalls Mentor Ripken Sr.," *Washington Post*, May 19, 2000; Cal Ripken Jr. and Mike Bryan, *The Only Way I Know* (New York: Penguin Books, 1997).

9. Jane Gross, "Yankee Veterans Find Different Style but Same Routine in Spring," *New York Times*, February 23, 1981.

10. *Atlanta Daily World*, February 24, 1974.

11. "Braves Trade Dick Allen, Johnny Oates to Phillies," *Atlanta Daily World*, May 11, 1975.

12. Ross Newhan, "Dodgers Obtain Oates; Sizemore Sent to Phillies," *Los Angeles Times*, December 21, 1976.

13. John Hall, "An Old Face, Warm Smile."

14. Dave Anderson, "Yanks' Johnny Oates Is in Good Spot," *New York Times*, April 23, 1981.

15. *Chicago Tribune*, May 31, 1984.

16. Michael Martinez, "He Had a Heart, and for Oates, That Was the Problem," *New York Times*, May 26, 1991.

17. Michael Martinez, "He Had a Heart."

18. Jane Gross, "Foote, Gulden Compete to Be Backup Catcher," *New York Times*, March 12, 1982.

19. "Around the Majors," *Washington Post*, August 23, 1988.

20. Ripken Jr. and Bryan, *The Only Way I Know*.

21. Mark Maske, "Orioles Cut from Top—Put Oates in for Robinson," *Washington Post*, May 24, 1991.

22. Mark Maske, "'Relax' Has No Place in Oates's Vocabulary," *Washington Post*, September 13, 1992.

23. Mark Maske, "Pressure Keeps Pounds off Oates, but Appetite for Managing Grows," *Washington Post*, April 5, 1992.

24. Ripken Jr. and Bryan, *The Only Way I Know*.

25. Frank Dolson, "For a Lesson in Confusion, Look at Position of Johnny Oates," *Philadelphia Inquirer*, August 9, 1994; Thom Loverro, "Maybe He Finally Can Find Peace," *Washington Times*, December 25, 2004.

26. T. R. Sullivan, "A Great Baseball Man . . . A Great Human Being," *Fort Worth Star-Telegram*, December 25, 2004.

27. Johnny Oates with Dennis Tuttle, "All I Can Do Is Be Excited about Today"; Thomas Boswell, "Oates Is No Longer Playing the Averages," *Washington Post*, March 26, 2002.

28. Thomas Boswell, "Oates Is No Longer Playing the Averages"; Jorge Arangure Jr., "Former O's Manager Oates Dies," *Washington Post*, December 25, 2004.

29. "Johnny Oates," Sports Encyclopedia, accessed online at http://www.sportsencyclopedia.com/memorial/tex/oates.html on November 18, 2008; "Rangers Honor Former Manager Oates," *Washington Post*, April 12, 2005.

30. "Former Texas Rangers Manager Johnny Oates Passes Away," Press Release, MLB.com, December 24, 2004.

43. September 1970 Timeline

1. *Baltimore Sun*, September 3, 1970.

2. *Baltimore Sun*, September 11, 1970.

3. *Baltimore Sun*, September 21, 1970.

4. *Baltimore Sun*, September 29, 1970.

44. Fred Beene

1. Fred Beene, telephone interview with Todd Newville, June 2005.

2. Beene, interview.

3. Beene, interview.

4. Beene, interview.

5. Beene, interview.

6. Beene, interview.

7. Beene, interview.

8. Beene, interview.

9. Beene, interview.

10. Beene, interview.

11. Phil Pepe, "Gabe Defends Hefty Outlay of Talent to Get Chambliss," *New York Daily News*, May 18, 1974, 5.

12. Beene, interview.

13. Beene, interview.

14. Beene, interview.

15. Beene, interview.

16. Beene, interview.

45. Chuck Thompson

1. Michael Olesker, "Thompson Brought Listeners to the Ballpark," *Baltimore Sun*, December 12, 2002.

2. Associated Press, "An Orioles Tradition: Limited Vision Can't Keep Thompson out of Booth," *Frederick News-Post*, June 23, 2000.

3. Associated Press, "An Orioles Tradition."

4. Chuck Thompson and Gordon Beard, *Ain't the Beer Cold!* (Lanham MD: Diamond Communications, 2002), 20.

5. Carl Lundquist, "Girl's Dare Started Thompson on Long Air-Waves Career," *The Sporting News*, May 14, 1966, 27.

6. Lundquist, "Girl's Dare."

7. Thompson and Beard, *Ain't the Beer Cold*, 32.

8. Thompson and Beard, *Ain't the Beer Cold*, 48.

9. Thompson and Beard, *Ain't the Beer Cold*, 49.

10. Thompson and Beard, *Ain't the Beer Cold*, 4.

11. Thompson and Beard, *Ain't the Beer Cold*, 4.

12. Thompson and Beard, *Ain't the Beer Cold*, 4.

13. Thompson and Beard, *Ain't the Beer Cold*, 5.

14. Thompson and Beard, *Ain't the Beer Cold*, 6.

15. Randi Henderson, "Memories Fill the Stands: Chuck Thompson Signs Off from the Ballpark," *Baltimore Sun*, October 3, 1991.

16. Thompson and Beard, *Ain't the Beer Cold*, 93.

17. Thompson and Beard, *Ain't the Beer Cold*, 94.

18. Thompson and Beard, *Ain't the Beer Cold*, 94.

19. Lundquist, "Girl's Dare."

20. Thompson and Beard, *Ain't the Beer Cold*, 9–10.

21. Thompson and Beard, *Ain't the Beer Cold*, 9.

22. Thompson and Beard, *Ain't the Beer Cold*, 101.

23. Thompson and Beard, *Ain't the Beer Cold*, 112.

24. Thompson and Beard, *Ain't the Beer Cold*, 128.

25. Jack Craig, "O's O'Donnell a Real Pro," *The Sporting News*, July 25, 1980, 53.

26. Thompson and Beard, *Ain't the Beer Cold*, 146.

27. Dave Ammenheuser, "Jon Miller and Tom Marr: Those Men inside Your Radio," *Frederick News-Post*, June 28, 1984.

28. Jim Henneman, "Go to the Hall, Miss Agnes: Thompson's Being Honored," *Baltimore Sun*, February 10, 1993.

29. Ed Waldman, "'A Class All to Himself'; Broadcaster: The Future Hall of Fame Announcer Came to Baltimore in 1949 and Won over the Hearts of the City; Chuck Thompson, 1921–2005," *Baltimore Sun*, March 7, 2005.

30. Associated Press, "An Orioles Tradition."

31. Associated Press, "An Orioles Tradition."

32. Thompson and Beard, *Ain't the Beer Cold*, 9.

33. Mike Klingaman, "Saying Goodbye to a Familiar Voice: Thompson Recalled Fondly at Cathedral Memorial," *Baltimore Sun*, March 11, 2005.

34. Associated Press, "An Orioles Tradition."

46. Bill O'Donnell

1. Jack Craig, "O's O'Donnell a Real Pro," *The Sporting News*, July 25, 1980, 53.

2. Scott Pitoniak, "O'Donnell Finds Practice Pays Off," *Utica Observer-Dispatch*, May 2, 1982.

3. Mark Decotis, "Bill O'Donnell Returns to Utica: Oriole 'Voice' Picks Yankees," *Utica Daily Press*, April 5, 1978.

4. Phil Spartano, "Bill O'Donnell: Baseball Prophet," *Utica Observer-Dispatch*, June 28, 1970.

5. Spartano, "Bill O'Donnell."

6. Spartano, "Bill O'Donnell."

7. Spartano, "Bill O'Donnell."

8. Pitoniak, "O'Donnell Finds."

9. Spartano, "Bill O'Donnell."

10. Pitoniak, "O'Donnell Finds."

11. Pitoniak, "O'Donnell Finds."

12. Spartano, "Bill O'Donnell."

13. Spartano, "Bill O'Donnell."

14. Chuck Thompson and Gordon Beard, *Ain't the Beer Cold!* (Lanham MD: Diamond Communications, 2002).

15. Thompson and Beard, *Ain't the Beer Cold.*

Smith, Curt. *Voices of Summer.* New York: Carroll & Graf, 2005.

————. *Voices of the Game.* New York: Simon & Schuster, 1987.

47. John Gordon

1. Pat Williams, telephone interview with author, April 22, 2010.

2. Williams, interview.

3. Williams, interview.

4. John Gordon, e-mail interview with author, April 2010.

5. Gordon, interview.

6. Dave Mona, e-mail interview, April 2010.

7. Moss Klein, "A.L. Beat—Twins Killing: Failure to Let Morris Go Home," *The Sporting News*, January 4, 1987, 60.

8. Gordon, interview.

9. Williams, interview.

48. Brooks Robinson

1. Ted Patterson, *The Baltimore Orioles: Four Decades of Magic from 33rd Street to Camden Yards* (Dallas: Taylor Publishing Company, 2000), 117.

2. Curt Smith, *The Storytellers: From Mel Allen to Bob Costas—Sixty Years of Baseball Tales from the Broadcast Booth* (New York: Macmillan, 1995), 204.

3. Brooks Robinson and Jack Tobin, *Third Base Is My Home* (Waco TX: Word Books, 1974), 20–29.

4. Patterson, *Baltimore Orioles*, 40.

5. Robinson and Tobin, *Third Base Is My Home*, 54–55.

6. Rick Maese, "Yea for York," *Baltimore Sun*, April 5, 2008; Patterson, *Baltimore Orioles*, xi.

7. Robinson and Tobin, *Third Base Is My Home*, 92.

8. Larry Stone, "The Most Wonderful Days I Ever Had," in *Rain Check: Baseball in the Pacific Northwest*, edited by Mark Armour (Cleveland: SABR, 2006), 106.

9. Robinson and Tobin, *Third Base Is My Home*, 126.

10. C. Joseph Bride, Bob Brown, and Phil Itzoe, eds., *Baltimore Orioles 1966 Yearbook* (Baltimore: Baltimore Baseball Inc., 1966), 10.

11. Tom Adelman, *Black and Blue: Sandy Koufax, the Robinson Boys, and the World Series That Stunned America* (New York: Little, Brown, 2006), 13.

12. Patterson, *Baltimore Orioles*, 83.

13. Patterson, *Baltimore Orioles*, 87.

14. Patterson, *Baltimore Orioles*, xii.

15. Patterson, *Baltimore Orioles*, 117, 133.

16. Patterson, *Baltimore Orioles*, 117, 120.

17. Patterson, *Baltimore Orioles*, 125.

18. Patterson, *Baltimore Orioles*, 134; Richard Kucner, "1983: Brooks Goes to Cooperstown," *Baltimore Orioles Official 1983 Yearbook* (Baltimore: FATA, 1983), 33, 36.

19. "There's Nothing Brooks Won't Sign," *Baltimore Sun*, April 19, 2009.

20. Patterson, *Baltimore Orioles*, xi; George Kell and Dan Ewald, *Hello Everybody, I'm George Kell* (Champaign IL: Sports Publishing, 1998), 205.

21. Peter Schmuck, "Brooks Robinson Was Treated for Cancer," *Baltimore Sun*, May 13, 2009.

22. Kucner, "1983: Brooks Goes to Cooperstown," 36–37.

49. The 1970 Orioles Postseason

Henkey, Ben. "World Series." In *The Sporting News Official Baseball Guide 1971*. St. Louis: Sporting News, 1971. 219–41.

Reidenbaugh, Lowell. "Birds Rule Roost Again." In *The Sporting News Official Baseball Guide 1971*. St. Louis: Sporting News, 1971. 205–11.

Epilogue

1. Rob Neyer and Eddie Epstein, *Baseball Dynasties: The Greatest Teams of All Time* (New York: Norton, 2000).

Contributors

MALCOLM ALLEN, a loyal Baltimore-born Orioles fan and former Memorial Stadium usher, is back in Maryland after a decade in Brooklyn, New York. Distributing vintage Jamaican music all over the globe has dominated much of his adult life, but he's currently focused on raising his young daughters, Ruth and Martina. Watch for his forthcoming biography of Dominican right-hander Joaquin Andujar.

MARK ARMOUR writes about baseball from his home in Oregon's Willamette Valley, where he lives with Jane, Maya, and Drew. His most recent book is *Joe Cronin: A Life in Baseball* (University of Nebraska Press, 2010), and he is currently writing, with Dan Levitt, a book on great baseball teams.

THOMAS AYERS has been a SABR member since 2004. A native Torontonian currently studying at the University of Toronto, he is a lifelong Blue Jays fan. This is his second contribution to the Baseball Biography Project.

MATT BOHN writes about baseball from his home in Milwaukie, Oregon.

WARREN CORBETT, a reporter and editor in Bethesda, Maryland, contributes to SABR's Baseball Biography Project. His first book, *The Wizard of Waxahachie: Paul Richards and the End of Baseball as We Knew It*, was published in 2009 by Southern Methodist University Press.

RORY COSTELLO always admired the great Baltimore pitchers of the Earl Weaver era. Speaking with two of the catchers who handled them gave him even more appreciation. Rory lives in Brooklyn, New York, with his wife and son.

CHIP GREENE is the grandson of Nelson Greene, who pitched briefly for the Brooklyn Dodgers. Chip is a contributor to SABR's Baseball Biography Project and several SABR book projects, Seamheads.com, and Maple Street Press publications. Chip lives in Waynesboro, Pennsylvania, with his wife and two daughters.

TOM HAWTHORN is a columnist for *The Globe and Mail*, Canada's national newspaper. He joined SABR in 1995. He lives in Victoria, British Columbia, where his sandlot nickname is E5.

MICHAEL HUBER went to his first Orioles game in 1968, attended Game Two of the 1983 World Series, and was in the Oakland stands on July 13, 1991, when four Orioles hurlers combined to no-hit the A's. He has been a SABR member since 1996.

MAXWELL KATES has lectured at the 2004 Limmud Conference at York University and the 2006 SABR Convention in Seattle, and his baseball prose has been published in several anthologies and periodicals, including the *Globe and Mail*. He is an accountant based in the Toronto area.

BEN KLEIN was born in Upland, California, and grew up in Rancho Cucamonga, California. He graduated from Etiwanda High School, where he was a member of the tennis team, and earned both his BA and JD from Georgetown University. He currently lives in Washington DC with his wife, Jennifer.

R. J. LESCH lives in Adel, Iowa, with his lovely wife, Christee. He works as a business systems analyst and information technology consultant. He is an avid saber fencer and coach, and a fan of the Chicago White Sox. He has never actually given anyone a hotfoot, nor wishes to, but understands why someone might be tempted to do so.

LEN LEVIN, a former editor at the *Providence Journal* (now retired), has had a role as a copy editor in many books for SABR. He is also the chairman of the Lajoie-Start Southern New England SABR chapter, which is consistently among the leaders in attendance at SABR regional meetings.

JOHN MCMURRAY is chair of the Society for American Baseball Research's Deadball Era Committee. Previously, he oversaw the SABR subcommittee that presents the Ritter Award, which is given annually to the best book on Deadball Era baseball written during the year prior. John has interviewed many current and former Major Leaguers for profiles published in *Baseball Digest*.

TODD NEWVILLE is a freelance writer from Plano, Texas. He has a wonderful wife named Melissa and a son named Jackson who was born in 2003. He is a proud member of SABR and sincerely hopes that his writings on baseball heroes do justice to all of them.

BILL NOWLIN is the national vice president of SABR and the author of some thirty Red Sox–related books, including *Red Sox Threads: Odds and Ends from Red Sox History*. Bill is also cofounder of Rounder Records of Massachusetts.

JACOB POMRENKE, a native Baltimorean, is a journalist living in Oceanside, California. He has been a member of SABR since 1998.

JOHN STAHL is a retired CPA with a lifelong baseball addiction. He and his wife Pamela will celebrate their fortieth wedding anniversary this year. They are blessed with two grown children (Jar-

ed and Rebecca) and one grandson (Noll). His entry in this volume is John's sixth SABR player biography.

STEW THORNLEY is an author of books on sports history for adults and young readers. He received the SABR-Macmillan Baseball Research Award in 1988 for his first book, *On to Nicollet: The Glory and Fame of the Minneapolis Millers*. In 2010 he received the Tony Salin Award from the Baseball Reliquary for commitment to baseball history.

ALFONSO L. TUSA C., a native Venezuelan, is a writer living in Los Teques, Venezuela. He has been a member of SABR since 2008. He has collaborated on several articles for newspapers and written several biographies for SABR's Baseball Biography Project and associated books.

ADAM ULREY is a lifetime Los Angeles Dodgers and Cleveland Indians fan. He works at Sacred Heart Hospital in Eugene, Oregon, and has been a contributing writer to *Deadball Stars of the American League* and SABR's Baseball Biography Project and associated books. He enjoys fly-fishing on his creek and in the lakes and rivers of Oregon. He lives in Dexter, Oregon, with wife, Jhody, his son, Camran, and his three dogs, Behr, Susie, and Montana.

FRANK VACCARO joined SABR in 1995 and has been researching baseball history since 1989. He contributes regularly to the SABR-L electronic bulletin board and writes biographies for the SABR Baseball Biography Project. He lives in Long Island City with his wife, Maria, and their black pug, Sophie.

JOE WANCHO lives in Westlake, Ohio, and is a lifelong Cleveland Indians fan. He has worked at AT&T since 1994 as a process/development manager, and has been a SABR member since 2005. He has made contributions to several SABR Baseball Biography Project books, as well as the website.

CHARLIE WEATHERBY, a native of Delaware, now lives in Novato, California, and is a semiretired adoption social worker. He follows the San Francisco Giants, is an avid softball pitcher, and once played a 1955 Little League game against Dave May.

RUSSELL WOLINSKY, a lifelong New York Mets fan, worked at the Library of the National Baseball Hall of Fame, where he was a frequent contributor to its publications and website, authoring a regular column, "Can of Corn," a collection of biographies of lesser-known Major Leaguers. He is currently working on a pair of baseball histories, and he resides in Rye, New York.